The Sedgwicks in Love

July 6, 2006

To Burr, the
scoundrel—
with warm
but suspicious regards

Tim Kenda

The Sedgwicks in Love

Courtship, Engagement, and Marriage
in the Early Republic

Timothy Kenslea

Northeastern University Press
Boston

PUBLISHED BY UNIVERSITY PRESS OF NEW ENGLAND
HANOVER AND LONDON

Northeastern University Press
Published by University Press of New England,
One Court Street, Lebanon, NH 03766
www.upne.com
© 2006 by Northeastern University Press
Printed in the United States of America

5   4   3   2   1

Library of Congress Cataloging-in-Publication Data

Kenslea, Timothy.
The Sedgwicks in love : courtship, engagement, and marriage
in the early republic / Timothy Kenslea.
p.   cm.
Includes bibliographical references and index.
ISBN-13: 978–1–58465–494–0 (cloth : alk. paper)
ISBN-10: 1–58465–494–5 (cloth : alk. paper)
1. Sedgwick family. 2. United States — History — 18th century — Biography.
3. United States — History — 19th century — Biography. 4. Courtship —
United States. 5. Marriage — United States. I. Title.
CT274.S44K4618   2005
973.5'092'2 — dc22   [B]   2005020244

for Mary

Contents

Acknowledgments   ix

Introduction: The World of the Sedgwicks   1

I. Nature and Custom: Five Marriages and a Ghost, 1774–1842

1. The Harvest Moon: The Unhappy Life and Mysterious Death   13
   of Pamela Dwight Sedgwick
2. The Power to Bind: Eliza, Frances, and Theodore   37
3. Bitterness in the Cup of Joy: A Stepmother, a Death, a Will   53
4. Brutal Conduct: The Watsons   70

II. Trifling and Badinage: Four Courtships, 1813–1816

5. The Heart That's Worth Possessing: Two Disastrous Courtships   85
6. The Perils of Badinage: Harry and Robert among the Friendlies   98

III. No Small Surrender: The Engagement Correspondence
of Harry Sedgwick and Jane Minot, October 1816–May 1817

7. The Only Consolation of Absence: Love Letters   129
8. That I Might Be Worthy of You: Roles and Responsibilities   155
9. To Translate Hope to Certainty: Setting the Date   172

Epilogue: Volumes Could Say No More   199

Appendix: Archival Sources   207
Notes   209
Index   259

Acknowledgments

This work has been in progress for a long time, and I have benefited from the advice, cooperation, and support of many friends, strangers, colleagues, and family members.

The good people who establish and maintain historical archives are the unsung heroes of historical research, and I am indebted to quite a few of them. Without the farsighted founders and benefactors and patient staff of the Massachusetts Historical Society this work would have been inconceivable. Peter Drummey and the library staff there (especially Virginia Smith, reference librarian, now retired) were good-natured, helpful, and encouraging during the many weeks I spent poring over and transcribing Sedgwick family manuscripts. Polly Pierce, curator of the Historical Collection at the Stockbridge Library Association (also now retired), was able to help me solve a thorny problem because of her encyclopedic knowledge of her collection. Bruce Abrams guided me through the intricacies of the old records at the New York City Hall of Records, and Catherine Fields offered good advice during my visit to the Litchfield Historical Society. Archive staffs at Yale's Sterling Memorial Library, Harvard's Houghton Library, the New-York Historical Society, the New York Public Library, the Williams College Archive, and the Massachusetts State Archives were all helpful and pleasant. In addition, I am grateful for the assistance of librarians at Boston College, Boston University, Wellesley College, the New England Historic Genealogical Society, and the public libraries of Boston, Brookline, Newton, Norwell, Wellesley, and especially Needham, Massachusetts.

This book began life as a series of graduate seminar papers and then a doctoral dissertation in the History Department at Boston College. Thomas H. O'Connor directed the dissertation, and he was generous and supportive. Alan Rogers offered advice that was always cogent. Carol Morris Petillo, a remarkable mentor, inspired me to take on the challenge of the doctoral program in the first place, and understood what I hoped to make of this project almost before I did. I composed an early version of parts of the introduction and chapter 1 in her biography seminar, where Victoria Byerly and Sandra Sandiford were collegial classmates and ideal first readers. Sue Goganian of the Bostonian Society sponsored a graduate student writers' group whose members were genial and welcoming. In the course of one twenty-minute conversation after a separation of several years, old friend Jack Zamboni offered two valuable analytical insights into material I was just beginning to explore; such conversations do not happen often enough, even when they are not so productive. A much earlier version of part of chapters 2 and 3 was presented to the New England Historical Association in a panel organized by Alan Rogers. Fellow panelist Ed Hanson and commentator R. Kent Newmyer made kind and constructive comments, as did audience members, in particular Richard Birdsall, the preeminent historian of Berkshire County of his time. I presented most of chapter 1 to the Twelfth Berkshire Conference on the History of Women; I am particularly grateful to Sarah Swedberg for inviting me to join her panel. Lucinda Damon-Bach, Victoria Clements, and all the members of the Catharine Maria Sedgwick Society offered encouragement when I participated in a panel discussion on Sedgwick biography at their triennial conference. Mary Beth Sievens read and critiqued the entire manuscript with great insight. With this much help and good advice, I must take complete responsibility for whatever flaws remain.

My students at Norwell High School challenge me daily to rediscover why history matters, and reward me with their enthusiasm. I would have difficulty imagining myself as either a teacher or a writer without the guidance and encouragement of a number of inspiring women who have served as my mentors over the years. In addition to Carol Petillo, these include Harriet Harvey and Ruth MacDonald. Now I must add to this list Phyllis Deutsch, my editor at the University Press of New England, who recognized the book that was hidden inside the vast manuscript I sent her several years ago and prodded me to carve away at that manuscript until the book was revealed. Her editorial skill is matched only by her patience and her tact, and I consider myself lucky to be guided by her.

Members of the Sedgwick family have been gracious and supportive of my work. In particular, John Sedgwick and Megan Marshall and their daughters invited me to present my research at a reunion of their extended family at the Old House in Stockbridge, and received me warmly there. Arthur and Ginger Schwartz were magnanimous hosts, and all the assembled Sedgwick descendants could not have provided a more enthusiastic welcome.

The stories of these Sedgwick brothers and sisters resonated with me in part because of my own experience as a member of a large, close-knit family, and I am grateful to my bothers and their families for their love and support. It seems almost unfair to single out Tom Kenslea, except that he provided invaluable computer help when a crashing hard drive could have delayed a summer of writing that was already much too short.

My father, Daniel Kenslea, died just as I was beginning this research, but his voice, his love of learning, his drive, his loyalty, his unswerving moral judgment, and his uncanny ability to ask the essential question continue to influence me in all my work. I count it a blessing, completing a first book at age fifty, to be able to present it to and share it with my mother, Clare Kenslea, who taught me to read, to write, and to love books.

Charlie Kenslea has grown up with this book and seen several summer vacations compromised by, if not quite sacrificed to, the demands of its research. I am grateful for his good nature and his curiosity, and proud to be his father. But no one has supported this work more thoroughly or unstintingly than Mary Sprogell Kenslea, who is as much a partner in it as in our life together. I cannot imagine how I would ever have completed this book, or even begun it, without her encouragement and her confidence in me, and I am more grateful for that than I can say.

The Sedgwicks in Love

Introduction

The World of the Sedgwicks

*I*n Berkshire County, in western Massachusetts, Pamela Dwight and Theodore Sedgwick were married on a spring day in 1774. Theodore—destined to become one of the Federalist Party's leaders in the United States Congress in the 1790s and later an influential judge on Massachusetts's highest court—was almost twenty-eight, and had been a widower for three years. Pamela was not quite twenty-one, and was marrying Theodore Sedgwick over the clearly stated objections of her widowed mother.[1] The courtships, engagements, and marriages of the sons and daughters of this marriage are the subject of this book.

Much of the story of these Sedgwick brothers and sisters takes place in Boston and New York, where several of them spent most of their adult lives. But for all the postrevolutionary Sedgwicks, *home* was Berkshire County, between the high ridge of the Berkshire hills and the New York border, and especially Stockbridge, the town their mother's family helped to establish. Their parents' families had arrived in Berkshire at different times, under extremely different circumstances.

Pamela Dwight Sedgwick's grandfather, Ephraim Williams, was one of four colonists granted land in the neighborhood of a new Indian school and mission in the 1730s. The mission was sponsored by the London-based Society for the Propagation of the Gospel in New England and run by John Sergeant, a young Yale-educated minister. It was located at a bend in the Housatonic River, about fifteen miles north of the village of Sheffield, Massachusetts, which had been settled in the previous decade. Some of the families who laid claim to this new settlement were linked by ties of blood and marriage to the "river gods," the wealthiest merchant and planter families of the Connecticut River valley towns in Hampshire County, about forty miles to the east. None was better connected than Ephraim Williams, who arrived in 1737, carrying his four youngest children in panniers on horseback. When the new settlement was incorporated as the town of Stockbridge in 1739, its charter called for government by selectmen, with the ninety or so Indian townspeople to choose two and the four English families to choose one. Ephraim Williams became the first English selectman.[2]

Abigail, then sixteen, was the oldest of the Williams children to arrive in western Massachusetts. Two years later, she married Reverend John Sergeant, bringing together in one household the missionary goals of her husband and the political and economic agenda of her father. While Sergeant lived, the mission and the town—that is, John Sergeant and Ephraim Williams—did not come into conflict. In 1744, when the town was separated into white and Indian sections, the Stockbridge Indians, still a majority and the immemorial tenants of the area, got title to less than a third of the land. Among the white settlers, Ephraim Williams was the largest landowner. By 1753 he had 1,500 acres.[3]

By then John Sergeant was dead, succumbing to what was described as a "nervous fever" in 1749, at age thirty-nine.[4] The search for a new missionary to replace Sergeant brought long-hidden conflicts to the surface in the town. The conflicts were not theological. Most white townspeople were orthodox Calvinists, as were nearly all the churches and ministers in New England outside Rhode Island. Most controversies within the church in colonial New England towns tended to be about access, membership, power, and property, not about fine points of theology. The mission controversy that followed Sergeant's death concerned power and money. Would the Williams family control and profit from the mission (as it had done in the past) or would the new missionary retain greater autonomy?

Ephraim Williams hoped to control the decision. His daughter Abigail was in full agreement with his goals. Everyone assumed that any young, unmarried minister who accepted the post would also have the opportunity to marry his predecessor's widow, and Abigail, with three children to care for, took an active part in the recruitment. But the Indians had veto power over the calling of a new missionary. Williams's opponents among the original white families made sure that the Indians knew Williams was trying to arrange a deal that would give him complete control of the town.[5]

The eventual choice of Jonathan Edwards as the new missionary thwarted Williams's plans. Several Williams cousins and nephews had been part of the congregation that had recently forced Edwards to resign from the pulpit at Northampton in a bitter dispute over standards for admission to church membership. In calling Edwards—a renowned scholar and preacher who was almost fifty, already married, and demonstrably willing to confront the powerful on spiritual grounds—the mission had sent Williams and his daughter Abigail a strong message.[6]

Two years later, Abigail married the recently widowed General Joseph Dwight, a prosperous merchant and landowner with eight children of his own, most of them grown. General Dwight had been one of Edwards's last defenders during the controversy in Northampton, but once he was allied with the Williams family in the contest over control of the mission, he turned against his old friend.[7] When Edwards left in 1758 to become president of the new College of New Jersey in Princeton, Stephen West, a young Yale graduate, succeeded him. West soon married Abigail's younger sister, Elizabeth Williams. Abigail and Joseph Dwight moved a few miles south, to the north parish of Sheffield, with their large blended family, including the two young children of their own marriage, Pamela and Henry.

Theodore Sedgwick was born in West Hartford, Connecticut, in 1746, the fourth child and third son of Benjamin and Anna Thompson Sedgwick. His father had been a storekeeper, but two years after Theodore's birth the family moved to the newly settled farming community of Cornwall, in Litchfield County, in the northwestern corner of the state. The land they claimed in Cornwall had only recently belonged to the Mohawks, who had mostly succumbed to white people's diseases or been forced into the wilds of western New York. Two more daughters were born in Cornwall. The family was neither rich nor poor, succeeding perhaps a little more than some of their neighbors. Then Benjamin Sedgwick dropped dead on a February day in 1757. Ownership of the farm fell to his oldest son, John, who was barely fifteen.

In 1761, Theodore, then fifteen, entered Yale College. Neither of his brothers had been sent to college, a luxury beyond most families' means. The sacrifice was considerable for John, a young farmer trying to support a mother and several young siblings in a country backwater where the tree stumps were still visible in the newly cleared fields.

During Theodore's collegiate years, Yale was plagued by frequent student riots. In 1765, his senior year, the British Parliament passed the Stamp Act. Students rioted in protests that were aimed not only at the hated new tax, but also at the upward spiral of tuition and fees and the tyrannical behavior of Yale's unpopular president, Thomas Clap. The night before the scheduled commencement in July 1765, a mob of students and townspeople attacked the president's house, broke thirty windows, carried the iron gates away, and injured Clap.

The student who injured the president was immediately expelled, the day before he was to have graduated. Although we do not know whether Theodore Sedgwick was that student, or even took part in the riot, we do know that around this time, very late in his senior year, Sedgwick was expelled from Yale.

A different person might have come away from this experience aggrieved over the injustice of his own treatment or the treatment of his fellow students. But despite (or perhaps because of) this humiliation in his youth, Sedgwick's later writings, and his entire career in public service, reveal an abiding devotion to what he spoke of as *authority*—the authority that made rules and laws, put down mobs, and punished or expelled miscreants.[8]

Being educated at Yale College in the eighteenth century often meant being trained for the ministry. Twenty of the forty-seven young men who graduated in Theodore Sedgwick's class eventually became ministers. Immediately after his expulsion, Theodore began to prepare to do likewise. But that plan was short-lived. Theology was not for Theodore Sedgwick.[9] In late 1765 or early 1766, he relocated to Great Barrington, Massachusetts. This was a new town, recently separated from Sheffield, where it had been that town's north parish. Theodore's older second cousin, Samuel Hopkins, had occupied the pulpit of the north parish for twenty years, but Theodore apprenticed himself not to the minister but to lawyer Mark Hopkins, Samuel's younger brother. Mark Hopkins had recently married Electa Sergeant, the daughter of Abigail Dwight and her deceased first husband.[10]

There were four ways a young man could prepare himself to practice law in England's American colonies. He could teach himself, through a self-chosen plan of reading and study. This was difficult, but manageable if he had the brains and drive of a Patrick Henry. If his family was wealthy, he might be sent to London to study at the Inns of Court. Sons of famiilies of the middling sort could begin as legal assistants, scribes, copyists, or deputy clerks in an American court, or serve as apprentices or clerks in an experienced lawyer's office.[11] Sedgwick became a clerk in Mark Hopkins's office.

Of Theodore Sedgwick's legal studies we know little, except that he must have been an excellent student. By April 1766 — a month before his twentieth birthday, and less than a year after his expulsion from Yale — he was admitted to the Massachusetts bar as an attorney. Great Barrington was the seat of the new Berkshire County, which had been broken off from Hampshire County and given a separate legal identity just four years earlier. Theodore briefly attempted to run an office near the courts in the county seat, but then chose to put some distance between himself and his mentor. He moved about seven miles south and opened an office in Sheffield in 1767. The chief business of a lawyer in western Massachusetts in the colonial era — as in most of the rural areas of the colonies, which meant most of the colonies — was collecting debts and arranging the sale or transfer of real estate. Theodore Sedgwick found more than enough business.[12]

Thomas Clap, the president of Yale who expelled Theodore Sedgwick, was forced to retire in 1766. Theodore received his degree retroactively in 1772, which enabled him to be listed as a member of his original class of 1765. He does not appear to have been asked to take any examinations or complete any additional work for the degree, which supports the view that his original expulsion came very late in his senior year.[13]

By the time Theodore Sedgwick got his degree, he was already a widower, and had probably begun to court, or at least to notice, Pamela Dwight, the teenaged daughter of the now twice-widowed Abigail Williams Sergeant Dwight. They would be married two years later.

In the course of their thirty-three years of marriage, Pamela Dwight Sedgwick gave birth to ten children, seven of whom survived to adulthood. In order of birth, they were Elizabeth Mason "Eliza" Sedgwick (1775–1827), Frances Pamela Sedgwick (1778–1842), Theodore Sedgwick II (1780–1839), Henry Dwight "Harry" Sedgwick (1785–1831), Robert Sedgwick (1787–1841), Catharine Maria Sedgwick (1789–1867), and Charles Sedgwick (1791–1856).

All but one of these Sedgwick children would marry. Because the marriage of Theodore and Pamela Dwight Sedgwick served as a model, for good or ill, for all their children, this volume begins with an account of it. Part 1 examines their marriage, characterized by Theodore's long absences

and Pamela's depression and mental illness. Part 1 also looks at the courtships and marriages of their three oldest children, Eliza, Frances, and
Theodore. These relationships offer a window onto changing perceptions
of the parental role in matchmaking. Eliza's and Frances's husbands were
chosen by their father, but Theodore was able to choose his own bride
over the objections of her family. They also reveal the shift, in the course
of the eighteenth and early nineteenth century, away from marriage as a
primarily economic arrangement to one in which the mutual attraction of
the partners balanced economic concerns.[14]

Part 1 concludes with a close look at two troubled marriages. The first,
Judge Theodore Sedgwick's ill-advised marriage to Penelope Russell,
barely a year after the 1807 death of Pamela Dwight Sedgwick, brought
emotional and economic tensions to the surface among the Sedgwick
children. To these brothers and sisters, Penelope Russell Sedgwick was a
usurper of their mother's place, and also one who might claim a sizeable
share of their father's estate. At the same time, Penelope Russell Sedgwick's
fate as a widow after Judge Sedgwick's death in January 1813 highlights the
increasingly tenuous financial situation of married women in the early
Republic.

In the decades following the American Revolution, more and more
states rejected the old European practice of primogeniture and adjusted
their inheritance laws to favor the division of estates among several male
heirs. These republican reforms led to greater equality among sons, but
they reduced the economic power of their mothers and stepmothers.
Many widows consented or were coerced to give up their dower rights
(the lifetime control of the traditional "widow's third" that had come
down though English common law) and accept fractional shares of their
husbands' estates, or small annuities. Courts upheld those agreements,
right up to the Supreme Court of the United States. As Linda K. Kerber
has noted, married women were in "a particularly vulnerable position" in
those decades.[15]

The second flawed marriage examined at the end of part 1 joined Frances Sedgwick to Ebenezer Watson (1776–1847). This union was arranged
by her father, who had opposed and forced her to end a six-year attachment to another man. Watson's early promise as a New York merchant
and publisher quickly gave way to business calamity. He vented his bitter
frustrations on Frances, subjecting her to a torrent of verbal, psychological, and almost certainly physical abuse that eventually forced her lawyer
brothers to respond.

Frances's plight exposes the vulnerability of married women seeking a divorce or legal separation from abusive or negligent husbands at that time.[16] The bothers counseled Frances, but even such skilled lawyers could not find a way for her to end the marriage *and* keep custody of her children. That they confronted the abuser at all was itself unusual, in an age when shamed silence was the most common response to domestic violence.[17]

Part 2 turns to the Boston-based courtships of Harry and Robert Sedgwick. Three of these courtships (two for Harry, one for Robert) were almost comically unsuccessful. The other, Harry's courtship of Jane Minot, resulted in a seven-month engagement, during which the two were separated but kept up a voluminous correspondence. They married in June 1817.

In Boston in 1815 and 1816, Harry and Robert Sedgwick courted a whole group of young women who called themselves "the friendlies." Female friendship in this era has been the subject of a small but important body of scholarly literature, but none of it describes a group quite like the friendlies.[18] The friendlies taught the brothers from Stockbridge important lessons about courtship, including the difficulties of navigating the subtle rules of social etiquette among the Boston elite. A premature gesture or expression, or even an inappropriate tone of voice, could be read as a pledge of commitment where none was intended. Most accounts of courtship rituals in this era have been based on letters exchanged between courting lovers while they were apart. The Sedgwick brothers' letters to each other and to their sister Catharine allow us to see in minute detail what actually happened when courting couples interacted in person.[19]

Part 3 focuses on the engagement correspondence of Harry Sedgwick and Jane Minot. A seven-month separation marked their engagement, with Harry in New York and Jane in Boston. During this period, they exchanged nearly a hundred letters. In them, they discussed their expectations of their marriage — its domestic, intellectual, and erotic possibilites — and attempted to define their roles as husband and wife. This extraordinary correspondence, undertaken in the spirit of absolute sincerity, shows a young couple envisioning for themselves a relationship of equals, despite the legal and cultural impediments of the day.[20] While the two discuss their future life together in terms in which the "separate spheres" of men's and women's lives can be discerned, both uphold the notion that those separate spheres are of equal value in creating a firm basis for a happy marriage.[21]

An epilogue considers the youngest sister and the best-known member of this generation of Sedgwicks, Catharine Maria Sedgwick. Catharine never married. Although she sometimes regretted her solitude and her childlessness, remaining single was a conscious choice. Devoted to her parents, sisters, nieces, nephews, and especially brothers, she became a well-known and successful author of novels, romances, and inspirational and didactic works. Catharine Sedgwick's reflections on her single state, both published and private, enrich this history of the married Sedgwicks by offering an early-nineteenth-century alternative to the marriage plot.[22]

The Sedgwicks were not the only members of their generation to rethink the meaning of courtship, engagement, and marriage in the new Republic.[23] But the records they left are extraordinary. They wrote hundreds of letters to each other and to their wives, husbands, parents, children, friends, rivals, schoolmates, and business partners. They also wrote journals, memoirs, diaries, recipe books, pamphlets, speeches, books, and articles. They saved these documents and passed them on to later generations. The family eventually deposited them with the Massachusetts Historical Society, where they form one of the largest extant multigenerational collections of a single American family's papers.

The Sedgwick family's papers have been cited in passing by many historians, but apart from a 1965 political biography of the elder Theodore and several scholars' ongoing work on Catharine's literary career, almost no one has drawn on them as a source for significant biographical narratives.[24] I discovered the collections when I was in graduate school, doing research on legal history. But it quickly became clear that these papers shed new light on more than just the legal profession that occupied the three oldest brothers. Casual family interactions and deeply personal reflections on religion, the arts, politics, business, technology, medicine, law, family life, and child rearing were recorded in hundreds of documents with grace and clarity. But for me, the most fascinating of these letters dealt with the family members' courtships, engagements, and marriages. Focusing on these subjects, I have tried to illuminate a much broader topic, the *idea* of marriage, at a critical moment in the history of American society. Taken together, the experiences of this wealthy, well-educated New England family illustrate the potential and the limitations of this relationship — and the extent to which it was possible to arrive at a new understanding of the roles and responsibilities of married life — in the first quarter of the nineteenth century.

I

Nature and Custom

FIVE MARRIAGES AND A GHOST, 1774–1842

1

The Harvest Moon

The Unhappy Life and Mysterious Death
of Pamela Dwight Sedgwick

*I*n June 1808, Judge Theodore Sedgwick, associate justice of the Supreme Judicial Court of Massachusetts and former Federalist Speaker of the United States House of Representatives, announced to his family that he intended to marry for a third time. To a reader in the extensive Sedgwick family archives who might not have first consulted a genealogy or examined the family's tombstones in the Stockbridge, Massachusetts, cemetery, this news would come as a shock. In eight different carefully arranged and well-catalogued collections of Sedgwick family papers, no clear reference to the death of the Judge's second wife can be found until four years after it occurred. Pamela Dwight Sedgwick, his wife for thirty-three years and the mother of all his children, died on September 20, 1807. But we only get a hint of her death when the Judge's eldest son (also named Theodore) mentions their father's plans to marry a Miss Penelope Russell in a letter to his brother Harry, written nearly a year later. After that Miss Russell (eventually Mrs. Sedgwick, or just "Mrs. S") appears regularly in the letters of her seven stepchildren to their father and to each other. But of Pamela Sedgwick we find only shadowy vagueness, a hollow where she should have been. Catharine Maria Sedgwick, destined to become one of the young Republic's most highly regarded authors, finally broke the silence and referred to her mother and her mother's 1807 death in a letter to a brother dated October 1811.[1]

Why this strange silence? How could, and why would, the Sedgwick brothers and sisters expunge all references to their beloved departed mother from their letters — not just years after the fact, but while they were writing them, in the weeks and months after her death?

Pamela Dwight Sedgwick's life was filled with suffering, especially in its later years. Her given name — Pamela — had been virtually unknown in the English colonies until the arrival from England of Samuel Richardson's 1740 epistolary novel, *Pamela*. For a few decades it was one of the most popular names for girls in England, although it was never quite so popular in America. When Abigail Williams Sergeant Dwight gave the name of an imperiled but ultimately triumphant heroine of secular literature to her daughter in 1753 (a time when the New England frontier was still full of young girls with such biblical names as Hannah and Bathsheba, or such pious names as Thankful and Electa), it was as if she were declaring an intention that her daughter was destined to live in a more modern world.[2]

Theodore Sedgwick, Connecticut-born and Yale-educated, was already a widower in his midtwenties when he began to court the teenaged Pamela Dwight. The lawyer from nearby Sheffield, Massachusetts, had married Elizabeth Mason (usually called Eliza) in 1767 or 1768, when he was in his early twenties, an unusually young age for a professional man to marry in those years. In 1771, Theodore caught smallpox. After surviving a term in quarantine, he was sent home. But he was not over the contagion, and soon Eliza was infected. The first Mrs. Sedgwick died April 12, 1771. She was twenty-six years old, and eight months pregnant.[3]

Grief devastated Theodore Sedgwick. Soon after Eliza's death, he lay on their bed, unable to sleep. "If I could but see her as she was," he thought, "in her everyday dress — see her once more, I should be comforted." Suddenly the room was filled with light — many years later, Catharine Sedgwick remembered her father calling it "a heavenly radiance" — and there was Eliza at the foot of the bed, "her face lit with love and happiness." The impression was so vivid that he made note of the buckles on her shoes. The young lawyer leapt to his feet, and rushed to embrace his wife, but (as Catharine told it) "she was gone — the light was gone — it was a dream." According to Catharine, this dream came back to Theodore Sedgwick every year throughout his life, "like a visitation of this girl-wife." Nor did he make any secret of it, for Catharine recalled him saying on certain mornings over the years, with a "sweet, tender expression" on his face, "I have had my dream!"[4]

Pamela Dwight might not have known, when she and Theodore Sedgwick began to court in 1773, that she was competing with an impossibly hallowed ghost. She had troubles of a more earthly nature on her hands.

Her mother opposed the match because Theodore Sedgwick, having never testified to or (apparently) undergone the requisite conversion experience, was not a church member. (Catharine believed her grandmother had opposed the match "on the score of family," and it is true that the Sedgwicks were no match for the Dwights and the Williamses in the provincial society of western New England; but one of Abigail's other daughters had already married Theodore's cousin Mark Hopkins, and the religious issue was the only one mentioned in Abigail's and Pamela's long letters.) Pamela shared her mother's concerns. "I would to heaven that there was no essential difference in our sentiments," she lamented to him. But there was, and, in Pamela's words, it consisted of "no Metiphysical nicety."[5]

In the spring of 1774, Abigail Dwight urged Pamela to stop receiving "Mr Such-a-One's visits."[6] But Pamela was undeterred. Just a month later, on April 17, 1774, she and Theodore Sedgwick were married. She was not quite twenty-one. Her new husband had been a widower for three years, an unusually long time for a widower to remain unmarried in those days, especially one in his late twenties. The long wait might have been a consequence of the obstacles Pamela Dwight's family tried to place in the way of the courtship, or it might have been a sign of his abiding grief.

A little over a year later, their first child was born. She was given the name of her father's beloved lost wife, Elizabeth Mason Sedgwick, and, like her, was called Eliza. For Pamela, naming her first child after her ghostly predecessor was a magnanimous action — the modern editor of Catharine's memoir speculates that Pamela did so "as if to signify the wifely role she and Eliza shared" — but it is not clear how full Pamela Sedgwick's consent was. Seven years later, in a letter to her close friend Elizabeth Mayhew, Pamela referred to this daughter as "your namesake," and of course, even the initials would have been the same. As Theodore in his dreams kept alive the ghost of his lost first wife, his new wife Pamela kept alive the polite fiction that their daughter's middle initial stood for something other than the family name of that first wife.[7]

Theodore's success in politics began immediately after his marriage to Pamela, when he became one of the leaders of the patriot party that sprang up in the Berkshires to protest the Intolerable Acts of 1774. In rapid succession, he was elected Sheffield's representative to the state legislature, a state senator, and one of Massachusetts's representatives in the Continental Congress.[8] As Theodore Sedgwick's career prospered, his family grew as well. An unnamed child born when Eliza was two had died after one day. Eliza was three when her sister Frances was born. A son, named after his father, followed two and a half years later. The next two children died as infants, both after living nearly a year. "Mrs Sedgwick feels this misfortune most sensibly," Theodore Sedgwick wrote to a friend on the death of a daughter named Catharine.[9] All three infants died in March—the gloomiest, most inhospitable time of year in the Berkshire hills. With sleighs, sleds, and snowshoes available, Berkshire residents never let winter's ice and snow interrupt their travel and socializing. But in most years, winter would have dissipated enough in March to clog the roads and fields with damp, chilly mud, dragging almost all travel to a halt. Spring, with its promise of warmth, growth, and renewal, would not return until many weeks later.

Theodore continued to practice law in Sheffield and around Berkshire County during these years, and his practice prospered. In his best-known case, he won a judgment in the Berkshire County Court of Common Pleas against John Ashley, a powerful neighbor. Sedgwick's clients were listed in the court papers as "Brom and Bett." Whether they could be held as slaves in the Ashley household was the point under dispute. The court records do not reveal any details of the evidence or argument Sedgwick offered on his clients' behalf, but according to long-standing local tradition, the law he and his clients urged the court to apply in the case was the Declaration of Rights in the Massachusetts Constitution, then less than a year old. It states that "all men are born free and equal, and have certain natural, essential, and unalienable rights." In light of that declaration, the argument went, no one could be held as a slave in Massachusetts. In a similar case heard during that same year, independent of Brom and Bett's case, the state Supreme Judicial Court explicitly rejected the continuation of slavery in Massachusetts on the basis of the Declaration of Rights, and determined that the state constitution had officially put an end to slavery in Massachusetts. The 1790 census counted no slaves in the commonwealth.[10]

The long-term effect of these cases was the abolition of slavery in Massachusetts, by judicial decree. The more immediate effect of Bett's case was that Bett—Elizabeth Freeman—came to live with the Sedgwick family, in whose service she would remain by her own choice for the next twenty-seven years. To the Sedgwick children she became something more than a servant—she became a second mother, "Mumbet," as much responsible for raising them as their two natural parents.[11] In Catharine Sedgwick's reminiscences, written from the perspective of old age, she recalled first her father's frequent absences from home and joyous returns; then her mother's frequent illnesses and afflictions; and then her love of "Mumbet, that noble woman, the main pillar of our household . . . the unconscious moral teacher of the children she tenderly nursed." Catharine's devotion to Mumbet was boundless. "In my childhood I clung to her with instinctive love and faith," she recalled, "and the more I know and observe of human nature, the higher does she rise above others, whatever may have been their instruction or accomplishment."[12]

Pamela bore her seventh child, Henry Dwight Sedgwick, in September 1785. He was given the same name as a brother who had died six months earlier, but he was usually just called Harry. Eliza was ten, Frances seven, and young Theodore, the closest to Harry in age, was about to turn five. Harry was a sickly child — "the most distressed sore little thing" his mother had ever seen.[13]

Theodore Sedgwick traveled frequently in the 1780s, attending the state legislature in Boston or the Continental Congress in New York. His failure to win reelection to Congress in June 1786 seemed to conclude the national phase of his political career. When he returned to New York for what he believed would be his last prolonged absence from home, he promised his wife, "I can and I hope without regret descend (if indeed it is descending) to private life." He then catalogued the things he would have time to do: "I can attend more than of late I have been able to the instruction of my children. I can enjoy more of the company and conversation of my dearest and best beloved. I can make a better provision for my family."[14]

In the last week of June, Theodore wrote to Pamela from New York expressing great concern about her health and inquiring, among other things, why young Harry had not been weaned. "I was in hopes a certain reason why he was not earlier weaned ceased when I came from home," he noted, hinting broadly that the infant's presence in their bed had kept him out of it.[15]

A knowledgeable historian of women's lives has used this complaint of Theodore Sedgwick's as evidence that the Sedgwicks, as a couple, had been using Pamela's prolonged breast-feeding as a form of birth control. In fact, the Sedgwicks and their friends were aware that lactation in and of itself did not prevent conception. This folk belief had some currency, but within fifteen years of this letter, in two separate instances, members of the Sedgwicks' circle would notice without surprise that women who were still nursing or had just weaned their infants were already visibly pregnant. In fact, the ideal implied in both cases was that the onset of a new pregnancy signaled that the time had come to *start* weaning the older child.

The folk belief that a nursing mother could not become pregnant persisted because prolonged breast-feeding almost certainly did reduce the incidence of conception. It allowed women to practice the oldest and most reliable form of contraception, abstinence. The constant presence of a nursing infant at its mother's breast and in its parents' bed made the resumption of marital relations more cumbersome and surely reduced their frequency. Scholars have found evidence of another folk belief, widespread at this time, that engaging in sexual relations would sour a mother's milk — a belief that might have given nursing mothers an additional cultural sanction for saying "no" to their husbands. Theodore's comment to Pamela probably meant not that Harry's nursing had kept her from conceiving, but that it had prevented them from even trying.[16] Wives had few enough ways to discourage their husbands' importuning. Pamela was thirty-three and in poor health. She had already borne seven children, and buried three of them.

In any case, Theodore Sedgwick was not complaining about *prolonged* breast-feeding. He had left his substantial new home in Stockbridge (into which he had just moved his family) in late May, to attend a session of the Continental Congress that began in New York on June 1, 1786. When he left home, therefore, Harry was eight months old. He learned that Harry was still not weaned, and wrote the letter that contained his complaint, less than a month later. Nowhere in the historical literature about colonial or early national times can evidence be found that anyone thought eight months was an appropriate age to wean an infant; mothers nursed their children for ten to twenty months, sometimes longer.[17] Theodore Sedgwick's letter does not illustrate a general truth about men and women taking responsibility for family planning, but a particular and personal truth: Theodore Sedgwick was impatient with his son Harry, and with his wife's excessive devotion to the "distressed sore little thing," when Harry was an eight-month-old infant at his mother's breast.

The summer session of the Continental Congress ended on August 22, and Theodore Sedgwick returned to Stockbridge shortly thereafter. Robert was born nine months later.

Around the time of Robert's birth in 1787, the state legislature elected Theodore Sedgwick to a new term in the Continental Congress. A few months later he was elected to the Massachusetts convention that would consider whether to ratify the new federal constitution. When that constitution was ratified, he was elected to a two-year term in the U.S. House of Representatives from western Massachusetts. Politics would once again keep Theodore Sedgwick away from his family.[18]

During the first session of the First Congress, in the spring and summer of 1789, and especially as the session's end became foreseeable, Pamela reflected on their separation with relative equanimity. "I have just been regaling myself with a little turn in the back porch of our house," she wrote to her husband one summer night, "the sky clear the full moon risen upon us in soft majesty — all silent around me. Nothing could then have added to the pleasure of my sensations but the company of my beloved, that I might have leaned upon his bosom — and softly stroked his cheek." As separated lovers ever have, she took comfort in the prospect that the same full moon would shine upon her distant husband.[19]

Theodore Sedgwick's first prolonged absence to attend the United States Congress marked the beginning of the most painful period in his and Pamela's married life. He had been away from home for weeks at a time when he served in the state legislature, and for up to three months at a time when he served in the Continental Congress. But for the twelve years of his service in the United States Congress, Theodore Sedgwick would be away from home almost exactly half the time. His sons Harry and Robert were three and a half and almost two when their father went to serve in the First Congress; they would be nearing the end of their first year of college when he retired. Catharine and Charles, the last two children, were born during their father's first and second two-year terms; they would be eleven and nine when their father retired from Congress. Between 1789 and 1800, Theodore Sedgwick would be away from home for at least three months every year, at least six and a half months in eight of those twelve years, at least seven months in each of three consecutive years (1796 to 1798), and more than eight months in one year (1790). And those absences almost always coincided with the bleakest months of winter, and the March anniversaries of the deaths of his and Pamela's three infants.

These were not like Theodore's earlier absences. Those had been distressing to Pamela, but she had been younger and stronger, had fewer children, and was surrounded by a supportive network of kin and neighbors, the most essential of whom was her mother, Abigail Dwight. By 1789, Abigail was nearing seventy and unwell. The long months without a husband, with six children to care for alone (three of them under the age of five) wore Pamela out. "I am tired of living a widow and being at the same time a nurse," she wrote. "I cannot possibly reconcile my feelings or make myself happy in this state of widowhood. . . . My children want a father." She continued to be supportive of Theodore's political career, but she missed his company. "Many very many cold nights I wake up enclosed by my children," she admitted, ". . . and long to be near your pillow that I may find you warm and sweetly sleeping. Then I would give you a gentle kiss—but lest I should be tempted to awake you or disturb your slumber I am not permitted to come near your bed."[20]

After the death of her mother in February 1791, Pamela Dwight Sedgwick's sanity started to unravel in the months of Theodore's absences.[21] Catharine Maria Sedgwick discussed her mother's plight in her reminiscences written sixty years later: "She was oppressed with cares and responsibilities; her health failed; she made no claims, she uttered no complaints; and she knew she was most tenderly beloved, and held in the very highest respect by my father, but her physical strength was not equal to the demands on her, and her reason gave way." In recording all this for her grandniece, Catharine repeatedly offered her father's pained rationale for his neglect: "I am sure that nothing short of a self-devotion to his country's good would have induced him to leave my mother, winter after winter, tottering under her burden of care."[22]

At least once during each of the six terms he served as a leading Federalist member of Congress, Theodore Sedgwick promised Pamela that this term would be his last.[23] Yet for a dozen years he stayed away from home for months at a time. In her study of the marriage of William and Elizabeth Wirt, a political couple of the next generation, Anya Jabour has pointed out how the burdens of such long separations fell disproportionately on the wife who was let behind. Yet Philip Greven, reviewing the careers of several of Theodore Sedgwick's contemporaries—men like Adams, Jefferson, and Franklin—speculated that certain types of men in the revolutionary generation sought out public life, with all its time-consuming travel, precisely *because* it ensured their absence from home, and so limited close contact with their wives and families. "Indeed," Greven concluded, "one might well wonder about the prolonged absences of such men from their wives in the light of their feelings about their own sexuality. Public life could have been a way to evade sexual passions, as well as to gratify the obligations of duty and political service so essential to many moderate men." The passion in the letters that passed between Theodore Sedgwick and his wife was usually found in her letters, not his. Greven's observation raises a ghost of a suspicion about the intensity of the passion felt by this man who, throughout his thirty-three-year marriage to his second wife, admitted to being haunted by phantom memories of his long-dead first wife.[24]

Pamela's first major episode of mental illness took place during the closing months of 1791, when she was preparing to deliver her tenth and last child, Charles. Theodore was attending a contentious session of Congress, and was unable to get home in time for the birth. This was not unusual, of course. Men in this era were rarely present for the births of their children, and their assistance was certainly not required. The servants (including Mumbet, who was among other things an expert midwife) took care of Pamela's physical needs, and Abigail Dwight's cousin Sarah Spring Gray (known as "Aunt Gray" to the children) came to live with the family, to provide the company of a "good matronly person" and the support Abigail had previously afforded. But the family's reports of his wife's derangement caused Theodore distress. "I should not think it any trouble to travel thousands of miles to administer to your comfort," he vowed to Pamela from Philadelphia, some two hundred miles away. Then a trusted political advisor in Berkshire visited Pamela and decided that things were not so bad. "Nothing but necessity ought to induce you to come home," he asserted. "*That necessity does not exist.*"[25]

A week later, Pamela herself finally addressed her husband: "Friends would persuade me I am not well but this I have no reason to believe but shall I tell can I tell you that I have lost my understanding what is my shame what is my pain what is my confusion to think of this what evils wait my poor family without a guide without a head for their sakes I wish you at home — for your sake I wish you not to come you must not come it would only make us both more wretched let me beg you my dear to make yourself easy don't be anxious about a creature utterly worthless to herself and to you."[26] When Theodore received this pathetic letter, his response expressed agony. "O my dearest Love," he replied, "my heart melts with tenderness inexplicable, I cannot be much longer separated from you. I will endeavor to dispel the cloud which shades your precious mind. I will administer comfort to your dear distressed heart." But two days later he was still in Philadelphia — promising assistance from afar. "I will not I dare not permit myself to believe that the painful gloom which overshadowed your angelic mind when you last wrote still continues," he wrote. "I know not what to say to you, if worlds were in my disposal, I would part with them without hesitation to purchase you peace and happiness."[27]

This first incident set the pattern for many later ones. Pamela would be stricken anew; her relatives and friends in the Berkshires would attend to her care; Theodore would write agonized and agonizing letters from the capital; and the friends and relatives would reassure him that it was more important for him to attend to his higher political calling. At least once, in the late summer of 1793, Pamela was stricken while Theodore was at home, and he remained there, supervising the household and caring for the children, while his wife was away, recuperating under a doctor's care. He missed the opening of the congressional session, but still managed to return to the capital before she came home.[28]

In December 1795, Pamela was being held in isolation under a doctor's care while Theodore was in Philadelphia debating Jay's Treaty, the Washington administration's attempt at a diplomatic settlement of long-standing conflicts with Britain. "If I could reconcile it to my sense of duty not an hour should Philadelphia contain me," he pledged to his law partner Ephraim Williams, who was also Pamela's cousin. "With what ardor would I fly to give to my beloved family what support I could," he assured his daughters, "but what I believe a superior duty fixes me here at present."[29] Pamela's half-brother, Dr. Erastus Sergeant, visited her several times and assured Theodore that his return was not required. "Your presence could not in the least contribute to Pamela's happiness," he wrote, "and I hope and trust you will possess yourself with patience while you reflect that the greatest *good* to your country is your object." Ten-year-old Harry saw his mother on a visit he made with his uncle, Dr. Sergeant. Ten-year-old boys in every age have used colorful terms to describe people who are afflicted as Pamela Sedgwick was then afflicted, but the word Harry used — "Mama is as [   ] as when she first went to Sheffield" — has been torn from his letter to his father. Reports of Pamela's recovery circulated over the next few months, only to be retracted or contradicted. When Theodore finally came home in June, so did Pamela, and by summer's end her relatives believed that she had been fully restored to health.[30]

On a few occasions, Pamela found ways to forestall these seasonal attacks of madness. In the spring of 1794, in the face of her husband's inability to move and in spite of her feeble health, she managed to travel to Philadelphia with her nineteen-year-old daughter Eliza. Pamela and Eliza enjoyed Philadelphia society. Shortly after they arrived, they stayed out one night at the theatre until an hour past midnight. When they were unable to get a carriage and had to come back to their lodgings on foot, Theodore feared that his wife would get sick, but she showed no signs of it. In fact, her health improved while she was in Philadelphia. Similarly, in the brutally cold Berkshire winter of 1797, preparing for Eliza's April wedding kept Pamela unusually healthy.[31]

During an extended stay at home the following fall, Theodore again agreed that he had devoted enough time to his country and needed to devote more to his family. Pamela felt unsure of her husband's resolve;

much as his unresisting attraction to the lure of public life pained her, she understood its causes. "You my love have ever had the pleasure of receiving the approbation of the wisest and most virtuous of your fellow citizens," she acknowledged. "You flatter me too much when you give me room to indulge a hope that you will soon leave public life. If you could feel contented, satisfied, and happy in retirement I should rejoice to have you quit it"—but, she allowed, "if the interest of your country should so far occupy your mind as to make you really uneasy I should then wish you had never resisted a station in which you are so useful and highly respected." Essentially, she was inviting him to go back on his promise, for she suspected that he would do so anyway. By the following summer, though, Pamela was again optimistic about the approaching end to her husband's political career. "It affords me pleasure," she wrote, "to reflect that this is the last season you will be obliged to pass in Philadelphia." She hoped he was getting ready to "spend the evening of your life far from the scenes of perplexity and strife which generally accompany public life."[32]

Their domestic life was filled with perplexity that summer of 1798. The children sent Theodore a letter about the state of his wife's health that caused him alarm. Pamela herself brought up the same subject. "The week before last I was very ill occasioned by a return of my old disorders," she wrote. She blamed this attack on the hot weather, adding plaintively, "this illness I hope will not be charged to my account on the score of impudence and indiscretion." But her condition did not improve over the summer. Aunt Gray's married daughter, Mary Bidwell, now a neighbor, wrote to her mother in late August that "Mrs. Sedgwick continues deranged in a degree, and the family are much alarmed." Pamela's afflictions may have been caused or exacerbated by a growing certainty that her husband's political career was *not* about to end. Indeed, in September 1798 a gathering of Berkshire Federalists formally drafted Theodore Sedgwick as the party's nominee for his old House seat. He won the election, and returned to Congress.[33]

Pamela Sedgwick suffered a relatively mild episode of her old affliction the following February, and reported to her husband her conviction that "my own unworthiness is the cause of depressing my spirits." Her husband urged her not to heap the blame on herself: "This we both know to be a disease—would to God we could discover a remedy." But she believed she knew a remedy, at least for the symptoms. "I trust in mercy I shall be better," she assured him, "when I again have the pleasure to see you."[34]

When Theodore Sedgwick went to Philadelphia for the first session of the Sixth Congress, late in November 1799, he was elected Speaker of the House. Every letter from Stockbridge assured him that Pamela was "recovering"—apparently from an attack in the fall, just before his departure. She traveled to Albany to stay with Eliza and her family, but then insisted on returning home, where she fell into a deeper gloom. She wondered why her husband would even bother to read her letters, and despaired of her efforts to care for her children. "I can do nothing to contribute to their happiness or to anyone's," she lamented. Every letter written in the early months of 1800 portrayed the attack as relatively mild, but a year later daughter Frances remembered the events of those days as grim.[35]

In Philadelphia, Theodore Sedgwick felt like "a prisoner returning to his confinement." He did not seek reelection in the fall of 1800. ("Be assured there is no earthly consideration which could induce me to consent to it," he had promised Pamela earlier that year.) After he attended the second session of the Sixth Congress, which opened in late November 1800 in the new national capital on the Potomac, he was relieved that he would never need to return to that raw new city.[36]

Pamela Sedgwick savored a quiet satisfaction that her twelve years of isolation were about to end. "She anticipates with all the life of youth your return," Frances told her father. Theodore Sedgwick's eleven-year-old daughter Catharine also made note of the upcoming end of his congressional career, a month before the Sixth Congress drew to a close. "You say in one of your last letters," she wrote to her father, "that the time will soon come when you shall take leave of Congress forever." Her feelings concerning this milestone were unambiguous: "That day shall I in my own mind celebrate forever yes as long as I live I shall reflect on that dear time when my dear Papa left a public life to live in a retired one with his dear wife and children." Anticipating her father's final departure from the new capital city, she reminded him that "you will have the pleasure to think when you quit the door of the House that you are going to join your family forever."[37]

Catharine was only partly correct. Theodore Sedgwick's congressional career was over, but his years in public life were not.

Just a year after Catharine Sedgwick celebrated her father's homecoming from Congress, the governor of Massachusetts appointed Theodore Sedgwick to a seat on the state's Supreme Judicial Court. It would have been unrealistic to imagine that Sedgwick would turn down this great honor. In fact, he was expecting it, having worked out a deal with the state's leading Federalist politicians before he left Congress. At the time, the entire court was expected to preside over every appellate proceeding, traveling as a group from county to county, and spending weeks in the capital, Boston. Massachusetts in 1802 still included the district of Maine, so this would make for significant travel time and responsibilities. Theodore Sedgwick's life of dutiful absence from home was about to begin again.[38]

Pamela was ill when her husband went to Boston in May 1802, and the following March she suffered another bout of her old illness while he was in Boston. During his vacation from Williams College that month, Robert Sedgwick passed up an opportunity to visit his older siblings in Albany and instead went home and read Tacitus to his mother. When he visited her again in May, he was able to send a glowing report to his father in Maine. "She really appeared this morning like a young lady endowed with all those captivating accomplishments which are calculated to inspire a young gentleman with love and adoration," he gushed. "If you had been here her youthful appearance would have recalled to you many former scenes of pleasure." *If you had been here.* At the end of a summer that saw the family home at Stockbridge filled with vacationing family members and visitors, including Judge Sedgwick, Harry commented, "The circle which rendered Stockbridge so agreeable is now nearly broken up, and Mama is left to solitude."[39]

Pamela's decline was virtually constant over the next few years, and especially severe in winter. In January 1806, Eliza Sedgwick Pomeroy and her family moved to Stockbridge from Albany, at least in part to be closer to the invalid Pamela. One night in February of that year, Mary Gray Bidwell across the street was interrupted in the middle of writing a letter to her husband. (Barnabas Bidwell sat in Theodore Sedgwick's old seat in Congress as a Jeffersonian Democrat, but their wives were distantly related, and their political rivalry did not prevent their families from enjoying warm relations.) Fourteen-year-old Charles Sedgwick appeared at her door, "trembling and pale," to ask for her help in attending to his mother. She ran for her cloak, but before she was ready to leave Harry appeared, "exhausted with agitation" — the situation had worsened. "The poor sufferer seemed sinking fast when I entered," Mary reported to her husband. But Pamela was revived, and when she came back to her senses she asked why so many of her neighbors were gathered around her. The next day, Mary Bidwell noted that Mrs. Sedgwick was "uncommonly wild." She suffered "repeated fits" that night, and Mary did not expect her to survive the following day. She did survive, though, and even recovered somewhat, only to be plunged again into fits of what her neighbors considered "derangement."[40]

Theodore Sedgwick contemplated giving up his judgeship to help his wife and family deal with the calamity of her ever-worsening illness, but he decided not to: "Owing to the importunity of the bar," he informed his son Theodore, "I have agreed to serve another year." He regretted that almost at once. In May 1806, Judge Sedgwick experienced one of his most bitter professional disappointments. The court's chief justice had stepped down. Sedgwick was by now one of the senior associate justices, and he felt that he had served his state and his party with distinction in Congress and on the bench. He expected to be nominated as the new chief justice. Governor Caleb Strong did not agree. He decided to look outside the court and named one of the leading lawyers of the Boston bar, Theophilus Parsons. Sedgwick was bitter: "I am, indeed, most infamously treated," he told his friend and political adviser Henry Van Schaack. "I will not patiently submit to this unmerited disgrace." He contemplated resigning.[41] That summer, Theodore Sedgwick received at least twenty-three letters from leading citizens of Massachusetts imploring him not to resign, many in response to letters he had sent threatening to do just that. He also received addresses from groups of the leading lawyers in Middlesex and Worcester counties.[42] After receiving the last of these (the memorial from the Worcester County bar), he drafted a generous response in which he thanked them for their kindness but informed them that he had made up his mind to retire — "forever." Then he filed that draft away and returned to the bench, where he would stay until the day of his death.[43]

It was at this point that Theodore Sedgwick's sons (and occasionally his sons-in-law, and at least once his daughter Catharine) began to refer to their father as "the Judge" in their letters. For the rest of his life, the brothers would use the term at least as often as "father" in their letters to each other, which were probably in this instance an accurate mirror of their conversations as well. The term implied a measure of respect, but also a mild lampooning, as if intended to deflate the pretensions of one who never came down from the bench.[44]

In the second of three spirited letters on the subject of the appointment of Parsons and the prospect of Theodore Sedgwick's resignation in protest, Henry Van Schaack expressed a sentiment that guided Theodore Sedgwick throughout his political career. He did not refer to public service, or even to fame and glory. Instead, this resident of the small town of Pittsfield simply said, "A man of your standing in society ought not to be buried alive in Stockbridge."[45] So, after a summer and fall of sulking, the

Judge went back to riding his circuit from county courthouse to county courthouse, and making his extended journeys to Boston. Live burial in Stockbridge was for people of lesser standing in society.

Pamela Sedgwick's health in the winter of 1806 and 1807 seemed remarkably good to friends and family who were used to expecting the worst.[46] Then, beginning in March 1807, they heard the worst. When Catharine expressed gratitude that her mother was comfortable, she admitted, "more we cannot expect." Catharine vowed in April that she would not leave while her mother was alive: "I am bound by every tie, to devote myself to her, the remainder of her life."[47]

The Judge returned to Stockbridge in late July. In August the family home was filled with the sounds of children and grandchildren. Frances considered it miraculous that her mother was still alive. Frances's husband came up from New York to visit, and Harry came home from Connecticut, on a break from Judge Tapping Reeve's Litchfield law school. The two men rose on the morning of Thursday, September 17, to go hunting for partridge in the Berkshire hills. Later that day Harry wrote a letter to his brother Theodore, which he closed by saying that their mother sent her love. The moon had been full the night before, the harvest moon, harbinger of the coming of fall. The Judge had gone to Boston, to court. Pamela, nearly buried alive in Stockbridge, asked to be remembered.[48]

Less than three days later, Pamela Dwight Sedgwick died, and her family's long, strange, self-imposed silence began. Many family letters survive from the months following Pamela's death. Consider only the ones from the remaining months of 1807: Less than a week after Pamela's death, the Judge began to make plans to send Charles (who was almost sixteen) to serve an apprenticeship with a merchant in New York, and discussed this in an exchange of letters with his oldest son, Theodore. In October, Robert announced that at the end of his term as a law clerk in young Theodore's Albany office he would be moving to New York to open an office of his own. When Harry, who now worked in his father's Stockbridge law office, tried to plan an October trip to New York to attend the sessions of that state's supreme court, his father objected that the trip would come while he was also away from home, and the servants would steal everything in the house. A week later, Robert discussed the state of the legal profession in Albany with Harry. The Judge wrote to Harry from Salem on November 7, complaining that he had not received a letter recently. Young

Theodore had written to Harry on November 1, wondering if he would go to New York, and he wrote again on November 17, describing the trip he had made without Harry. ("We have all regretted your absence as much as you could wish," he wrote. "We never sit down to the wing of an ox, but that your name is mentioned.") Frances wrote the next day to describe a gathering with Theodore and Robert in New York.[49] On Christmas day, Catharine wrote to tell Frances that she and Mumbet had been present for the arrival of a "youthful stranger" a week earlier — sister Eliza's seventh child. Three days later Catharine wrote to Frances again. Most of this letter concerned the great misfortune of Harry being stuck in Stockbridge. Catharine put this letter down on December 28 and did not finish writing it until New Year's Day.[50]

Not one of these letters contains a mention of Pamela Sedgwick, let alone of her death.

There is no requirement, of course, that every letter a person writes in the months following the death of a mother or wife must contain a mention of that death and the letter-writer's own grief. But the complete absence of any such mention seems bizarre — as if the family had decided that it must never discuss the death or the person who had died. In contrast to the epistolary silence surrounding Pamela's death, the Sedgwick family's letters after the Judge's death six years later were liberally sprinkled with memories of the dead man's life and expressions of sorrow and grief.[51]

Particularly haunting is the letter that Catharine finished writing to Frances on New Year's Day, less than four months after their mother's death. In it, she expressed her hopes and good wishes for the year just beginning, but made only a passing reference to the one that had just ended. How could Catharine resist the opportunity to comment on her mother's death? Two years earlier, on the day after New Year's, her father had written to her, "On this anniversary, every correct mind will, of course, retrace the events which have intervened since the last — our improvement of the time, the mercies we have received, the dangers we have escaped, the sufferings we have endured, our social sympathies, our indulgencies and our self-denials, with all the serious scenes in which we have acted an interesting part." The family members were all familiar with the genre of the New Year's letter. Harry had extemporized on the reason people write such letters when he had written one to Frances three years earlier. "In these points of time marked by successive revolutions," he had observed, "there is an almost universal impulse to abstract ourselves from the scene and occupations of the moment, to retire as it were upon an eminence whence we can view the road which we have hitherto traveled."

But no Sedgwick family member was to climb that hill at the beginning of 1808 to look back on the difficult road they had all traveled in 1807. And their silence on their mother's life and death continued for years thereafter, broken only intermittently — never before 1811.[52]

Why would a family resort to this silence? Had their mother's long illness been such a drain on them that they were relieved to see her die? There is ample evidence that Pamela's death did cause her family real and long-lasting grief. Catharine wrote to a friend fifteen years later, "The name of Mother is sacred with me. I remember the language that was in the beam of my own dear Mother's eye — the feeling of shelter near her — and all those impalpable and indescribable effects that like light pervade every thing." Fourteen years after that, when she heard that a young acquaintance's mother had died, Catharine shared some of her memories with a sister-in-law: "Even now after this long passage of years there is nothing actual and present that I *feel* like that ray of ineffable tenderness from my Mother's eye." Catharine even carried out a visible demonstration of her devotion to her mother's memory. Pamela Dwight Sedgwick had been dead for almost a half century when Catharine wrote her reminiscences of childhood for her grandniece, and, in speaking of her own great love of flowers, mentioned "above all, the pinks, my mother's favorite, and till now the memorial I wear through all the summer months for her."[53]

In those 1853 reminiscences, Catharine Sedgwick transcribed what appears to be the only family document written at the time of Pamela's death that makes reference to it: a five-paragraph obituary, written (according to Catharine's recollection) by Harry. He wrote of Pamela's patience and "submissive piety," but also mentioned that "she was often afflicted with the severest anguish, from an apprehension that her life was useless." Was that a clue? Had Pamela, in despair on her final night, taken some drastic action to end this anguish? As if anticipating that he might have implied as much, Harry drew back. "Her sufferings, in degree and duration, have been perhaps without a parallel," he noted, "but they reached not the measure of her faith and her patience."

Of his fellow survivors, Harry wrote: "What her friends, and, above all, what her husband and children have suffered, must be left to the conception of the reader — *it can not be told.* But it is hoped that they will try to dismiss all selfish regards, and to rejoice that she is now where the righteous have their reward, and the weary are at rest."[54] All that they had suffered in response to her suffering, all that unimaginable sorrow and pain — *it can not be told.* In light of the unearthly silence that followed

Pamela's death, the phrase takes on the aspect of a solemn pledge: *it can not be told.*

One account does survive of the last day of Pamela Sedgwick's life: a letter from Mary Gray Bidwell, the neighbor across Main Street in Stockbridge, to her husband, Barnabas Bidwell, then the attorney general of Massachusetts. He was in Boston, as was Judge Sedgwick, when his wife wrote to tell him that "our excellent neighbor is numbered with the congregation of the dead."[55]

Mary Bidwell reported that Pamela Sedgwick had been unusually well, "or rather comfortable," until Saturday morning, September 19. Mumbet, to whom Mary Bidwell credited much of her information in this letter, "was alarmed while dressing her that morning by the appearance of a livid spot over her right eye." The rest of the family considered this "some slight contusion," apparently the kind of thing they were used to seeing on their mother's weakened body. "She supported her customary pleasantness through the day," Mary Bidwell reported, again crediting another eyewitness, a neighbor by the name of Sally Fairman, who had visited Pamela "towards evening." Several of Pamela's children and their friends were in the front parlor, "in a high scene of mirth." Sally Fairman wondered if the noise disturbed Pamela, but she replied, "No, I am pleased to find they are cheerful and happy." Pamela went to bed that evening "without special complaint." The moon shone brightly in the sky. It had been full — the harvest moon, the last full moon before the autumnal equinox and the beginning of fall — just three nights earlier. The looming presence of that nearly full harvest moon would certainly have caught the eye and lighted the way of any family member who might have rushed through the streets later that night, searching for a doctor, or a messenger to send to Boston or Albany, or a helpful neighbor.[56]

At two o'clock on the morning of Sunday, September 20, Pamela Sedgwick suffered a seizure "similar," Mary Bidwell wrote, "to those which have so long afflicted her." After she had experienced about twenty "distressing paroxysms," Bidwell confided to her husband, "nature yielded under this severe conflict." Messengers were sent at first light for the Judge in Boston and for Theodore and Robert in Albany, but a little before eight o'clock that morning, Mary Bidwell reported, "Mrs. Sedgwick closed a life of uncommon suffering."

So Mary Bidwell's account provides reassuring confirmation that Pamela's last night, though filled with "distressing paroxysms" and "uncommon suffering," included no events or incidents of the type that would force the family to adopt its vow of silence — *it can not be told.*

Or does it? It is as close as we will ever get to an eyewitness account, but it is not an eyewitness account. Mary Bidwell did not visit Pamela Sedgwick on her last day of life. Her report of events in the Sedgwick house that day was pieced together from, and duly attributed to, other sources: Mumbet (to whom Bidwell refers as "her attendant Betty") and Sally Fairman. She did not name her sources for the events of the middle of the night, but she was not present herself, as she was careful to tell her husband: "The unconfirmed state of my health" (she was pregnant at the time) "prevented my going over while Mrs. S was living, as the street was very damp from the rain of the preceding night." She did go over Sunday morning to offer her condolences and her assistance.

Catharine (we know from her own much later report) sobbed inconsolably over her mother's lifeless body. Only Mumbet could reach her, shushing her with what Catharine recalled as "still, solemn sadness" as they comforted each other. "We must be quiet," the old woman said. "Don't you think I am grieved? Our hair has grown white together." Forty-six years later, Catharine could still address her beloved mother with an anguished lament: "The thought of what I suffered when you died thrills my soul!"[57]

Catharine had fainted "repeatedly" that Sunday, and Mary Bidwell found her still "very ill" and "distressed deeply" two days later. Robert and young Theodore came quickly from Albany, and Mary Bidwell reported that all the family members were "deeply afflicted." The Judge did not arrive until late Tuesday afternoon, in time for Wednesday morning's funeral.

And that was all Mary Bidwell reported to her husband—a window from across the street, opening Saturday morning with the discovery of a spot that looked like a bruise over Pamela's right eye, and closing Tuesday afternoon with the arrival of the Judge for the funeral. Where are the grounds for this mysterious silence? Did Pamela cry out some unforgivable blasphemy, or disclose some terrible secret, on her deathbed? Did she plead for death to come and relieve her sufferings, and did she—or anyone else—take any action to answer those pleas? What was it, that night, that made Harry and Catharine and all the family take their vow? As far as the record of the family's correspondence takes us, it appears that the Sedgwicks all clung to that solemn pledge: *it can not be told.*

Catharine Maria Sedgwick *may* have written an account of her mother's death, or perhaps of the death she would have wished for her mother on that night when the harvest moon lit up the sky. Though her first published book lay fifteen years in the future on her mother's last night and morning, a few tantalizing clues indicate that the final scene of *A New-England Tale* might well be a magical, heroic reimagining of the sufferings Pamela Dwight Sedgwick endured that night.

A New-England Tale is a conventional romance in which a plucky orphan girl encounters adversity and peril before she is rescued by a kindly hero, whom she later marries. The tale is set against the backdrop of a lovingly described but unnamed Berkshire village that has many of Stockbridge's landmarks.[58]

In the final pages of the novel, though, an important but minor character steps forward, takes over the tale, and makes it her own. Catharine Maria Sedgwick was a well-educated and well-read woman, and a highly professional author. She understood the importance to a romance of a satisfying and powerful conclusion. Yet in her first published work of fiction, she considered it more important to let the madwoman have her death scene than to observe the conventional unities.

Catharine admitted in the last words of her preface that "the writer has attempted a sketch of a real character under the fictitious appellation of 'Crazy Bet,'" the madwoman who appeared from time to time to utter prophetic truths to the other characters. Pamela Sedgwick might not have been the only madwoman Catharine knew as a "real character"; several scholars have noted a resemblance between Crazy Bet and a well-known Berkshire eccentric of the early 1800s.[59] But Pamela was certainly the first and most memorable madwoman in Catharine's life. Moreover, the author gave Crazy Bet three attributes that suggest just how closely she sympathized with this troubled character. Each of these attributes associated Crazy Bet with one of the three people from whom Catharine Sedgwick learned everything she knew of parental love.

First, she gave her the name Bet. Mumbet was the only person Catharine addressed as *Mother* other than her actual mother and her oldest sister. She considered Mumbet a second mother, and after Pamela's death she used the term *Mother* frequently, both to refer to Bet and to address her. Her brothers and sisters used it as freely, and Charles wrote the epitaph that would be engraved on Bet's tombstone in the Sedgwick family burial plot, ending, "Good mother, farewell."[60]

In giving the name Bet to the madwoman, then, Catharine Sedgwick gave her a name that had always appeared to her in the company of the word *mother*. The use of the name was particularly appropriate because the real Bet had been so close to Pamela Dwight Sedgwick, even during her bouts of insanity.[61] To seal the connection, Sedgwick had the character Crazy Bet transform another character's racial characteristics, mimicking the authorial alchemy by which Catharine herself had given the name of the perfectly sane black woman to a wildly deranged white character. Crazy Bet worked her transformation on a black servant girl named Sukey, reaching from the street through a window to tear a hole in the ticking of a bed, shaking out all the feathers, throwing them at Sukey, and dusting her with the lint to turn her white. "Now Sukey," Crazy Bet had cried to the girl, "look in the glass, and you'll see how white you'll be in heaven; the black stains will all be washed out there!"[62]

Second, Catharine Sedgwick gave Crazy Bet her father's ghostly lover. She had many times heard Theodore Sedgwick's tale of his grief at the death of his first wife, and of his enchantment by the lifelike apparition of her that haunted his dreams.[63] Again there was a crucial transformation in Catharine's tale: the *woman* was the survivor, and the *man* had gone to an early grave. But the vigil of the fictitious Bet, who "would watch for whole nights by the side of a grave in her native village, where twenty years before were deposited the remains of her lover, who was drowned on the day before they were to have been married," echoed the vigil of Catharine's father waiting for his ghost dream to revisit him. Then, at almost the exact midpoint of *A New-England Tale*, Crazy Bet took the heroine Jane Elton on a nighttime pilgrimage that required them to climb a mountain. After Jane crossed a lower ledge, she looked up to the summit and saw Bet in a kind of trance, "standing between heaven and earth," and "wrapt in some heavenly vision." When Bet came out of the trance, she uttered words that Theodore Sedgwick might have uttered after one of his dream encounters with Eliza's ghost: "Oh! . . . messenger of love, and omen of mercy, I am content."[64]

Finally, Catharine gave Crazy Bet the harvest moon.

Catharine Sedgwick did not conclude her first published work of fiction with the heroine's rescue, or her marriage to the hero, or the arrest or reform or death of the villains. Instead — after all those other resolutions — she ended with a rambling scene in which Crazy Bet, the madwoman who had Mumbet's name and Theodore Sedgwick's ghostly lover, died Pamela Sedgwick's death. Perhaps it is better to say that she died the death that Catharine might have wished for her mother. But what held the deaths together was the harvest moon, lighting up the sky:

> The last time Mary [Hull] saw her, was a brilliant night during the full harvest moon; . . . the wildness of her eye was tempered with an affecting softness; her cheek was brightened with the hectic flush that looks like 'mockery of the tomb' — Mary observed her to tremble, and perceived

that there was an alarming fluttering in her pulse. "You are not well," said she.

"No, I am not well," Bet replied, in a low plaintive tone; "but I shall be soon — here," said she, placing Mary's hand on her heart — "do not you feel it struggling to be free."

Mary was startled — the beating was so irregular, it seemed that every pulsation must be the last. "Oh!" she exclaimed, "poor creature, let me put you to bed; you are not fit to be sitting here."

"Oh, no!" Bet replied, in the same feeble, mournful tone; "I cannot stay here. The spirits of heaven are keeping a festival by the light of the blessed moon. Hark! do you not hear them, Mary?" — and she sung so low that her voice sounded like distant music:

"Sister spirit, come away!"

"And do you not see their white robes?" she added, pointing through the window to the vapour that curled along the margin of the river, and floated on the bosom of the meadow.

Mary called to her husband, and whispered, "The poor thing is near death; let us get her on the bed."

Bet overheard her. "No, do not touch me," she exclaimed; "the spirit cannot soar here." She suddenly sprang on her feet, as if she had caught a new inspiration, and darted towards the door. . . . The door was open, and she passed through it so suddenly that they hardly suspected her intention before she was gone. The next morning she was discovered in the church-yard, her head resting on the grassy mound that covered the remains of her lover. Her spirit had passed to its eternal rest![65]

Did Pamela Sedgwick, like Crazy Bet, break free from her friends and family in her last night of life, and soar with the spirits in the light of the harvest moon? It is highly unlikely that she did so in any literal sense — such an escape would surely have caused enough of a stir in the town that Mary Bidwell would have heard of it, and reported it in her letter to her husband. But by allowing Crazy Bet to hear the spirits of heaven keeping their festival, and to rush out of the house to join them, Catharine Sedgwick strove to use her art to redeem her mother's suffering, which so closely resembled Crazy Bet's. By calling the madwoman *Bet*, she associated her with the dynamic woman who represented everything strong in the word *mother*. By letting the harvest moon shine on Crazy Bet's death as it had shone on Pamela Sedgwick's, she linked the death of the fictional character with the death of her real mother. And by bringing Crazy Bet to a final resting place at her lost lover's grave, she united the character with her own father in experiencing the transforming power of a lifelong grief, even as she implicitly acknowledged the pain that grief for a lost wife had caused his second wife, her mother. The miseries of that night in 1807, when the harvest moon looked down on the wretched paroxysms of a dying invalid — while her husband the Judge slept 120 miles away in Boston — *could not be told*. In telling of the death of Crazy Bet, though, and in giving that tale its surprising pride of place at the end of her first published romance, Catharine Sedgwick found a way to tell them — and to transform them.

2

The Power to Bind

Eliza, Frances, and Theodore

A host of historians of the period after the American Revolution
have found that in those decades, the ideal of romantic love
came to guide the choice of marriage partners. Couples more frequently
chose their own mates, according to judgments based on virtually every
available type of written source: letters, diaries, periodicals, and literary
works. Within some limits, young people were expected to choose on the
basis of affection. Parents hoped to be consulted about the choice, and
lovers hoped for their parents' approval, but the choice was left more and
more to the partners themselves.[1]

In every age, direct parental involvement in this decision was more
likely to be seen in wealthy and powerful families, for whom marriage
determined the course of inheritance of that wealth and power. Tradition-
ally, those parents were understood to bring a more realistic, dispassion-
ate sense of a couple's prospects, and to seek out matches that were eco-
nomically advantageous to the whole estate. But to put it in commonsense
terms, both in Europe and in America, personal attachment was not as
unimportant as one might fear before the revolutionary era, and parental involvement did not just vanish thereafter. "Republican" marriage,
in the words of Carole Shammas, "seems more a continuation of than a
departure from the eighteenth-century colonial institution, especially as
it concerns parental consent."[2]

Still, the way people made decisions about marriage, even in wealthy
families, was changing noticeably in the decades after the American Revolution, and the older children of Theodore and Pamela Sedgwick (Eliza
and Frances, married in 1797 and 1801, and young Theodore, married in

1808) provide us with opportunities to study those changes — especially the changing meaning and importance of parental consent. At least one and probably both sisters married men chosen for them by their father. Frances left behind a man she loved passionately and married a man she disliked, at her father's insistence. Their brother married a young woman of his own choosing, despite the strenuous objections of her wealthy and powerful family. The stories of these three Sedgwicks reveal a great deal about attitudes toward courtship and marriage in this generation.

Eliza, the oldest daughter, was courted for a while in her late teens by her mother's cousin Ephraim Williams, the junior partner in her father's law practice, who was then in his early thirties. Williams kept Theodore Sedgwick apprised of affairs in his home district while he was away at Congress. Catharine later claimed to believe that her "Uncle Bob" was "abstemious in eating and drinking," but her father's constituents did not think so: his reputation as a tippler was generally understood to be the reason the Federalists could not get him elected to his patron's old seat in the House of Representatives. Catharine also believed that Williams did not propose to Eliza for fear that she would have refused him. This fear was well founded. Theodore Sedgwick would never have consented to the marriage of his oldest daughter to Williams, and Eliza would not have married him without that consent.[3]

Dr. Thaddeus Pomeroy of Albany got that consent in late 1796, and he and Eliza were married the following April, a week before her twenty-second birthday. Pomeroy was a Harvard graduate ten years older than his bride. He had been trained as a physician, but gave up the practice and earned a fortune as a druggist in Albany. Although he had been raised in meager circumstances, he would do well enough to retire to Stockbridge while still in his early forties to live as a gentleman farmer.[4]

Fewer of Eliza's letters and papers survive than those of any of her brothers or sisters. It is easy to imagine why. In a span of less than twenty years, she gave birth to twelve children, eleven of whom lived to become adults. The time between their births ranged from sixteen to thirty-one months, and was typically nineteen or twenty months. Only twice in these two decades did an interval longer than two years pass between births.

Appearing as they do during the first two decades of the new century, Eliza's many children provide a backward glance at an older pattern of childbearing. What historians and demographers refer to as a "fertility transition" to smaller families was already under way, directed in large part by women's own conscious actions in limiting or postponing reproductive behavior.[5] Five of Eliza's brothers and sisters became parents after her. Their average number of children was five (the exact number for three of them), and the next-largest family to Eliza's twelve was Robert's eight, two of whom died in infancy.

Eliza's survival and continued good health through all her pregnancies and deliveries amazed her family. On a few occasions she was critically ill just before or after a delivery, most notably in 1805, when her fifth child was born just two months after the death of the fourth at twenty-one months. But by the time the ninth child was born in 1812, the business of childbearing seemed routine. "I have a new daughter N° 9," Dr. Pomeroy reported to his brother-in-law Harry, "so we go on." (His count always included the daughter who had died years earlier.) When the tenth child was born a year and a half later, Charles informed his brothers that for their sister "in this as in all other instances habit has rendered it easy." It is worth noting that of the eleven Pomeroy children who survived to adulthood, six — two of the five daughters and four of the six sons — never married. Thaddeus and Eliza Sedgwick Pomeroy, who had twelve children, had only thirteen grandchildren. No one in the entire next generation of Sedgwicks would come close to Eliza's twelve children, or even match their grandmother Pamela's ten. Three of Frances's devoutly evangelical children would have families of eight or nine, but only one other Sedgwick cousin (Theodore III) would have as many as seven children.[6]

According to her younger sister Catharine, Frances Sedgwick was a great reader of "poetry and romances," and "excitable, irritable, enthusiastic, imaginative . . . [and] sympathetic and diffusive beyond anyone I have ever known." The family's references to her, both contemporary and retrospective, hint at a ferocious temper. When she was eleven, her father considered her a good girl who nevertheless had "a vivacity of temper which . . . will frequently push her into extremes of impatience," and Catharine concluded her posthumous recollection with this thought: "dear sister Frances shone widely and irregularly, but, if ever a soul was kindled with holy fires, hers was."[7]

Pamela Dwight Sedgwick contemplated sending Frances away to a boarding school for young ladies before her daughter had turned twelve. As a mother who was at home with young children and whose husband was absent for months at a time, she was not confident of her ability to monitor her headstrong second daughter and keep her out of trouble. She was pleased to read her husband's report that at one school they were considering, "the utmost attention is paid to purity of morals and decency of conduct." Frances appears to have attended a school in Philadelphia, at least in the fall of 1792, when she was fourteen.[8]

Frances was still just fourteen when Loring Andrews, one of her father's political operatives, began to court her after her return to Stockbridge that winter. Andrews served as the Stockbridge postmaster, but his most important work for the Federalists in Berkshire County was to edit and publish their newspaper, the *Western Star*. Theodore Sedgwick appears never to have written directly to Andrews (except once, on business that was not political), but rather included in every letter he wrote to Ephraim Williams a paragraph instructing him to "tell Andrews" to do this or that. Andrews and Frances found themselves in each other's company at first largely because of their respective closeness to Williams and Eliza. Theodore Sedgwick's disapproval of Williams as a match for Eliza can only be inferred from a few cryptic remarks in Catharine Sedgwick's later reminiscences and from the fact that they both eventually married other people. But Sedgwick's distrust of Andrews in any matter relating to his daughters is amply documented.[9]

In spite of her father's disapproval, Frances's attachment to Loring Andrews grew over the next several years. When she was sent back to Philadelphia in the fall of 1796, her parents' stated reason for removing the eighteen-year-old Frances from her home was to distance her from "an affection which may prove unhappy."[10] While Frances and her father were in Philadelphia, Andrews sent Theodore Sedgwick an apologetic letter about his involvement with her. He admitted that he should have addressed Sedgwick earlier, regretting that his imprudence had caused the older man such pain. Then he asked for Frances's hand in marriage.[11]

Andrews mentioned a prediction of Theodore Sedgwick's that his "degrading habits would gain the ascendancy" over him. Whatever those degrading habits were—and it is possible that they were the same bibulous ones rumored to afflict his good friend Ephraim Williams—Andrews claimed to be hopeful of achieving "a lasting reformation." Nevertheless, he was in some kind of serious trouble in Stockbridge that winter. He planned to resign from the post office and move across the state line to Albany, New York, forty miles away. Pamela Dwight Sedgwick, who had witnessed Andrews's entire courtship of Frances, retained a fondness for him. "He is certainly in many respects an amiable character," she wrote to her husband, "and is greatly attracted to Frances."

Although Pamela was saddened to learn of Andrews's planned departure, her husband was not. Loring Andrews must have recognized that his proposal of January 1797 was not going to win Theodore Sedgwick's consent. He wrote to Frances about the same time he wrote to her father, and told her of his plans to move. That letter left her "very far from being happy," her mother reported to her father. It is revealing that Pamela, at home in Stockbridge, served as an intermediary between her husband and her daughter, who were both in Philadelphia nearly two hundred miles away from her, but who apparently had not spoken to each other on this subject.[12]

In the weeks following Andrews's proposal, all the other parties involved waited expectantly for Theodore Sedgwick's decision. Pamela was so sensitive to the delicacy of the subject that she sent her husband a long letter after two weeks in which she did not mention Andrews or the proposal, or even inquire after Frances, who was still in Philadelphia.[13] A few days later, Andrews received Theodore Sedgwick's negative response. Pamela saw that he was "greatly affected" by this letter, and reported that as a result he had begun to make his final arrangements to leave Stockbridge. Pamela knew how unhappy Frances was, but also believed that she would not disobey her father. Mother and daughter both retained the hope that once it became clear that Andrews had reformed, Theodore Sedgwick would relent and allow Frances to marry him.[14]

Over the next weeks, Loring Andrews was required to be in regular contact with Theodore Sedgwick to discuss such issues as his resignation from the editorship of the *Western Star* and the appointment of a successor at the post office. He also needed to request letters of introduction to the leading Federalists of Albany. He continued to humble himself before the man who had dashed his expectations. "May I yet indulge the hope," he pleaded "that I have not given you offense? To a cooler judgment, and to a more deliberate reflection, it may appear that I have done amiss; but when I listen to the responses of my heart, it does not accuse me of guilt. If that heart, in its indulgencies, has forced a passage thro' the bounds of propriety, let its feelings forcibly urge the plea for pardon. If the wish which it dictates could be complied with, I think my share of human happiness would not be small. But you, Sir, must determine — all rests with the decision which your goodness, wisdom and judgment shall prescribe."[15] In private, however, Andrews harbored a resentment of Sedgwick's decision. "Poor A—— is really very unhappy," Pamela Sedgwick observed, "and appears to believe that his ill fortune is owing wholly to want of property."[16]

His belief might have had some merit. After all, as he was preparing to move out of Stockbridge, Eliza Sedgwick was preparing to marry Dr.

Pomeroy, a college graduate and a man who had achieved a considerable fortune in commerce. Andrews knew that Theodore Sedgwick had chosen Pomeroy to be Eliza's husband over his friend Ephraim Williams, a fellow laborer in the vineyards of Federalist politics. It might have seemed that Theodore Sedgwick was determined his daughters should not marry a man like himself—a man whose efforts were passionately devoted to the battles of politics and the business of governing, the hardships of which were all too real and the rewards all too intangible—but instead, that they should marry men of business, men with sound material prospects.

Frances's enforced absence from Stockbridge until Andrews had left town meant that she missed her older sister's April 1797 wedding. Her father left her with family friends in New York while he returned to Stockbridge.[17] At the end of that year, when she was back in Stockbridge and her father had returned to Congress in Philadelphia, she exchanged argumentative letters with him on the subject of Andrews and his prospects. She insisted that her father's treatment of Andrews was unjust. Pamela Sedgwick looked on in dismay. "She seems to be very much fixed in her affections," she reported to her husband, "and nothing that is said by way of objection has any weight with her." Frances could not imagine being separated from Andrews forever: "the very idea fills her mind with distress," Pamela noted. When Pamela traveled from Stockbridge to Albany in February for the birth of Eliza's first child, Frances went with her, pleading with her mother that she might otherwise never see her beloved sister again. Her devotion to Eliza was genuine, but her overriding purpose seems to have been to see Andrews, which she arranged to do as soon as she got to Albany.[18]

Pamela Sedgwick was present for Frances's meeting with Andrews in Albany, and was pleased that Frances had behaved "with more propriety than at some other times." Then Frances returned to Stockbridge to look after the house and the younger children—and Andrews followed her. Pamela was forty miles away in Albany, still waiting for Eliza's baby to arrive, but at least to her husband she affected unconcern. "I did not write anything to Frances on the subject of Andrews' visit," she admitted, "as after all that has been said to her I thought she had better act for herself." Frances sent a letter a few weeks later, just after the birth of Eliza's baby, in which she reported that all was well at home.[19]

The following winter, Andrews visited Stockbridge again. Something happened early in that new year of 1799: Theodore Sedgwick sent a letter from Philadelphia in which he used dramatic and highly charged language to express his relief and gratitude "that we have rescued a beloved daughter from impending ruin." He mentioned news he had received "on the subject of her escape." If this "escape" had been from abduction against her will, Andrews would certainly have been arrested when he dared to call at the Sedgwicks' home shortly thereafter. It was more likely an attempt to elope that her relatives managed to prevent. The notion of her voluntary participation is reinforced by her father's assertion that "she has been to blame much to blame in her transactions with Andrews." Her brother Theodore, who was always eager to defend his headstrong sister and mediate between her and their father, replied that "she has acted with the best possible motives. . . . [S]he has been guilty of a great many imprudences and is willing that they should be imputed to her. But she can not be brought to think that she has been to blame."[20]

When Andrews did pay that bold call, Frances refused to see him. His response was bitter—so bitter that he began to express it aloud. "Andrews speaks of Frances with the utmost scorn and contempt," Theodore told their father. "He abuses her shamefully upon every occasion." The frustrated suitor began to tell tales about her around town, and to claim that he had never loved her. Young Theodore, with all the wisdom of an eighteen year old who had just graduated from college, pronounced that "Frances's attachment founded upon extravagance and enthusiasm and not upon virtues could not exist long after the object of it was removed." Her feeling toward Andrews, Theodore reported, was now "a proper resentment which has already cured her of all love."[21]

Andrews went back to Albany, and traces of his later life and work are elusive. But young Theodore's confidence about the change in his sister's affections seems simplistic. For more than six years—from a few months before her fifteenth birthday until a few months before her twenty-first—a passionate attachment to Loring Andrews was part of Frances Sedgwick's everyday experience of the world. When Andrews had once before started spreading rumors about Frances, in Albany before Frances's visit there, Pamela (who had observed them longest and may have known them best) had been appalled at his insincerity. "If he does not indeed sincerely love F——," she insisted, "he has duped himself as well as others."[22] When it ended at last, bitterly, with what appears to have been a failed attempt to elope, Frances was ready to do her father's bidding and marry the kind of prosperous businessman he had found for Eliza. But not before she had a last word on the affair, in a letter she sent to her father:

> Unkindly as he has treated me yet my parent neither time or memory or approving conscience, could afford me happiness, if I had been capable of insulting his affections—or even in wounding his pride. I could only be unhappy. On my knees and with a heart the most grateful, I thank

heaven, that it is not *in my power* to interrupt his happiness. I had infinitely rather be the object of his hatred — of his stigmas — than the source of his regret, and even now I would spare no exertion (if his peace required exertions) to make him completely happy. I will my father in one principle be capable of a virtue that is practiced for its own sake — I will never feel a resentment towards him however he aims to stimulate all my just displeasure, and he shall not have it in his power, to render me indifferent to his well-being and happiness. My prayers shall unalterably be offered for both, and weigh all the circumstances that you know my parent relative to both. Suppress the partial Father. Judge as well of Andrews as he can merit. I would not be the cause of diminishing one deserved friendly sentiment towards him. I would have him possess all that can add to his enjoyment. For this line of conduct I can never be sorry. The time will come, when we shall all be seen justly. The veil that is rended hereafter, will place all our actions in their just light — and then it will be known that Frances (however little she merits) never played to A——s — the parasite and never feigned sentiment she did not feel. I have now done with the subject.[23]

Frances, according to her sister Catharine, had always been a reader of romances, and she would certainly not be the only young woman to model her behavior on the sentimental literature she had read. Indeed, one of the leading historians of human sexuality and romantic love in the English-speaking world discerns a strong correlation between the rise of literacy, with the opportunity it brought for such independent reading, and the rise of romantic love as an individualistic ideal in the making of marriages.[24] This vision of the young Frances as a reader of romances is part of what makes one cringe to read the next chapters of her life. By the time she had written her gracious and self-sacrificing valediction, playing out the last scene of her own romance, and sent it to her father, he had already selected a prospective husband for her — in fact, she had already met him. And for a passionate young woman like Frances, Ebenezer Watson would be no romantic hero.

He was, her father believed, "a man of virtue, of unblemished character, and of happy prospects."[25] Frances might have met him as early as April 1797 when she was staying with a mutual friend's family in New York, while in Stockbridge Eliza was marrying Thaddeus Pomeroy and Andrews was packing his bags.[26] Watson was involved in a variety of businesses, including the sale of food; his letters are filled with inquiries about the availability of cider and the cost of hams. But his major business was publishing. His family had founded and owned Hartford's *Connecticut Courant*, but Ebenezer sought success in New York, becoming involved in several bookstore and book publishing ventures that might well have impressed Theodore Sedgwick.

The letter of February 1799 in which Frances urged her father to think kindly of Loring Andrews also contained an account of a recent exchange of letters with Ebenezer Watson. Ebenezer had been dissatisfied with a statement Frances made to him in her letter. Her noncommittal version of it was, "That if esteem, founded in the *principle* of valuing worth for its own sake, could in the intercourse of acquaintance secure the first interest of the heart, mine might in that intercourse and acquaintance be secured to him." Ebenezer's disappointment at this half-hearted compliment had reached her father's ears. He had in turn sent Frances some admonitions about the forwardness of her behavior toward Ebenezer that angered her. "His suggestion of my treating him with uncommon attention is indelicate, for it is entirely unfounded," she informed her father defiantly. "Indeed there were many whom I treated before him with more preference than I did himself." Frances stated flatly to her father that she had no qualms about Watson's discomfort. "I cannot regret it," she fairly spat out, "for not as you suppose my dear Papa—attached to him I am not." She knew he was a respectable character, and in keeping with her father's wishes she would struggle "to coalesce the affection and approbation of my heart." But if her behavior had led Watson to threaten to end their "alliance," she assured her father, "I must and shall be perfectly satisfied." Her only lament was that her father and brother would be disappointed.[27]

The brother in question was young Theodore. He spoke highly of Watson in ways he knew his father would appreciate: "I think him a man of business, which is saying almost everything of any man in any profession or occupation." But Frances was less impressed. "I must love him, I believe, because my friends do," she summed up (using "friends" in its eighteenth-century sense to mean members of her immediate and extended family), "but in this case nature and custom seem to be inverted." Frances identified the first rising up of a passionate new love as part of "nature," and friends' traditional willingness to accept the people whom their friends had chosen to love as "custom." To her, this underscored the perversity of her situation: Her father and brother had fallen in love with the idea of Watson as her husband, and she was expected—unnaturally—to conform to their passion because of her devotion to them.[28]

Frances continued to find Watson cold and stiff, his abrupt manners distasteful, and his lack of warmth distressing. In January 1800, young Theodore saw her when she received a letter from Watson that "nearly created such a disgust as almost to obliterate all her former friendship for him." He had written "in his cool moderate manner" asking her to select a date when they should be married. "She was offended at the indifference, with which he treated such a subject and hinted it to him," Theodore reported to his father. "He returned for answer that she would not have him address her in the baby cant of a whining lover." To Theodore it seemed a trifle, but it gave rise in Frances to "an almost unconquerable aversion." Her brother believed he could see the point of conflict. "Frances has a warm affectionate disposition," he knew from experience, "and she cannot be won by anything less than that warmth of love and esteem for her, which she professes for others. Eben is undoubtedly jealous from the representations which have been made of her character" — that is, from her long history with Andrews — "and is unwilling to commit himself by any profuse exhibitions of tenderness and love, lest a bad use of them should be made by her at some future period." Theodore knew this was the wrong approach for a man to take in wooing his sister, "but as you say," he commiserated with his father, "who can tell him, that such conduct will deprive him of Frances inevitably?"[29]

In March 1800, Loring Andrews appeared for a last gasp, and may have done his rival Watson an unintended favor. Frances had heard from a cousin that Andrews was telling anyone in Albany who would listen that "he would not marry Frances or any other woman for he is unable to support a wife." Frances, who had been courted by Andrews for six years, appears to have considered this an insult, and she made up her mind to go to Albany (where her sister and brother now lived, and where her mother was already visiting) "to convince our wise gentry," young Theodore supposed, "that she is not a hopeless lover." Theodore was eager for her to come, "for I take so much pride and pleasure in contemplating her worth," he confessed, "that I want the world to know what a sister I possess."

Her more astute father knew his daughter well enough to dread this visit, and its effects on Watson's thinking. "I do not know what reflections a recommencement of intimacy with Andrews may produce," he admitted. He asked with trepidation: Did she see him? But Frances's visit to Albany produced no new encounter with Andrews; "they both endeavored to shun each other," young Theodore surmised. Frances returned to Stockbridge "with a firm determination to love Watson, if possible," he informed his father. He acknowledged that while this was certainly "a dutiful resolve," it might be a difficult one. "From what little I know of him I suspect that he will make a better husband than lover," he added optimistically. "Few of either sex at my age are willing to connect themselves, with one, to whom they are not passionately attached."[30]

By the fall of 1800, Frances's resolution had yielded a change of heart: "I am more happy than I have ever been with regard to a subject which must influence the affections and happiness of the heart," she wrote to her brother concerning Ebenezer. "The qualities he has now revealed make me regard a connection with him as desirable in every view. . . . In short — the best thing I can say is that I really love him, and feel as much respect for his character as to confide that I may be stimulated to virtue by the force of his example and the earnest desire of contributing to his happiness."[31]

Frances and Ebenezer made plans to be married in the spring, shortly after her father concluded his tenure in Congress. Theodore Sedgwick still basked in the recollection of his arrival in New York that fall, when "I was congratulated by all my friends on the prospect of a connection between my daughter and a young gentleman of such a character and such prospects." Frances fell into the spirit of the wedding preparations in the spring of 1801 with great zeal. "Indeed," concluded brother Theodore after spending some time with his sister and Watson, "I think she is as enthusiastically fond of him as she ever was of Andrews." After Frances visited with his daughter, old friend Henry Van Schaack wrote to observe, "I dare say [she] is grateful for the firmness you have manifested in preventing her from going down a ruinous precipice."[32]

Frances Sedgwick and Ebenezer Watson were married on April 9, 1801. Six weeks before the wedding, the bride-to-be wrote to her father:

> I never sit down to write you, my beloved parent, without antecedently reflecting that I can perform nothing worthy of you. The sense of your excellence rises in my heart, and the feeling it there raises, sends one of those warm suffusions to my face, which speaks the force of an affection and admiration, that no language can copy. . . . I cannot express the affection, esteem, and respect I feel for this excellent young man: I wish I thought my own merits proportional in any fit measure to his. . . . As for me insignificant as I am, I can hope to cause little happiness anywhere, but through countless time you will be remunerated for all your goodness to me. How great then must the whole sum of your reward, since I am only one, and equal excellence has animated your conduct to all your children.

It is hard to find the voice of the once-fiery Frances in this letter. Loss, unworthiness, and submission were its overriding themes. Frances reminded her father that he still had a daughter to entertain him at home. "Catharine is a lovely child," she assured him, "and will much more than compensate my loss." With all its emphasis on loss, on being remembered and rewarded through eternity for one's goodness and kindness in life, it reads more like a funeral elegy than a wedding hymn.[33]

Eben and Frances took up residence in New York, and the couple's first child, a son, was born on George Washington's birthday, just over ten months after they were married. It is a mark of their determination to honor the baby's maternal grandfather that amid the holiday commemorations, this staunch Federalist family managed *not* to name the newborn after the late president. Theodore Sedgwick Watson was joined by a brother, Ebenezer, two years later, and by a sister Catharine two years after that. Meanwhile, Eben's businesses prospered so much that his brother-in-law Theodore marveled to his father that "the assurance of *his* prosperity, would almost make *me* rich." Even Catharine felt it necessary to acknowledge to her mother that "Mr Watson . . . is one of the best men in the world."[34]

The family could not have been more surprised when Eben's business was announced to have stopped payment of its obligations—the first step down the precipice to collapse—on September 1, 1806. But even that setback proved temporary. "I feel great consolation," Theodore told his father, "in knowing that his worst enemies cannot impute to him dishonor, or reproach him with anything but misfortune. . . . When I consider his youth his health his talents and integrity, I do not suffer myself to doubt that a short time will place [him] in an eligible and independent situation." Watson was back in business, shipping wine, brandy, oysters, brown sugar, coffee, and four kinds of tea up the Hudson from New York, before three months had passed. At the end of the following summer, as the harvest moon signaled the coming of autumn, Ebenezer Watson enjoyed a delightful hunting expedition in Stockbridge with his brother-in-law Harry. They wished brother Theodore could have been with them. "We know no one," Harry wrote playfully later that day, "who would more faithfully *stay* by the baggage."[35]

Young Theodore had much to celebrate as that summer of 1807 wound to a close. His legal practice in Albany was flourishing, and while he and his brothers realized that this was not so momentous an accomplishment as winning the Revolution in which their father and many of their neighbors had fought for the freedom of the new Republic just thirty years earlier, he was happy to have the reputation of a successful lawyer. "The truth is Harry," he confided to his brother that year, "that great men are only made by great occasions. There are few opportunities for digging up witnesses. The occasions in which a bold stand may be made for the liberties of the country are very rare. Libel suits seem now to be the only road to fame."[36] To add to his happiness, Theodore had recently become engaged to a woman he had courted persistently for three years.

Theodore probably met Susan Ridley in Albany some time in 1803 or early 1804. Years later, Catharine Maria Sedgwick had vivid memories of the day she went with her oldest brother to Mrs. Bell's school in Albany to be introduced at the start of her studies. Some of the girls offered to teach her to jump rope during the noon recess. As she left, she recalled, one of the "mannerless girls" shouted out to her, "Give Miss Ridley's love to your brother!" Catharine turned and saw "a delicate, fair, and elegant girl overpowered with confusion, and blushing up to the roots of her soft brown hair." The blushing girl called out to try to overrule her teasing friend, "Oh don't, don't!"

The fateful encounter had a natural appeal to the composer and inveterate reader of romances, for the blushing girl was Susan Ridley, of course, and they were destined to be lifelong friends. Susan was not quite sixteen, almost two years older than Catharine, and was concluding her studies at Mrs. Bell's just as Catharine was beginning hers. Her blushes were significant, for what Catharine called a "mutual interest" between Susan and the twenty-three-year-old Theodore had begun months earlier.[37]

Susan's mother was Catharine "Kitty" Livingston, a member of the powerful New York family whose manorial holdings covered much of the Hudson River valley. Her father, Matthew Ridley, who served during the American Revolution as a commercial and diplomatic agent of the Continental Congress in Europe, had died at forty in 1789, leaving his widow with two infant daughters. After seven years as a widow, Kitty married again. Her new husband was one of her Livingston first cousins, John Livingston, who already had ten children of his own from his first marriage.[38]

Livingston wanted Susan Ridley to marry one of his own sons, and therefore bitterly opposed Theodore Sedgwick's courtship of his stepdaughter.[39] Theodore appears to have proposed sometime in 1805, but by October of that year he had given up any attempt to go against John Livingston's wishes. Harry and Robert Sedgwick greeted the news of their brother's submission to the will of the powerful Mr. Livingston with chagrin. For Susan's sake as well as his own, Harry and Robert believed that Theodore should have pressed his case and saved her from a loveless marriage. Susan would have married him even without her stepfather's consent, they were sure. Susan's mother did not share her husband's wishes, and Susan preferred Theodore to her stepbrother, or to any other likely suitor. What was he waiting for?[40]

Theodore reestablished a relationship with Susan some time in 1806, but his brothers still chastised him for his irresolution. "They say you have not got the *grit* to ax a gal," Harry complained to Theodore as the year drew to a close, and then unburdened himself of an allusive sermon on the theme of procrastination as a thief of time.

It will suck the marrow from your backbone, and the mucus (if there be such a thing) from your knee pans. Your cheeks will soon lose their down of peaches and will be forsaken by the bloom of roseate virginity. Why, ak! why will you waste your sweetness on the desert air? Why like the virgin lily will you droop in obscurity? When adversity comes like a ploughshare you will be cut down like a solitary reed, unlike the myrtle interlaced with a sister plant, supporting and supported. Think of having children, those sweet little prattlers, sitting on your knees and charming away all your cares, especially about pecuniary matters. Think also of having a beauteous, kind, comfortable, loving, sympathetic, amiable, judicious wife to whom you can unbosom yourself every night of all worldly cares — and who will take care of you and clothe you, and feed you and the little hungry bonds of union between you and her. You are desirous of acquisition and there are many who very seriously affirm when clasping their charmers that they have the whole world within their arms. Some of them most certainly have a large part of it. I have mentioned some of the most powerful and most common motives to matrimony. You may find many others of a similar nature in *books*.[41]

Still Theodore dithered. Robert, in Albany working as a clerk in Theodore's law office, heard reliable information that Susan had turned down at least one other proposal, from a merchant who had come all the way from Baltimore to ask. Harry wondered if Theodore's reluctance to press his case was based on "none but pecuniary considerations" — the clear threat that Susan would be at least partly disinherited if she defied her stepfather. "Your present determination," he lamented, "seems to be founded on an idea . . . that Miss R. would consider nothing she could find in this connection as counterbalancing the loss of fortune," — an idea Harry was sure was incorrect. If she were to marry Theodore, the threatened disinheritance by stepfather John Livingston would not leave Susan poor: she was already in possession of some of her father's estate, and the Sedgwicks were not without resources. It was time for Theodore to give up the single life. "No man who lives (as you propose) sullenly for himself alone, can be happy," Harry warned his older brother.[42]

In April 1807, Theodore again expressed a belief that the affair was over. (His father learned of this by breaking the seal of a letter that Theodore had addressed to Harry. "Whether it be that my curiosity grows stronger or my morality more feeble I know not," he rationalized, "but so it was that I felt myself unable to resist my strong desire to see the contents.") The family despaired of Theodore's resolve. "Let me . . . ask you," his father demanded in May, "whether you think you can be happy in your passage thro life in the solitary state of a bachelor? If you can I have been miserably mistaken as to the social affections which I supposed you to possess. If a chaste and indissoluble connection with a worthy and virtuous woman is essential to your happiness," the Judge argued, "is there any reason to hope a more pleasing one than with the lovely charming girl I have in my mind?" The elder Theodore was sure that by his inaction, his son was "laying a foundation for lasting future regret."[43]

All this family pressure eventually wore young Theodore down. Much as he dreaded risking rejection and its associated embarrassments by forthrightly proposing, he had come to fear his family's condemnations, and the "lasting future regret" they forecast for him, even more. In July he went to New York, where Susan Ridley had been staying since May, and asked her to marry him. She accepted at once. Her stepfather fumed, but her mother, who did not dare give her overt consent, quietly informed them that she would not stand in her daughter's way, and that Susan should act as she pleased.[44] "Yes my dear brother my ribs are parted," Theodore told Harry. "Susan Ridley has one of them." Harry wrote to Theodore from Litchfield, where he had begun attending Judge Reeve's law lectures, "I rejoiced to hear that you went to New York and that you behaved so manfully when there."[45]

Theodore proposed to Susan Ridley while he was staying with his sister Frances and her husband. Catharine had kept Frances informed of the earlier progress of the affair with regular letters from Albany and Stockbridge. Ebenezer Watson's reactions to Theodore's plight were occasionally quoted by his father-in-law or one of his brothers-in-law. But how did Frances Sedgwick Watson react to this story — to Susan Ridley's rejection of a parent's command forbidding her to marry an "unacceptable" man? We can only guess. The elder Theodore Sedgwick does not seem to have been troubled by any sense of inconsistency while urging his son Theodore to do what would have caused him indignation if his daughter Frances had done it; but of course, Theodore was his son, and he was marrying up the social ladder.

At first the lovers planned to wait two years before marrying, in hopes of softening John Livingston's resistance. Harry quoted Ebenezer Watson's reaction: "This business of two years is fudge." The elder Theodore agreed with his son-in-law, writing the following spring that "the sooner the thing is concluded in my opinion the better," because "the hostility of L. will not only continue but be increased as long as it shall hang in suspense."[46]

Theodore and Susan finally decided on a November 1808 wedding. "I am rejoiced that an end is put to the state of suspense in which I have been," Theodore wrote to his father once the date was set. "Indeed I hardly know why we were not married a year ago." When Susan fell ill in early November, the wedding had to be postponed. It finally took place on Monday evening, November 28. Susan's uncle, Supreme Court Justice Brockholst Livingston, presided. Kitty Livingston did not attend her daughter's wedding.[47]

Judge Sedgwick's prediction proved to be only partly correct. John Livingston's hostility to the marriage lasted years beyond Susan and Theodore's wedding. Kitty Livingston visited and corresponded with her daughter and her daughter's husband, and even asked young Theodore to handle some legal business for her, but her husband would not let the young couple into his home, separately or together. Only when her mother was on her deathbed did Susan Ridley Sedgwick, after five years of marriage and the birth of two children, receive what her husband called the "inestimable blessing that the heart of M^r L was so far softened, as to permit her to enter his doors."[48]

Over the course of a little more than a decade, the three oldest Sedgwicks of this generation married. Their courtships, weddings, and marriages show an institution in transition. In 1797, Eliza fell into step with her father's choice easily, and left behind her earlier attachment to Ephraim Williams without apparent complaint. Her younger sister was a different story. Twenty-seven years after he had married Pamela Dwight against her family's wishes, the elder Theodore Sedgwick had become wealthy and powerful enough (at least in part as a result of that marriage) to be one of those fathers who expected to preside over his daughters' marriage decisions. But Frances had plans and attachments of her own, and their conflict was only resolved after years of angry and bitter confrontation. Theodore and his traditional view prevailed, and in 1801 Frances married Ebenezer Watson, her father's choice.

Frances was not the only young woman of her generation to suffer from a father's attempt to force her to marry a man she did not love. In 1808, Susan Ridley faced down the demands of her even wealthier and more powerful stepfather. She gave up much of her fortune when she married the man she loved, Frances's brother Theodore. But even the elder Theodore Sedgwick had to applaud her spirited defiance, her insistence on marrying only for love. It is not at all clear that he understood what had changed in those intervening seven years, but from a distance of two centuries it is hard to miss.

3

Bitterness in the Cup of Joy
A Stepmother, a Death, a Will

Like Susan Ridley's mother and stepfather, Judge Theodore Sedgwick did not attend the wedding of his son and namesake. His reasons for staying away, though, were unlike those of the Livingstons. Two weeks earlier, he too had gotten married.

Throughout history, the reactions of grown and nearly grown children to a widowed father's sudden introduction of a stepmother into their midst have frequently been stiff and awkward. Such a change has economic as well as emotional repercussions, and no one would be more aware of these than a judge's sons who had themselves become lawyers or were studying to become lawyers. The responses of Judge Sedgwick's children to the Judge's plan to remarry ranged from astonishment to depression to stunned silence. Most of all, they feared Penelope Russell Sedgwick's effect on their home and family. Young Theodore expressed his horror at the Judge's plans to remarry in June 1808, when their mother had been dead a little more than eight months. (In nearly every society, widowers have been quicker to remarry than widows, but at least some of the Sedgwick brothers and sisters knew that after the death of his first wife in 1771, Theodore had waited and grieved for more than three years before marrying their mother.)[1] "I see in it the certainty of the breaking up of the family," Theodore wrote to Harry. "That Miss R. will not live in Stockbridge is I think certain and that the Judge will be little disposed to remain there is as much so." For one of the only things the brothers knew of the thirty-nine-year-old Penelope Russell was that she was not made for country life.

Penelope Russell was born in 1769 to a Cambridge family whose sympathies during the Revolution were so firmly with the Tories that they had moved to England. They returned to Boston after the war, and Theodore Sedgwick was one of the lawyers who argued for her uncle, William Vassall, in his attempts to recover property that had been confiscated by the state of Massachusetts during the Revolution. Catharine Sedgwick later said that the Judge "was flattered into this marriage by some good-natured friends who believed he would be the happier for it, and knew she would."[2]

Even before the Judge married Penelope Russell, Harry sensed problems ahead. "I am more confirmed in the opinion that he does not anticipate his approaching connection with pleasure," he told brother Theodore on the last day of October 1808. He was troubled by a recent quarrel between his future stepmother and her neighbor Mrs. Tucker, who a few years earlier had been a gracious hostess to Harry, Robert, and Catharine during a prolonged visit to Cambridge and Boston after the boys had graduated from Williams College. When young Theodore got Harry's letter, he had probably already received his father's letter of ten days earlier, and he must have marveled at Harry's perceptiveness. For the Judge had made a remarkable admission: "There is much, in my circumstances, in this solemn event, to make me thoughtful and gloomy; and it does make me gloomy. I have, indeed, a high opinion of Miss R. but I hardly know what to say or think. She is sensible, and I believe amiable, yet I can foresee events which would render the connection a source of uneasiness and misery."[3]

A week after expressing his doubts to his older brother, Harry sent a note of congratulations to his father on his impending marriage. The note could be described as lukewarm at best, sounding at times like a legal brief:

I know of no right which children can have in any mode to interfere in the conduct of so excellent a father, with respect to an affair so important as his marriage. Their interests may possibly be affected, but they are affected by the exercise of a perfect right in their father. . . . You certainly must have understood the character of Miss Russell in all those points which would most probably affect your happiness and that of your children, and unless you had believed it suitable in both these respects, you surely would not have proceeded to form the connection. You may be assured that we all feel disposed to treat her whom you shall introduce in the place of our mother with the utmost affection and respect. With regard to the whole affair, it is certainly a very fortunate circumstance that there seems to be not the slightest shade of difference in opinion or sentiment in the minds of the children with relation to the subject. Some of us affect not to have feelings on this occasion which we believe to be natural and unavoidable, yet none of us pretend to question that you have a most undoubted right to remarry, and that you are the sole judge with respect to the propriety of the choice.

None of the children knew when the wedding was to take place, and none of them attended it. Most of them were getting ready to attend young Theodore's wedding in New York. Harry closed his long letter of November 7 by extending a greeting "to Miss Russell (which name I presume she yet retains)." A week later, sixteen-year-old Charles closed a letter to his father very grandly, "with my warmest love and wishes for your happiness and that of Miss Russell." On the same sheet, Robert asked his father to "remember me very affectionately to Miss Russell," and Eliza informed him that "Dr. P. unites in fond remembrance to yourself and your good dear friend." But unknown to them all, in Boston on the day Harry had written the first letter, their father's friend had become his wife. Miss Russell no longer retained that name; she had become the new Mrs. Sedgwick.[4]

Catharine never would use any form of the term *mother* in referring to her father's third wife, and in these first few weeks she even had a hard time calling her Mrs. Sedgwick. "The family all unite with me in the fondest remembrance *to you and yours,*" she closed her first letter to her father after receiving the news. Like most other members of the family, she heard the news from Harry, to whom the Judge announced it in a letter almost a week after the wedding. Judge Sedgwick acknowledged that the family had not discussed his remarriage, but he assured his children that they had nothing to fear from his introduction of a stepmother into the family. "Had I imagined it possible that the harmony of the family could have been disturbed by this event, or the happiness of my dear children impaired I would have preferred death to it," he promised. "I believe my companion to be kind, gentle, affectionate and good."[5]

The first unpleasant news for the family that could be attributed to the remarriage of the Judge had come a week before that event, when Mumbet announced that she was leaving the family's service. Not only had she been close to Pamela Dwight Sedgwick, she had also been given considerable freedom to manage both the household and her own time during Pamela's long illnesses. With the arrival of the new Mrs. Sedgwick imminent, she became "resolutely determined to leave the family." Catharine believed that she "felt that she could no longer maintain the authority into which she had gradually grown." Mumbet remained closely connected to the family — "a necessary link in the family chain," Catharine called her.

She attended at the births of most of their children, and eventually came to be buried in their family burial plot. But as of November 1808, she was no longer a member of the household. The Judge had no idea what a wrenching loss this was for Catharine and her brothers. "I hope you will be able to procure a successor to Bet," he wrote blithely to Harry, "so as to prevent the necessity of taking a woman from Boston."[6]

On her first visit to Stockbridge as the new Mrs. Sedgwick, Penelope made a favorable impression. "We have for a considerable part of the time since her arrival passed our time in that hilarity which usually characterizes the meetings of our family," Harry informed Catharine (who was staying with Frances's family in New York) a few months after the wedding. But there were some reassurances he could not deliver, as Catharine must have realized with a pang when she read on. "The only unpleasant circumstance which I had not precisely anticipated," Harry wrote with an almost visible blush, "was to see our revered father caressing a woman with any other sentiment than that of paternal affection."

The new Mrs. Sedgwick occasionally stayed in Stockbridge in the Judge's absence. More frequently, she traveled from court session to court session with him. The children recognized her distaste for life in the country. "She fluttered gracefully enough through the inanities of town drawing-rooms," Catharine later remembered, "but the reality and simplicity of our country life was insupportable to her."[7]

It was probably natural and understandable that the appearance of a stepmother in their midst should provoke a man's grown sons, especially grown sons who were lawyers, to urge their father to make plans for the eventual division and distribution of his estate. They did not expect that their father and his thirty-nine-year-old bride would have children, but it was within the realm of possibility, and even without bearing stepbrothers and stepsisters, Penelope would be able to make claims of her own. Young Theodore raised the subject with the Judge just three months after they both got married, prompted (he said) by "the late change in our family," and at least in part by reports he had heard that his new stepmother's own property was "vast." A year later, when he was planning a move to Boston after an unsuccessful campaign for a seat in the state legislature, Harry made a similar request to the Judge, and an additional one: that the Judge should divide up his property and distribute his children's shares right away, presumably to prevent the new Mrs. Sedgwick from complicating that distribution. Two weeks after receiving Harry's letter, the Judge drew up the will that would eventually be executed at his death. He did not divide his property up at once, though. "My expenses are enormous, and I know not how to retrench," he admitted to Harry. (Two years later, Charles would assert that Mrs. Sedgwick was "a spendthrift.") He had hoped to retire from the court, but claimed he could not afford to because his assets could not be sold, or at least not without great inconvenience. He assured Harry that his inheritance was secure. "You have a good deal due to you," he promised, "and it will be a great relief to me that you should leave none of it behind." True to his word, the Judge wrote a will that gave his sons every option for protecting their property and enjoying the fruits of all their father's hard work and shrewd investing.[8]

As these requests seemed to hint, so later developments confirmed: the Sedgwick children were deeply suspicious and mistrustful of their stepmother, and by late 1811 they were disgusted with her. All the letters of 1811 mentioned the new Mrs. Sedgwick's precarious health, and as her illness dragged on, Catharine spoke more and more openly of her suspicions regarding the causes of that illness — her intemperate misuse of alcoholic beverages. "Mrs. Sedgwick had a very ill turn yesterday in consequence of indigestion," she wrote to Robert near the end of May. "She is certainly seriously out of health, but I believe it is almost entirely the consequence of her mode of living." Their father feared that her death was imminent, and his treatment of her seemed to Catharine to be a model of compassion. "Her wants and sufferings inspire that tenderness which she has no qualities to excite," she told Robert.

When Mrs. Sedgwick had finally recovered enough to leave Stockbridge with the Judge, Charles heaved a sigh of relief. "I consider it a piece of good fortune to get rid of the society of one for a little while whose selfish and uneasy temper is death almost to domestic comfort." He even referred to his "detestation" for his stepmother, "who sacrifices every worthy and honorable and delicate quality of the female character to her own *miserable* gratification." The brothers mocked Mrs. Sedgwick openly in their letters. Charles's exasperation came through clearly in his assertion the next time he saw her that "Mrs. S. is in her usual state of health." Charles's bitterness grew over time, until he could write to Harry, "At home we are all well except one member of our family of whom it is painful and sickening to speak."[9]

The fall of 1811 brought a crisis, which finally elicited from the grieving Catharine a mention of their mother, now four years dead, in a comparison that was brutally unflattering to the woman their father had married in her stead. Something the Judge said while visiting young Theodore in Albany led Catharine, Harry, and Theodore to believe that Mrs. Sedgwick was using "her blasting influence" to prejudice her Boston friends, and even the Judge himself, against Harry, at a moment when Harry was struggling to establish a legal career and reputation there. In writing about this to Robert, Catharine heaped scorn on her stepmother with such vehemence that the subsequent comments about their dead mother seem almost to have been shaken loose:

> The miserable half gratification of an insatiate vanity, and the bustle of impertinent trifling make up the sum total of Mrs. S's happiness. If this is true and every day's observation proves it, is not she an object of commiseration? Let us together my dearest Robert thank our God, that that purity which is now sainted in Heaven, shed its blessed influence on the formation of our characters, and early taught us to love the light of virtue and the favor of Heaven.
>
> May the memorial of her excellence, the treasured recollection of her patient endurance of every evil preserve us from even a momentary forgetfulness of our filial duty. That duty must be paramount to all earthly ones, and it is made easy and delightful to us by the parental virtues of the best of fathers. If *we* do *right* Mrs. S. cannot invade the sacred circle of our happiness. . . .[10]

Whatever imagined or self-inflicted injuries caused Mrs. Sedgwick's frequent ailments (and Catharine continued to suspect that her physician's "brandy and laudanum system" was the cause rather than the cure), her husband in 1812 suffered from a series of real, painful, and eventually debilitating illnesses. In February his gout was so bad that Ephraim Williams and Charles had to carry him from room to room. At the end of March, he and Mrs. Sedgwick left for Boston to attend court sessions. "Mrs. S. was sick when she left home, but I believe the last view of the mansion restored her," Charles informed Catharine waspishly. The Judge returned home alone and feeble at the end of April.[11]

In June the Judge's health appeared to improve a little, and Mrs. Sedgwick (who had returned shortly after her husband) was spared any of what Catharine referred to as her "spasms." But the Judge's improvement was temporary, and conflicting prescriptions from doctors in Boston and Stockbridge did not make things easier: the steam that one recommended for gout only worsened the asthmatic condition that the other was trying to treat. The Judge was so ill that Frances's children had to skip their usual summer-long visit with their beloved grandfather in Stockbridge.

By the end of summer the Judge's pain was so great that he could not sleep without opium, but he refused to take the drug because it interfered with his appetite. All his children made an extra effort to get to Stockbridge for an end-of-summer reunion, and by the last week of August everybody was there but Harry. "Pray come and complete our family circle as soon as possible," Robert wrote to him. "I want to settle the destinies of our country with you." Young Theodore's law partner, Harmanus Bleecker, was with them, and he felt a premonition that he was seeing the Judge in the midst of his family for the last time.[12]

A traumatic dispute flared up sometime during the family reunion. The only specific reference to its cause is young Theodore's expression of regret that so many members of the family had made occasional remarks that were injudicious and "calculated to excite ridicule." It seems likely that, with all the bright and occasionally sharp-tongued Sedgwick children gathered together, with even mild-mannered Charles by now completely out of patience with Mrs. Sedgwick, and with the added anxiety of the Judge's grave illness facing them, one or more of the younger Sedgwicks must have exchanged bitter words with their stepmother (who else did they ridicule?), which then escalated into a major incident, possibly even involving the Judge himself. "Had I imagined it possible that the harmony of the family could have been disturbed by this event, or the happiness of my dear children impaired," the Judge had written just after he married Penelope Russell four years earlier, "I would have preferred death to it. I may be mistaken — it is possible; but if I am I am sure that my life will cease with the disappointment." In September 1812, with death approaching, the Judge appears to have found himself involved in a corrosive family dispute caused by the stepmother they were supposed to consider "kind, gentle, affectionate and good."[13]

Catharine gave up her plans to spend the winter with Frances in New York in order to stay home to care for her father. She expected that he would be unable to attend the court sessions in Boston in November, but despite a sensation in his stomach that he could only label "indescribable," he wrote to ask Harry to secure lodgings for himself, Catharine, and Mrs. Sedgwick. "I am more and more convinced that my going to Boston is almost necessary to papa," Catharine explained to Robert. *"You know Mrs. Sedgwick."*

Family and friends were astonished and frightened by the Judge's determination to attend court in Boston, but he made the journey. When he got there, everything — the damp vapors in the courthouse, his medicines, his restricted diet, his uncomfortable lodgings — conspired to weaken and dispirit him. Harry found his father's condition alarming, and Catharine wished she had tried harder to persuade him not to come.[14]

Sometime in December, Harry and Catharine began to wonder whether they should summon their brothers and sisters to Boston for what was

looking more and more like a final farewell. Charles arrived from Stockbridge on December 24, and Robert came from New York before the end
of the year. Theodore was unable to come because of Susan's "critical situation": they were expecting the birth of their second child in early January.
The two married sisters expressed concerns about the state of their father's
religious faith—the kind of concerns their mother had raised forty years
earlier. Dr. Pomeroy spoke to Harry of a vision of the Judge being borne to
heaven by angels, "there in heaven to meet his wife and our mother who
has gone before him. How glorious it will be for them to unite again in the
blissful regions above," he rhapsodized. But they all knew that the Judge
was not a religious man, not even a church member, and had never made
a profession of his belief. For Eliza, Frances, and Ebenezer this was a real
worry. Frances urged her brothers on the scene to bring to their father's
bedside "a ministering servant of the Redeemer" to guide him.[15]

Shortly after the new year began, the Judge told Catharine "that he had
for many years been desirous to make a public profession of religion."
He had never done so before because he refused to join the church at
Stockbridge, where Pamela's uncle Stephen West, who had objected to
their marriage nearly forty years earlier, was still the minister. For fear
of offending West and other family members who were members of the
Stockbridge church, though, he could not bring himself to join any other.
Catharine offered to send for her friend William Ellery Channing, one of
Boston's most liberal young clerics, but the Judge demurred, telling her
that instead, "if it should please God I wish to do it in the face of the
world." Nevertheless, Channing visited a week later. "Papa imparted to
him his earnest desire to unite himself to the visible church, and his reluctance to defer it," Catharine reported. He and Channing discussed the
meaning of "the sacrament commemorative of the death of our Lord," and
found that they agreed, so Channing administered it "in the most solemn
and affecting manner."

The younger Sedgwicks—Harry, Robert, Catharine, and Charles—had
all been gathered by their father's bedside for weeks. Catharine sometimes
had the feeling "when we are all assembled around our Father as if our
sainted Mother watched and *approved* us." The new Mrs. Sedgwick was
there, too, but the family only noted her presence by commenting occasionally that she had gone out.[16]

In mid-January, the older married sisters decided that they, too, ought
to go on the journey to Boston. Eliza made it to Boston on Friday, January 22. Judge Sedgwick hung on through the weekend and died, "almost
without a struggle," a little before seven on Sunday evening, January 24. "I

trust he is now with our sainted mother," Harry wrote to Theodore. Frances and Ebenezer arrived later that night, and they made arrangements for a funeral in Boston at Channing's Federal Street church on Wednesday. To their friends and relatives, Catharine in particular appeared inconsolable.[17]

"Every one who has followed a dear friend to the grave, remembers with shuddering the hollow sound of the first clods that are thrown on the coffin." Thus did Catharine Sedgwick the novelist describe the experience of the burial of a parent in her first book, nine years later. The Judge's funeral was one of her two major sources for that observation. The family returned to the Tuckers' house after the funeral, and Catharine remembered clinging to her brother Robert. Her heart "quivered with the pang of separation" as she said to him simply, "You must be my father now." Robert's reply was immediate, and when Catharine recalled it decades later, she underscored it to convey its decisiveness: "*I will.*" Robert offered "a most fervent prayer to God, that I might in some degree supply your loss, and be what you asked of me." Six weeks later, he admitted that he could not think of this exchange "without its thrilling every nerve of my heart." He felt what he described as mingled sensations, "on one hand the strongest feelings of tenderness, of which my nature is capable; and on the other, a deep sense, of my unworthiness of the confidence it implied, and of the awful obligation it imposed."[18]

After the funeral in Boston, Catharine was relieved to get back to Stockbridge. "Our beloved Father seems still to exist in every object around me here," she wrote to Robert. But amidst the tranquility of their country home, they also had to deal with what Catharine simply referred to as "the bitterness that has been infused, into our cup of joy," by which she meant the continued presence of Mrs. Sedgwick. Penelope Russell Sedgwick's residence in the Stockbridge house during February and the first weeks of March was a nagging reminder of past unpleasantness, and of the future task of settling the Judge's estate. Their suspicions of her were so profound that Thaddeus Pomeroy had delivered the Judge's will to the office of another lawyer in Stockbridge a month before the Judge died, "with orders to be delivered to no one during life without a written order." The will had been read to the family at Stockbridge, just a week after the funeral.[19]

According to a long-established tradition in the English law from which the laws of Massachusetts and the other states were derived, Mrs. Sedgwick was entitled while she lived to a one-third interest in all her late husband's property, and in the income derived from it. This principle, known as *dower*, had been gradually falling out of favor in some of the American colonies (and now states) for more than a century at the time of Judge Sedgwick's death. It had depended on the English practice (derived from Roman law) of primogeniture—the custom of leaving an estate to one heir only, usually the eldest son, and not dividing it. In England this practice served to preserve the power and status of a wealthy landed and titled elite, on whose loyalty the power of the monarchy had come to depend. In some northern American states, great fortunes were being built in the late colonial and early national periods out of property other than land—fortunes based on commercial success, on industrial innovation, and even on supreme legal skills. Such estates were partible—as even great landed estates could be in the United States, because land was so plentiful, and because the sovereign power of the Republic did not depend on the loyalty of a titled nobility. It drew instead on the independent participation of a great body of virtuous and productive citizens. Indeed, the Constitution of the United States expressly prohibited the granting of the kind of titles that had been attached to the great estates of English tradition. Every major change in inheritance law and custom in Britain's American colonies, and in the states they became, had as its overriding purpose the end of primogeniture and an increase in the partitioning of estates, not necessarily equally, but *relatively* equally, among all heirs. And when estates could be partitioned, it made less sense to grant a widow one-third of the income from the bequests made to all the other heirs than to treat her as one of those heirs, with a testamentary settlement specified to ensure her continued support.[20]

Thus the republican reforms that led to greater equality among sons and heirs also led to a reduction in the power, and sometimes the wealth, of their mothers and stepmothers. Such changes happened gradually, more often driven by custom and by judicial decisions in contentious lawsuits than by explicit legislative action. Most states still recognized dower rights in principle in 1813, but arrangements in lieu of dower were becoming more common and less controversial. One scholar of legal history has said that the renunciation of dower rights was the single most frequent civil law action women engaged in during the years just before and after the Revolution, other than marriage itself. At least in Europe, men who left cash bequests in lieu of dower usually did so in the belief that their widows would be better off. But in the United States many widows were settling, or being forced to settle, for much less than their traditional third. Theodore Sedgwick handled at least one such case, for a widow who was one of his wife's relatives, in 1794.[21]

While inheritance reform in the new Republic thus limited one of the ancient privileges of women under English law, it did nothing to mitigate their ancient disabilities. A married woman was still a *feme covert* according to the laws of all the states: she was subject to coverture by her husband, which in essence meant that her whole legal existence vanished while she was married. In explaining this principle to his sister Catharine around the time their father drafted his will, Harry Sedgwick had used this homely illustration: "A little brook loses its name and distinct being after its confluence with a mighty river." A married woman had no power to act on her own in any legal or commercial transactions; her every action was seen as an expression of her husband's will. This condition of coverture was the rationale behind the prohibitions against women voting and serving on juries. (In a few places, married women who owned property were allowed the franchise.)[22]

When a woman married she also surrendered her claim to any property of her own. Her property became her husband's property, unless she or her birth family made arrangements to lock it up as a separate estate, usually held in trust by a male relative, and thus legally untouchable by the husband or the husband's creditors. When income from such separate property was delivered to a woman, it became part of her property — which is to say it became her husband's. But the principal — the land or securities or other assets — remained under the woman's control, at least indirectly.

Such a premarital exclusion of some of the last Mrs. Sedgwick's property probably did not take place, but it might have been planned or implied before she married the Judge in 1808. The disposition of Penelope Russell Sedgwick's English property became one of the most contentious issues in the controversy over settling the Judge's estate, so it is unlikely that any clear legal document existed. In the case of the third Mrs. Sedgwick, another complicating factor (in the eyes of her stepchildren, but not necessarily in the eyes of the law) was the brevity of her marriage to the Judge, and his long prior marriage to a wife whose property had added considerably to his fortune, and who had left him with seven lawful heirs among whom that fortune was now to be divided.

Harry believed that the will read to the family at Stockbridge was an "admirable disposition" of their father's property. Mrs. Sedgwick was to receive an annuity of $550. "She has also her bedroom with necessary appurtenant privileges in the cellar, kitchen, and gardens during life,"

Harry noted, "and one third of all except the law books." (Given the chilly state of relations between her and the Judge's children, the enforcement of those boundaries and privileges promised to be a constant headache.)[23] Eliza, Frances, and Catharine received large cash bequests, with Catharine's significantly larger than those of her married sisters. Charles inherited the house and most of the land the family owned in Stockbridge. His three older brothers, the residual legatees and executors, were to divide up the balance of the property equally. This consisted of lands in upstate New York, various canal stocks, and other securities the Judge had accumulated over the years. Theodore immediately saw the wisdom of the Judge's apportionments. "Those have most, who wanted most," he explained to his law partner, Harmanus Bleecker, referring to the unmarried Catharine and the unschooled Charles. Since we know that the exact value of Catharine's bequest was $8,500, we can calculate that Theodore believed the residuum to be divided among the three executors must have been no more than $25,000 (just under three times what Catharine got), and the total estate a little over $50,000.

Theodore made no comment on what a shrewd lawyer like Bleecker must have noticed as the will's most conspicuous feature: It attempted to settle on Mrs. Sedgwick less than was her right under the principle of dower. Depending on the rate of return expected, Mrs. Sedgwick's annual $550 would have represented the income on property of anywhere from $8,000 to $14,000 — even at the generous end of the spectrum, significantly less than a third of the Judge's estate. According to a later reckoning after he had identified and valued all the assets, Harry put the residual value to be divided among the three executors at close to $38,000, making the total estate worth considerably more than $60,000, and Mrs. Sedgwick's annuity much less than a widow's third.[24]

With Robert in New York and Theodore weighed down by family responsibilities, the burden of negotiating an acceptance of these terms or some alternate settlement with Mrs. Sedgwick fell on Harry. The widow remained among her stepchildren for a little more than a month. She stayed in her own room, occasionally joining the family at dinner and never otherwise. She complained to the servants about her treatment by her stepchildren, thinking they offered a sympathetic ear; but the servants despised her, and everything she said went right back to Catharine. "She has even said in so many words, that she had made no money by marrying, that she had lived a life of slavery, and got nothing for it at last," Catharine reported to Frances in astonishment. No one was disappointed when Penelope returned to Boston at the end of the first week of March.

"We never varied nor abated in our respect and kindness to her," Catharine insisted, "but where there is no heart, it is in vain to try to reach it."[25]

Harry returned to Boston with Mrs. Sedgwick, to resume his legal business. He and his family knew that he would eventually be required to meet with her lawyers in an attempt to induce her to accept the bequest in the Judge's will instead of asserting her legal claim to dower rights. The Sedgwicks were well aware that their stepmother had no intention of settling without a fight. "Poor Harry has some scenes of difficulty to pass through that will require all his firmness and integrity," Catharine reminded Robert, thinking not only of the inherently tense negotiations but also of Harry's uncertain prospects in the Boston legal community. "You know the character of those persons whose censure he may innocently incur and whose good opinion must be particularly valuable and desirable to him. Those persons would not censure him without believing they had good grounds for it, but misstatements will be made to them, and unfounded complaints poured into their ears."

For weeks the brothers had been discussing a strategy for negotiating with Mrs. Sedgwick's representatives. Ebenezer Watson urged a hard line, demanding that Penelope Russell Sedgwick's English property (which was worth at least $5,000, and which was not mentioned in the will) be included as part of the Judge's estate, rather than excluded and returned to her before any other calculations were made. He told Harry that he feared "that the restoration of her original property was a clear evidence that you were conscious there had not been an adequate provision made for her by your father" — which was, of course, true, though Harry could never admit it. Watson insisted that if the family's claim to the English property was forfeited, the loss ought to be borne by the three executors (Theodore, Harry, and Robert) and not by the whole family. But Watson was in debt to the Judge's estate for a large sum he had borrowed in 1811; he had reason to want to keep as much property as possible within the estate, because if the executors needed money to pay off the cash bequests, they were likely to demand the final repayment of his loan. Robert urged a more conciliatory approach, and for a good reason. "I would sacrifice half I am worth," he admitted, "than have her take up her abode at Stockbridge, or even be there any portion of the year." Charles, who acknowledged that his heart was "sometimes corroded by angry passions" toward Mrs. Sedgwick, wished Harry a speedy ending to his journey in their stepmother's company, the circumstances of which he could not contemplate without disgust.[26]

Soon after Harry got back to Boston, he picked up a hint of what was to come when he called on Isaac Parker, his father's fellow justice on the Supreme Judicial Court. When he rose to leave, Judge Parker followed him out of the room, and informed him that he had already heard from Mrs. Sedgwick's brother-in-law, who asked if she was legally entitled to her English property in addition to the annuity granted in the will. Parker, according to Harry, was "evidently disgusted by the indelicacy of the application, and the rapacity it evinced." [27]

Stephen Higginson, Jr., called on Harry a few days later. Higginson told Harry he and George Cabot would represent Mrs. Sedgwick's interests, and that he thought the will was essentially just, but wanted a compromise. He believed that the English property (which Harry had not yet agreed to exclude from the Judge's estate) was much more valuable than the $550 annuity, and said he was sure that the Sedgwicks did not want to enrich their family with Mrs. Sedgwick's own money.

Harry gave Higginson his family's proposal. It included the return of the English property *and* the complete annuity paid out of income from the Judge's estate. In other words, it might well have been more generous than what Higginson was asking for. In return, he asked that Mrs. Sedgwick give up everything that did not belong to her before the marriage, especially her third of the Judge's library, any personal property of the Judge's that she had taken from Stockbridge, and a portrait of the Judge painted by Gilbert Stuart in 1807 or 1808. (The will granted Penelope custody of the portrait during her lifetime, and required her estate to turn it over to Eliza and her heirs.)

Cabot assured Harry that the return of the English property was all he and his client sought, and even agreed to give up her claim to the picture. But when Higginson informed Mrs. Sedgwick of Harry's insistence that the books and the portrait be returned, she flew into a rage and suffered what Harry called "a more violent set of fits than she had ever before been known . . . to have."

Harry believed he knew the cause, and it had nothing to do with the value of the property. "If anything but rum operated to produce this effect it was doubtless the demand for restitution of the articles brought from Stockbridge," he informed Charles. Mrs. Sedgwick had been telling her friends in Boston how much the children, the servants, and the people of Stockbridge were attached to her; that three servants, including Mumbet, had told her they were losing a best friend when she left, and had even said that they wished they could go to Boston with her. Harry was both pleased and a little frightened when he realized that his demands had proved to her friends that she had lied.

Foremost among those friends was Penelope's older sister, Catharine Russell. (She was the one who was so surprised at the severity of Mrs. Sedgwick's fit.) Harry had a conversation with Miss Russell in which she was also surprised to learn of the bad feelings that had existed in Stockbridge; her sister had said she was always treated well by the Sedgwicks, especially by Catharine. When Harry mentioned Mrs. Sedgwick's intemperance, Catharine Russell professed surprise a third time — she "never had the slightest suspicion."[28]

It took almost a week for Harry to learn the consequences of Mrs. Sedgwick's violent reaction to his insistence on the return of the personal property. Then he learned from Higginson that she planned to contest the will and to sue the estate, demanding the return of her English property *and* the annuity *and* her one-third dower rights in the Judge's entire estate.

The case thus came to concern an issue that would be addressed by the United States Supreme Court later the same year: whether a widow's claim to her one-third dower rights in her husband's estate came *in addition to* any other property specifically bequeathed to her, or whether the value of any specific bequests ought to be counted toward her dower. In the case of *Herbert v. Wren*, Chief Justice John Marshall, writing for the majority, would decree that specific bequests ought to count toward the one-third dower claim. Among the justices voting with Marshall was Bushrod Washington, nephew of the former president, who as a young man serving as coexecutor of his father's estate had negotiated with his own mother the surrender of her dower rights in exchange for the protection of an enslaved family she wanted to save from being sold.[29]

When he received Mrs. Sedgwick's ultimatum from Higginson, Harry, who had been successfully playing the part of the reserved, temperate young lawyer, became enraged. "This novel claim was so offensive in itself," he informed Robert, "the terms of his letter so objectionable, and the suggested resort to legal means so irritating after the liberal course we had taken, that I wrote him in a style not the civilest in the world as you may well suppose." Higginson's reply was in turn so offensive that Harry felt he could not send it on to his brothers and sisters. Harry sent back another furious reply stating "that we could never for an instant suffer the implication that our father had not in all things dealt justly by his wife." He urged Higginson to tell Mrs. Sedgwick that her friends knew nothing of the true circumstances of the case — which appears to have been a veiled threat that he was willing to tell them much more. His last words to Higginson were that he and his family had already offered Mrs. Sedgwick more than she would get in court.

It worked. "This change in my style immediately produced its effect," Harry told Robert with evident surprise. Higginson came to call and offered an apology. "Upon the whole I entirely forgave his waspishness," Harry recalled grandly. He again offered the original terms: the English property plus the annuity in exchange for relinquishing dower and returning the books, portrait, and other personal property. He was willing to fight on the issue of dower, because while it would not have been worth "more than a trifle" to Mrs. Sedgwick, "yet it would seriously incommode Charles" as the owner of the Stockbridge house and lands.[30]

All the distant family members were astonished and appalled at the unfolding saga. Rumors had begun to circulate in Boston that the Judge had left his widow a much larger legacy than he actually had, and that his son was now trying to wheedle her out of it. "It is difficult to determine how far a sense of justice and of respect to your own character, will enable you to go in vindicating it from wicked aspersions," Charles sympathized. "It is almost impossible for a virtuous man to be silent when his reputation is malignantly assailed." Yet even after all that had passed between the family and their stepmother, Charles could not forget his manners. He added in a postscript, "If it is necessary tell Mrs. S. I wish her well. I hate to mention her name."

"The business of Mrs. S. haunts me day and night," Harry admitted after the meeting in which Higginson had apologized and relented a little. Eliza urged him not to let the portrait stand in the way of a settlement. "If it would be as valuable to her as such an article would be to a real and sincere mourner," the Judge's oldest daughter allowed, "it would be hard to take it."[31]

On April 10, Harry finally informed the family that the settlement had been achieved. "Mr. Higginson expressly relinquished dower," he assured them, "and promised that it should be resorted to under no circumstances." Higginson was probably acting in his client's best interest to accept this settlement. If she had pressed her claim to dower, any court that might have recognized it almost certainly also would have added her English property to the Judge's estate and (following the new precedent of the *Wren* decision) applied the $550 annuity toward the computation of her widow's third. Harry even let Mrs. Sedgwick keep a disputed interest payment on the English property. "I did this," he told his sister Frances, "because some people might think it hard that she should derive no part of her support from the family she had entered, and because, wasteful, helpless, and sick as she is, she will need the income of the whole for her support." Harry learned that as a result of his reports to Catharine Russell and Stephen Higginson about Penelope Sedgwick's drinking, her doctor had "utterly forbidden her the use of ardent spirits." He recognized that the key to his victory in the negotiations was Mrs. Sedgwick's reluctance to have her Boston friends learn the true state of her reputation in Stockbridge. "Her evil conduct has been overruled to our good," he boasted. "She feels herself in our power, and besides is obliged to support the consistency of her former assertion, that all our family and everybody else at Stockbridge were delighted with her."[32]

By the middle of June, Harry was able to write a long letter to Robert that contained no mention of estate-related business. And at year's end, Harry could even congratulate himself that his timely revelations had done some good for the woman he had come to despise. "Mrs. Sedgwick is better than she has been," he was able to tell his sister Catharine. "She rises earlier, walks more, and drinks less than she ever has." But when she asked through a mutual friend about the possibility of getting the Stuart portrait back — insisting "how extremely she idolized our father and how much her feelings were consequently hurt in being deprived of his picture" — Harry refused without further comment.

Harry was satisfied with the outcome of his angry legal squabble with his stepmother, and with his ability to settle the estate without granting her the kind of burdensome dower payments that would keep her in frequent, uncomfortable contact with the family. His hope, like that of his brothers and sisters, had been that they could keep their stepmother from invading the sacred circle of their family's happiness. (And they did: Penelope Russell Sedgwick sailed for Naples in the fall of 1815, not to return for many years.) Now he wanted to get on with building a career and a future in Boston. He had no way to know that his seemingly trivial decision to allow Mrs. Sedgwick to keep the interest on the English property (a demand he had originally derided as "novel" and "offensive") would lead to a bitter quarrel within the family two years later. But it would not take him long to discover that some of his other actions, and the rumors about them, even though unfounded, would have lasting consequences.[33]

4

Brutal Conduct

The Watsons

$\mathcal{E}$benezer Watson owed a large debt to the estate of his father-in-law, Judge Theodore Sedgwick, because he had borrowed from the Judge in 1811 to finance a new business venture. He needed to borrow from his father-in-law because his previous business had failed, and he had unhappy creditors throughout New York and New England. In 1809 Watson had suffered severely from the reduction in New York's business caused by Jefferson's embargo on all trade with England and France. He and his family had been forced to move to a less expensive house, much farther from the center of the city's commercial and social life. Then he went out of business altogether in March 1811, closing merchant offices in both Albany and New York. Harry at that time had considered Watson's fate as proof that "there is in this life no apportionment of reward and punishment to merit and iniquity."[1] The Watsons moved to Stockbridge for a while, until Ebenezer accepted an offer to go into partnership with Samuel Whiting as Whiting & Watson, printers, publishers, and booksellers. His share of the partnership's capital was to be $10,000. He borrowed the entire amount from Judge Sedgwick. "The business in question is as safe as anything in the shape of trade can be," Robert assured Harry. The amount was substantial, but Robert pointed out that any smaller business would not be enough to support a growing family, and the Watsons by then had five young children.[2]

Ebenezer Watson still owed his father-in-law that original amount plus interest when Judge Sedgwick died in January 1813. As executors of their father's estate, the three oldest Sedgwick brothers knew that anything their sister Frances inherited became her husband's property. They initially planned to have her share of the estate (about $6,000) deducted from Watson's debt, and his bond rewritten at a face value of just about $4,600. At Watson's suggestion, the bond would be made payable to Catharine, and it would make up a little more than half of her share of her father's estate. She would receive that amount, plus any additional interest, when Watson paid the bond off in installments. This arrangement appealed to the brothers as executors, because they believed they would otherwise have to sell some securities at a loss in order to make a large cash payment to Catharine. But Harry insisted that if Catharine were to take Watson's bond, she would have to receive "*absolutely perfect security*" that it would be repaid, and he and his brothers would provide that security. If Watson were unable to make the payments, the executor brothers, as residual legatees, would pay her, and Watson would owe his debt to them.[3]

By the time the estate was ready to be settled, the brothers had raised or uncovered enough in the way of cash that Catharine only needed to take Watson's bond for $3,500; the rest would be payable to the estate. Harry floated a novel legal maneuver past Robert, probably as part of a plan to keep some money reserved for Frances in case her husband should fail again: Instead of Frances's inheritance simply being deducted from Watson's original bond, the deduction from Watson's bond would be considered a new loan from the estate. Watson would still have to pay that debt to the brothers, who would then turn around and pay it to Frances as her inheritance. This seems to have been a doomed attempt to do with Frances's bequest what the Judge did not do when he could have: to set it aside as a separate estate in trust, untouchable by her husband, to be used for her benefit only. It did not work. When Robert collected the rewritten bonds from Watson, he also collected a receipt, not a bond, for Frances's bequest.[4]

Watson's next crisis came the following year. "I am obliged to communicate to you unpleasant news," Robert wrote to Harry immediately after returning to New York from a visit to Stockbridge. "On my arrival here I found that Mess.rs Whiting & Watson had stopped payment." Two other businesses whose principals owed large sums to Whiting & Watson had gone under. If Whiting & Watson's creditors, in the face of this crisis, decided to call in their loans, Watson and his partner would have to close up shop. "This will depend entirely upon the banks and their friends," Robert reminded Harry. The banks seemed likely to want to wait out the crisis and let them go on. The "friends" — the individual and commercial creditors, one of whom was Catharine Sedgwick — would make the decision.[5]

When Catharine learned of this situation a few days later, her first thought was of Frances. She wrote to Frances of her admiration for "the heroic resignation and heavenly fortitude, with which you bear all great trials." Throughout the rest of 1814, her lawyer brothers were involved in a series of small transactions in which they lent money to Whiting & Watson, collected money that was due to Whiting & Watson from other merchants, and collected money that was due to them from Whiting & Watson. By November, Charles and Robert had begun to harbor some suspicions about Watson—not so much about his integrity as about his attention to the details of his business. "He certainly is not so particular about paying his debts as he is about many other things," Robert told Catharine when Watson's payment on his bond was late.[6]

In April 1815, when Harry visited New York, he and Ebenezer Watson discussed the unpaid debt to Catharine and other nettlesome financial issues. Perhaps feeling threatened, or certainly at least uncomfortable, Watson brought up his displeasure at Harry's relatively easy agreement two years earlier to restore Penelope Russell Sedgwick's English property to her, and especially to let her keep the interest that had already been paid on that property. The other brothers had been unanimous in their agreement with Harry's desire to settle. Watson was still irate about the settlement and its slight diminution of the estate; to use Harry's word, he had "brooded" over it for years. (Since it would not have affected the amount of Frances's inheritance, Watson must have "brooded" about the different amounts he would owe to different family-member creditors based on the changing size of his bond to Catharine.)

After Harry and Ebenezer exchanged angry words in New York, Ebenezer wrote Harry a long letter, which was delivered to Harry the same day, while both were staying in the same house. "To my view matters between us could hardly be left on a worse footing than that on which they now stand," he began. "I feel myself to have been very injuriously treated," he complained, and then listed all the ways.[7]

Harry took nearly two weeks to reply. He had already returned to Stockbridge before he finished drafting a full response to Watson's angry letter. He sent his reply to Robert, asking his brother to read it first and then, if he thought it would be wise, to hand-deliver it to Watson.

Watson had closed his letter with a conciliatory wish: "I sincerely desire to retain and cherish the cordialities of an affectionate brother." Harry's reply exploded any chance of that. "I shall seek no reconciliation with you," he wrote, "until I have some evidence that you prefer affection to its reverse." Shoving aside their whole discussion of bonds, debts, estates, and property, he moved on to what was really troubling him.

> Have a care that you do not suffer your feelings in regard to me to vent themselves upon my much injured sister. The state of your mind towards me is an evil the less to be regretted because it was unavoidable, for I could not hope to excite the sentiment of kindness in one who exercises it not towards those who are much more its appropriate objects than myself. But for your wife — who never has never will complain — remember that your marriage vow, your oath to God to love and cherish her — is upon your soul. Its continued violation will, be assured, meet with awful retribution. Commune with your own heart — reflect upon the terrible passions of your unsubdued nature. . . . In your prayers — which I do not like to hear — you say that the essence of religion is love. What then must be the state of him . . . who tramples on the submissive and defenseless. Your powers are great but great has been their perversion. I pray God to work in you the work of reformation.

The silence had been broken. For at least the past several years, Ebenezer Watson had been violently abusing Frances. Now one of her brothers meant to make him stop. And, since Harry had provided security for one of Watson's single largest debts — the bond to Catharine that he had guaranteed at the end of the estate settlement — he had a weapon at his command that could force Watson to do so, as long as Watson remained in business.

Harry believed he was writing about abuse that had gone on for quite a while. Perhaps in the spring of 1815 he had just begun to piece together the meaning of signs he had been seeing for years, or perhaps he had simply never before been angry enough to raise the issue. "I do not consider that the present time has afforded any peculiar reason for the foregoing remarks," he noted at the end of his letter. "On the contrary I am rejoiced that your domestic conduct has improved. I only think that your *letter* has furnished a justifiable occasion for saying what I have long thought ought to be said."[8]

Harry's letter of April 1815 was the first mention of Frances's abuse in writing. Robert had read and responded to the draft; he had also boarded with the Watsons in New York for a large part of the year over six or seven years. Other family members appear not to have learned of Watson's abuse of their sister for several more years.

Robert refused to deliver Harry's letter. He said that Ebenezer's behavior toward Frances had been "*good*" since Harry left New York (and he underlined "good" four times); he noted that Harry admitted in his own letter that Watson's recent behavior had been unobjectionable. He also reflected, thinking of Watson's other recent displays of anger (especially toward Harry), that it might not be judicious to bring up the subject. It might set him off again, and cause a renewal of his "numberless injuries to our dear sister." Robert insisted that Watson would receive his "chastisement" for these injuries elsewhere, and "with all the majesty of *impartial justice.*" He urged Harry to write instead about their specific quarrel concerning Watson's debts and the settlement with Penelope Russell Sedgwick. "I will however put your letter in the Post Office," he granted, "if you think it advisable."

It is tempting to be cynical and say that Frances Sedgwick Watson had one brother who only attempted to stop her abuse when her abuser owed him money, and another who would not do so even then, but to say that is to take Harry and Robert Sedgwick out of their time. Fifty years would pass before most state courts would begin to reject arguments based on a husband's right to "correct" his wife by physical punishment. In addressing another man's violent treatment of his wife openly and in writing, and in such passionate terms, Harry Sedgwick was prepared to take a bold and unusual stand.[9]

The tone of Watson's next letter implies that he had never received this chastisement, but that next letter was composed and sent a full six months after the initial exchange of accusations. All through the summer, Ebenezer and Harry would not speak to each other, or exchange letters, or even extend the informal greetings that were usually included at the end of a family letter. When Harry had written to offer to escort Frances on a journey back to Stockbridge, she had been obliged to ask for her husband's permission to respond, and for his advice about what to say. "I asked him this morning what I could reply to your letter," she wrote back to Harry, and "he said anything that my inclination and sense of duty dictated." This stony silence might have been attributable to Watson's indignation over Harry's frank letter, but the accusations leveled over the bond and the handling of the will by themselves could have been more than enough to cause the rift.

Ebenezer Watson finally broke the silence and addressed a letter to Harry. His salutation addressed "My Dear Brother," and in the first line he added, "Thus I sincerely desire ever to address you, thus ever cordially to feel towards you." He admitted that his earlier letter had been written "with asperity," but insisted that the feeling had been only temporary and superficial. Harry's angry response had surprised him, for Harry should have known that he was not "stubborn, stupid, perverse, or malevolent." It seems unlikely that a man who had received Harry's scathing April letter about his treatment of his wife would have made such an assertion.[10]

Harry was favorably impressed with Watson's near-apology, and he intended to write an acknowledgment of it. Before he was able to resume communication with his brother-in-law, though, the word came from Robert in New York that Whiting & Watson would finally be going out of business. The partners had assigned their entire inventory to another publisher, who they expected would sell it at auction. The proceeds of the auction would be used to pay Whiting & Watson's creditors. As one of Whiting & Watson's creditors, and a fairly large one, Harry Sedgwick and his brothers as coexecutors of their father's estate would have to get in line with the other creditors once this auction had taken place. The slow dissolution of Whiting & Watson proceeded through the spring and summer of 1816. Watson gave some thought to applying for protection under New York's new bankruptcy law, but he decided against it, believing until the end that he would be able to pay off all his debts in full—an amount that a skeptical Robert estimated at more than $90,000. In March 1817, one of Whiting & Watson's creditors forced the partners to seek bankruptcy protection in New York by demanding timely payment of their debt in full. That virtually guaranteed that no creditor would collect more than pennies on the dollar.[11]

In the meantime, the Watsons made plans for Frances and the children to move to Stockbridge, where life would be less expensive. Charles and Catharine visited them in New York in April 1816. "It may be the last opportunity I shall have of seeing Fanny in her own house," Charles wrote to Harry, "and I am not disposed to withhold any gratification from her that is in my power to bestow." Robert commented on a favorable change in Ebenezer Watson's behavior. "Mr. Watson in his domestic life seems another man," he wrote to Harry. But on two counts Robert still found Watson remiss in his actions: he had not made any provision for the support of his wife and children after Whiting & Watson closed, nor had he attempted to secure any property for Frances's separate and protected use.[12]

Sometime before Frances moved to Stockbridge, she shared her thoughts on her family's predicament with Harry. She expressed relief that the collapse had not been caused by any dishonesty on Watson's part, and a conviction that the financial setback was having "the most salutary influence in our domestic circle." She assured him, "I have in a good measure already felt these blessed effects." Watson was not only ill (as he had been that entire winter and spring), he was humbled. Frances referred to him as one of "those who are ground down by excessive care — whose spirits are always agitated by defeated plans — whose days and nights are given to fearful anticipations of the future, and who cannot even consider the blest relations of life — since even wife and child present claims which are a dagger to the heart." Still, her sympathy with her husband in his hour of distress did not sweep away the bitterness in their marriage. After Frances and her children moved to Stockbridge, she wrote a sympathetic note to a young relative who was newly engaged, in which she commented, "I can recall as the cherished inmate of my own bosom every emotion you express, even those, which most imperially, most extravagantly exalt the beloved object above yourself." That relative would have had no way of knowing that Frances was probably referring to Loring Andrews when she wrote that sentiment, but he might have picked up a strange hint a month later when Frances wrote again and said, "I can only say that those *only* who have felt the atmosphere of chilling coldness can know what it is to vivify in the warm beams of love and kindness."[13]

Frances and her children lived with her brother Charles from May 1816 until sometime in 1820. Ebenezer Watson did not live with his family in Stockbridge, partly because he still had work to do in New York, and at least partly because there was considerable danger that his creditors in Massachusetts might have him arrested and jailed until he could pay his debts or surrender his property. (Imprisonment for debtors was coming to an end in New York.) Several times Watson did come to Stockbridge secretly to see his family. On one of those occasions, in early September 1816, he had what might have been his first face-to-face conversation with Harry since their blowup in New York almost a year and a half earlier. It did not go well. A few weeks later, Watson wrote to Harry of his deep regret for all the bitterness that had passed between them, including the events of their recent meeting. "I hoped that personal intercourse would put a finishing hand to the healing of the unhappy breach which had taken place between us," he wrote, "and restore that affection which we formerly cherished towards each other." He admitted to a painful awareness of "the evil propensities of my nature," but expressed his desire "to cherish the spirit of harmony and affection towards you, and to avoid everything that can tend to continue the painful alienation which has taken place between us." But Harry was unmoved by his "fit of remorse."[14]

Harry had indicated, in the aftermath of his first bitter argument with Watson, that he knew Ebenezer was treating Frances violently. That situation had probably only become apparent to Harry since his father's death in 1813. Not all Harry's brothers and sisters shared his belief that there was a problem, or if there was, that it was serious, or that they had any power to address it. Robert had refused to deliver Harry's letter or to take any other confrontational action in April 1815, and as late as March 1816 Catharine could say, in anticipating Watson's visit to Stockbridge, "I have no pleasure in expectation that would be a parallel to seeing him." A year and a half later, Catharine was less pleased with Watson. When he planned one of his occasional visits to his wife in October 1817, Catharine worried about the risk, both that he might be arrested, and that he might take Frances away to live with him somewhere in New York, where he would mistreat her. "Poor Frances!" Catharine wrote to Robert, "my heart bleeds for her, when I think to what thralldom her noble spirit is subjected." When Watson came for a brief visit, Catharine reported that she was "in a continual trepidation" and wished he would leave quickly. Another family member reported watching him constantly with "eyes which are as sharp as those of the lynx in spying his faults" when he visited two years after that.[15]

The Watsons were reunited in 1820, at the time of the death of their eighteen-year-old firstborn, Theodore Sedgwick Watson. Catharine believed that Ebenezer's presence was a great consolation to Frances. They were separated on and off again throughout the 1820s, and his violence became less of a secret and more of a problem to be discussed openly within the family. At the end of 1822, Catharine informed Eliza of what she called Watson's "*brutal*" behavior. "I hate to tell you how much our dear Frances is oppressed and afflicted," she acknowledged, "for it seems to be one of those hopeless miseries over which we must mourn without being able to remove it. But we may all alleviate it, for she is touched and comforted by kindness. Mr. Watson is *brutal* in his conduct to her and does and has for a long time rendered her miserable. It is one uniform system of degrading oppression, and she bears with scarcely ever a word of reply, patiently and uncomplainingly. What is to be done, I know not, but something must be done. . . . He has a stubborn oppressive temper — that temper essentially diabolical which delights to trample on that which is in its power." Eliza, closest in age to Frances and her companion in youth, was apparently one of the last members of the family to learn of (or at least to admit) these horrors — though even in this letter, Catharine warned her not to tell Charles. She also anticipated the question that must have occurred to Eliza almost as quickly as it occurs to a modern reader: "She would leave him," Catharine noted, "but she cannot bear a separation from the children."[16] In December 1822, four were still living. Eben was nineteen, Catharine almost seventeen, Robert thirteen, and Frances eleven. At least the youngest three would be Ebenezer's to do with as he pleased, and Frances would have no influence over them — no right even to see them — if she attempted to leave her husband.

Divorce was not an option for Frances Sedgwick Watson in either of the states in which she and Ebenezer had lived as a married couple. Because of the Puritans' view of marriage as a civil contract rather than a religious one, Massachusetts in early colonial times had one of the most accessible divorce laws in the English-speaking world, but significant restrictions had been added in the eighteenth century. New York had always been an extremely difficult place to get a divorce; they were only available by special legislative enactments, which were rare and expensive, or (after 1787) by decrees granted in the state's equity courts. Cruelty and abuse were not grounds for an absolute divorce in either state. In New York, adultery was essentially the only ground for a divorce. In Massachusetts, cruelty would have qualified as the ground for a separation *a mensa et thoro* ("from bed and board"), which would not have ended the marriage but would have empowered Frances to live apart from her husband.

In nearby Vermont it was much easier to get a divorce than in Massachusetts or New York. There the state's supreme court granted divorces, and the grounds included adultery, fraud, seven years' absence, and three years' desertion. In 1787 the legislature had added "intolerable severity," and in one large county over the next fifty years more than a third of the women who successfully sued for divorce did so on that ground. But even in Vermont, people who intervened to protect victims of spousal abuse were known to be beaten, threatened, and shot at by enraged husbands. Perhaps more intimidating, in an 1820 custody case in which community sympathy was clearly with a wife who had charged her husband with intolerable severity, the husband successfully sued for damages the community members who had testified on her behalf.[17]

In Frances's case, the economic power her brothers held over Ebenezer Watson as his creditors could have effected a separation even without a declaration from a court or from the legislature, if she had so desired. So could her permanent relocation to one of her brothers' homes in Massachusetts, where disgruntled creditors might still have been happy to have Watson arrested. (Charles lived in Stockbridge and then Lenox during this period, and in 1824 Theodore retired from full-time legal practice and moved from Albany back to Stockbridge.) But from the time of their first reconciliation after their son's death in 1820 until almost the end of her life, with only a few interruptions, Frances and her husband remained residents of New York. For most of that time, she chose not to pursue a separation.

She was well aware, as Catharine had noted to Eliza, that even if she were able to win a legal separation or divorce from her abusive husband, both states would almost certainly have granted him custody of their children.

Recent studies of the law of child custody have demonstrated an unsettling confusion over exactly what the courts of the several states were likely to decide in the early decades of the nineteenth century. Michael Grossberg found an 1809 South Carolina case (*Prather v. Prather*) in which a divorcing mother won custody. The judge there specifically cited her husband's adultery, one of the only grounds for definitively ending a marriage. But even then, he only granted the mother custody of her youngest child, mentioning the infant's attachment to her mother during her "tender years," and acknowledging the unstable legal ground on which his decision stood. Grossberg also cited the 1813 *Addicks* case in Pennsylvania. Taking the "tender years" principle at face value, though, when the child was two years older and its years not so tender, the court ordered that custody should revert to the father. Hendrik Hartog has shown that it was technically possible in the equity courts of New York for a husband to lose custody of his children to a court-appointed custodian, who might or might not be his wife or ex-wife. Hartog cited the 1816 *Codd* case, in which a separated wife was granted such custody in order to protect the safety of the children. Michael Grossberg found another, the 1815 *Bedell* case, where the father's drunken abuse was the deciding factor.[18]

Frances Sedgwick Watson's three oldest brothers, all successful New York lawyers by 1817, must have been aware of these precedents, but certainly knew how rare such findings were. It seems likely that Watson's conduct toward Frances included physical violence along with anger and severity; the letters in which her brothers and sisters refer to the abuse contain again and again such verbs as *trample* and *persecute,* and such adjectives as *harsh, brutal,* and *oppressive.* But somehow the three brothers conveyed to the rest of the family that Frances's chances of getting custody were bleak, as that was the only thing any family member said when separation or divorce was suggested. And if any of the Sedgwick brothers thought of trying the case in Massachusetts, where they had all grown up and received their early legal training, that state's chief justice, Lemuel Shaw, emphatically reasserted fathers' presumptive claim to custody in 1834. Until the 1840s, in just about every state, fathers enjoyed those presumptive custody rights. By that time the issue was moot for Frances, whose youngest daughter reached the age of majority in 1832.[19]

Four years after Catharine's 1822 letter to Eliza about Watson's brutal conduct, Robert Sedgwick would lament that Watson's treatment of

Frances continued to be as violent as ever. "That brute to whom God, for wise and merciful purposes without doubt, has suffered her to be united — continues to persecute her with that implacable and inhuman temper of which she has so long been the victim," Robert noted in August 1826. "It is high time they were separated forever." Harry had written to her, earnestly suggesting just that course of action, but she had refused. "From the nature of my own character, I must *be driven* to the measure you recommend," she informed him, "and present circumstances do not warrant that." Frances did separate from Ebenezer briefly at the end of that year ("I trust that after her severe conflicts, she will enjoy some serenity," her sister Catharine wrote), but by the following summer she was back with him, to Catharine's evident disgust. "For my own part I have been for years hopeless of any favorable change in Mr. Watson," Catharine warned Frances. "I do not believe it is in his power to change his habits of mind which of course govern his conduct as certainly as the rudder does the ship." [20]

Catharine's hopelessness proved warranted. Within six months she wrote a bitter letter to Watson, "to discharge a duty which has long been on my conscience and which I have sinfully deferred because it was painful to me." Perhaps stimulated by the recent death of her sister Eliza, she wrote with directness and with fury. (Catharine's criticism of Watson, like so many of Harry's, includes an implied Unitarian critique of the orthodox Calvinism to which only the Watsons and the Pomeroys still clung in this generation of the extended Sedgwick family.)

> I would make all due allowance for an unhappy physical constitution, for whatever may have been adverse in your life — still I do not see how a man can rationally entertain a hope of Heaven and at the same time *cherish* bad passions; how he can expect the peace and love of God, when he is continually violating peace, and sinning against the law of love.
>
> The kingdom of Heaven is within you saith Jesus. Mr. Watson is that kingdom within your breast? I solemnly appeal to your conscience. Look back upon your life upon your daily and hourly treatment of that being whose happiness was entrusted to you and to whom you promised love and fidelity and kindness. . . .
>
> Our lives are drawing to a close. We must all soon appear before the tribunal of God and in the solemnity of this truth — I intreat and I admonish you to compare your character with the requisition of Christ — and in the name of our blessed Saviour I pray God to enlighten, to guide, and bless you. [21]

Painful as her periods of life with Watson were, Frances suffered almost as much while they were separated. A great deal of this was attributable to their economic woes. Watson never recovered from the failure of Whiting & Watson, and spent the rest of his life working for low wages in a series of clerical jobs, many of them arranged with the help of his brother-in-law Theodore Sedgwick. During one period of separation in the 1820s, Frances confided to Harry that she was frequently "harrowed" by the feeling that perhaps she ought to be earning her own living. But she had no idea how to do so. "I lament now bitterly my own miserable education, which would render it impossible for me to do it except by the needle — and in this humble employment I should have many competitors who would probably be very justly preferred to me." Nor was economic hardship the only peril of separation. Another letter Frances sent to Harry admitted to the devastating loneliness of her predicament, especially after the death of her son. "I am much separated from my earthly friends," she noted somberly, "and I carry about in my heart remembrances that seem like the sepulcher of a first born — for whom my heart had cherished the fondest love and highest hopes."

At least one separation came against her will. On December 19, 1828, Watson threw his wife and children out of their house in Albany because of their defiance of his commands. Robert Watson, who was nineteen, traveled nearly forty miles to Stockbridge to fetch his uncle Theodore, who returned to mediate. Ebenezer allowed the family back in three days later. "His I consider a case of partial insanity," Theodore wrote to his own teenage son. "What use in talking of reason, when reason no longer regulates our actions?" Catharine regretted that her sister had returned to her husband yet again. "For your own sake dear sister," she wrote, "we should have been better pleased if the connection with Mr. W. had been severed forever now." But she understood that the fate of the children was still the impediment. Even though the youngest was now seventeen, the girls in particular would depend on their father's support until they were married. The following spring, Frances fled briefly to live among her brothers in Stockbridge. They would have been happy to let her stay indefinitely, but within two months she was back with Watson.[22]

So it went throughout the 1830s: brief separations followed by returns to ever meaner and more desolate circumstances. Catharine Sears Watson, the middle child, married in 1832 and left with her new husband to serve as a missionary in Burma. Young Frances did not marry until she was thirty, and immediately after her wedding trip she visited Stockbridge in order to wait with her Aunt Catharine at her dying mother's bedside.[23] Ebenezer Watson was not with Frances in her final months, or when she died on June 20, 1842, but they were still married, and he was buried beside her in the Sedgwick family plot in Stockbridge when he died five years later. The inscription on his tombstone reads:

Elevated in Sentiment,
True to his sense of duty,
Fervid and loyal in friendship
Philanthropic, Benevolent, Generous
His memory is warmly cherished
In many hearts.

It is not known which of his children composed the epitaph, which is more remarkable for what it does not say than for what it does. In its address to posterity, the inscription allows the same public silence that marked the early years of Ebenezer Watson's abuse of Frances to descend again — a silence that was typical for abusive marriages at the time. What is noteworthy is that, however briefly and irregularly, some of Frances's brothers and sisters attempted to break that silence. The laws and customs of the time, and Frances's own combination of stubbornness and shame, doomed their attempt to failure. But the record of their efforts to help Frances and to influence Ebenezer bears witness to their struggle, and to hers.

II

Trifling and Badinage

FOUR COURTSHIPS, 1813–1816

5

The Heart That's Worth Possessing

Two Disastrous Courtships

*I*mmediately after his father's death in 1813, Harry Sedgwick became serious about finding a wife. Perhaps the Judge's death at age sixty-six had reminded Harry of his own mortality, and he felt a need to make the kind of human connections that would lead to the opportunity to immortalize himself in his progeny. Perhaps the realization that at age twenty-seven he was a moderately wealthy man gave him a new sense of confidence in social situations, and a sense that some young woman might consider him worth marrying. Perhaps he was just glad not to have the Judge looking over his shoulder, second-guessing him at every turn, *judging* him.[1]

Harry considered some young women his friends, and dealt with them with an almost complete and sometimes refreshing obliviousness to their gender. Mary Channing, sister of the cleric who had visited the Judge on his deathbed, was one such friend. She was three years older than Harry. Their letters were as frank and open as Harry's to his brother Robert or his sister Catharine. She acted as a kind of surrogate big sister to him in Boston in the months after his father's death.[2] Almost all Harry's other references to young women in his letters up to that point had been either ribald (those were rare) or avaricious. Jokes about the desirability of marrying a young woman of great fortune were fairly common in letters exchanged by the brothers in the years just after Harry and Robert graduated from Williams College, but they had not ended then. The year before the Judge's death had brought a spate of such references. Robert reminded Harry, though, that their joking on this topic should remain mere joking—because of "the native repugnance" that their sister Catharine would feel if they made money "the moving cause of the most important and most sacred connections." Apparently intending to reassure himself as much as his brother, Robert expressed confidence that neither he nor Harry could ever do that, "notwithstanding all the slang which has passed between you and me on this point." Nevertheless, he insisted, "this aversion to all mercenary considerations, ought not to suffer (and I am not sure but it would) a lady's estate so to intervene between you and her charms, as to obscure if not hide their lustre." In other words, neither Harry nor Robert would object to falling in love with a young woman who was rich, as long as he did not fall in love with her *because* she was rich.[3]

In the summer of 1813, Harry fell in love with the richest young woman in Boston.[4]

Harry was introduced to the Phillips family by his father when he first moved to Boston, and he saw the family socially once or twice a year. William Phillips was the president of the Massachusetts Bank, which he had helped to establish in 1784. In 1812 he was elected lieutenant governor, a position to which he would be reelected every year, under two different Federalist governors, until 1823. Phillips was unlike most of the men with whom Harry and his father had professional and social connections in Boston, in that his religious beliefs encompassed the devout old-school, fire-and-brimstone Calvinism that, among Boston's leading congregations, was by then preached only at Old South Church, where he was a member.[5]

Harry had received "particular and kind attentions" from the Phillips family during his father's last illness. When he called on the family at their home on Tremont Street after his return to Boston, William Phillips's twenty-three-year-old daughter caught his attention. Abigail was the youngest of the lieutenant governor's four surviving children, and the only one still living at home with him. Harry noted that Abigail's life with her parents was "secluded from all society suited to her age and the natural cheerfulness of her temper." Still, he was surprised that she returned his interest.

Harry was coached in his courtship of Abigail Phillips by an expert on young women, his friend Mary Channing. She and Harry had discussed the subject of love enough for her to have laughed at some of his infatuations, and to know that he believed "*that love (for a time at least) is the death of friendship.*" Nevertheless, she was determined to help him find love, even if it meant putting their friendship at risk. And Abigail Phillips provided the ideal opportunity: "For the first time since I have known you," Mary Channing told Harry, "I think your heart is touched."

She decided (as an act of "disinterested benevolence," she said) to do all she could to help Harry win Abigail's heart. She wrote him as blunt a letter as any his brothers or sisters ever would. "Now Harry," she demanded, "be willing to believe that I know more of a woman's heart than you do and listen to some *sage* advice. I would caution you against being in a hurry, it is a great mistake of yours that a heart can be taken by violence. Trust me the heart that's worth possessing is worth and *requires* something more than being asked for — it must be sought — it must be won. Let the lady see that you are not merely a general admirer, we are not much flattered by attentions that are paid indiscriminately to all — but show her that you have *particular exclusive* feelings and that she has called them forth. This seldom fails of awakening an interest." But what Mary Channing saw of Harry in that summer of 1813 led her to believe that he was moving too fast. "I think you have nothing to hope if you are precipitate," she warned. "Something more is necessary than asking, to obtain this prize."[6]

Harry was sure that Abigail Phillips was "one of the most amiable of her sex." But the fact that her father was the president of the bank and widely known to be the richest man in Boston certainly crossed Harry's mind. As he later phrased it, "I suffered my imagination to be excited and influenced by visions of wealth and splendor." He proposed to Abigail Phillips at the end of August 1813, just seven months after the death of his father. She sent him a letter declining his proposal, and he gave up his pursuit and went away. Surely Mary Channing shook her head in bewilderment and dismay.

Just a month or two after this disappointment, Harry began to see the two unmarried Sumner sisters socially — Mehetable, who was a year older than Harry, and Elizabeth, who was the same age as Abigail Phillips. Their late father, Increase Sumner, had been governor of Massachusetts in the 1790s. Their mother was dead as well, so they lived in the home of their unmarried older brother, Colonel William Sumner, a state representative and a military adviser to the governor during the War of 1812. Harry had known William Sumner for several years.[7]

Harry later claimed to have been interested in both sisters, citing "the dignity of character — the fine manners and intelligent conversation" of Mehetable, and "the sensitiveness the diffidence and reserve" of Elizabeth. His acquaintance with Mehetable was greater, because Elizabeth was "timid and reserved" (though Harry crossed that judgment out after he wrote it). "She always seemed repressed by the prominent part her sister took in conversation," he recalled, "and by an habitual deference towards her," something that he thought might have been explained by the six-year difference in their ages.

One or both of the sisters served as bridesmaid at a wedding at about that time. Harry visited the family soon after, and found Elizabeth Sumner in unusually high spirits. She gave him a piece of wedding cake, and asked him to be sure to tell her what he dreamed. Ever the man to comply with a lady's polite request, Harry composed what he called a literary rhapsody of a dream and sent it to her: a vision of a wedding on a distant planet, where three goddesses (the bride and her two bridesmaids, as at the recent wedding) presided. He remembered the letter with vivid embarrassment three years later. "In portraying the ideal representation of Miss E. S.," he admitted, "I certainly employed all the warmth and glow of coloring which my imagination could supply, and contrived to make the fiction a medium for the conveyance of compliments which were to be sure somewhat hyperbolical as applied to any maid of mortal mould, but which in the main, I thought were just." Harry remembered his epistolary creation as a lighthearted trifle, "a piece of piquant gallantry." He enclosed his dream in a note addressed to both sisters, "to avoid the appearance of particularity." But he could not avoid it: Elizabeth Sumner had asked to hear about his dream, and Elizabeth Sumner responded. The tone of her response led Harry to conclude that she had taken his flattering portrayal too seriously. In the very serious game that was courtship in Boston in 1813, with its intricate and carefully monitored rules, Harry feared he had made a move without realizing it. Reports reached his ear that the town had begun to link him romantically with the younger Miss Sumner. Rightly or wrongly, Harry believed that the source of those reports was the elder Miss Sumner. He wanted to convey to both sisters that his efforts had been more literary than amorous, but he feared that even calling on them to say so would have been seen (by the anonymous people whose "reports" kept circulating in Boston) as an indication of further interest. He froze, did nothing, and wrote to Catharine in Stockbridge for advice.

In her response, Catharine told him not to worry so much about the reports, which she considered "the offspring of the idle garrulity of the world." She reminded Harry that he had absolutely no reason to believe Elizabeth Sumner herself had initiated the reports, or done anything to circulate them, or committed any other indelicacy. She and Robert (who both had a chance to read Harry's transcriptions of all the letters in December) were sure Elizabeth Sumner had not taken the dream as seriously as Harry feared. She had seen it, Robert insisted, as a "poetic excursion — as you had gone into the heavens, and carried her with you, it became necessary to make her a goddess." Her reply was as playful, Robert believed, as Harry's original letter purported to be. Catharine insisted that Harry go back again to call on the Sumners and atone for his indiscretion by "as graceful and adroit an extrication as possible."

Catharine also pointed out to Harry that, despite the overreaction, Elizabeth Sumner had clearly "made an impression on [his] heart." She even went so far as to say that, if the connection should amount to anything, she hoped Miss Sumner was worthy of her brother. She must have conveyed that sentiment to other family members in Stockbridge, and even as far away as New York, because within two weeks of her mid-November letter of instruction and advice to Harry, three different family members indicated that they expected Harry to announce his engagement imminently.

Harry did not follow Catharine's advice to call on the Sumners at first. Instead, he sent Elizabeth Sumner a second note — what he thought was "a very distant and delicate reproof for construing commonplace civilities into serious expressions of attachment." Robert would later claim that Harry had turned the whole matter too "*serious* entirely" with this second note, and Elizabeth Sumner said as much in her reply, complaining that he had accused her of indelicacy. Again, Harry panicked. "In a fit of frenzy," he recalled three years later, "and, as I then imagined, with something of the magnanimity of a martyr, I wrote her a furious declaration of passion, at the same time however requiring an instantaneous and decisive answer, and expressing my expectation that it would be in the negative."[8]

A version of that letter survives. Harry began, strangely enough, by mentioning his courtship of Abigail Phillips the previous summer:

> Last summer led on by some fatality by some malignant influence which had a temporary possession of my mind at a misguided moment I offered marriage to Miss Phillips. Heaven knows how immediately how deeply and how constantly I have suffered. Her answer declining the proposition relieved me from apprehension, but not from remorse.
>
> I could tell you what influence was exerted over my mind by the importunity of others. I could hatch out some miserable apology for my *crime*—but I disdain it. My heart had and long been yours, and no motive should have had the power to sway it a moment from its truth.
>
> Forgive — Let me see by your manner that you have pardoned me, but say nothing to me on the subject. I shall not have the fortitude to hear it. Trust me, I will never put your goodness to such another test.[9]

This might be an unsent draft of a letter that was very different in its final form. It is not exactly a "furious declaration of passion," nor does it demand an immediate response. But it does, as Robert noted soon thereafter, reveal that Harry's head was "somewhat bewildered by the perturbations of [his] heart." It also implies that Harry's devotion to Miss Sumner predated the current series of interactions by at least several months.

A day or two after Harry sent his third note, he received a reply — not from Elizabeth Sumner, but from her sister. He was puzzled by its contents, but he copied it over for inclusion in a letter he sent to Catharine, describing the whole affair. A portion of his copy survives in a fragment of that letter. "I am so sensible of Mr. Sedgwick's entire unwillingness at any moment to give offense, and of the correspondent return which his ingenuousness merits," Mehetable Sumner had written, "that I cannot hesitate in yielding him an immediate compliance with his request — and it is with the more pleasure acceded to — as I can with sincerity assure him that there is no transgression for which he requires 'forgiveness.'" She concluded by assuring him that "every *mistake* is now rectified," and that the whole matter had been nothing more than a misunderstanding.

But Harry was not mollified. "If in truth 'every mistake is now rectified,'" Harry beseeched his sister, "I do most humbly implore you to inform me how, for I am as ignorant of the matter as the babe unborn." Though both Catharine and Robert saw Mehetable Sumner's letter as an attempt to allow Harry the opportunity to resume his contacts with Elizabeth Sumner in a more level-headed fashion, Harry believed that its intent was to declare the whole affair ended, and to warn him politely to stay away from her sister. He considered its manner "so dry . . . as to awaken my resentment."[10]

When he looked back on this whole series of events three years later, Harry admitted, "I should myself now think these things incredible, if they were not engraven in my mind in characters as imperishable as the mind itself." He was so stunned by the latest developments that at about this time (during the first few weeks of December) he withdrew from social life completely. "Parties are on foot for almost every night," he informed his brother's law partner, Harmanus Bleecker. "I have taken the outrageously rational resolution to abstain from all such amusements for the present, not that I dislike or disapprove them, but partly from whim, and partly to increase the zest of future enjoyment."

The Sumners began to wonder why Harry stayed away; then, after more time went by, they began to wonder if they should take offense, if he had simply been trifling with Elizabeth. Again, reports reached Harry's ear, so he ended his brief self-imposed period of asceticism and went to call on the Sumners, "not in the most unperturbed manner in the world," he informed Catharine, "but still manfully." He found that they were not at home, and when he learned that they were at a small party at a neighbor's, he went there and was invited in. "They received me as usual," he reported. "I said nothing to Miss E. S. except in general conversation."[11]

Mary Channing was still on the scene in Boston to reinforce the sisterly and brotherly messages Harry received from his family. She sent him twelve letters at the time of his encounter with the Sumners, offering advice, commenting on Catharine's advice, and asking to be let in on any news of the latest developments. "Trust me Harry you are in a dangerous state," she informed him in exasperation. When he neglected to deliver a message as he had promised, she blamed it on his distracted state. "What a selfish, absorbing passion must this love be," she lamented, "when it can make *you forgetful of the interest of another*." And it is tantalizing to try to imagine which of Harry's encounters with Elizabeth Sumner and her family might have produced this announcement from Mary: "From your own account, I pronounce you 'Lost Lost Lost.' You describe yourself as having all the symptoms of a malady, you have been praying for months to be a victim to and still lament your 'forlorn condition'—and seem as far from a contented state as mortal need be."[12]

With the beginning of the New Year, all the Sedgwicks in Stockbridge and New York were again awaiting the announcement of an engagement. But Harry was sure the affair had ended. His sister and confidante agreed. "My dear brother you have been too precipitate," Catharine lamented. "On this subject I cautioned you particularly. Believe me for I speak very sagely from experience, a woman's heart must be entirely won before she makes that awful affirmative decision." Catharine had been particularly distressed when she learned that Harry had committed his most passionate statements to paper rather than delivering them in person. "How after all your eyes have seen and your ears have heard," she wondered, "how could you trust to a letter? This was indeed launching your bark on the ocean of uncertainty."[13]

The chastened Harry's resentment toward Elizabeth Sumner and her sister, which had been keen, eventually diminished. "I had at length sense enough to reflect," he admitted, "that I had been the sole carver of my own fortune, and that I had even put it out of her power to bring the adventure to a different termination." Harry continued to avoid social situations where he might encounter any of the Sumners, and did not speak to Elizabeth Sumner when they were present at the same parties, out of embarrassment and what he would later call "morbid pride."

Then Abigail Phillips sent *him* a letter. They had passed each other when they were both out riding on Sunday, January 16. In her version of what happened, she attempted to catch his eye and acknowledge him, and he returned a frown. In his version, he had attempted to catch her eye, but she appeared or pretended not to see him, which caused him to frown. Whichever version was accurate, she took advantage of the occasion to resume the contact he had broken off after she had declined his proposal the preceding summer. Her first letter came at the end of that week. "Why should you give pain to one for whom you have professed an esteem?" she asked.

> Has that profession been laid on so slender a foundation that a negation to a single question should obliterate from your heart that delicate feeling of sensibility. . . ? Had those professions arisen from flattery, a thing to which a female judgment can discern you a stranger, it would not have been surprising if disappointed pride should have embraced the first opportunity of discovering on the street and on the Sabbath the frown of displeasure. But to come from one whose motives were of so much more honorable a nature could not be received in any other light than a sharp rebuke. Have I committed the deed or said the word meriting it? I can hear your reply to be yes. When you passed in the carriage it did not need a very penetrating look to discern your altered countenance.[14]

Harry scribbled a frenzied note to Catharine after receiving this letter. "Strange reverse — I have divested myself of all pique against my old friend Miss Phillips," he began, "and request that you will do the same." The letter had been so kind, so clever, and so inviting that Harry was sure he now understood that Abigail had not rejected his earlier proposal — only her father had. "Oh my dear sister, I would to Heaven that you were here," Harry sighed. "In the present imbecility of my mind I would yield myself entirely to your counsel."[15]

Harry wrote and delivered his reply without benefit of Catharine's counsel. "You can readily conceive," he told Abigail Phillips, "that after what has passed between us, and particularly as I am not much skilled in the forms of etiquette I should feel a momentary embarrassment at a sudden view of your countenance. If I recollect the occasion to which you allude, I had not recovered from this embarrassment until you had passed." He was not content just to explain and apologize for the frown; he returned to the subject of the previous summer. "I have long been tired of the heartless dissipation of fashionable society," he claimed. "My heart earnestly desired domestic bliss, and I imagined that your character was in every respect calculated to render that state respectable and happy. My hopes, you well know, were blasted."[16]

She responded almost immediately. The letter was witty and wordy (as were so many of Harry's), and it informed or reminded Harry that the incident on January 16 had not been the only time he had ignored or turned away her glance since August. But a passage near the conclusion surely caught his attention and raised his hopes. "Your acknowledgment of innocence in the intention as I thought of wounding my feelings has been a relief to my mind," Abigail had written. "I can assure you it was not my pride, but my tender feelings which were wounded, and I acknowledge my partiality for you which commenced with your first attentions has not in the least abated, though I did refuse you I did it with reluctance, and I was influenced so to do, but I must clear the charge laid on my friends, and reduce it to the influence of one only for the remainder were in favor, and that one which first objected would now be entirely satisfied with my choice." Apparently, not only had Harry been correct in his assumption that William Phillips alone had rejected his earlier proposal, he was now being invited to ask again, and offered a virtual pledge by Abigail that her father would respond differently this time. She closed (as she had in the first letter) by inviting him to deliver his reply at a time when her father would not be home ("if it is not inconvenient to send it about three or past it would be most agreeable") and even specified that he should deliver it to the kitchen door, "as by that means I shall receive it in my own room." The letter was dated January 24, 1814—the first anniversary of Judge Sedgwick's death.

Harry's second reply is lost, but Abigail Phillips's response—the third of four letters, three of them quite long, that she would write to him in the span of nine days—revealed how quickly the affair had progressed. "I find on conversing with my father that he is desirous of having the first interview with you himself," she informed him, "and as I am not under the least apprehension from any desire on his part to make an objection it will be agreeable to me that he should be gratified." She would let him know as soon as her father was ready to see him, "which I hope will be very soon." Her next words were even more promising: "I will leave my feelings to be expressed when we meet." She went on to describe her recent restless inability to sleep—agonizing, no doubt, over the outcome of her bold gesture in contacting him—for which she had found it necessary to take laudanum the night before.

A fourth letter, apparently written the next day, is even more explicit in its invitation. "I expect to be alone this afternoon," Abigail informed Harry, "and shall be glad to see you if you can make it convenient, little after three." And there seemed to be still better news: "If you please Papa will see you on Monday." Harry met with Abigail that day, and she told him in person that she would accept his proposal.[17]

The news spread to family members in Stockbridge and New York almost as soon as Harry himself knew it. Theodore sent a letter before the week was out congratulating Harry on "a prospect, so fair and so near, of your being connected with so excellent, so amiable, and so respectable a woman." Even Eliza took pen to paper to express her pleasure, and to warn Harry "to behave with *great wisdom*, and not to destroy your future success by rashness."[18]

Then Harry did a most rash and unwise thing, one that he was still at a loss to explain more than two years later. In what he came to see as a "paroxysm of distempered magnanimity," he demanded an interview with Mehetable Sumner, informed her of his as yet unconfirmed engagement to Abigail Phillips, and — most bizarre of all — "told her that I preferred her sister." She said some harsh things; so did he. He wanted to be just to her, though he felt that she had been unjust to him. She would not change her mind; or, perhaps in her view, would not admit that she *had* been unjust to him. She expressed her disapproval of his news, though, "using harsh language." The bitter feelings this meeting occasioned in the Sumner family would trouble Harry for many months.

When Harry met with William Phillips on Monday, Abigail's father still refused to give his consent to their engagement, despite his daughter's assurances — "so dreadfully did she deceive herself," Harry lamented afterwards. William Phillips insisted that he had not given his daughter "the least encouragement." He had no objections to her receiving calls from Harry Sedgwick, or seeing him on social occasions, but he would not consent to an engagement.

Why did William Phillips say no? Maybe he was hostile to Harry's liberal religious views, or troubled by Harry's inability over the previous three and a half years to establish himself in the legal profession in Boston. Perhaps he had heard rumors of Harry's alleged mistreatment of Mrs. Sedgwick during the settlement of his father's estate. He may have suspected that Harry was a treasure hunter, or disapproved of his hasty courtship of Abigail. Whatever the reason, the decision was delivered in such a way that Harry concluded it would be worthless to appeal, so he went away — again.

The rest of the family was as distraught as Harry to receive this news, but they urged him not to give up. "It is in your power to marry the young lady and with her father's consent," brother Theodore insisted. "A man with your character and advantages, can never be opposed with success." He placed the responsibility for the next step squarely on Harry. "If you desire to marry her and fail to do so, on account of this obstacle," he assured his brother, "I shall set it down to the account of sheer want of spirit." Thaddeus Pomeroy had a more earthy view, one that compared the exertions required in a successful courtship to those required in establishing oneself in business. "This is a great bargain," he proclaimed, "and is not to be completed without a struggle equal to its magnitude."[19]

Nevertheless, Harry gave up the struggle. Perhaps he knew that William Phillips suspected him of being more interested in his money than in his daughter, and perhaps he already knew in his heart that Phillips was right. He would admit this suspicion of his own motives when he reflected on these events two years later. But to the other Sedgwicks, Harry's passivity in the face of Phillips's refusal made no sense. Frances referred to his conflict with Phillips as a "combat with age and parental prejudice," and urged, "*Perseverance is* the motto." But her brother seemed unwilling to persevere. Frances even thought the struggle to change William Phillips's mind would add a *frisson* to his relationship with the man's daughter. "Such circumstances are very favorable to an excitement," she solemnly informed Harry, "which every one would wish previous to the consummation of a love affair." This was *Frances*, whose experience of such an "excitement" had led to the banishment of Loring Andrews and her eventual marriage to a man she did not love. Frances's sympathies with Abigail Phillips were deep. "I sincerely commiserate her," she informed her addled brother. "She has displayed so generous a frankness in her second communication to you — so delicate and high principled a consideration in not even alluding to the person who objected in the first — as is indicative of no vulgar or ordinary soul." That Frances herself had done something similar to this with Andrews was the unstated context. She had ended up doing her father's bidding anyway. That she believed Abigail Phillips's affair ought to end differently was a sign that she felt the rules of "the combat with age and parental prejudice" should have changed in the decade and a half since her father had driven Andrews away.[20]

Meanwhile, the Sumners were still angry. They were convinced that Harry had resumed his courtship of Abigail Phillips before he had ended his contact with Elizabeth Sumner — in effect, that he had made two proposals at the same time. Harry sought out an interview with William Sumner in an attempt to explain what had passed between him and the colonel's sisters. He drafted a long written explanation of the events of the preceding fall and winter, which probably gives a fair indication of what he wanted to say to Sumner. The most important claim was that his attachment to Abigail Phillips had ended entirely before he began paying serious attention to Sumner's sister. Harry stressed that point several times, and offered to produce evidence of it — presumably, Abigail Phillips's letters rejecting the proposal in late summer and resuming the correspondence in January. His summation of his new dealings with Abigail and her father in January was blunt: "I have been treated as a puppet." One cannot help but wonder what William Sumner — a soldier and a scientist five years older than Harry, who would not marry the first of his three wives until he was forty-six — thought of all Harry's elaborate literary posturing and lawyerly exposition. But he accepted Harry's explanation, and indicated that it would be appropriate for Harry to contact his sisters again and "resume the acquaintance upon the customary footing of civility."[21]

Harry returned to Stockbridge, for the first time in nearly a year, in late April or early May 1814.[22] His family could not believe that he had courted two different women so assiduously and come away unattached. It seemed, as Frances put it to Harry, that "though you have been compassed about by the waves of matrimony, you are not . . . born to be drowned in them." Harry professed to have no regrets about coming out of the whole fiasco still uncommitted. "I fear my love was too much the effort of effort," he informed Catharine. "I always knew though I tried not to confess it to myself that neither of the ladies were sufficiently intellectual to spend a life with." Catharine agreed. She was relieved that the affair with Miss Phillips had ended, even though she thought "a little patient and manful perseverance would have won the prize." She had not considered Abigail Phillips good enough for her brother. "His habits are literary, and his pleasures intellectual," she had reminded their sister Eliza just as the affair was breaking up, "and though he certainly could not have been unhappy with Miss [   ], still there would have been rather more mental discord, than is admissible in the full harmony of domestic life." Just before Harry returned to Boston in June, Catharine had a conversation with him, "a very full conversation," about his tangled courtships and his future dealings with Miss Sumner and Miss Phillips. "I advised Harry whenever he met them to seem to forget that anything extraordinary had ever passed between them," she informed Robert. "If he was *indifferent* I think he would not feel so much on the subject. He is reluctant to meet them at all."

Catharine suspected that Harry would eventually be reunited with Miss Phillips; Robert was sure it would be Miss Sumner. Robert was also sure that the more important lesson of Harry's turmoil in Boston concerned the way a man ought to choose a marriage partner. Reviewing the events of the whole year, he focused on the intervention of Mehetable Sumner in Harry's relationship with her younger sister, using the language of a lawyer to draw a lesson. "She has been made a principal, when she ought to have been second," he complained. "A negotiation has been carried on through her, which all laws human and divine required to be conducted in '*the very presence*.' This has been a great mistake," he admonished Harry. Robert insisted that he was only pointing out this mistake to his brother "for future improvement."[23]

A few years later, Harry would have reason to recount the whole story in all its embarrassing detail to another young woman to whom he had proposed. He hoped he would not be judged on the isolated incidents. "If I know anything of myself," he pleaded, "I am not mercenary, and I am persevering in the continuance of friendships." And to this young woman, who he feared might judge his behavior harshly, he admitted, "You cannot pass a sterner censure than I have sometimes passed upon myself."

The best thing Harry could hope for, in reviewing his once-promising courtships, was that they would be forgotten. "In a few years the events I have related will have passed away with all their train of consequences," he hoped, "without leaving any more trace than the shadows of yesterday." He would look forward, not back. In that resolve, he retained the confident support of his family. Catharine had expressed this best back in November, when Harry believed he had been rejected by Abigail Phillips and was beginning his encounters with the Sumner sisters. She told Harry she was certain "that in a second case, you will act worthy of yourself, and proceed but upon *one ground*: that of an affection unequivocal in its nature, and promising to be stable as the everlasting hills — Yea that shall endure when they have passed away as a scroll." In the summer of 1814, when Harry Sedgwick returned to Boston from his brief sojourn in Stockbridge, such an unequivocal affection still eluded him. But, like his sister, he was sure it was the only ground on which a stable, lasting marriage could be built.[24]

6

The Perils of Badinage

Harry and Robert among the Friendlies

While being consoled by Catharine and Robert in Stockbridge after the humiliating events of the winter and spring of 1814, Harry Sedgwick thought seriously about staying in his hometown and never returning to Boston. He did go back to Boston in June, then took a long late-summer trip to Stockbridge. When he returned to Boston in November, he stayed only a few weeks, then returned to Stockbridge for the winter. He did not say how long he intended to stay in Stockbridge, but to his brother Charles it looked like a permanent move.[1]

At first Robert believed Harry was staying away because of the difficulties he had experienced getting his law practice established since he moved to Boston in 1810, difficulties that had been intensified by the controversy surrounding the settlement of their father's estate. He was sure that the failed courtships of Abigail Phillips and Elizabeth Sumner contributed to Harry's reluctance to return, but he did not see them as its main cause. In Robert's view, Harry was passing through "hours of tumult," and to come to a more sanguine view all he needed was time. "I beg therefore," he concluded, "that you will not consider the present moment as a sort of sample of future time."[2]

Harry went to New York to visit Robert and to confront Ebenezer Watson in April 1815, but returned to Stockbridge and gave no indication of any intent to leave. His friends in Boston legal circles wondered what was keeping him in the country. He assured them that he intended to come back, but when summer passed, and the end of September — and Harry's thirtieth birthday — rolled around, he still stayed in Stockbridge. He had been away from Boston, idling in the country as a country lawyer, for ten months, and for thirteen of the last fourteen. "Has Boston lost all its attractions?" one friend and college classmate wondered.[3]

Robert, who had visited Harry in Stockbridge in late May or early June and again in late August, knew better. In the first week of October, he sent a blistering letter from New York to Harry in Stockbridge, virtually order-ing him to return to Boston. By now he had deduced that the setbacks that loomed largest in Harry's mind and most impeded his return to Boston concerned love, not law. One of the women Harry had courted (as always, Robert left a blank where the name ought to have been, but a reference to her great wealth makes it probable that it was Abigail Phillips) had requested that he come see her to tell his side of the story.

Harry dreaded the prospect, but Robert reminded him, "When a lady *comes forward* and expresses a desire to see a gentleman with a view to an explanation, he has no right to presume that that explanation will not be sufficient—he cannot refuse an interview." Robert was beginning to realize that Harry had lost touch with even these fundamental rules of etiquette; that a paralyzing fear froze him in place and prevented him from returning to Boston, lest he encounter either of the women he had courted. And Harry's fear of those prospective encounters, according to Robert, arose "not from your having suffered wrong, but from your hav-ing done it."

Here was Harry's chance. Robert was about to go to Boston on personal business. Would Harry and Catharine leave the family's country seat and meet him there? And so, some time before October 15, Harry, Robert, and Catharine Sedgwick found themselves in Boston together, staying as guests of the family of William Minot. Harry told his Stockbridge friends he would be back in about three weeks.[4]

The Sedgwicks had known the Minots for a long time. Harry and Robert had encountered and been impressed by the "good natural understand-ing and . . . very considerable acquirements" of the slightly older William Minot during their six-month stay in Boston after their 1804 graduation from Williams College. Their fathers had been political allies at opposite ends of the state. Judge Minot was a decade younger than Judge Sedgwick, so he was still in his forties when he died in 1802. His widow, Mary Speak-man Minot, died nine years later, leaving her sixteen-year-old daughter Jane an orphan in the care of Jane's newly married older brother and his wife. That wife, Louisa Davis Minot, was also a member of a family that had enjoyed a long professional and personal relationship with the Sedgwicks. Her father, Daniel Davis, had been the state's solicitor general during all the years Judge Sedgwick sat on the Massachusetts Supreme Judicial Court. Louisa first caught sight of her future husband in January 1802, when she saw him walking in his father's funeral procession. According to Minot family tradition, her reaction was immediate: "He was the handsomest man I ever saw." She was almost fourteen at the time, and he was eighteen, a senior at Harvard. They were married eight years later, in July 1810.

The Minots lived in a large house in the new and fashionable neighborhood of Charles Street, at the foot of Beacon Hill. Until about 1804 the area had been part of the Back Bay, where the tidal basin of the Charles River widened before it flowed into Boston Harbor. Then the riverfront was filled and extended about two hundred feet to the west, using landfill from Mount Vernon, just above, which was being leveled to accommodate more new construction. This whole upsurge in development had been set in motion by the construction of the new State House, which opened at the top of Beacon Hill in 1798. The Minot house was just a few steps from Boston Common, and a long block from the ropewalks that had been located across from the common since the ones closer to the harbor burned down in 1794. At low tide, what was left of the Back Bay was marshy enough (especially near the ropewalks, where the Boston Public Garden would be constructed when the rest of the Back Bay was filled in the midnineteenth century) that duck hunters could walk out on its flats. One of William and Louisa's teenage sons would lose a thumb in a hunting accident on the flats in 1833.

Over the years, Harry and his brothers had been involved in legal business with both the Davis family and William Minot. But what probably brought about the invitation to stay with the family on Charles Street in October 1815 was a chance encounter between the Minot family and Robert Sedgwick in the late summer of that same year.[5]

After his summer trip to Stockbridge, Robert had journeyed to the mineral springs at Ballston, New York. The account of his days at Ballston that he later sent to Catharine dwelt on matters more social than therapeutic. At Ballston at the same time had been Louisa Davis Minot and her sister-in-law Jane, who were nearing the conclusion of a two-month journey across upstate New York to Canada, and returning through Ballston. Jane Minot found that the only thing people seemed to remember about each other at Ballston was their apartment numbers: "It is a fine place to learn your own insignificance," she wrote in the travel journal she kept for friends to read when she returned.

The Minots left Ballston and steamed down the Hudson several days after Robert had, staying in New York to visit with old friends. Foremost among these were the Murrays (clients of Robert's), and it was at their elegant home that Robert paid them a call.[6] Another guest who arrived at about the same time played the flute for them, "much to Mr. S's annoyance," Jane reported, "as he hates any interruption to conversation." After the musician finished one tune, Robert applauded the tune's brevity. "I admire Robert Sedgwick," Jane reported in her journal. "He is very sensible and good natured and so droll in conversation that you may be sure of laughing when you see him." Robert took some time over the next few days to act as "a companion and directory," guiding the Minot women around the city, and saw them off when they boarded the steamer to New Haven for their return to Boston. Nearly a year and a half later, Jane would remember him as being "all sufficient to fertilize New York with charms to my eyes."[7]

When Robert set out for Boston a month after the Minots had visited New York, the language he used to justify his journey gave a strong hint of his purpose. "The expense I disregard. The loss of business I must put up with," he notified his brother Harry. "The chance in my favor is next to nothing, but in a matter of so much importance at my time of life, I think it right to *do* a great deal upon chances." The reference to "my time of life," along with the playing out of subsequent events, confirms that the chance Robert intended to take involved courting someone — either Jane Minot, or some other young woman Jane or Louisa Minot had called to mind. The fact that he left New York so quickly after the Minots' visit, and with such dry-mouthed determination, would seem to indicate that the object of his attentions was someone he had at least seen, if not met. We have no indication that any other unmarried Boston ladies were traveling with the Minots or visiting in the Murrays' parlor in those early days of September. The Minots might have mentioned some young lady he already knew in Boston, who might have been the stimulus for his hurried visit; but it is also possible that Robert was the first member of the Sedgwick family to court Jane Minot.

Robert arrived in Boston a few days before Catharine and Harry did, and left after "a delightful visit" of about two weeks. He was determined to return soon. Harry and Catharine dallied. "Boston is so pleasant to us," Harry reported to Frances, "that I think it not impossible that we may extend our visit here beyond the time we originally designed." They stayed until the middle of November, returning to Stockbridge just in time for Thanksgiving. This time when Harry went back to Stockbridge he had already made plans to return to Boston early in the new year, and to stay there.

Something happened in Boston in the closing days of October and the early days of November that caused both Harry and Robert Sedgwick to believe that they were about to enter into courtships whose prospects of success were both significant and pleasing. "You must be almost as surprised I think, at your present state of being, contrasting it with what you were six weeks ago — as one of those crawling gents is, who all at once finds himself robed in the luxurious plumage of a butterfly," Robert wrote to Harry a few weeks after the younger brother had returned to New York. "In sober truth, I cannot tell you how much delighted I am to see you in a new world."[8]

By the time he left Boston in November, Harry had closed the book on his previous courtships by calling on Elizabeth Sumner (their conversation was "*merely friendly*"), and probably also on Abigail Phillips (Robert appears to have concluded that Harry "did right" by her).[9] More important, he had opened up a whole new courtship, one that his brother and sister believed would conclude speedily and successfully — and Robert was only a few steps behind him in a courtship of his own.

The only problem is that it is impossible to tell for sure *who* the brothers were courting in the late fall of 1815. Their visit to the Minots brought them into close and frequent contact with Jane Minot's circle of friends in Boston, and at various times, beginning with Robert's first encounter with Jane in early September, each brother appeared to be actively interested in at least two or three of the young women who made up that circle. They might, in fact, have believed it necessary to appear to court the whole group without a particular preference. This might have been what Robert meant when he wrote to Harry the following spring to say "that you cannot be in love till you are engaged."[10] As in the case of Harry's earlier courtships, the problem is compounded by the brothers' unwillingness to write out the ladies' first names, and usually their last names as well. This reluctance was rooted in social convention, specifically in a taboo against addressing a lady familiarly by her first name, but it also seems to draw on the brothers' own penchant for secrecy in their personal affairs. Nevertheless, it is possible to identify most of the young women Harry and Robert encountered. They devoted their attention to all or almost all of the unmarried "friendlies," the collective name by which Jane Minot and her circle of female friends referred to themselves.[11]

As a group, the friendlies had elastic boundaries. They seemed at times to consist of as many as eight or nine women, a few of them already married. Their interests and activities were personal, emotional, and domestic. As such this group differed from another form of female-directed social group that has attracted the attention of scholars: the political salons seen, for example, in Philadelphia when it was the Republic's capital in the 1790s. Women in those more mixed groups used their social access to powerful men to exercise some influence, albeit limited, on the world of politics and government. The salon was a much more public setting (in many senses of that word) than the intimate circle of the friendlies in Boston two decades later. Carroll Smith-Rosenberg and Nancy F. Cott have written of intimate female friendships around this time (Smith-Rosenberg refers to a "female world of love and ritual" in which men "made but a shadowy appearance"), but their subjects mostly played out exclusive, one-on-one friendships at a distance of many miles, in exchanges of passionate letters or shared diaries. Jane's commonplace book, and the letters she wrote to friends who were just outside her circle, especially to Catharine Sedgwick and her brothers, provide a glimpse of the friendlies sharing such an intimate connection in person, several decades earlier than Smith-Rosenberg's rich examples.[12]

At the core of the group, with Jane Minot, were three other young women. Jane, who was probably about to turn twenty-one in the closing months of 1815, was the youngest.[13] Mary Ann Gray Fales was a year or so older, but she was married and had at least one child at the time of the Sedgwicks' arrival in their midst, so her involvement was diminishing. Margaret Champlin Jones was almost a year and a half older than Mary Ann Fales. She was the oldest daughter of one of Boston's wealthiest merchants, John Coffin Jones, and his third wife, Elizabeth Champlin Jones. Jane referred to her at various times as "Gretty," "Greta," "Gretna," and "Gretina." Caroline Danforth — "Crough" or "Cro'" to Jane — was the daughter of Dr. Samuel Danforth, the prominent Boston physician who had cared for Judge Sedgwick during his final illness. Her mother, Martha Hall Gray Danforth, the doctor's third wife, had died while Caroline was an infant. Caroline was Mary Ann Fales's cousin. Records of her are sparse, but she was the oldest of the friendlies, almost exactly the same age as Catharine Sedgwick, and possibly more than five years older than Jane Minot. Mindful of her position as the youngest in the group, Jane reproached herself for having the presumption to take pleasure in being welcomed into the company of such "superior persons."

Margaret Champlin Jones had three younger sisters. Elizabeth was twenty-two, Mary twenty, and Martha Ellery just fourteen in the fall of 1815. All three of them occasionally participated in the social gatherings of the friendlies, as did their mother, also named Elizabeth, who hosted many of them. Mary, the Jones sister closest in age to Jane Minot, also came closest to joining in the intimacy of the inner circle of the friendlies.[14]

The friendlies did not live especially near each other in Boston, nor had their parents been the closest of friends. All of their families but the Minots had some historical connections to Newport, Rhode Island, but their connection seems to have been made and strengthened at the Brattle Street church, a liberal Boston congregation where Mary Ann's family were longtime members and the Joneses and Minots occasional members or frequent visitors. (The ease with which a family like the Joneses might drift from the Brattle Street church one year to King's Chapel another comes as something of a surprise, although both churches were decidedly liberal in theological terms, as was the third church the friendlies attended with any frequency, William Ellery Channing's Federal Street church.)[15]

The fullest descriptions of any of these women can be found in a notebook Jane Minot used from 1811 to 1815 as her commonplace book. There, probably around the end of 1814, she wrote lengthy sketches in which she attempted to capture the dispositions and behaviors of her two closest friends in the group, Caroline Danforth and Margaret Champlin Jones. Together with some later references in Jane's letters, and a scant few letters of their own, these sketches are almost all we have to reconstruct the lives of these strong, complex women.

Nancy F. Cott has written of the development of an ideal of female "passionlessness," first in evidence around the time of the friendlies' births, which enabled some women to accomplish significant work by furnishing them with a sense of a higher destiny, and thus with a rationale for keeping away from the traditional roles of wife and mother.[16] A great deal of the portrait of Caroline Danforth that emerges from Jane's sketch matches Cott's image of this "passionless" female. Jane noticed most Caroline's solitary aloofness. "A fertile imagination has molded most of her ideas," she wrote, "and as much of her life has been passed alone her warm feelings have been mostly exercised on these beautiful visions." But Caroline's receptiveness to beautiful visions was different from openness to real-world pleasures. Jane was surely thinking of Caroline's loss of her mother in infancy when she wrote this assessment: "Not early accustomed to sympathy, she hardly seems to expect it and she shrinks from it from the fear that she cannot impart pleasure." Jane noted that Caroline's reserve "screens her social feelings, but when warm interest discloses them you perceive a heart that may be touched when its excellence is appreciated." Appreciators of such excellence were rare, but when Caroline found them her face told the tale. "She is very susceptible with regard to the opinions of her friends as you may perceive by the variations of her color," Jane had observed.

Jane also saw in her friend Caroline a piety that gave her character an "elevated tone" and a "moral sublimity which the consciousness of rectitude gives"; an excellent memory that gave her conversation an allusive charm; a taste for philosophical works; and a devotion to duty. "Her taste however is still for those beautiful regions of fancy to which she is indebted for all the pleasures of early life and for which her pure spirit seems indeed a fit inhabitant," Jane concluded. "There is still about her an air of poetry and spirituality—which animates her loveliness and excites your imagination." [17]

While Caroline Danforth typified the ethereal pure spirit, Margaret Champlin Jones was more worldly. "Having been brought up without restraint in the expression of her thoughts and feelings," Jane noted, "she had the free use of her understanding. She was never repressed except when she did wrong. There was no cold silent look to send the bursting sentiment of youth to its own bosom. Her energy and enthusiasm were shown in her manners. She made friends wherever she was seen. . . . She enjoyed the happiness of a virtuous heart when it is permitted to yield to its own impulses." Jane went on to write of Margaret's ability "to afford a fund of most animated pleasure to her friends," of her "clear and remarkable" mind and her "quick perception of truth." She commented on "a luxuriance about her mind and feelings" which to Jane looked like genius. "It makes her the constant object of attention and emotion in the circle of her acquaintance and renders her conversation always delightful," Jane observed. "Very candid in her disposition, she prevents those misunderstandings which often arise among the best friends. Her countenance conveys an invitation to examine her whole heart but it is not necessary to investigate farther, whatever is frank generous intelligent and tender is there expressed you read in it the nobleness of her nature and while you feel you enjoy her superiority."

Over the next few months, the Sedgwick brothers were to experience the effects of the unrestrained candor and impulsive freedom of expression to which Jane referred in so many different ways in her sketch of Margaret Jones. But there was more to Margaret. Around the time Harry and Robert Sedgwick came to Boston, she seems to have suffered some grave disappointment in life—most likely a broken engagement, perhaps even the death of a suitor—which added a certain gravity to her demeanor. As Jane noted in a letter to Catharine Sedgwick the following spring, "now that affliction has turned her mind to the most exalted views she is more winning without being less splendid."[18]

Jane also wrote enough about herself in her commonplace book — her thoughts, hopes, fears, curiosities, and anxieties — to give an extensive introduction to her own personality and upbringing. Although the only formal education to which we find specific reference is her study of the piano, beginning when she was about ten, her notes reveal that at some point she received the kind of broad, comprehensive schooling that was just becoming a possibility for wealthy, city-dwelling young women in the early years of the nineteenth century. Her commonplace book contains extensive entries in her own hand on chemistry, metallurgy and mineralogy, geology, plant and human biology, English history, theology, philosophy, grammar, and rhetoric.[19]

Sometimes Jane derived moral lessons from the simple details of her everyday life. "A walk on a fine morning is calculated to set in operation some of the best and most important powers of the mind and heart," she wrote once, without further elaboration. On October 31 of an unspecified year she recorded a lesson in diligence: "I mended my stocking this morning and put it on without examining it very closely because I was tired of my work," she wrote. "Just as I put it on a thin place caught my eye it would not have become a hole for many days — but I knew it would be more trouble to darn it then than now, yet it was not without some reasoning and effort of mind, that I persuaded myself to do it." She recognized that the lesson was not a heroic one. "That I darned my stocking was not virtue in me," she acknowledged, "but it was upon the same principle as virtue — and little exertions of this sort very much smooth the way for difficult virtues."

She recorded some thoughts on child rearing that imply a deep-seated disapproval of the kind of free-spirited upbringing her friend Margaret Jones had enjoyed:

> It is becoming fashionable to make children happy in order to make them good. The argument in favor of this measure is plausible, that we are always amiable when we are happy — it is expected that habits of well doing will be so fixed in childhood that misfortunes in after life will not shake them. I would not cause children any superfluous pain but I believe that the earlier they are familiarized to their condition in the world the better they will act in it. Nothing is plainer than that this is a state of probation, and sorrow would not have been sent to us if it was not a means of improvement. It is not by turning away from thoughts of misery that we can make our lives most happy but by considering how we may lessen it.

If we are constantly receiving happiness in youth when we are older every attention to misfortune will be an effort of duty. Our first impulse will be to shun it when it comes to others or ourselves.

Some of the most revealing passages in the commonplace book concern Jane's self-image. She considered herself slow and reserved in conversation, not because of any defect in understanding, but because all her reading had been in books that were "more useful in conduct than in conversation"; her difficulty in conversation arose "either from having too many ideas and feelings or not enough." In company, she found that "all the sense I have is of no use but to keep me from saying silly things." But she was sure she could improve this. She worried that she provoked the brother and sister-in-law in whose home she lived by her "independent spirit" and "opposition to their taste," even though William and Louisa had "never once intentionally hurt my feelings while they have given me daily proofs of their desire to promote my happiness." She believed that she was not as attractive or admired as her friends, and she feared that she loved praise too much and put forth "counterfeit" qualities in order to secure it. But in another entry, she expressed the belief that she had wrestled with this love of praise and subdued it. "I have some strong but indistinct desires of what is purely intellectual and holy which prevents my being entirely satisfied like most of my friends with what are called the pleasures of life," she claimed. "I am not subject to being delighted as they are. I always like to claim less than I deserve." Jane valued her independence — "therefore it suits me to have some excellence in reserve that nobody knows of but myself," she wrote. "I should like to be generous and yet only appear to others not mean. I admire to see people possess power without the desire of displaying it."

Perhaps most intriguing are Jane's ruminations about her destiny. Close as she was to her brother and sister-in-law and to the friendlies, she worried in the months before Harry and Robert Sedgwick's arrival in Boston about the impact that being orphaned in her teens might have on her ability to experience and demonstrate affection. "We must have the habit of loving," she asserted, "or however strong our natural feelings may be they will not have that enthusiastic interest in others which gives so much happiness to life. I am twenty and this power is almost dead in me. I may have preserved some of the innocence of youth," she lamented, "but the radiance of its feeling is lost." At least in the privacy of her commonplace book—which is not, of course, as inaccessible as the privacy of one's mind or heart—she confessed that she did not believe she would ever marry. She envisioned her own early death after a few more years of life as a reserved maiden aunt to William and Louisa's children. "I think I shall remain in this family with little addition or diminution of intercourse," she prophesied. "I shall probably be a kind of second mother to a little rising generation — and when I get to be about thirty I expect to die — remembered a little while as a respectable woman."

In Jane's imagination, her death seemed almost piquant, as she envisioned what it would be like to take a last look at the places where she loved to walk, "to watch the last bound of my little Mary" (William's oldest daughter, probably three years old at the time), and to say a tearful goodbye to her family. "How tight should I grasp William's hand," she imagined. "What a kind look I should give to Louisa." In this vision of single life and early death, Jane freed herself in her imagination from the demands and responsibilities of the married state, and from the loss of independence it implied.[20]

At the center of the friendlies' life together was the regular Sunday evening gathering at the Joneses' house on Pearl Street, to which a small and carefully selected number of male guests was sometimes invited. At these and other gatherings, the three women described most fully in Jane's commonplace book — Caroline Danforth, Margaret Champlin Jones, and Jane Minot — became (along with Margaret Jones's sister Mary) the objects of Harry and Robert Sedgwick's amorous hopes in the waning months of 1815 and on into the new year. Harry had almost certainly met Caroline Danforth three years earlier, when her father had cared for the dying Judge Sedgwick, and Robert probably had as well. Jane Minot would later refer to herself as someone Harry had known and seen for years "without notice." At different times in 1816, both brothers seemed to be most intrigued by Margaret Jones, who may have been previously unknown to them. But what emerges from the brothers' letters is a clear impression that the two of them acted as Robert had suggested, in a way that allowed them to engage in some forms of courting behavior with the whole group without appearing to indicate a particular preference for one or the other until almost the last possible moment.[21]

Harry returned to Boston around January 10, and entered into an office-sharing agreement with William Fales, Mary Ann's husband. Though he would be a frequent visitor to Stockbridge on vacations and family business, Harry would not return there to live until ill health forced him to retire from his law practice a dozen years later. Robert made three lengthy visits to Boston from New York between October 1815 and June 1816. In addition to the two weeks of his late October visit, he came for virtually the entire month of February and for two weeks beginning Sunday, May 26. He was in Boston and away from his New York office so frequently (with two to four days of travel time at each end of each trip) that he worried about the impression residents of both cities must have had of him. Harry, for his part, worried that Robert was crowding him, and that their respective courtships would interfere with each other. He urged Robert to stay away until he had reached some kind of resolution.[22]

The brothers consulted with their younger sister on the progress of their courtships, but Catharine shared only enough of their secrets with other family members to give a general sense that something important was happening, and that it might soon lead to a change in the marital status of one or both of them. Poor Charles was left out of the discussion completely, and sent several letters to Harry begging to be told what was happening. Frances knew that Catharine and her brothers had been discussing matters related to courtship. By February, Thaddeus Pomeroy once again believed he might hear the announcement of an engagement at any time. He also believed, when Robert went to Boston for the whole month, that Harry and Robert were courting the same woman (or women), and his advice to Harry was blunt. "I would not allow him to infringe upon your soil," he warned. "He is after her no doubt and wants courage to pop the question. Every day he is determined to do it and every sentence falters upon his tongue."[23]

Catharine traveled to Albany to stay for the winter with Theodore and Susan. Her account of the goings-on in Boston provoked the lengthiest and most revealing response from a family member outside the trio who had traveled to Boston together in October. "Dear brother," Susan Ridley Sedgwick implored Harry, "what are you about? I do not mean with your hands, but your heart; are you any nearer that desired haven to which your wishes and your promises have so long pointed? Or are you still afloat on the 'tide of *un*-successful experiment?' Recollect your repeated assurances to us, our hopes and expectations of you; reflect on the horrors of old bachelorhood, and the comforts of a good wife and a snug home; and above all remember that you cannot say in the words of the song 'Time has not thinned my flowing hair.' 'Be wise, redeem the time, for the days are evil' while you continue as you now are. I should have considerable hope of you were you not in pursuit of so many." She concluded in exasperation, "How long will you halt between two opinions?" Catharine echoed the sentiments (and the allusiveness) of her sister-in-law. "What are you doing?" she inquired of her brother, and then answered her own query: "Sucking your thumbs, and building castles while all the birds of the air are building their nests."

It took Susan two weeks to find enough time to finish her call to action and send it to Harry in Boston. When she picked up her pen to resume the letter, she informed Harry of all the conversational raw material his affairs had provided for family members in Albany, especially Catharine and herself. "Whenever we can excuse ourselves from the press of par- ties," she told him, "we do really enjoy ourselves round our dear, ugly, comfortable close-stove. We then talk over *you*, and *your affairs*; discuss Bob, and touch upon Charley; and at length retire in as sweet a delirium of hopes, fears, and impressions, as if we were *ourselves in love*." Theodore was sometimes caught up in their enthusiasm, but more often than not Susan believed that he extinguished it along with the stove, "covering the fires, and shutting up the doors," before he marched his wife and his sister off to bed with the sage admonition, "Girls don't humbug yourselves."[24]

Robert was especially interested in securing Catharine's approval for his plans. In December, Catharine knew which one of the friendlies Rob- ert had in mind when he told her that "the simple fact of having your approbation my dear Catharine, not to say your sympathy, is enough to send me through fire and water." Ten days later he added, "I should have felt very differently towards ——— if after *knowing* you she had thought or felt differently with regard to you."

In the course of his long February stay in Boston, Robert suffered some experience that he referred to as a "disaster," and compared himself in those disastrous circumstances to Don Quixote. At the end of the month, he left without bidding farewell to anyone but his brother. It is possible that he made some expression of interest, maybe even a proposal, to someone during that month and was rebuffed—but it is also possible that his quixotic disaster was only the bad weather that kept his return voyage from leaving Newport for days, during which time he was able to reread his innkeeper's copy of *Don Quixote*. After all, he also referred to his stay in Boston as "felicitous" and the place itself as "magic." And as late as the end of February, Catharine was certain that she knew which of the friendlies Robert was pursuing; she cited him to Harry as an example of single-mindedness that he should follow.[25]

By the beginning of April, Jane Minot told Catharine that she believed she knew which of the friendlies had piqued Harry's interest, and kept him from concentrating on his legal practice; "a certain magical mourner of our circle who presents to his inspection an animated pair of black eyes when he wishes to study a case." "Mournfulness" and "black eyes" may refer to Margaret Jones, but a day later Harry informed Catharine of his intention to "relinquish all further *views*—nay those I never formed—*imaginations* of Miss J." A month after that, Catharine was still imploring Harry to make up his mind. "No wise man would launch upon an ocean sailing about it and about it, towards every '*friendly*' mist that arose to his view, and never directing his ship to a port," she reminded him. "Determine my dear Harry on some specific object, *shut out all others*, and pursue it resolutely . . . and you will attain it."

The slippery allusiveness of the family's correspondence reflected the brothers' own indecision. Jane Minot seems to have inspired Robert's initial interest in coming to Boston. Harry was at first believed to be in pursuit of Margaret Jones. Each would eventually devote more serious attention to another of the friendlies, with differing results. In Boston in the winter and spring of 1816, the Sedgwick brothers' amorous interests changed so quickly, as Susan Ridley Sedgwick had lamented, that it is impossible to make any inferences from a letter written in June or July about what passions a lover might have felt in February.[26]

One thing can be said with certainty about the identity of the woman who aroused Robert Sedgwick's interest in the early months of 1816: she was *not* Margaret Jones. In March, after the quixotic disaster of February, Catharine tried to direct Robert's attentions toward Margaret. Robert's dismissal was devastating in its candor: "There is an air of repulsive desolate majesty about that old earth which is enough to haunt one's imagination."[27] Nevertheless, when Robert returned to Boston in late May, he found himself entangled in an embarrassing series of misunderstandings involving not just Margaret but also her sister Mary. Robert's attempts to convince Harry of "the propriety of my conduct" and to extricate himself from this puzzling situation fill three long letters, all written within two weeks of his departure from Boston in June. The controversy is worth exploring for the light it sheds on what the brothers and their friends believed could and could not be done in a courtship, and in a friendship between a man and a woman.

Robert arrived in Boston on Sunday, May 26, and he and Harry called on the Joneses, who were hosting their regular Sunday-evening gathering of the friendlies. The brothers were invited to dinner at the Joneses the following Tuesday, and stayed for a pleasant evening of conversation. They went back, again in response to invitations, on Friday, May 31, and Monday, June 3. Robert also called on the Joneses once in the company of William Fales, who went to deliver an invitation for the sisters to visit his house, and on two other occasions about which he provided no details, except that one of them was the night before he left. In other words, Robert called at the Joneses' house on half of the fourteen days he spent in Boston.

Sometime during the weeks in which Robert paid these frequent calls, the notion arose — it is not clear exactly how — that Robert was courting Mary Jones. The report spread quickly among the friendlies and their acquaintances. On the day he arrived back in New York, Robert took pains to deny it to Harry. "I declare in the presence of my Maker," he stated, "that I have not the least recollection of ever having said anything either seriously or in jest to M——y which by any construction whatever could be considered as an expression of attachment or anything like it. I feel the utmost confidence that I am correct in this," he assured his brother, "because I never said anything at all to her by way of badinage."

The last word was an important one, so important that Robert used it three times in these letters. *Badinage* was the clever wordplay by which a gentleman and a lady could hint to one another of a deeper interest, and allude to events or experiences in history, nature, or literature, in whose parallels a deeper message could be found. In Robert's view, badinage was the key to courtship, for if one of the speakers experienced a change of mind or heart, all that was necessary was to argue ingenuously that the conversation was only about its literal subject and contained no deeper meaning. In an age in which conduct manuals envisioned women as the passive objects of zealous male pursuit and warned women not to allow men "improper familiarities," badinage was a way for a clever young man and woman to sound each other out, to see if there was any interest without making a commitment or even appearing to make a direct overture.[28] For commitments were easy to fall into as soon as one passed from the formal to the familiar or from the allusive to the literal; and too many commitments made and broken could damage a person's reputation for forthrightness and sincerity. Badinage was a way of testing the waters without appearing to do so.

Despite his disclaimer, by the end of Robert's visit Mary Jones had heard enough of his badinage to believe that he had expressed a genuine interest in her and a desire to form an attachment with her. Robert did not understand how this could have happened, insisting that "if any inference at all could have been drawn by her on a subject which ought not to be left to inference, it must have been directly the reverse from that which has been drawn." He wondered what "imprudence" he might have engaged in. Then he decided to look instead at who else might have been whispering in Mary's ear, suggesting interpretations of whatever Robert might have said during those seven calls. "I feel perfectly *sure*," he concluded, "that no impression of this kind would ever have entered the mind of M——y, much less have been suffered to remain there long — unless the spark had been most industriously fanned by her sister." And then came a remarkable admission: "If her sister has made the mistake I should have thought myself to blame, for my trifling and imprudence." (Ten days later Robert would go even farther, saying that his flattery of Margaret was so open "that if *she* had made the *mistake* my case would seem very criminal, and one in which I had been, to say the least, wickedly careless.") Whatever Robert might have thought of Margaret Jones in March, by late May he was calling on her home freely and attempting to engage in the badinage of courtship with her. She, apparently uninterested but without an acceptable means of declaring it, decided instead to parry his advances by interpreting them as being intended for her younger, plainer, and less outspoken sister.

Robert cited for Harry some instances when Margaret might have done so. "The day we dined there," he recalled, "she asked me what was the matter with me, and said if I would state my case she would prescribe for me." Margaret had written her "prescription" on a slip of paper: "delicate perseverance." After that, in a "long encounter of wits" while they sat together on a sofa, Margaret had attempted by hints and indirection — by badinage — to imply that she did *not* mean Robert should persevere in pursuit of her, *nor* of her sister. "You will perceive," he told Harry, sure that Harry shared his notions of gallantry, "it was impossible to disclaim either of these objects with great seriousness because that would have looked too much like its being possible that they might have been had in view." In his efforts "to satisfy her . . . that I entertained neither of those suspicions," he had then "indulged a good deal in a kind of wild play of imagination" with Margaret, "almost without knowing whither it tended." He later remembered "laughing very heartily" and saying "extravagant things" to her. "All the gallant particular speeches which I made to her afterwards related exclusively to herself — as far as I can remember," he told his brother, "nor do I suspect that she had any idea that they had any other bearing whatever till . . . after a good deal of conversation about my heart under the allegory of a terra incognita, . . . she said that her object in making discoveries in that territory was to be able to make a just report about it to any friend who might be interested. Even then," Robert insisted, "I had no distinct idea that anything she said related to M——y." On one later occasion, Robert recalled, Margaret had offered to give him her counsel — a remark he found puzzling at the time. "But most assuredly," he insisted, "there was no ground for putting serious interpretation upon anything that passed between us — because everything was said in a style of badinage and pleasantry and known to be so said."

That Saturday night before Robert left Boston, Margaret forthrightly urged him to put an end to his disingenuousness, and "asked with some emphasis what was the matter with me." His reply, he felt, was serious — "Nothing is the matter with me" — but Margaret kept asking him to disclose his "disorder."

That same last evening, Robert had a conversation with Mary Jones. "Nothing could have been more guarded — more cautious," Robert claimed. Mary asked why he would leave his friends, and he replied that his business required it. She asked when he would visit again. Two wildly incompatible versions of his reply can be found. Robert's version was that he said he could not tell, "that my reputation had already suffered from my long absences from my business." Margaret Jones's version of Robert's reply went beyond mere badinage: "I shall return at least to gaze on what I love."

Whichever was true, Mary Jones then offered him a gift to remember her by — a ring. "My heart I confess almost leaped from my bosom," Robert recalled. "I could scarcely refrain from the warmest confessions of acknowledgement" — until he realized that his statements "might easily have been construed to mean that I was hers." In such misconstructions, of course, lay the perils of premature or unintended commitment. "I saw my danger," he insisted to his brother. He paused for a moment to collect his wits, and then said to Mary, "I thank you. I do not need anything to remember you." Despite the implicit flattery of the reply, Mary wondered later if Robert considered it improper for her to have offered the gift. He insisted, of course, that he did not.

So Robert left Boston in June as he had in February — unattached, embarrassed, behind in his business, and unable or unwilling to give even his closest relative a hint of where his true amorous interests lay. "It is impossible not to be interested in the simplicity — delicacy — ingenuousness — purity — and warm-heartedness of M——y," he admitted. "There is certainly a loveliness about her which might melt harder and colder hearts than mine."

Here lay Robert's problem: Enough badinage had passed between him and Mary Jones, or had been reported by her sister to have transpired, that "reports" in Boston were of an imminent announcement. "But my dear Harry," Robert pleaded, "that union is too sacred, too lasting in its consequences to be ventured upon so short an acquaintance. I know but very little about the stamina of her character. . . . Still I am by no means sure that a longer acquaintance might not have refined the interest I felt into an ardent love. Without this in my heart, I never never will take that sacred vow upon my lips."

Nevertheless, on his return trip to New York, Robert experienced "many a reverie about this lovely girl." He wondered what occasion might give him a legitimate excuse to return to Boston without neglecting his work any more than he already had, and promised "that these *events* would enable me to decide." If a decision was required immediately, "I say no—once and forever. My heart is too stiff to shape so soon."

Robert's long letter to Harry—one of the longest he had ever sent to his brother, written immediately upon his return to New York—ended with a plea that resonates over the years. "If I have as you say gone too far already," he complained, "then I do not see how I could go farther and reserve the right of retreat. I do not understand the laws of honor or manhood—the feelings of a gentleman or of a man—the laws of social intercourse—nor the rules of common discretion; if such an intimacy as is essential to a just estimate of character, must necessarily commit a gentleman under any circumstances." In Robert's view, at least one more visit to Boston would be necessary before he could decide whether he wanted Mary Jones to be his wife. In Harry's view (shared by Catharine), another visit would be a matter of "extreme delicacy," and tantamount to an announcement of their engagement. After all, Mary's interest had been made public—she had offered him the ring. If he came again to do anything but commit himself, Robert would be deemed to have "trifled" with Mary. "If you think it quite so," Robert conceded, "and think that after farther acquaintance and another visit—I should have no right to decide—then the affair must be considered as entirely at an end. I say again I never would see her without being free as air, by honor's law—and laws much more sacred." Even more than the affair, Robert wanted the discussion of it among the friendlies to end. "*The conversation on* this subject has broken the charm," he admonished Harry. "If nothing had been whispered about it, all would have gone well."

What went almost unnoticed here is that the stratagem of the ring (even though he had declined it) had diverted Robert's erratic attentions again, this time from Margaret Jones to her younger sister, as Margaret had all along intended. Robert was sure that Mary Jones's interest in him owed its origins to "the anticipations which M——g taught her to indulge respecting the object of my visit—and to the belief with which M——g

must have inspired her of the unquestionable thralldom of my heart." He
was not yet enthralled by Mary Jones in June, but he was interested in
exploring the possibilities of the relationship, in getting to know more of
her character. Two weeks after he left Boston, he made an urgent request
of his brother:

> You know me—you know my dispositions—my levity, my serious-
> ness—my love of amusement, my love of sense—my ambition, my mod-
> eration—my admiration and value of talent, my fondness for, and love
> of integrity, good principles, good dispositions, kindness, warmhearted-
> ness—you know that I require a great deal in the character of that person
> who for life is to be pillowed on my bosom, and be nearest my heart—you
> know I have formed high expectations, and rejected moderate ones—in
> fine you know my head and my heart. Now my dear brother, I do not
> ask your advice—it would not be just to cast such a responsibility on
> you—but I do ask your deliberate, well weighed opinion of the character
> of M——y, and of her capacity for filling a station of less ease and more
> responsibility than any she ever knew, that of my ———. Give *me* her
> character unvarnished, good and bad as far as you know it. I am sure you
> will not shun the trouble. The subject is one of great moment. It is one on
> which I ought to have all the light I can get.

Robert had known all along that the Jones sisters believed he was courting Mary—or at least his brother believed Robert had known this. Harry
said as much in a letter to Catharine, a report of which reached Robert.
"This Harry is really cruel," Robert complained. "I had no more reason to
be aware of it than you had." Then Harry read to Margaret Jones and Mary
Ann Fales passages of Robert's long letter describing the events of his June
visit; promised Margaret that he would not tell Robert he had done so;
and told Robert, both that he had read it and that he had assured Margaret
he would never reveal as much. Each action of Harry's made Robert more
indignant, especially because Harry had confided in Margaret. He knew
that Margaret was shrewd enough to mistrust Harry's promise to keep
the reading secret from him. The next time he saw her, she would be fully
aware of his interpretation of what had happened on the evening Mary
offered him the ring, and of what he had said to Harry later about Mary.
She would also have a strong (and correct) suspicion that Robert knew
what she knew. Under such circumstances, badinage with either of the
Jones sisters would be nearly impossible.[29]

Robert thought about returning to Boston in September. This time,
though, he decided that the object of his wayward attentions would not
be either of the Jones sisters, but the most exalted and unapproachable

member of the friendlies, Caroline Danforth. In July, Robert experienced "something like a second sight conviction" that he and Caroline were destined to wed. "Were it not for a fear of something not seen, which in relation to her has always lurked about me," he admitted, "I have no hesitation in saying that I would place my heart in her custody." In a little more than a month, Robert had soured on his prospects with Mary Jones, or on her suitability, probably in response to Harry's judgment of her. He knew that Harry held Caroline in higher esteem. (Harry had even compared Caroline to Catharine, who like her at age twenty-six stood as a prime example of "*unappropriated* excellence.") Still, he was hesitant to court her, fearing, with some apparent justification, that "she may think me strange, whimsical, unintelligible — possibly insincere." In the last week of July and the first week of August, Robert's resolution to go to Boston or not during the following month changed regularly. Catharine even suggested that she might invite Caroline to come to Stockbridge in September, so Robert could court her there. But Robert never made it back to Boston that year, and Caroline Danforth either was not invited to Stockbridge or declined the offer. Still, by that fall the inevitability of a connection between Robert and Caroline had become an article of faith for Harry, and some none-too-subtle hints of this possible connection had reached the ears of the friendlies.[30]

Margaret Jones whispered to Caroline of Robert's attentions to an otherwise unnamed "Miss E," and of the embarrassment her sister had suffered during Robert's last visit. (Could Caroline have missed that?) Harry let Robert know whenever some suitor or other pressed his attentions on Caroline, so that Robert might be goaded into speedier action. Rumors of Caroline's imminent marriage — and even that it had already taken place — seemed to sweep Boston. "Mrs. Snow heard she was married and called on her as a bride," Jane Minot reported once. "Not knowing the new name she inquired for Miss Danforth *that was*." Jane had a suspicion in December "that some matrimonial opportunity has lately been open to her."[31]

In January 1817, Robert had a chance to go to Boston on legal business. But to Harry's surprise, Robert demurred and asked someone else to handle the case. Harry believed Robert would have made the trip but for his embarrassment — "mere shame-facedness," he called it — over the events of the preceding June and the attention he was sure would now follow his every move. "He has been so many times — thinks that everybody would know his business — the lady too would be apprised of his intentions — and the whole affair would be of an awkward, coarse and embarrassing nature. Such are his misgivings," Harry reported. "He has as much shrinking delicacy on the subject as C. herself would have."

The fear of a new wave of rumors, and the shame-faced suspicion that everybody would talk about any courtship Robert might undertake, had some foundation in experience. Margaret Jones had continued to spread rumors of Robert as a two-timer who had "coquetted" with her *and* her sister while actively pursuing the elusive "Miss E." Robert likened the prospect of a journey to Boston that winter to having to "go through a courtship on the Boston stage with pit, boxes, and gallery for spectators." Harry had no doubt that if Robert were to go to Boston, "the affair would come to a decisive result — so far as depended on him."

On a Friday evening in early February, Harry and Robert had "a long and very interesting conversation" in New York. "The substance of the matter," Harry reported, "is that Robert will come to Boston, and will not come for nothing — so far at least as depends upon him." He was determined to go before June, but was still looking for "some apparent motive which may veil his ulterior designs."

But something had changed — again — in the nature of those "ulterior designs." The previous summer Robert had expressed the "second sight conviction" that he and Caroline Danforth would wind up together. Throughout the winter of 1817, showing "a reserve which was never wont to exist" between himself and Harry, he had never mentioned Caroline by name in all his equivocation about a visit to Boston. Harry had *presumed* Caroline was still his object, but during their Friday night conversation Robert was vague enough to arouse his brother's suspicions. Two weeks later the brothers spoke more openly. "I now know, and most deeply regret, that I have been mistaken," Harry reported. Robert was not interested in Caroline Danforth but in someone else (he had demanded Harry's pledge not to say who), and "the reason of his reserve to me was a knowledge that I should not sympathize with him."

And that was the end of Robert's flirtation with the friendlies. Even as Harry defended his brother's choice, and kept his secret, he could not help but be disappointed. "I much fear that the period is far distant when he shall be happy," he lamented. At about the same time, Jane Minot wrote of her friend Caroline, "*That man* would be too much blest for this world who should have the worth to deserve, the discernment to perceive, and the glory to obtain her virtues."[32]

Both of them were right. Another five and a half years would pass before Robert would marry. Caroline, nearly twenty-seven at the time this imagined courtship ended, apparently never married. Her name seems to have disappeared from history, except for a recollection of her father that she wrote at the time of his death a decade later, and a namesake in Mary Ann Fales's youngest daughter.[33]

The experience of the Sedgwick brothers among the friendlies reveals much about the dizzyingly complex nature of relations between the sexes, and especially of courtship, among the wealthy, educated elite in the young Republic. To say too much was to commit oneself too soon. Even the most sophisticated suitors found it difficult to understand the exact meaning of their own gestures and utterances. Carefully worked-out strategies of indirection — of badinage — were needed to determine if a member of the opposite sex was interested in pursuing an amorous relationship, and to extract oneself where desires did not match. In light of all this, and of his own indecisiveness, it is no wonder that Robert Sedgwick came away from his interactions with the friendlies unattached. What is surprising is that his brother Harry did not meet a similar fate.

The Jones sisters were not the only friendlies on whom Robert Sedgwick paid a call on his last night in Boston in June 1816. He and Harry also called at the Minots' house. When they left, had Robert not been too distracted by his own preoccupations, he might have noticed in Jane's expression toward his brother the outward signs of a deep inner emotion. "I often think of that fine night when Robert left us," Jane would tell Harry six months later, "how much I wished to shake your hand at parting but dared not." She remembered offering Harry such a "formal shake of the hand" in January, when he had returned to Boston from Stockbridge. Apparently such contact was appropriate when a lady encountered a gentleman she had not seen for a long time, or expected not to see again for a long time: Jane might well have shaken Robert's hand that night, but could not offer her hand to Harry, whom she would see again in a day or two. She felt tears welling up in her eyes. For by the early weeks of June, according to clues that make sense only in hindsight, Harry Sedgwick and Jane Minot were not only actively courting each other, but were beginning to fall in love.

Perhaps Harry had been influenced by Catharine, his most trusted advisor in these matters. "I have no doubt myself that Jane has more intrinsic worth than any of them," Catharine had lamented in April, when she and Jane had both thought that Harry's attention was captivated by Margaret Jones. "But the beauty of her soul will never triumph over the beauty of another's person, and I do not like to waste wishes upon what would make me happier than almost any other event, because my dear brother I am sure it would most contribute to yours." As late as mid-June, Catharine had received no indication that Jane Minot held any special place in Harry's heart.[34]

We cannot know how Harry and Jane fell in love. We have just a few words about the badinage that passed between them. Some entries in Jane's journal recorded what Harry later described as "the first opening of your affections," but all that survives is Harry's response to them, when he was given the opportunity to read them six months later. He told her that "it is and ever will be a mystery that such affections should have been bestowed upon me. . . . What had I done, what could I do to deserve it? How much anxiety would it have saved me to have known that I had found even such a measure of favor in your eyes." He quoted a few passages from Jane's journal entries. "*Occasionally* I believe he has felt something like tenderness for me," Jane had written, "but I never could have the power to make his interest permanent" — revealing again the tendency toward self-depreciation that was seen in her commonplace book.[35]

We do know that just a month after Robert's visit, sometime before Tuesday, July 16, 1816, Harry proposed marriage to Jane Minot, and she accepted his proposal.

Robert and Catharine were the only people to whom Harry would communicate the news until he had received the consent of Jane's brother, who as her guardian stood in a father's place. The news of Jane's acceptance "went through and through me," Robert reported, and brought "bounding joy and exultation" to his heart. Still, both Harry and Robert feared that William Minot might withhold his approval. Minot might have doubted Harry's ability to support his sister; or he might have been influenced by his father-in-law, Daniel Davis, who was still suspicious of Harry's treatment of Penelope Russell Sedgwick during the settlement of Judge Sedgwick's estate. But William Minot did not overrule his sister's choice. Harry received his approval, and sent the news to his family, on Friday, July 26.[36]

Robert had already warned Harry that "you cannot be in love till you are engaged." A much wider range of expressions of intense affection became available to Harry and Jane once their engagement had been announced. (Such a change from caring to love would even be recognized by the highest court in Massachusetts just two years later, when a young woman sued her lover for breach of his promise to marry her. He denied they had ever been engaged, but the overtly passionate language in his letters proclaiming his love for her was all the evidence the court needed to find that they must have been.) The night before Harry received William's consent, he and Jane took a walk on Boston Common with Louisa Minot and her three-year-old son, George. Harry headed the group, running backward down a hill, perhaps in an attempt to amuse or just to keep up with little George. Jane and Louisa lagged behind. Jane's gaze had been cast downward, but at one point she looked up. Her eyes met Harry's for a moment. She withdrew her gaze almost immediately, but her expression of love in that moment remained fixed in Harry's memory. "That was the *perpetual moment*," Harry would assure her the following winter.[37]

Jane left Boston for a visit to her cousin Mary Speakman's country home in Quincy, a few miles to the south, a short time before Harry learned of William's consent. Her excursion did not separate the couple, though. Bostonians could travel to and from Quincy on the same day, at least in summer, and still have time to enjoy a visit. A few days after Jane left, Harry joined a small party of friendlies on a day trip to have tea with Jane in Quincy. It was the first time they had seen each other since their engagement had been announced. Harry found himself tongue-tied in Jane's presence. "I respect and absolutely fear her more than all the queens princesses and potentates in the world," Harry admitted to Catharine. "How we conducted I know not—foolishly enough no doubt. After tea we walked—and began to find our wits a little." (The following spring, Jane would also admit that "tremulous doubts . . . agitated my happiness" when she had seen Harry in Quincy.) The next day Harry accompanied Louisa Minot to tea at the home of a mutual acquaintance in Dedham, where Jane was also present. When the time came to leave, Louisa jumped into Jane's seat in the chaise of the party that had come from Quincy, "declaring that Miss M. might get along as she could," and drove off, leaving Harry and Jane alone together, to their "inexpressible confusion," for the first time since they had been engaged, and leaving Harry with the pleasant task of transporting Jane back to Quincy. "I will make no attempt to describe my feelings," Harry reported to his sister. "It seems to me that till I knew *her*, I was as dull as the weed that rots in Lethe's wave."[38]

Jane returned to Boston sometime before the middle of August. She and Harry resumed their round of social interactions with the friendlies, but they also began to enjoy the privileges of private association that belonged to them as an engaged couple. Jane remembered that her evenings had been his exclusively during this time, and they spent many hours together in "scenes of love" on the sofa in the parlor on Charles Street. "We have already the pleasures of memory," she would remind Harry a few months later, when they were separated by many miles, "though compared with what it will be our intercourse has been short."[39]

Catharine came to Boston in the middle of August to congratulate the engaged couple in person and to bring Jane back to Stockbridge to meet the rest of the family. Harry followed them a few days later, and in the beginning weeks of September they enjoyed more pleasant intimacies in the Berkshire hills. Harry particularly remembered sitting by the fire in the parlor, and the moonlight that shone "softly and . . . sweetly" on them during their evening walks, as they crossed the bridge over the gently flowing Housatonic.[40]

Stockbridge was also the scene of their first important disagreement. The only evidence of it is an undated, unsigned letter, written in Harry's hand and addressed only to "Miss Minot." The absence of any additional address information, or a postmark, or any folds or other signs of wear indicates that the two were in the same place when Harry wrote and delivered it. (Apparently the Sedgwicks believed that some intimate communications were so weighty, and needed to be prepared with such care, that they had to be written out even when both parties were under the same roof. This was not the first time a family member had written a letter to communicate with another family member a few rooms away. Ebenezer Watson had done the same with the angry letter that initiated his long quarrel with Harry just over a year earlier.)

Jane had written a letter to Catharine early in the summer, before Harry had proposed. In it, she asked some candid questions of Catharine about her brother and the prospect of a marriage to him, and requested a confidential and equally candid reply. Jane was worried because she was so little acquainted with Harry outside the constrained world of Boston society. Someone had been spreading reports about Harry in Boston — probably about his courtships of Abigail Phillips and Elizabeth Sumner, two and three years earlier. "If I know anything of my heart," Harry promised when this issue came to its resolution, "it is that I am totally incapable of the character which has been ascribed to me."

Harry had gotten wind of the letter to Catharine. Perhaps Jane told him about it, or perhaps Catharine sent it to him with a request for his advice. He had urged Catharine in the strongest possible terms not to reply — he "solemnly charged her to say nothing in my favor." Harry wanted Jane to make her own judgment of him, not to depend on others' opinions, even the inevitably favorable opinion of Catharine. He dismissed the idea that they did not know each other well enough to make such judgments. "You are not acquainted with me!" he exclaimed to Jane in the letter written at

Stockbridge. "Would to Heaven that I could lay my heart naked before your eyes. You would find that its highest and warmest impulse is love for you." This probably marked the occasion on which Harry delivered to Jane the earlier letter containing his excruciatingly complete account of his two courtships in the year after his father's death. "Whatever my faults may be," he insisted, "insincerity or reserve is not among them. You will perceive that the communication was intended to have been made previously to the sacred relations which exist between us. Circumstances rendered this difficult if not impossible," he admitted. "Indeed I forgot everything but yourself."

In that earlier letter he had insisted on his sincerity as well: "I would rather lose than deceive you," he had pledged. "There shall be no hidden recess—no dark shrouded corner of my soul into which you shall not penetrate." If Jane read his account of the earlier courtships in Stockbridge that September, she would have had to respond to his plea in that letter for understanding. "Do not judge me hardly," he implored, "and yet you cannot pass a sterner censure than I have sometimes passed upon myself." The archives contain no clear indication of Jane's response, either to the hurried letter written at Stockbridge or to the longer letter about the earlier affairs, except that she and Harry remained engaged, and continued to walk together on the bridge in the moonlight.[41]

When Harry and Jane returned to Boston after a few weeks in Stockbridge, he faced a decision. He had been back in Boston for nearly a year, and though his marital prospects were happy, he had achieved little in the way of professional success. Robert offered a solution. Since his arrival in New York the year after their mother's death, he had laid plans to induce Harry to join him in a partnership. For years Robert had considered it "a melancholy thought that so much of our existence should pass away as if it had no reference to each other."[42]

Robert had pondered the faults that interfered with Harry's success. When he finally invited Harry to come to New York to be his partner, he prefaced the invitation with a catalog of Harry's seemingly infantile behaviors ("ten thousand little ticks such as picking your teeth with pen-knives and forks—running strings through them . . . putting your hands on a certain part of your pantaloons") in hopes that Harry would mend his ways. "Now Hal you know you can avoid these things," he continued, "but you do not try. You seem to have a fatal indifference on the subject. Why can you not *constantly* bear in mind till habit shall supersede attention, that you must have the manners of a gentleman?" Despite this litany of complaint and criticism, Robert concluded, "I do with all my heart invite you to join forces with me here if you think of leaving [Boston]. Nothing would give me more happiness than to ally my fortune to yours."[43]

Harry had already considered leaving Boston again. One concern he had raised with Catharine the previous winter, as he contemplated courting one of the Boston friendlies, was that he might find it necessary to move, and that his hypothetical wife might find it unpleasant to move away from her family. "Oh Harry 'you goose too romantic,'" Susan Ridley Sedgwick had written when Catharine told her of this concern, "your knowledge of the sex is small indeed if you imagine this to be an insuperable barrier. Crossing the ocean might I grant you stagger a good daughter, but the circumstance of removing to a place equally pleasant, and within a moderate distance, would never be an obstacle were the heart interested. It is a thing done every day." Susan and Catharine had enjoyed a laugh over Harry's conception of "the Passion," and Susan warned him that "we greatly doubt your power of inspiring it, while so far from it yourself."[44]

Harry received Robert's invitation just three or four days before Jane accepted his proposal of marriage, so he did not respond right away. The brothers discussed the move when they were together in Stockbridge in September, but Harry was not ready to make a decision. One reason for Harry's indecisiveness can be seen in a letter he received from his future brother-in-law just before he returned to Boston. Harry had apparently mentioned to William Minot that he was considering relocating to Albany, or even Stockbridge, as alternatives to Boston or New York. William advised him that his feelings were "strongly opposed to my sister's removal to the country." William, who was only two years older than Harry and had been running a successful law practice in Boston for more than ten years, continued in some puzzlement. "You left Stockbridge a few months ago, because it did not offer sufficient encouragement for business, and came to Boston as I understood, with an intention of making a permanent establishment here," he reminded Harry. "Can any change in the former place have made a settlement more eligible, and do you think you have made a fair experiment of your chance of success in Boston?" William felt it necessary to ask about the potential change in plans, he said, because his sister, "in leaving Boston, must relinquish a great many sources of happiness and comfort, besides the enjoyment of her family and a large number of friends here." Jane was "accustomed to a town life," William wrote, "and I think her mind and feelings require it." His motive in raising this issue, he insisted, was love for his sister. "I most sincerely believe it would be a most serious misfortune to her, to remove to the country," he wrote. "Of all the places you mention I think New York much the most eligible."[45]

William's letter must have been the decisive factor. A few days after hearing from Jane's brother, Harry accepted Robert's offer of a New York partnership—as "an experiment." Robert, perhaps to Harry's surprise, rejected the idea of an experimental association. He had been building a practice and a reputation for nearly eight years, and he needed to approach this change with great seriousness. He told Harry to come for good or not at all. Harry took several more weeks to ponder this choice; not until late October did he make up his mind to accept Robert's offer. He made plans to arrive in New York on November 1.[46]

Moving to New York would separate Harry and Jane for months — possibly for as much as a year. Harry knew that joining his brother in the fast-growing commercial center of New York would be the best way for him to prepare to support a wife and a family. Still, the prospect of separation stung. A few nights before his departure, he and Jane sat out behind the buildings on Charles Street, in sight of the common and the Back Bay. There was a chill in the air, and Harry took off his coat and wrapped it, and his arm, around Jane, to shelter her. She heard in his voice "the tenderness which the dread of parting gives to tones of love." When the time came for them to part a few days later, she was eager to give him some appropriate testimony of affection. Her parting look, with its "agonizing sentiment of loneliness," as the front door on Charles Street closed behind him for the last time, remained indelibly fixed in his memory. After Harry left, Jane walked over the bridge near her home that crossed the Charles River, experiencing a "melancholy tranquility." When she awoke to her first day without Harry, she filled it with writing a long letter to him — the first of more than forty she would write before she saw him again.

Harry traveled overland by coach to New London, Connecticut. At 6:30 on the same evening he found himself seated at a desk in a crowded barroom, waiting for the steamboat whistle to call the passengers for boarding. He was trying to write a letter of his own to Jane—the first of more than fifty he would write during their separation. He felt disoriented. He was sure he had lost or forgotten his keys. But he also felt renewed. "I feel now a new stimulus," he wrote, "a new governing motive for all my actions—that of deserving you, and making you happy." He knew now that the best motive to animate his exertions toward success and fame in this world was "an ardent and reciprocated affection," and he was confident that he had found that in his love for Jane and Jane's love for him. "If therefore I shall ever come to anything good," he promised, "you may consider yourself as the creator of a new character."[47]

The whistle blew, the passengers boarded the steamboat, and it steamed away into the night, bound for New York.

III

No Small Surrender

THE ENGAGEMENT CORRESPONDENCE
OF HARRY SEDGWICK AND JANE MINOT,
OCTOBER 1816–MAY 1817

7

The Only Consolation of Absence

Love Letters

*I*n his letters to Jane Minot during their engagement, Harry Sedgwick intended to narrate his quest for fame in New York City, a
quest that began, with mythic appropriateness, in a journey by water. But
Harry's plan for his letter writing went beyond mere narration. In explaining himself to Jane, he would reinvent himself for her. As he had written
while waiting for the steamboat in New London, he meant to become
"as worthy a man as I can render myself" — the hero of his own life. His
letters to Jane would be his epic telling of that quest, and she would be
his muse.[1]

Both Harry and Jane expected that they would live in New York after
they were married, so one of his tasks would be to explain that city to
her. New York was, as a traveler would describe it a few years later, a "city
surrounded with masts." Virtually every settled place was in sight of the
harbor or the rivers. A traveler approaching the city by water noticed its
"swamps of shipping, piles of buildings, and seagulls flying around us,"
and on arriving at the city's docks was immediately struck by "the huge
masses of buildings the burr of the hacks and the ringing and chiming of
the bells." When Harry arrived in 1816 the city was thickly populated from
the Battery at its southern tip only about as far north as what is today
Canal Street. Greenwich Village was the site of farms and country estates.
Still, the downtown areas of what Harry called "this whirling, mercenary,
money-loving, and money-getting city" teemed with human activity. Wall
Street, home to bankers, brokers, and insurers, was hazardous when merchant ships arrived in port. As the news of their arrival began to spread,
people who had an interest in their cargoes, or who thought they might,

would rush pell-mell to the docks. Pearl Street, where many merchants had their offices, was mobbed with such foot traffic almost as frequently. Harry settled into "a large thronged boarding house" on Pearl Street.[2]

Reminders of what he had left behind in Boston ("this land of good habits," as Jane referred to it) reached Harry in the letters that arrived every few days from Jane and in the frequent visits of Boston acquaintances. Harry encountered in New York a woman he had met in Boston. He recalled her as always appearing rather plain in Boston, but in New York he was struck by her beauty — no doubt, he concluded, because of the pleasant association with that more hospitable city. "I believe there never was a genuine, old-fashioned native Bostonian who loved the place better than I do," he claimed. To prove it, he extolled the virtues of Boston's most obvious flaws. "I begin to imagine that there is beauty even in its narrow and serpentine streets, its scanty, broken, and irregular sidewalks, and in the nocturnal obscurity which its partial illumination is not sufficient to dispel," he wrote. "It seems more sociable to have the houses near to each other; the state of the sidewalks makes a gentleman's approximation to a lady and his vigilant protection of her the more necessary; straight lines have too formal and unvaried an appearance; and lovers, you know, ever court the shades."

Harry was not the only New Englander to take a chance on New York. In fact, the old Knickerbocker aristocracy of Dutch and Huguenots was beginning to fade in New York in the years after the War of 1812, even as the city underwent the unprecedented economic growth that would place it at the center of the nation's business. Immigrants from all over were coming to New York to find success. The most determined of these immigrants were not yet from foreign countries, but from nearby New England. "The city swarms with Boston people," Harry wrote to Jane in late January. "They all seem like near and dear relatives."[3]

Between October 29, 1816, and May 14, 1817, Harry Sedgwick wrote fifty-one letters to Jane Minot, all of which survive among his family's papers. Jane Minot wrote between forty-two and forty-five letters, thirty-nine of which survive. The letters were written in longhand, on large, folded sheets. All but two covered at least all four sides of one folded sheet, sometimes more. The longest letter ran ten sides. Except for a space left for the address, every speck of paper was usually filled with Jane's fine, precise handwriting or Harry's dramatic, sometimes blotchy script. Often when they had filled a sheet they would turn it sideways and scribble postscripts in the already tiny margins.

The volume of the correspondence, in a little less than seven months, is astounding.[4] But the noticeable impact of the letters on the correspondents was even more remarkable. More than their engagement itself, these letters changed their authors, and prepared them to cross over from single to married life. Writing the letters became not just a form of communication but a ritual celebration of their love, an anticipation of their expected marriage. That ritual deepened their understanding of each other and of themselves. It empowered them to take on the responsibilities of married life.

As in all rituals, the writing and reading of these letters required a predictability of form. This involved not only the words on the page but the settings in which they were written and read. For Harry, letters were written and read in his law office, in the evening or on Sunday. The office had a large window, very nearly at street level. Passing foot traffic was constant. During weekdays, the traffic into and out of the office could be steady, too — a stream of clients, clerks, out-of-town callers, messengers, and fellow lawyers. But in the evening the crowd was absent, and he could close the street-facing window. On Sundays he could also open the rear window, which looked out on a calmer, more scenic view. "The day is mild and gloriously serene," he wrote on one such Sunday, the first day of December. "I have closed the large street window thus excluding the world and its concerns. The sun beams brightly but not fiercely through the south window. It is the sabbath of rest and joy, and I devote it to love and you." He looked out on a French Protestant church and churchyard just behind their office. The sexton, unmindful of the sabbath, was digging a grave. A "most venerable goat" seemed to be "silently pondering upon the reflection that our species is as mortal as his own."[5]

More than once Harry began a new letter on the same day he had closed an earlier one, and occasionally he spent as many as six days working on continuations of the same letter. "I have now done what I thought was impossible," he wrote after filling ten pages in a little more than three days. "I have nearly written myself out." But he wrote another page and a half before closing that letter. Except for a ten-day gap in January when he was silenced by measles, he never let more than a week pass without sending a letter, and only twice did the interval run longer than five days. The typical gap between his letters was from two to four days. Once he apologized for his neglect after allowing four days to pass without writing.[6]

Jane sometimes wrote or read letters by the fire in the parlor of her brother's house (especially on Sundays), and occasionally in the children's nursery. Her preferred setting, though, was her own room, "that sanctuary of all my emotions." She never let more than a week pass between letters, and let that full interval pass only three times. Even during the long silence caused by Harry's January illness, she wrote a letter to Robert, intending him to read it to the suffering Harry. "I think a week's silence rather too long for lovers under fifty," she remarked on one of these occasions. "About two days short of that time I begin to be fidgety." Like Harry, Jane frequently drew the composition of a letter out over several days, the longest taking more than five days. Her longest letters were not as long as Harry's longest, nor did she ever write any as short as Harry's briefest. She filled a reliable four pages every four or five days from October 30 until at least May 4.[7]

Jane's letters are more challenging to a researcher because she often neglected to date them, or just as often got the date wrong. "I always remember the *propriety* of a date if I do not always hit the day," she quipped in an inaccurately dated Thanksgiving Day letter. But even that was not true; many letters showed only a month, or a day of the week, in their datelines, and a few got no dates at all. Harry made a point of congratulating her the first time she got the date exactly right, in her ninth letter to him. She made a similar point of gloating a little when he got a date wrong early in the new year. She wondered, "Is it in compliment to me that you continue to write 1816?"[8]

Jane was not the only member of her family to date letters to Harry inaccurately. He remarked that he had miraculously received a letter from Louisa Minot two days before it had been written. "Destiny anticipates the benevolence of women," he marveled. The frequency with which these educated women got dates wrong or did not use them at all suggests that calendars were still of little real importance outside the male-dominated world of business. Jane was usually reliable on days of the week, though, and like Harry she quickly began numbering her letters in sequence. Many letters bear legible postmarks as well; so, especially with the evidence of Harry's letters to which she was responding, it is possible to piece together the order and deduce the date of all her letters within a day or two.[9]

The city offered opportunities for dramatic adventure of all sorts. Late on the night of December 3 a fire broke out not far from Harry's boardinghouse. Hearing the alarm, Harry and the other boarders rushed outside.

It was a windy night, and the fire spread quickly to the other wooden buildings nearby. "I never saw a scene of so deep interest," he reported later to Jane.

> The astonishment and distress of the inmates of the houses who were forced into the street shivering and half-dressed in a cold night — the nonchalance — the gaiety of a part of the citizens — the active zeal of others — the expertness and courage of some of the firemen — and the stupidity of the rest — the great fury of the element — its rapid extension — the vivid blaze and strongly illumined faces of thousands of gazers — the breaking furniture, crashing beams, and falling walls, the hurry, the confusion, the thwarting flames, the press of some to save furniture, of others to extinguish the flames or to satisfy their curiosity, and all in different directions — all this presented a variety and combination of circumstances with which those accustomed to great fires may be familiar, but which impressed my mind with great force.[10]

The furniture from the threatened buildings had to be carried across the street ("a tolerably wide street," Harry noted) and still much of it was lost. Some that was saved had to be moved two or three times as the fire advanced, and Harry volunteered to help. The first thing he moved was an elegant lamp; in doing so he spilled lamp oil all over his coat. Next he went to move a mattress, which he "pulled with such violence that it was opened from one end to the other by a nail which unhappily came in contact with the ticking." Much of the "cloud of feathers" that flew from the ripped bed attached itself to his oil-stained coat, "which . . . rendered it quite visible and highly picturesque."

But the fire was still not out. Harry and his neighbors had work to do. (It was, in fact, a big enough fire that Jane and her family would read about it in Boston newspapers several days before she received Harry's letter about it. "I wonder if you were burnt up in the late New York fire," she would write, noting the passage of an unusually long time since his last letter. "I think at least your right arm must have been badly scorched.") Harry assisted with the fire engines for a while, then helped a storekeeper carry some of his merchandise and furniture to safety. At about two o'clock in the morning he felt exhausted and decided to head home. As he walked past the door of a shop, he recognized the shopkeeper, Mr. Blunt, the father of a clerk from his office. An entire waterfront block across the street from Mr. Blunt's shop (which was also the man's home) had been destroyed. Wooden houses on either side of Mr. Blunt's were already on fire, and he stood in the doorway directing volunteers who were carrying his furniture out to the street. At Blunt's urging Harry went up to the roof, where he joined young Blunt and others in their attempts to keep the flames from spreading. "The danger was by this time chiefly over," Harry reported. "We remained for nearly an hour inactive spectators of the magnificent scene beneath us."

Magnificent, indeed. The energy, the single-minded purposefulness, the camaraderie of this group of young men shines through in Harry's account of both the fire and its aftermath. "At length we descended and spent a merry half hour in a room below where rum, brandy, and water were served to a company of about twenty or thirty in pails," he wrote. "We then had a most delicious repast of cold beef, smoked salmon, and bread, with hot chocolate and coffee. . . . A sailor who had been very daring and useful was the hero of the circle. We had no chairs or spoons nor any knives or forks except for the carvers — our handkerchiefs were around our throats, and one napkin served for all — but what of that — we had fine coffee and chocolate which seemed the better for being without milk — excellent beef, and most delicious salmon, and appetites upon which I need not expatiate."

But what of that — food eaten with the hands? Liquor drunk from pails? A single shared napkin among a few dozen gritty, sweaty men? Coffee drunk black, of all things? For a few hours, a battle against the ancient and elemental terror of a raging fire made this group of lawyers, shopkeepers, laborers, sailors, clerks, and firefighters feel socially equal, and heroically alive. Harry did not get to bed until almost four in the morning. When he awoke, he immediately wrote down an account of the fire for Jane.

When she read this letter, Jane could easily envision Harry with a cloud of feathers stuck to his oily coat. "I think your accident at the fire completely characteristic," she wrote. "Had the anecdote been related without naming the person I should instantly have ascribed it to you."[11]

Letters like the one in which Harry described these events, once finished, were folded so that only the middle third of the back page was visible, and that panel (always left otherwise blank) was used for the address. They were then sealed with an adhesive wafer or sealing wax, remnants of which still stick to many of them. This left part of the fourth page visible, and correspondents were always careful not to include anything too private or personal on the part that would be, as Harry put it, "*inspectable.*" In March, Jane received a letter of Harry's that was sealed in a way that allowed it to be opened without breaking the seal. She related the suspicion of the family's cook, Mrs. Wood, "that the postmaster thought Miss Minot had so many letters it was best to see what they were about."

Most of the letters were sent by United States mail. The postage would vary depending on the weight of the letter and the distance it had to travel; sending a standard one-sheet letter between Boston and New York cost 12½ cents, and Harry and Robert's expenses for office postage ran to about $150 to $200 a year—more than their rent. Postage on personal letters was usually paid by the recipient. (When Jane suggested that she might pay the postage on a letter she was sending to Harry's sister Frances, whose family was struggling after her husband's business failure and their separation, Harry disapproved, fearing that it would embarrass Frances. "This is never done except on business letters," he informed Jane.) Harry addressed his letters to Jane in care of her brother William at his law office. William brought them home when he came for dinner at midday, or at the end of the day, and Jane sent her replies in the morning or when William returned to his office after dinner. Jane's letters to Harry were addressed to his office as well, though in his eagerness to receive them he sometimes went to the post office to pick them up. Letters sent between Boston and New York by way of the post office were usually delivered on the third day after they were mailed, Sundays included. When a letter that Jane had closed on Sunday, February 23, arrived in New York on Wednesday evening, February 26, instead of earlier in the day, Harry assumed that William Minot must have forgotten to put it into the first mail of the day, until he remembered that the bitter winter storm they had just endured would have slowed the mail from Boston.[12]

On a number of occasions, the lovers trusted their letters to "private opportunities" or "private conveyances"—acquaintances who were traveling from one city to the other, usually on business, who they hoped would make personal calls to deliver the letters. The urge to scribble a quick note on hearing that an acquaintance was traveling into the neighborhood of a loved one was nearly irresistible, even if the letter was cursory. "Presuming the frequency of my letters to be more important than the novelty of their contents," Jane wrote, she would hurry a quick note for a business traveler to carry. Her network, only in part relying on her brother's business contacts, was excellent. "If I were only a man I could find opportunities every hour," she lamented, but she did a remarkable job of locating travelers and getting letters into their hands before they left.

She discovered, though, that the travelers who offered these private opportunities were consistently unreliable. Sometimes they left town before a letter was ready to be sent, as the normally procrastinating John Coffin Jones did in mid-November, preventing Jane from sending a watch chain she had made for Harry, along with an eight-page letter. Sometimes they did not leave town as quickly as they had expected, as in the case of Mr. Coolidge, who took Jane's letter of December 21 but still had not left Boston when she closed another letter on December 26. Coolidge delivered both "long-delayed" letters to Harry on December 28. "Unluckily you cannot animate everybody with your own feelings," Jane wrote in her next letter. "Mr. C. has studied his own convenience unconscious of bearing sentiments which were panting for his departure."

Sometimes the lovers found themselves imposing on travelers they barely knew. On New Year's Eve Jane asked the Heards, a couple returning to New York from a visit to Boston, to deliver a letter to Harry. On New Year's Day she sent a letter to Harry by mail and asked him to call on the Heards to retrieve the letter, so the favor would be less of an imposition. Before Harry could do so, Mr. Heard delivered the letter to the Sedgwick brothers' office on the afternoon of January 6 — taking just about twice as long as the post office would have.[13]

Sometimes travelers with letters to deliver simply forgot them. Jane entrusted her letter of January 14 to a Mr. Munson. Harry had been incapacitated with measles since around January 13, but by January 23 he was feeling better, and beginning to wonder why he had not had a letter in two weeks. He kept careful track of the departure times and expected arrival times of his letters. He knew that John Popham, a suitor of Louisa Davis Minot's younger sister Helen, ought to have delivered his letters of January 9 and January 10 through 13 (which he had sent together) on Saturday, January 18, at William Minot's office. Robert's letter informing Jane of Harry's sickness ought to have reached her by mail the following day. Why had she not written back instantly? Why had she not written since January 8? "Every day," he complained, "the unconscious penny-post has come unladen, or bearing only trash."

Harry finally learned of the existence of the Munson letter when Jane's January 21 reply to Robert arrived by mail on Sunday, January 26. The letter Munson was carrying had probably spent the better part of two weeks "quietly reposing in the bottom of his trunk at New Haven," Harry fumed, "unconscious of the long protracted pleasure it might have given." Munson finally got around to delivering the letter on January 28, two weeks to the day after Jane had written and sealed it. In addition to her January 21 letter to Robert, her January 24 letter to Harry had also reached its destination by then. Harry's irritation with the delay led him to resolve not to rely on such private opportunities any more. "The mail is the only conveyance that can be trusted," he insisted. Even before Munson's arrival, he advised Jane, "The mail is much the safest and most expeditious mode of conveyance, and after a considerable interval between letters has passed, none other should be trusted." The cost was not important, the savings virtually meaningless. "Letters from one's friends," Harry insisted, "are the cheapest luxury we can have."[14]

But there were advantages to sending by private opportunities, and despite Harry's resolve, both he and Jane kept using them. The most efficient travelers could usually beat the mail by a day, as Mr. Cunningham did with a long letter he collected from Jane on Sunday, February 2, and delivered to Harry two days later. Moreover, a friend who had been entrusted with a letter could deliver much more than the post office could. He could tell the recipient about the health and spirits of the sender at the moment he had collected the letter, and, if he were to make a return trip soon, report on the reactions that the letter itself had stimulated. Such an advantage would be especially valued by a lover sending love letters to a beloved after months of separation. Harry even trusted Munson to carry another letter when he left New York on February 6. The wayward messenger was consistent: Jane received two of Harry's later letters before Munson finally delivered. To make up for the long silence Harry had experienced in January, Jane inundated him after his recovery from the measles, sending ten letters between January 24 and the end of February.[15]

Throughout his first months in New York, Harry stayed late at his office, working or writing and reading letters to and from Jane. He had little interest in accepting social invitations. It was no sacrifice, he assured Jane. "I have grown to be a very old gentleman as to all great parties and gay society especially of strangers."[16]

Shortly before the New Year, Margaret Champlin Jones had written to urge Harry to arrange some social contacts for Jane in preparation for her eventual arrival. She reminded him that her friend, soon to start a new life in an alien place, would not be able to take advantage of the ready-made network of professional contacts that a man of business like Harry could. Without an introduction to an appropriate social circle, her world would be limited. For Jane's sake, Harry resolved to accept more invitations, and began to do so. He warily informed Jane of his plans to attend his first New York party, on the Saturday before New Year's Day. He resolved to arrive late and, "if I find the party too splendid for my costume," to "take refuge" with some "plain" friends.

On New Year's Day itself, Harry got a chance to take part in a New York tradition that baffled him at first. "After church which is out at half past twelve and before dinner at three," he told Jane, "you are expected to call on all your friends and everywhere to get a glass of wine and a cookie (small cake). You cannot stay at any one place more than three minutes. It is as if all the town gave wedding parties." Despite his initial skepticism, Harry changed his mind about these visits after taking part in them. "The custom I think is a very excellent and delightful one," he admitted, "though somewhat fatiguing. Everybody is delighted to see you, and kind feelings are everywhere promoted. We finished our rounds or rather exhausted our time at a quarter past three having made more than thirty visits in every part of the city. There were still several omissions which [Robert] very much regretted."[17]

"It appears to me that you have made some valuable new acquaintances lately," Jane wrote that same month, "and should therefore speak well of New York." And so he did. "I think I should like New York very well if Jane were here," he had admitted to Charles as they took an absent-minded stroll about the city during that brother's December visit. But whenever he met someone whose manners and habits really impressed him — "not all gew-gaw, flourish, and nonsense, but good-humored and intelligent people" — his response was the same: "They really put me in mind of Boston."[18]

In late February, Harry discovered one New York social setting where he was eager to be welcomed. A group calling itself the Greenwich Club gathered regularly at the home of one or another of its members. Harry was pleased to be invited as their guest. The Greenwich Club was "a coterie of the most rational, literary and accomplished ladies in the city with a few beaux whom they know by their particular selection." Harry was invited by several of the members. "If I find it as agreeable as I anticipate," he predicted in a letter to Jane, "I shall exert myself to find favor in their eyes and get a *season ticket*." The first time he attended, he saw "several very fine women," but the gathering was more crowded than he expected. Worse still, in Harry's view, the conversation was interrupted by dancing. His next visit was more to his liking. "I am sliding very kindly into this society," he informed Jane. She might not have been surprised. She had seen how comfortably he fit into her friendly circle in Boston during the days of their courtship, and had watched him become an unusually trustworthy male companion and confidant to more than one of her friends. "This would be just the society, and all the society of that description I should want," he had asserted when he was first invited to the Greenwich Club.[19]

Both Jane and Harry preferred to read the letters they received in the private places they had chosen for writing, and usually did so.[20] Occasionally, though, the act of reading a letter would itself become an adventure, and material for another letter. On Sunday, February 16, Harry was so eager for a letter from Jane that he went to the post office twice, and after "jostling half an hour with the crowd," finally collected the letter Jane had mailed the preceding Thursday.

Harry left the post office in a rush to get to dinner at the home of a friend and important client. The weather was "cold and tempestuous," and he knew nowhere to stop on the way to finish reading the letter. But he was determined to do so. All the way to the Wilkinses, he walked, stopped to read a little, walked more, stopped to read more, and walked and read on. "You recollect," he reminded Jane of her letter, "that it was not written in such character as that he who ran might read, and if the wayfaring man were a fool he would stand a great chance to err therein." Dinner started late and took forever. Harry got into a discussion with "a scientific gentleman," but "scarcely knew what I said," he confessed in his next letter to Jane, "as my mind was more than half occupied in rioting upon the half-enjoyed treasures of your letter." When he hinted at his interest in finding a moment of privacy to finish reading the letter, Mrs. Brush, a widow who lived with the Wilkinses, led him to her chamber, "where alone and by a good fire I perused and reperused it to the fullness and satiety of delight." Days later, in his second letter since that stormy Sunday, he still relished the experience: "I have never enjoyed a letter from you so much as last Sunday."[21]

Any delay in the production or delivery of their letters deserved attention and comment. "I have spent hour after hour in conjecturing the cause of your silence," Harry wrote while waiting to receive the early letter that John Coffin Jones had left behind in Boston. "I *know* it has some good cause — but I cannot imagine what." He knew how childish it was on his part to suffer from this delay, "but I cannot help it — I *do suffer*." He wondered if he had done something to deserve her silence. Had he offended? Had he been carelessly frank? During his wait for the letter that had gone astray with Munson, Harry insisted that he didn't want to dwell on her seeming neglect of him. "But remember," he wrote, "that I am a stranger and far removed from almost all those I love — that I have little society, and none with which I entirely sympathize. Robert is everything that a *brother* can be, but you have taught my heart to yearn for more. . . . You have become necessary to me." When Jane expressed a feeling of "unaccountable diffidence" lest she write too much and distract him from his business, he replied, "Such fits of rationality never come over me." The idea that she might distract him from more pressing matters was laughable. "There is seldom a moment when I could spare you from my thoughts," he assured her. For her part, Jane felt any delay intensely, and anticipated her relief at its end. "If I could only obtain a letter now," she wrote near the end of April, "I should have nothing further to desire — except seeing you."[22]

Jane feared that her planned March excursion to the country, to stay with her cousin Mary Speakman in Quincy, would delay their letters. Harry first raised the question more than a month before her expected departure. He wondered if she ought to rely on the milkman, who came from Boston regularly to collect milk from the dairy farms of Quincy, as a courier to and from the Boston post office. Jane assured him that if there were any problem with their letters getting to or from Quincy, she would leave after a week. They suspected that the mail to and from Quincy would be as unreliable as it was in other rural areas, where, as Harry had reason to know, it was nowhere near so prompt or predictable as in a city.

Quincy in 1817, though, had something that few other country villages could claim: a living ex-president of the United States. Perhaps because of the presence of the Adamses, mail was delivered to the Quincy post office three times a week. It would actually be faster, Jane determined shortly after she arrived, for Harry to address his letters to her at Quincy than to send them to Boston and have them forwarded.

Neither mode of delivery seems to have slowed their correspondence in any meaningful way. A letter that Harry addressed to Jane in Boston apparently arrived in Quincy just three days after leaving New York, and Jane's letter mailed at the Quincy post office reached Harry's office in New York in three days. Even private conveyances reached Quincy in good time. Harry sent a letter on Wednesday, March 26, in care of an acquaintance who was returning to Boston. On the following Tuesday, April 1, Jane had been in the midst of writing to him, lamenting her isolation. "What a fool I was to trust to this stupid country mail," she complained. "These moderate people are satisfied provided they read a letter in the course of their lives — they are not the least particular about what time." But even as she wrote, "without the slightest hope of hearing from you before Thursday," the Boston stage stopped with Harry's ten-page letter.

The biggest problem Jane encountered while in Quincy was the difficulty of writing to Harry from a place that, familiar as it was to her, was not her customary setting for letter writing. She portrayed herself sitting on the floor as the sun streamed through a window, propping her letter up on a rocking chair, trying not to turn her letter into a mess — and running out of paper when she felt she could still write for another hour, and not knowing where to get more. She was relieved to return to Boston a few days later to help Louisa prepare for the birth of her new baby.[23]

For Jane Minot and Harry Sedgwick, their love letters themselves became one of the great subjects of their love letters. Given the huge amount of time and energy that they both invested in the act of writing and reading, it is no surprise that they came to write about the act of writing them. The letters were more than letters. Writing was more a physical *act* than almost any other intellectual endeavor can be.

When we write a love letter to a lover from whom we are separated, we remake ourselves, and we remake our lover. The act is a performance, an invention, and its affirmation comes only days or weeks later, if and when the lover replies in kind. This would of course have been even more true in the 1810s, when letters and the occasional secondhand accounts of travelers might be the only contact one had with a distant lover for months at a time. Written words, carefully crafted, make a distant lover present. Writing a letter gives each individual a degree of control over his or her presentation of self that is nearly impossible when we are in each other's presence.

"Imagination will surpass *any* reality," Harry Sedgwick had written in commenting on what Jane had come to mean to him, and what he had come to mean to her, during the first three months of their separation. Through those three months of letter writing, he believed, they had come to love each other far more intensely than they had in the months they were together in Boston. But more than imagination was at work. Astonishingly, the lovers' new perception of each other had become a new reality. Jane Minot and Harry Sedgwick sensed themselves becoming new people to each other as their correspondence progressed in the winter and spring of 1817, and marveled at the newness.

Friends asked Jane "how I bear my widowhood," she reported just a week after Harry left for New York. "In truth I am rather happier than I expected, especially when I receive your letters." She had only received two of them, and was just sitting down to write her third, but she felt their power already. "It is the only consolation of absence to be able to trace in letters every movement of thought," she added a few days later. "Write then dear friend until I *complain* of your letters." She had a sense that she was seeing a Harry different from the one she might experience if she were with him in his daily business activities in New York. "It surprises me that you are able to keep up two such opposite states of feeling," she confided — "that at this time there should be any current from your heart for *these* beautiful volleys which embosom the affections."

Harry, for his part, clearly sensed that he was a much better, stronger, more complete person in his letters than he had ever been in his life, which was why he considered the great investment of time to be no sacrifice. "I had much rather stay where I am," he wrote during one of the many long nights spent composing a letter to Jane at his office, "or I should go out." [24]

They both took note, as their friends had, of the extraordinary length of their letters, and of the hours consumed by writing and reading them. "The time I take in reading your letters steals away like the sand in the hourglass," Harry insisted. "I have no perception of its departure." They quickly ceased worrying that they would run out of things to say. "I sometimes fear that my letters will be uninteresting to you from the monotony of my life," Harry claimed in March. "I have little to tell you but what I feel, and the feelings of a lover whose life passes without incident, or change of affection, however ardent, have not variety enough to admit of copious narration." He was not alone in this thought. "Robert wonders what under heaven I can have to say," Harry revealed late in the correspondence. "He says that everything must be understood, and that he is sure I only write the same thing over and over." But this was where Robert revealed himself to be a stranger to the ways of love. "I believe it is very much so. I can only say that I *do love you*. No circumlocution or flourish of epithets can add any thing to that." [25]

As scholars who have studied the meaning and importance of nineteenth-century love letters have noted, this absence of "circumlocution" was essential. "Dear Jane," Harry wrote when the long silence caused by his illness and Munson's delay finally ended, "I do love you with all my heart, and you must suffer me to tell you so without any circumlocution or softening of phraseology." When her letters arrived, he was tempted to describe his reaction figuratively, using "images derived from the gratification of physical wants." But whether he tried hunger satisfied, thirst slaked, or rest attained after great exertion, they were all "incapable to express perceptions of a nature so exquisite." At first he had feared that his "inelegant" and "careless" style might put her off. "The truth is," he told her early in their separation, "that I have entertained towards you, in a degree which I believe is uncommon even between persons who are engaged to each other, a secure *home* feeling—an undoubting trust—a firm confidence that you were mine and I was yours, which seemed to render all form and ceremony unnecessary and frivolous. The stream of affection has flowed uniformly and copiously from my heart, but I have taken no care that it should meander in graceful rivulets." Jane too disparaged any but the most direct and heartfelt language. She had no taste for artifice, she insisted. "I care not how carelessly you write," she informed him in the letter Munson carried. "Elegance was never a requisite to my feelings but sincerity and truth however hard are indispensable." And Harry provided her with those indispensable virtues. "Few men write such delicate and tender letters who write so sensibly as you," she assured him.[26]

The regular Sunday evening gathering at the Joneses' house on Pearl Street remained at the center of the friendlies' life together in Boston. Their talk, at least as much of it as Jane reported to Harry, was of beaux (with a particular focus on what made one unacceptable), of books, of religion, of their future lives and prospects, and of their own cherished friendship.

Shortly before Christmas, Jane and Margaret spent a day with Mary Ann Fales. "It was one of those heart-felt pleasures which unite friends nearer than ever," she reported. This was typical of Jane's accounts in the first few months of Harry's absence. The friendlies' conversations were "free," "eloquent," "enchanting," and "heartfelt," and they were certainly frequent, but the details were often not shared with Harry in writing. Then, as Jane warmed to the task of letter writing, she shared more. Often the friendlies would evaluate a suitor who had turned his attentions to one of them or to an acquaintance, or discuss women they admired, in an attempt to cultivate female role models.[27]

Their attention often turned to their absent friend, and in Jane's account these mentions were always bright with compliments, except when they complained about his plans to move Jane to New York. Harry had been the favorite gentleman for the friendlies to include in their gatherings during his year in Boston. He was amusing, sympathetic, and well-mannered all at once. At the announcement of his engagement to Jane, the friendlies celebrated "the new and delightful tie, by which our late friend is bound for life to the circle," and they genuinely missed him when he moved to New York. "Many an *evening* sigh is breathed for our loss," Jane informed him wistfully, and that "our" was sincerely meant. This must have come as a pleasing realization to Harry. He who had been uncomfortably inclined to bluster, faux pas, and irresolution in the male worlds of business, law, and politics appears to have been effortlessly gracious — and recognized as such — in the company of women. "You are the nearest to a woman in your feelings of any man I know," Jane told him, and the remark was a profound compliment. Feelings and emotions were the cultural territory of women. Nancy F. Cott has written that the language of the emotions was the only language in which an intimate relationship of equals could be achieved, which is why women enjoyed such close bonds of passionate friendship as the ones the friendlies shared. Men *could* learn to speak it, but few did. Harry's fluency in this language of the heart gave him the rare opportunity to enter such a friendship with the woman he intended to marry. The friendlies understood this. Now Harry's new status as a man safely engaged to one of their friends enabled them to speak more freely than ever of the esteem in which they held him, "since there is now no danger of a wrong construction to their language."[28]

Several references make it clear that Jane was regularly reading Harry's letters aloud — "all that is not particular" — to the friendlies.[29] Her reading of his first letter had almost become a performance set-piece around Boston. Aboard the steamboat, Harry had encountered and engaged in a lengthy conversation with a fellow passenger. Laurent Clerc, who was deaf as a result of a childhood accident, had lectured on the education of the deaf in Boston in early September. He had just left the faculty of the school for the deaf in Paris, and was on a fund-raising tour to support a new school in Hartford. Harry and Clerc conversed in writing on the nature of deafness and its effect on human personality and consciousness. A fairly large crowd gathered around them, and Harry served as Clerc's interlocutor with the crowd during the entire exchange. Harry narrated the encounter to Jane in his first letter from New York the following morning. He included more than a page of dialogue between "S." and "C."[30]

Jane was delighted with the report. "I ran directly to Miss Danforth with your interesting picture of her friend," she informed him, choosing Caroline because she had attended one of Clerc's Boston lectures. "Charming" was Caroline's repeated response, "exclaimed at every other line." (For a woman well past her twenty-sixth birthday, Caroline sometimes revealed what the much younger Jane saw as a surprising ingenuousness. She once asked Jane "if it were not embarrassing" to write her frequent letters to Harry. "I laughed at the primness of the question," Jane told Harry in her next letter.) Jane read Harry's account of his meeting with Clerc aloud at the homes of two or three other friends. Then one of the eminent ladies of the city, Mrs. William Sullivan, heard of it and asked that Jane come and read it to her. "Thus have I the honor," she announced to Harry, "to be the instrument of your fame."[31]

Still, after a little more than a month, Harry begged Jane to "suppress his letters," insisting despite his dislike of "squeamishness" that they ought to be kept confidential. This request must have been hard to honor, coming as it did in the letter in which he gave his account of the great December fire.[32] For his part, Harry shared large portions of Jane's letters with Robert, from whom he had never in his life kept anything secret. But Jane and Harry were quick to lay claim to each other's private attention only. Harry insisted that "my letters are written in the careless and easy security of entire confidence" when he asked Jane to stop reading them to the Sunday gatherings of the friendlies. Just a few days later, Jane tried to forbid Robert's reading of her letters. "Have the manners of chivalry so far passed," she inquired, "that you don't know the difference between my showing your letters and your showing mine?" As it happened, despite their enthusiasm and their honest delight in each other's writings, the growing intimacy of the letters gave them all the illustration they needed that they ought not share them with their acquaintances, friends, or even family. In the view of Karen Lystra, who has studied nineteenth-century love letters closely, the sincerity required in those letters went hand in hand with privacy. The initial willingness of Harry and Jane to share each other's letters with their friends seems to argue against this assertion, but the promptness with which each staked a claim to privacy for his or her *own* letters, and educated the other in the importance of that privacy, suggests that we are witnessing an early instance of a notion of privacy that Lystra refers to as "Victorian."[33]

Jane and Harry moved with surprising speed to a powerful sense that the arrival of each other's love letters constituted a kind of physical contact—a contact so real that they began to experience them as actual visits. "Good night then my own dear friend," Jane closed one of her earliest letters, and then whispered, "Can you not hear me say good night?" At about the same time, leaving his office and his letter for a required social call, Harry complained, "It seems like tearing myself from you to rise from my paper."[34]

They saw attributes of each other's character in the content and physical appearance of the letters. Describing a letter in which Jane had added a postscript and then crossed it out, Harry noted that the passage "was hardly obliterated enough to have been done in earnest. This is true woman, ever hiding to be sought and seen." When Jane read his strident denunciations of what he thought of as the hypocritical religious practices of some New Yorkers, she wrote, "I can hardly believe that the fiery hand which wrote that epistle has *touched* me without scorching." A week before that she had written, "I think of you as usual, but my faith in you is not the substance of things hoped for. I do desire the reality of your presence. Write often and believe me always yours entirely." Clearly a thought or a recollection alone would not suffice; to experience the reality of Harry's presence, Jane required a letter.[35]

They described the experience of these visits to each other in loving detail. Sitting in the parlor on a Sunday so stormy that she had not gone to church, wondering why she had not received a letter in so long, Jane read a collection of sermons, "vainly endeavoring to turn my mind from the New York mail to heavenly things, when a loud ring from a shivering servant was the signal of a packet to my weary and watching spirit." John Popham had arrived from New York, bearing not one but two letters from Harry. William had gone out, and Louisa lay asleep on the nearby sofa. "How cheering to me were the hours I then passed with you," Jane assured Harry. "Every sentence in your letter has invigorated my whole system," she informed him a week (and two letters) later. "How delightful it is thus to stimulate each other." Looking back on his long silence a few days later, she confessed, "I know of no delight more exquisite than relief from such a state. . . . After such painful occurrences are over, we realize more deeply our constant importance to each other." His letters had increased her feeling for him. "To say the truth," she admitted, "I never expected to have quite such sensations by your means."[36]

One letter in particular had given rise to powerful sensations. In the first week of February, Harry had begun to think about house hunting in New York for a place where they would live together the following year. He interrupted an otherwise dry account of neighborhoods, expenses, and the customs of the New York housing market to inform her that "I am almost sick to see you," and to remind her, "Dear *you know* that I love you."

When Jane read that last line, she reported, "I felt a thrill like that which ran through me when I received '*le premier*' etc on Cambridge bridge." (It is not clear whether "*le premier*" is a first letter, a first gift of some sort, a first avowal of love, or a first kiss—which seems most likely, especially since we have another account of a first letter.) "I was alone in the nursery," Jane continued, "sitting on the floor and leaning hard against the fender, the wires of which moved by the beating *of my* heart." She went out a short while later to a party hosted by Harry's friend Mary Channing, who lived with her brother the minister and his family, but she didn't enjoy it. "I was full of your letter," she explained.[37]

Harry sometimes experienced a sensation that can only be described as a trance while writing a letter to Jane or reading one from her. In one of his letters of late February, he gave a lengthy account of that almost hypnotic state.

> Dear Jane, when as now in the late and silent hours of the night I sit, and think of you, I almost forget you in intensity of thought. The time which precedes our marriage is annihilated; my imagination becomes fixed; my thoughts and feelings are too concentrated for variety or succession; I remark not the lapse of time, and scarcely note my own perceptions. I start from this mental enchainment, reflect that all this is unprofitable, and again sink into the same voluntary trance. Can any reality be equal to this imagination? Tell me, dear, does your face now beam with kindness, and is it touched with love as my fancy paints it to me? . . . I would not represent that this state of mind is habitual; but I feel it sometimes; I have felt it most strongly tonight. If you were with me now, I should scarcely speak to you. I would for hours press you silently to my heart.

Jane "devoured" this letter when it reached her a few days later. "I love you more than ever for this letter," she burst out in her reply. "Every line of it is intense with feeling and yet it is so gentle that I feel as if I were reposing in your arms while thinking of its contents." A few days after that she wept at the thought of their growing closeness, and of her inability to suppress any thought or feeling from him. Then she paused. "I have harrowed up my feelings unnecessarily," she admitted. "Perhaps this may give you pain, and yet I think you would like to know how much you are capable of exciting me."

Harry felt such excitement as well. When he got one of her letters from Quincy, he wrote back, "I wish, my love, that you could feel my beating heart, and let *that* tell you how I thank you, for neither my tongue nor my pen can." Jane "turned deadly pale" when her brother handed her this letter, even before she had a chance to read it and be "overpowered." The letter worked a physical change in her appearance, she insisted. "I thank you dear," she told him, "for the improvement you have given to my face for the evening."[38]

It is possible to overstate the sense in which these letters represented symbolic physical visits. On one level, after all, they were the self-conscious literary creations of highly educated people with strong motives to impress their readers. One of the most vivid of Harry's imagined epistolary visits underlines this point.

Harry sat in his office on a Friday night in January, relieved to be alone. He had been out several evenings that week. He was suffering the effects of what he thought was a cold, but would soon reveal itself as a severe case of measles. It was ten o'clock. On Charles Street in Boston, as he envisioned it, William Minot had just retired for the night. Jane had placed her feet on the fireplace fender, and Louisa was about to put away her work and sit down with her young sister-in-law "for an hour's chat over the decreasing embers."

> I am there also among you. I was born and bred a domestic creature. At this hour so sacred to friendship, to confidence, and every kindly affec-tion, my spirit is wont to leave my sluggard frame either at my solitary office, or among the equally lifeless bodies of the boarders at my lodgings; it recreates itself for a while in your society — then darts to Stockbridge like a volume of detached flame — then returns to Charles Street, and at last, having expended nearly all its fire and energy, revisits its owner and invests me with just life enough to conduct me to my bed.

Perhaps the reader of this letter experienced the visit Harry described in the same personal way. If so, it tells us nothing about the experience of romantic love, for this letter was written not to Jane but to Louisa. Harry, it seems, having fallen into the convention of experiencing Jane's letters and his own as symbolically freighted visits, could not fall out of the mode simply because the letter he was writing was to be sent, not to his beloved and intended wife, but to his future sister-in-law.[39]

The months of separation gave Jane and Harry an opportunity to review and reexamine the meaning of the erotic experience they had shared dur-ing their courtship, and to begin to explore the erotic possibilities of the married state they expected to enter soon. In discussing the erotic experi-ence of unmarried couples in the upper middle classes in the early nine-teenth century, it is important to keep in mind Ellen K. Rothman's assess-ment of the nature and limits of that experience. "Flirtation and sexual playfulness remained common features of male-female social life," Rothman has written. Both men and women were willing participants, sparked by mutual desire and with ample opportunity to be alone. Both spoke of the difficulty of restraint. Nevertheless, normal premarital experience in these classes almost never included sexual intercourse. "What happened," Rothman has written, "might be called the 'invention of petting,' or the removal of intercourse from the range of premarital sexual behavior. . . . [I]ntercourse was posted as not only 'off limits' but as a separate territory, accessible only to married people. Courtship did not lose its erotic elements, but boundaries were drawn so as to contain sexual expressiveness and minimize its consequences." Rothman pointed out that in the seventeenth century such boundaries were set by family and community. In the early nineteenth century they were self-imposed by couples, providing them with "a *self-guided* transition to marriage." Women and men used these self-imposed limits to preserve the free contact and interaction that had been available to couples in the eighteenth century, when rates of premarital pregnancy were higher than in the seventeenth or the nineteenth.[40]

The references to past pleasures in the letters of Harry and Jane are occasionally cryptic, as seems appropriate. Why elaborate on them when just the mention of the setting, or the occasion, was enough to call them fully to life in the imaginative memory of the only other person who could experience them? Nevertheless, these references give a glimpse of the pleasures already in Harry and Jane's memories, and of their anticipation of pleasures to come.

Evenings spent together in Boston were the source of many of these memories of delight, calling forth in Jane a "deserted feeling which always arises when I am alone in the evening, because these hours were peculiarly yours." Harry felt a bittersweet melancholy at those hours as well. In his office at ten o'clock on a December night, he wrote, "I have been sitting and thinking sometimes of the parlor fire at Stockbridge, but more frequently of the sofa in Charles Street till my heart is sick with the contrasts it is compelled to draw between those scenes of love and my solitary office. Oh that I could tell you how every impulse of my nature impels me toward you at this moment! You would think no more of the ties of honor." Almost startled by his own boldness, he quickly closed his letter with "Farewell — my best friend."[41]

"Do you remember," Jane asked in her second letter of the new year, "how much you once complained of my rationality in leveling our attachment to that of all other lovers?" Whenever she had made that comparison, Harry was sure to remember it. But after just two months of his letters, she had more experience to draw on. "I begin to think there is something higher than usual in our sentiments," she admitted.

"There are certain expressions of your face which are indelibly fixed in my memory," Harry wrote in one of the intensely passionate February letters that so often moved Jane to tears, "and when I think of you, they always first recur." He recalled, and described to her in detail, the "momentary glance" she had sent his way on that hot July evening on Boston Common, shortly after she had accepted his proposal and just before she had left for Quincy — "the *perpetual moment*" when she lifted her eyes from the ground and ever so briefly locked them with his. Jane had never admitted that the glance had any special meaning. "Perhaps it was fancy in me," Harry allowed. "If so it is a fancy that has become as fixed and habitual almost as consciousness itself." To Harry, that glance resonated with sweetness, with love, and with promise. Just writing about it contributed to the trancelike experience of her personal presence that Harry went on to describe later in the same letter.[42]

A month later, gazing up at the night sky over New York while Jane was staying in Quincy, Harry had pondered "how different would be this beautiful moonlight with the congenial accompaniments of friendship sentiment and love, from what it is in this crowded and coarse city. Still," he consoled her (and himself), "the same moon now shines that lighted us on the bridge at Stockbridge, and if we were there, we should say, as softly and as sweetly" — but Robert interrupted Harry with a legal question before he could remind her what they would say, or had said, and he never returned to the subject. The recollection of the setting alone would have to suffice to remind Jane of their exchange of endearments during their visit to Stockbridge the previous September.

The day of their parting in October and the days leading up to it were a rich source of erotic memories. "I love to think of you on that evening when we sat behind the buildings a few days before we parted, when you took off your coat to shelter me from the cold," Jane wrote in late February. "How sheltering did your arm seem that evening. How closely shall I always cling to its affectionate support." At other times, she was sure just a mention of the occasion would serve the purpose of stimulating his memory. "Remember dear when I bade you farewell," she urged. "Think that I love you now as I did then." Harry agreed that her parting look was among the expressions "indelibly fixed" in his memory — along with some more physical contacts. "Have you not told me that you loved? have you not *looked* your love? have I not *felt* the throbbing of your heart?" he reminded her. "I never can forget that."

Jane began this cycle of references to memories of physical expressions of their love just hours after that "parting look" at Harry's departure. "I walked over our favorite bridge," she informed him in her first letter, written later the same day, "where the mild freshness of the air or some soothing remembrance gave a melancholy tranquility to my mind." Again, she felt no need to remind him what that "soothing remembrance" might be, instead informing him that the sounds of his tender affection "creep on the ears of my memory like touches of sweetest harmony."[43]

"I certainly could give the same testimony of affection if you were here," she told him three months later, thinking again of that day of their parting. This was but one of many frequent wishful expressions of erotic intention that the lovers sprinkled through their letters. "Were you here you would have a seat on the sofa at my side," Jane promised in one of her earliest letters. "As it is, you must think of those moments when our souls have enjoyed the most perfect repose in the consciousness of yielding affection to each other — an affection which makes me yours and you mine however distant." Often she associated a promise of such wishful experience with his performance of some minor task. "I wish you were here now to make my fire," she wrote, as "this is my greatest difficulty in housekeeping. . . . If you could but slip over here and pass this fortnight in Boston I should certainly *treat you well*."[44]

Sometimes their wishes seemed to be synchronized in a way that is startling. "O that you could but breathe with me this pure warm air," she wished, after receiving his ten-page letter in Quincy. "It opens the feelings to every happy sentiment, above all it makes them ardent for sympathy." At the very moment she wished for his company and his sympathy in Quincy, he was closing another letter in New York and rushing to get it to the post office, assuring her that if she were in New York with him, "we should be heightening each other's love, and perhaps each other's virtue, by a walk this beautiful moonlight night. There are no bridges here, but love does not depend *absolutely* on place."[45] It is striking that their remembered erotic encounters, so hazily recalled and so sketchy in details, contain at least four references to bridges, two of them real and specifically identified bridges.

Dreams, both waking and sleeping, and other unconscious reveries occasionally contributed to the lovers' sense of each other's presence during the months of their separation, and revealed a little more about their erotic expectations. When Harry finally got to sleep after staying out late one night in December, he dreamed of an encounter with Jane. "You were at Quincy," he told her, "and there was a good deal of company in the house. I heard your voice as you were standing and talking on the stairs, and to avoid coming upon you by surprise I spoke loud to give you notice of my approach. You instantly ran up to your chamber telling cousin Mary you had left something there. I caught the expression of your face as you turned," he concluded, but rather than describe that expression, simply noted, "it was all I wished it." Harry was the pursuer, but in fair and gentlemanly fashion, giving advance warning. Jane made excuses and fled, but gave him encouragement to continue the pursuit. Catching sight of her face in the dream apparently jolted Harry awake, or at least ended the part of the dream he could recall. "The dream you sent me is very natural," Jane concluded, agreeing that under such circumstances "we should both have acted as you thought." When she closed that letter she expressed her hope that they would both have more such dreams. "What would I not give to meet you in a dream and say God bless you dear," she sighed. "Good night — may visions of happiness visit your slumber — may they be prophetical and may I fulfill them."

Jane had a dream of her own to report a month later. In her dream she did more than just say "God bless you" to Harry. "I dreamt that we *were* married but that we were separated as we are now. You came home however to make me a visit and I thought you appeared the kindest of human beings and on some occasion I was so transported with what you had done that I threw my arms around you and thus awoke." Perhaps because it startled her awake, Jane was able to report to Harry, "This is the only dream of you which I ever remembered." It is most notable for Jane's dream presentation of herself as the initiator of their contact.[46]

Harry and Jane surely had physical experience, then, of the touch of each other's hands, the press of each other's arms, and the beating (even the "throbbing") of each other's hearts, and almost certainly of the kiss of each other's lips. Even then, they both wrestled with the whole question of erotic aspiration — with expressing their expectations of their erotic future together. Neither had ever been in this kind of relationship before. Both had been involved in courtships, according to their own admission. Harry, a man of thirty-one, might have had some sexual experience, although there is no real evidence of it; the only hint in any of his letters is his involvement in a friend's failed (and possibly spurious) attempt to smuggle "cundrums or cundums" into the country ten years earlier, and even that might have been for the benefit of brother Theodore, who they believed was about to be married.[47] But neither Harry nor Jane had ever been so close to crossing over the bridge into married life.

On a chilly Monday in late February, Harry, lacking any new letters since the previous Thursday, took out the twenty-eight letters he had received from Jane since his departure from Boston and began to read through them.[48] He stayed up very late and read twenty that night, stopping with the one that had taken Munson so long to deliver in January. He read four more the next night. The four most recent, including the one he had read on the run on the way to the Wilkinses, he did not bother with, as they were so recent he had "perfect recollection" of them.

Harry noticed a "progress of feeling" in Jane's letters. "I know not that you have felt of late any greater glow of tenderness or warmth of emotion, than at earlier stages of our engagement," he informed her, "but your confidence and even affection itself is more entire and habitual, and you feel your heart more at home in mine. Is not this true? Do you not with less fluttering of ill-defined fear regard me as one who is to be, and whom you are satisfied should be — let me say in one word all that language can say — your husband?" He lamented that he had not brought with him to New York the letters that he had received from her in Boston, when they were first engaged. "They would be a treasure to me now," he assured her. "The first I used to read every half hour long after not only every word was fixed in my memory, but after my eye was familiar with the formation of every letter."[49]

Just days earlier, in a letter Harry had not even received yet, Jane made a similar acknowledgment of the change in the meaning of their letters. Though Sunday had been stormy, the previous Friday had been "a most glorious morning," one that reminded her of a morning in the first weeks of their courtship when they had taken an early walk together. "That walk produced the first note I ever received from you," she recollected. "I remember that I destroyed it because I thought myself too much pleased with its complimentary strain. I heard you laugh at some ladies for taking compliments seriously and I took warning by your observations."

How much had changed in the ensuing months! It is impossible to imagine that the Harry of February 1817 would even have considered moving to a new city without taking Jane's letters with him, or that this Jane would ever have thought of destroying one of his letters. But less than four months earlier he had apparently not remembered or seen fit to pack her first few letters when he moved to New York, and just a year earlier she had in fact destroyed not just any letter, but his first to her. Those letters, of course, were written during a time when they were frequently in each other's company, so they had not taken on the representational power of the letters they had exchanged since his move. Each of them now had a sense of their letters as great and personal gifts, special creations that each had made for the other, and that each had made possible in the other. How could they ever give appropriate thanks for such a gift? "*That*," said Harry a week later, after receiving three more of the most heartfelt letters, "shall be the task, the duty, the pleasure of my whole life." [50]

8

That I Might Be Worthy of You
Roles and Responsibilities

"Dear Jane, I hail you as happy among women," Margaret Champlin Jones began her congratulatory letter on Jane Minot's engagement to Harry Sedgwick. "You have gained a treasure invaluable, the affections of a heart rich in every virtue which can adorn humanity, and beating high with those exalted, tender, sacred feelings which must shed a light over the existence of that woman whose blissful lot it is, to be guided through life by such a protector."[1]

Harry and Jane devoted a great deal of attention in their letters to the roles they would take on as husband and wife. They used their seven months of correspondence to educate themselves and each other in the nature of their mutual expectations. Throughout that exchange, both of them repeatedly rejected Margaret's model of the husband as household god who sheds light over the existence of his wife, guiding and protecting her, and of the wife as his adoring, unquestioning devotee. Margaret's letter reveals a view of marriage that we might have expected to find in a genteelly educated woman of the 1810s. Harry and Jane were hardly presenting the kind of radical view that would make of marriage a relationship of pure equals, but they moved farther in that direction than we might anticipate.

And they were not alone. In her survey of love letters from around the United States written from the 1830s to the end of the nineteenth century, Karen Lystra noticed a surprising fluidity of gender roles. "Letters between men and women suggest that nineteenth-century sex roles in actual interaction were less rigid than any description of their content might imply," Lystra concluded. "Although most of the correspondents affirmed their belief in the ideology of domesticity, the cult of true womanhood, the doctrine of separate spheres, and the ideals of true manhood, they also demonstrated that sex roles did not necessarily remain one-dimensional and static in everyday life." The letters of Harry and Jane, written two decades before the starting point of Lystra's study, support Lystra's view.[2]

Even Margaret Jones found it wise to pay lip service to the idea of equality in one small detail in her letter — "You truly deserve all your happiness, the exchange will be equal, the happiness mutual" — but her consistent theme was the husband's near-divinity and the wife's adoration. Still, on one subject her congratulatory letter was very much an expression of the latest changes in popular sensibility: Her description of Harry Sedgwick's heart as "rich in every virtue which can adorn humanity" reveals an understanding of *virtue* as something wholly private and domestic, an idea that would have startled her revolutionary forebears, for whom personal virtue was the cornerstone of the public life of the Republic. This shift in the locus of virtue from the forum to the fireside is amply documented in Harry and Jane's letters — again, a full two decades earlier than recent scholarship would lead us to expect. This was a significant departure from the model of masculinity prevalent during the founding era, which was a time of transition away from an older patriarchalism.[3] Harry and Jane's expression of such an ideal does not prove that it was widespread. Studies indicate, for example, that as in many other matters, the South and the North differed. Jan Lewis has pointed out that women in Virginia in these years merely "characterized ideal husbands as those free from a host of flaws."[4] But it does show that in 1816 it was possible and fairly natural for wealthy, educated young New Englanders from elite professional families, with Unitarian sympathies, to arrive at a new understanding of the roles and responsibilities they would take on when they entered into a marriage.[5]

One constant theme throughout this exchange was Harry's worthiness — intellectually, spiritually, and professionally — as Jane's partner. But at every turn Jane diminished the importance of outward success and turned his attention to the intellectual and emotional support that she claimed were her real expectations of a marriage partner. Toward the end of winter Harry experienced a brief crisis of confidence ("a festering anxious sensation which I cannot well define") about his own worthiness to be Jane's husband. "I wish I could look into destiny," he wrote, "merely to know one thing — whether I shall ever become unworthy of you and forfeit your esteem. If I thought so (and I sometimes have an obscure and undefined but dreadful apprehension of it) I would now abjure you forever."

Jane began her reply almost as soon as she had finished reading his letter. "I was a little startled at the undefined obscure apprehension you say you sometimes feel lest you may become unworthy of my esteem," she wrote. "I trust it has no foundation in what you know of your own character. I rely on your virtue even more than on your love." She knew he was not perfect, of course, but she thought he had "a fine foundation for perfection." At several points during their months of correspondence she had been reminded how little acquaintance they actually had with each other. "We have not much chance of seeing each other's dark sides at present," she admitted. "I trust they will come upon us too gradually to produce much shock."

Harry assured Jane that he was not worried about revealing a hidden dark side to her; he simply had a sense of "the magnitude of the responsibility I assume," and looked forward to it with anxiety. "Every night since our engagement," he informed Jane in March, "I have proffered a petition to the giver of every worldly blessing, and of every right affection — of all good and perfect gifts — that I might be worthy of you — that I might render you happy here and conduce to your happiness hereafter." His anxiety was proof of the intensity of his devotion, not of its variability. "If I loved you less," he asserted, "these feelings of timidity and occasional apprehension would never visit me." Jane agreed. Ultimately, worth of character was all she looked for in a husband, and that worth of character was best demonstrated not in the public forum but in the privacy of the relationship between husband and wife. Harry's very anxiety about attaining it proved to her that he had done so.[6]

Honesty was another preeminent characteristic in a worthy husband, and Jane had come to expect it of Harry. "I would rather lose than deceive you," he had vowed in the long letter in which he explained in detail the complete history of his courtships of Elizabeth Sumner and Abigail Phillips.[7] As much as his honesty, Jane let Harry know that she would depend on the utter genuineness of his love for her. But Jane felt as much anxiety on this matter as Harry did in the area of his worthiness. "Shall I tell you the truth?" she wrote, when he had been gone just a month. "I had a notion that you were more important to me than I could be to you. . . . It seemed to me a part of the weakness peculiar to my own sex to give more than it received." A little over a month later she concluded that his love was indeed something she could rely on. His "delicate and tender" (yet still sensible) letters were what led her to that conclusion. In answer to her question why he had not been subject to the same kind of "fluctuations" of confidence in *her* devotion, he attributed it to his calmer, more trusting nature in matters of the heart. A woman, "who if she be deceived is lost forever," had to be more cautious. Jane feared that raising the whole question of her emotional "fluctuations" and Harry's lack of them sounded like a condemnation of him, "because I am not quite so old in the ways of the world nor so wise as you are," and she qualified her comment in her next letter. "Do not think I mean that you ever feel less than you should do," she assured him. "I only wish to say that you feel like all very thinking people — that is just what I desire. Your affection is much more flattering than if it were less guided by your judgment."[8]

Confident as she had become in his virtue, his worthiness, his honesty, his sincerity, and his love, Jane still retained one great fear about Harry Sedgwick as she prepared to enter into a marriage with him: his temper.

On one level, Harry's temper was no threat to Jane. She never feared for her personal safety, and had no apprehension that he would ever do her any physical harm. On that point her faith was absolute. "You have . . . the power of inspiring my confidence to a degree of which I am almost *ashamed*," she admitted in an early letter. "Long before I knew you as I do now, I had the impression that you were a man entirely to be trusted, that no temptation could shake you when you were entirely relied upon." She mentioned his "great consideration" as one of the features that drew her to him, and thanked him for never judging her hastily. But when she heard of what seemed to be a steady stream of his confrontations over religion in New York, she sent back cautionary messages.[9]

Harry was appalled by the religious beliefs and practices of the New Yorkers. "The theological ignorance of this city is very gross, and its bigotry exceeding bitter," he wrote to Jane's brother William a few weeks after his arrival in New York. "The truth is," he had told Jane a few days earlier, "that in almost everything of an intellectual nature, and specifically in theology, this city is at least a century behind Boston."

Boston in 1816 was the home of what Jane and Harry and their families referred to as "liberal Christianity." This set of religious beliefs would begin to be widely identified as "Unitarianism" after their friend William Ellery Channing claimed the label in a widely publicized 1819 sermon. Harry and Jane, however, used the term frequently in 1816 and 1817 when referring to their own religious ideals and beliefs.[10]

While substantial theological disagreements divided Unitarians from orthodox Calvinists, a cultural and behavioral chasm nearly as great stretched between them as well. Unitarians were (in their own view) moderate in temperament, tolerant, inquisitive, and receptive to change — all characteristics that were understood in their appropriation of the adjective *liberal*. They considered the orthodox Calvinists intolerant zealots. In

Boston, where liberal Christianity was widespread, it was generally seen as the province of the elite, and especially of the upwardly mobile.[11]

As a young man trying to establish himself, Harry hoped to avoid religious squabbles.[12] Still, he managed to get himself enmeshed in two separate church-related controversies within his first four months in New York.

The first came in December, when the Young Men's Missionary Society rejected a candidate who had hoped to be sent west to the frontier, because his beliefs were insufficiently orthodox. His fellow moderates in the Missionary Society sought to bring the matter up for a vote of the membership. "While the controversy was pending," Harry informed Jane, "both sides beat up for recruits to out-vote each other." Robert had joined the Presbyterian church on Murray Street during the years he boarded with Frances and Ebenezer, before Frances moved to Stockbridge with her children. A member of that church came to the Sedgwicks' office to recruit Robert for the Missionary Society. "We both agreed to do it," Harry wrote, "but of course cast our weight on the side of toleration."

The participants soon recognized where the brothers' allegiance lay. Harry observed that "the great champion" of the moderate faction (which he referred to as "the New England side") was Rev. Gardiner Spring. Finding himself outnumbered by the more orthodox Calvinist speakers, he ·asked Harry and Robert to join in the debate — "which we did," Harry informed Jane. The debate went on until eleven o'clock Monday night, December 16, and then resumed and lasted until the same late hour on Wednesday, still with no vote.

The debate was scheduled to conclude Friday. In a letter written to Jane on Thursday, Harry told her that some of the orthodox members of the Missionary Society had raised "a hue and cry," saying that "Mr. Spring procured two Socinians . . . to support his side of the controversy." (In the language of the ancient church, Socinians were heretics who believed that Jesus Christ was essentially and only human, though he was an especially blessed and perfect human.)[13] A bit sheepishly, Harry admitted to Jane that in order to join the society and participate in the debate, he had "signed, without scruple or examination, the constitution which expressly recognizes all the doctrines which at Boston you call Calvinistic," the teachings that gave rise to the liberal Harry's illiberal rage. As the debate proceeded, he began to realize that he might have acted rashly. "I perceived that we had signed a constitution," he acknowledged, "and that all who had done so were considered as pledging themselves to the adoption of the principles of faith therein contained."

So on Thursday morning, Harry called on the president of the Missionary Society, told him that he had signed this constitution "inadvertently," and promised that he would abstain from speaking and voting at the next night's meeting. Still, he was intensely curious to hear the conclusion of the debate. The president agreed that he should not debate or vote, "but that if I abstained from doing so, I was perfectly at liberty to attend."

On Friday night both Sedgwick brothers were present when the society reopened the debate. A clergyman named Matthews — Harry called him "the great champion of orthodoxy" — objected that "a person who was avowedly opposed to the true and proper divinity of our Lord Jesus Christ" was present in the room, and threatened to move for Harry's expulsion if he did not leave voluntarily. Harry stood to defend himself. He described his meeting with the society's president, and the president confirmed the account. Matthews began to back away from his complaint, but Harry had never allowed a person who had insulted him to find a graceful way of retreating. He pressed his demand that something be done about the insult. "If you had been there you would have given me credit for my temper," Harry wrote to Jane, probably with more hope than conviction.

The evening of debate about Harry's continued presence had postponed the vote on the original issue, which was now rescheduled for Monday, December 23. Monday night's vote came at half past eleven, and the orthodox Calvinists carried it by a margin of nearly two to one. When the result was announced, the Missionary Society voted "immediately and unanimously" to split itself into two societies, "and thus they separated in true orthodox charity a little after midnight."

The entire controversy left Harry feeling gloomy and homesick a day later, as the city around him celebrated Christmas. "The bells are ringing their cheerful peal," he recounted. "All seems to be joy and gladness. This is a holiday here" — in Boston it was not celebrated with anything like the New Yorkers' enthusiasm, because both the liberal Christians and the orthodox Calvinists there shared a hostility to its papist overtones — "but my obstinate head rejects all their consolations; my unsympathizing heart will not soften to their merriment, and I have retired from the social throngs, proud, sullen and solitary to my lonely office." He stayed there all day, reading the Gospels and thinking of Jane.[14]

Jane went that day to King's Chapel in Boston. The contrast to the zeal of the New Yorkers could not have been more pronounced, and Jane and her sister-in-law Louisa Minot had enjoyed a good laugh over Harry's account of the first two nights of the Missionary Society debate. A few days later, when she received Harry's letter describing the controversial events of Friday night, Jane's reaction was more cautious. Had he done anything to damage his prospects in New York? Had he even considered that he might be doing so? Though she began her admonition lightheartedly, she soon turned her attention to an important question about Harry's judgment. "From curiosity and love of *amusement* quite as much as of *toleration* you signed the paper of a party whose principles you knew were opposite to your own," she admonished. "I see you do not put much value upon the ornament of a meek and quiet spirit. I admire to have your ardor raised by any means more dignified than your own imprudence." And then, having deftly taken him to task, she reverted to whimsy. "I am thankful you confine yourself at present to theological disputes," she remarked, "as the nature of subjects will secure you from a duel."

By this time, some glimmering of the same thought had occurred to Harry. "I have now cooled down and feel quite comfortable," he wrote, a few days before receiving Jane's letter. "I suppose however that as I pass in the streets people whom I don't know are staring at me to see cloven feet or some other palpable mark of my belonging to Satan's kingdom. All that I care about the matter is that it may possibly prevent my getting business." Jane was glad to learn that Harry had considered this possibility — finally — even before she raised it. "For the future," she offered hopefully, "I know you will keep as quiet as you can." Still, Harry missed the perceptiveness of her complaint. He told her at great length that Matthews and the Calvinists offered him no threat of physical danger or injury. He simply did not acknowledge, and may not have understood, that it might not be good for his growing business in New York to be perceived by *anyone* as a theological brawler, or to be in the middle of a controversy that had originated when he had signed his name to a statement that he did not believe.[15]

Sometimes Jane's warnings to Harry about his temper were indirect. A Major Romagno was fined for violently beating a soldier under his command. Everyone in Boston was talking about the case. Jane was not pleased with the sentence. "I am dissatisfied that mere money should be the atonement for such a crime," she informed Harry. "It is just as bad as the practice of selling indulgences. I would decree that the major should be beaten as he beat the soldier, and pay the two thousand and fifty dollars besides." Her next comment let Harry know that this was not just an idle remark on a local incident. "I wonder how this conduct affects the lady to whom he is engaged," Jane continued. "As one of the fair sex she ought to reject him. If she does not she places herself on the level with the soldier, and deserves to be treated like him."

It must have been sobering for Harry to receive this veiled warning in the midst of the Missionary Society controversy. Ten days later, with the controversy over, Jane made the connection a bit more explicit, even as she moved beyond it. "I have at least granted a long *suspension* to all my misgivings of you," she told him. "When my alarms rise again that will be from some cause of a new nature but you are so economical in affording me subjects of pain that the prospect is rather barren."

"I foresee what an excellent monitress I shall have!" Harry acknowledged. "Indeed the reflection that I no longer act for myself alone has already begun to have an influence on my conduct."[16]

In matters of theology, Jane was in perfect agreement with Harry, but less hostile to the beliefs of their orthodox rivals. A few years earlier, writing a comparison of liberal and orthodox Christians in her commonplace book, she had noted that "the doctrines which they most contend about have no practical effect or at least very little connection with the business of life." With this in mind, Jane's concern was for the intemperate actions Harry might take to defend his beliefs against real or imagined opponents in New York. "Honor is not so often in danger as young men wish her to be," she admonished. She knew that Harry would act honorably in any "scrape" he was involved in, "but," she cautioned him, "you don't avoid one sufficiently."[17] So when Harry's second great religious "scrape" of the winter occurred, two months to the day after the conclusion of the Missionary Society debate, Jane's anxiety grew.

On Sunday, February 23, Harry went to the Presbyterian church on Murray Street with Robert. The guest preacher was a Dr. Romayne. He might have been "one of the most eminent and highly vaunted clergymen in this city," but to Harry he was an "eminently ridiculous" man. His sermon was an attempt to argue that the unregenerate (the many who were not predestined to be saved) were "strictly and literally in bondage to the devil." Romayne appeared "fidgety" to Harry, as if he were aware of the incoherence and contradictions of his argument, "but tried to supply the defect of reason by vehemence of assertion." Harry and Robert sat in the seats nearest the pulpit. "My attention was riveted," Harry claimed. "I think it very probable that my face expressed contempt, but upon my honor I was perfectly unconscious of it."

After the service, Dr. Romayne pointed to Harry and asked who "that young man" was. "Now he knew me as well as he did his own deacon," Harry insisted. "On being informed that it was Mr. Sedgwick he said that he had never been so insulted in his life, as by that man during the whole sermon — that he had a great disposition publicly to reprimand me which he certainly would do if he should ever again receive a similar provocation." Harry took the minister's indignation as a tacit admission "that he had sense enough to know that he was a fool," and he joked that he felt "a little vanity that he did me the compliment to observe that I perceived it. I shall take no notice whatever of it," he declared magnanimously. "Robert is determined to call on him for an explanation."

Some time within the next two weeks, Robert did so. Romayne told Robert why he had made the complaint. It must have occurred to Jane, as she read Harry's account of his brother's meeting with the offended minister, that he had left a crucial detail out of his original letter. As Harry had stared intently at the flustered homilist from the front pew, he had been doing something else as well. "What do you think my crime consisted in?" he finally asked Jane. "The heinous offence of cutting my nails in sermon time." Robert had expressed his exasperation with Harry's habits many times; he had even gone so far as to criticize them in writing eight months earlier, in the letter he sent to Harry before they launched their New York partnership.[18] He was therefore able to explain to Dr. Romayne that Harry had meant nothing personal by staring (no mention was made of what must have been his ill-concealed contempt) and cutting his nails during the minister's sermon. Romayne, perhaps unexpectedly, agreed that he "would *untell* the story he had been gossiping."

Harry was surprised at the "rumpus" this incident had caused. "For fear lest I should fall into some seeming irreverence," he told Jane, "I have not dared to show myself in the convocation of the saints since the impious moment, when heaven-forsaken, and hell-influenced, I was guilty of the sacrilegious audacity of cutting my nails in the very sight of the preacher, and in sermon time." Harry believed he understood the true nature of his offense: "If it had been during the prayer — or if I had held down my hands so that the minister could not have seen me — or had not been an Unitarian, it would have been no matter." That last point, he was sure, had given rise to the whole incident: Romayne was using his distaste for Harry's habits as an indirect way of attacking his liberal beliefs. "A gentleman said the other day that if he wanted a rascal, he could find him anywhere, but if he wanted a d——d rascal he would go to the communion table," he complained.

Jane fretted that, "however unjust or ridiculous," Romayne's displeasure "might have some influence" against Harry. And by this time, she was not merely worried about his business prospects. "I know it sounds old womanish," she acknowledged, "but I will say it, sometimes I think the warm contempt you feel for the prevailing religion in New York may weaken your attention to its important interests." A few days later she was still worrying. "I have discovered since our engagement that you have more temper than I expected," Jane concluded. "I do not fear in the least that it will ever be vented against me or any of our friends but I do fear that it will often get you into difficulties with strangers. I do not trust so much to my influence over you in future as you do," she admitted with great prescience. "I have seen enough of characters to know that it is impossible for that influence ever to be so great as it is now." Harry was chastened. "In this, and in a great many other things," he acknowledged, "I expect that you will make me better."[19]

Each warning about the dangers of his hot temper was coupled with the qualification that she did not fear its being turned on her. If she had, she assured him, she would have ended their engagement. "I do not think I shall ever fear you," she wrote in the midst of the Romayne controversy. "If I did think so I would never marry you—love's plumage once ruffled can hardly be smoothed again. I am sure you could not restore to me the charm of entire confidence if once I had the wish to shun you." But she never came close to experiencing that wish. She was aware of the bitter experience of Harry's older sister Frances, and shared his revulsion for Ebenezer Watson; but she knew Harry Sedgwick was no brute. "I am sure Harry dear," she insisted as their separation drew near its conclusion, "that I shall never be more afraid of you than of a kitten."[20]

"Dear Jane," Harry wrote in April, "if I were master of the world it should be yours—as it is I must be contented with proving to you that I will do for you all that I can—that every power, every faculty and every affection will be called into your service."[21] While Jane's most exacting standards for Harry concerned his private behavior—his love, his honesty, his even temper—she relied on his letters for assurance that he was destined to achieve some measure of material success as well.

Jane had seen Harry flounder professionally in Boston. The region's economy was not conducive to the growth of new businesses in the immediate aftermath of the War of 1812, but Jane knew that Harry was the source of some of his own problems. She was aware of the suspicions his conduct during the settlement of his father's estate had aroused in many leaders of the legal profession, including Louisa's father, Daniel Davis. She knew that he had drifted back and forth between Boston and Stockbridge for more than five years, unable to settle permanently in one place or the other. Certainly she was in the best position to assess the impact of his clumsy and very public courtship of the daughters of two of the city's most prominent families.

New York was to be a new beginning. In the postwar years its economy was taking off, and within a decade it would achieve preeminence as the nation's commercial capital. And where commerce was growing, legal business was growing: there were contracts to be drafted, estates to be bequeathed, properties to be divided, debts to be collected, claims to be filed. The prewar years had been dismal in New York. No city was hit harder by Jefferson's 1807 Embargo Act, by which American merchant ships were prohibited from trading with Britain and France in an attempt to put a stop to those powers' violations of the neutral rights of the United States. But in the postwar years the city's central location, superior natural harbor, and rapidly improving connections to the hinterland provided an irresistible impetus to economic growth.[22]

Full as the letters were of testimony to Harry's character and industry, they also contained warnings of the horrors that might befall the young couple if he let up in his efforts to succeed. Several times Jane reported from Boston on the newly announced insolvency of some friend or professional acquaintance of her brother. Business disasters struck the families of the friendlies as well. In March, a Mr. Brower defrauded William Fales of $1,500, even though Fales had been "a benefactor to this man's family." Mary Ann Fales, still nursing her new daughter, said she did not regret the loss, "as it may learn her husband to take better care of his affairs." And not all the horror stories came from Boston. Looking over his and Robert's growing legal practice, Harry acknowledged, "A great, and indeed the greatest portion of our business has resulted from mercantile failures." All these stories of failed ventures, dishonored debts, and lost reputations served to reinforce the countervailing ideal of worthiness, and to link Harry's professional achievement with his attainment of the virtuous state of honest, loving, and temperate compassion that would make him a worthy husband.[23]

In the course of her correspondence with Harry Sedgwick during their engagement, Jane Minot developed a new understanding of her role as a wife. Mutuality and reciprocity were the keys to that role. Just as Harry depended on her to validate his worthiness as her husband-to-be, she would insist on his cooperation and active participation in her creation of a new model of wifeliness. The surprising thing about this is that Jane implied her intention to create such a cooperative ideal of reciprocity even before she was engaged to Harry Sedgwick, in journal entries in which she expressed her frustration about his failure to reciprocate her ideas. She expected that a successful relationship would require equality of minds *and* hearts, even when she despaired of achieving that with Harry.[24]

Virtue, in its newly domestic and personal sense, was as central to Jane's role of wife as it was to Harry's role of husband. Religion did not give definition to this idea of virtue, although religious observances were understood to be the obligation of both partners, and Jane admonished herself as frequently as she did Harry for inattention to those duties. Three times in her letters Jane claimed to be acting in the role of a preacher to Harry, and though she gently mocked herself on each of those occasions, she saw her attention to Harry's worthiness as a necessary prerequisite to her own attainment of happiness.[25]

Virtue meant something new to Jane; it was *not* what an older friend, Mrs. Metcalf, had meant when she tempered her congratulation of Jane on her engagement with a warning that "it was good for the virtue of women to be married but not for their happiness." Jane was not willing to separate the two. As for marital happiness, "if there should be any deficiency," she wrote, "I most solemnly believe the fault will be my own. If I only have enough employment, something to satisfy my moral nature I have no fears."

What was new here was not the attention to virtue but its identification with personal happiness. When Harry expressed those curiously satisfying feelings of unworthiness, Jane recognized the virtuous aspirations that inspired them, and reciprocated. "I hate to use a hacknied expression," she offered, "in saying that I have felt as if I could die were it necessary to make you perfect, but the sincerity of the feeling will induce you to pardon the want of originality in the expression of it." Just as his worth was measured by his ability to make her happy, her happiness was founded in her ability to make him worthy.[26]

True, mutual love was the most essential element of the wife's role, and Jane and Harry, both comfortable with the idea that they could be in love, used their letters to define such love. Jane knew that the dominion of reason over love, as over religious belief, was severely limited. Despite her rejection of Margaret Jones's ideal of wifely adoration, she was willing to admit some similarity in the two impulses. "To women there are but two powerful sources of feeling," she informed Harry, "religion and love." All her friends were regulated by what she called "religious habits," but few of them had felt the "secret animating influence" of religious belief so early or so intensely as she had, or "seemed to receive the pleasure . . . from piety" that she did. Now she was ahead of her older friends in experiencing another "secret animating influence." At the beginning of April she told Harry, "I have had some feelings for you very like those I have had towards my maker; the same openness of heart and sometimes the same wish of being devoted to you, and the same sort of reliance though in a less degree upon your kindness and protection."

Within the context of their liberal Christian theology, this is a bold statement. Jane had chastised Margaret Jones for her assertion that as a wife Jane ought to "adore" her husband, "that guardian angel, which heaven has bestowed upon you, to share your destiny on earth." For Jane, *devotion* was not the same as Margaret's *adoration*, and the difference was not just one of degree. For one thing, devotion allowed (and almost required) the possibility of constant reciprocation. So did the kindness and protection she expected to rely on, as Jane believed Harry had reason to know. "There is something even in your unhappiness which gives me pleasure," she had written in response to his earlier expressions of apprehension about his worthiness. "I presume it is for the selfish reason that I know I can then give you the sweetest delight — that of sharing in those feelings in which no other can entirely participate — giving you a realizing sense of the union of our destinies — that your hopes and sorrows are mine, and that I will solace and love you so long as I shall retain the consciousness of your feelings or my own."[27]

Jane and Harry both knew that their exchange of dozens of passionate and revealing letters had laid the foundation for this mutual love. The Harry she now envisioned when she anticipated her marriage to him was the Harry who had written and read those letters, far more than he was the Harry she had known during his months in Boston. She admitted as much in March, in what may have been her most passionate outburst in the entire correspondence.

> I think I shall feel that you are even more necessary to me when after this intercourse I shall see you daily — and having no friend about me *but you* shall look forward with impatience for dinner time and evening to call you from the office. My love, my best friend, my future husband receive from me in these imperfect words all I am capable of feeling all I desire to feel. I believe I am yours beyond the power of recovering myself. My confidence in you is so entire that I will not withhold even this expression of

it. While I make this confession my whole soul is solemnized. I can make no greater surrender when I join you at the altar — it is a surrender which puts me entirely in your power, it is no small surrender for me, for I have desired independence more than even love itself. My tears flow while I write, it is because I feel the sense of my own weakness in my inability to suppress anything from you. Harry you never can have deceived you never will deceive me. I shall always have cause to love you as I do now. If any change be possible in futurity Oh my God may I die before that hour.[28]

A shared religious faith was essential to Jane's and Harry's view of their ideal marriage. Jane worried that being in love had made her less religious because she found herself staying home from church some Sundays, or let her mind wander to thoughts of Harry during the worship service. Still, her faith never wavered, nor did her certainty of Harry's. "Harry dear," Jane wrote on a stormy stay-at-home Sunday in February, "I should not have loved you if I had not thought you were religious." And as much as she disapproved of his controversies, she shared his fervent rejection of the orthodox beliefs of his opponents. She deplored his tactics, not his principles. "If I saw you acting contrary to the general principles of religion," she admitted after the controversy with Romayne, "I should indeed be a dead weight, apathetical and useless."

Harry valued their shared faith as much as Jane did. Her love was a miracle that could only serve to increase his faith. "You feel for me more than I deserve, more than I could have believed, more than I could hope," he wrote in the depths of winter. "You say so frequently that you do not deserve my affection," Jane replied, "that I am inclined to think you are converted to the orthodox doctrine of total depravity." She warned him against this pitfall. "I know of no other requisite for deserving affection," she assured him, "but the power to return it."[29]

They genuinely expected their marriage to unite them for eternity. Harry began the new year with a letter describing 1817 as the year that would "decide our destiny for that portion which is marked by the regular revolution of those orbs which now do so gloriously move around and above us — and perhaps also for the eternity which will remain when our disenthralled spirits shall soar beyond their spheres." He then posed a question concerning that disembodied eternity: "Shall we love each other then as we do now?" He knew the theological arguments that would support the negative answer to this question. "But nature, sentiment, affection—the impressible yearnings of the heart say no" to such arguments, he insisted. Jane passed off her agreement as a joke—"I believe it to be one of the punishments as well as the blessings of another existence that we shall be doomed still to love what we have loved here"—but her faith was no less optimistic.[30]

While Harry was wondering in New York whether their love would last for all eternity, Jane was in Boston listening to William Ellery Channing preach his New Year's sermon at the Federal Street church. Channing was one homilist during whose preaching Jane's mind never wandered, even to thoughts of Harry. On this occasion his topic was the effect that every single incident in a person's past had on that person's present and future life. Now she and Harry were part of each other's past, she thought. They had already changed each other in countless ways, and their life together was just beginning. "We must be responsible for each other as well as for ourselves," she resolved.

Jane did not hear Channing preach his sermon on marriage during the winter of her engagement, but she learned about it from a number of friends. "I am told by the manner of people that they never received a more affecting representation of their respective duties," she wrote to Harry, "and it is presumed that the young lovers who were present will in futurity be patterns of conjugal virtue and felicity." The sermon serves as a summary of the ideal of marriage that Jane Minot and Harry Sedgwick spent seven months constructing in their letters.[31]

Channing was five years older than Harry Sedgwick, and had been married for about two years. So when he began the sermon by looking around to seek the causes that had contributed "to elevate among us the female character, to render woman the associate of man's most refined pleasures and pursuits, and to confer on the conjugal connection a tenderness and dignity which have rarely distinguished it," he spoke from within the same postrevolutionary generation. To Channing, the education of young women was one factor. Another, perhaps less novel, was the respect Americans accorded to the marriage vow. The one that stood out, though, was "the habit by which we are marked, of looking to our homes for the greatest part of our happiness"—in which one can hear an echo of the domestication of *virtue* that Harry and Jane had celebrated in their letters. For all these, Channing believed that American women ought to give thanks for being born at the time and in the place they were.

The reverence in which Americans held marriage imposed obligations on people who were considering such a union. "Let not the most solemn engagement of life be an act of rashness and unreflecting passion," Channing warned. "Let the heart take counsel of the understanding. Let the future as well as the present be brought into the account. Let not the eye or the imagination be trusted." In essence, Channing was charging young men and women who wanted to be married with the responsibility to "arrange" their own marriages — to temper the urges of their own passion, which in earlier times would have been restrained by their parents.

Channing went on to list the noble purposes of marriage: "to awaken the heart, to exercise and strengthen its sensibilities and charities, to train it to the perfection of social virtue, to confer the highest enjoyments of friendship, to secure to each party the benefit of the other's strength, intelligence, and virtues, and to unite both in forming useful and virtuous members for the community." The differences between men and women prepared them "to supply each other's deficiencies, to perfect each other's character, and to bear distinct, yet equally necessary, parts in that most important work of the present state, the support and rearing of a family." This last is the only item in Channing's catalog that did not earn any mention in the letters of Jane Minot and Harry Sedgwick. Channing, whose firstborn child had died twenty-four hours after her birth in October 1816, was understandably more attentive to this aspect of married life than Harry and Jane, who were impatiently awaiting their wedding day.[32] Yet the letters are so comprehensive that the absence of any reference to prospective children of their own is intriguing. Perhaps it is related to the delicacy that prevented any overt mention in the letters of several friends' pregnancies.

To those who would marry, and to those who were married, Channing recommended "a thousand nameless, indescribable offices by which the heart expresses its interest, and which serve as a continual nourishment to the affections." He feared that many long-married couples saw "the fervor of youthful affection cooling into indifference," and urged them to cultivate "opportunities of mutual services" and to "multiply expressions of affection." Then he prescribed a requirement would have been impossible for Theodore Sedgwick, John Adams, and all the traveling statesmen of the revolutionary generation, for whom absences from home of months and even years were routine: Husbands and wives "should cultivate each other's society. They should avoid long and unnecessary separations, for these generate unconcern and produce an independence on each other which marks a declining attachment. As far as is consistent with their duties, they should include each other in all their plans. . . . They should often read together the same books, view together the same scenes of nature, enjoy the same society."

Channing concluded his catalog of the requirements of the married state with what he believed to be "the noblest purpose" of marriage. Husbands and wives "should labor to improve each other's characters," he insisted. "They who sustain this near relation . . . should regard one another in the light which the gospel throws on our nature as immortal beings, capable of great improvement, and whose highest interests are in a future state. . . . Let them watch over each other's hearts and minds with affectionate concern, mutually inviting honest and friendly admonition, and aiding and strengthening religious and benevolent sentiments."

When all these requirements were met — when married couples acted as "sources and cherishers of virtuous sentiment" — that, Channing urged his listeners to understand, was "a felicity almost too pure for earth" and "a foretaste of the attachments of a better world."[33]

In his focus on affectionate love and companionship, on mutual improvement of each other's minds and hearts, on shared responsibility for the cultivation of domestic virtue, and on preparation for a shared eternal life of cozy domesticity, Channing prescribed an ideal of marriage that was virtually identical to the one his friends Harry Sedgwick and Jane Minot were working out for themselves. By re-envisioning the roles of husband and wife, these New England Unitarians consciously set themselves apart from their forebears, and set out together toward the future.

9

To Translate Hope to Certainty

Setting the Date

*S*etting a wedding date was an immediate topic of discussion, and occasional contention, in the exchange between Harry Sedgwick and Jane Minot. Harry was eager to marry as soon as possible. He had no interest in a long engagement. Jane urged Harry to have patience, to practice the virtue of restraint, and to enjoy the privileges and blessings of being engaged.

Part of this difference in their relative senses of urgency may have stemmed from their ages. Jane was twenty-one or twenty-two when Harry left Boston. She claimed to have had "love affairs" before, although she recorded no specifics. She was younger than her unmarried close friends—five years younger than both Caroline Danforth and Catharine Sedgwick. Harry was nearly a decade older. His older sisters had both married at twenty-two; his older brother married shortly before turning twenty-eight. Harry had been involved in two earlier courtships that he thought might result in his engagement.[1]

The disagreement over the timing of the wedding also fits into a larger pattern of relations between men and women in the early decades of the nineteenth century. Once an engagement was announced, most men wanted to hurry the wedding. It seems likely that men's relative eagerness to set the date can be linked to what Ellen K. Rothman has described as the effective "removal of intercourse from the range of premarital sexual behavior," and its posting as "not only 'off limits' but as a separate territory, accessible only to married people." No doubt some men urged the speeding up of marriage plans at least in part out of eagerness to cross the bridge that led into that separate territory. Women often encouraged delay. Sometimes a specific external demand (the agricultural cycle, some other scheduled work, or a planned trip) was the reason for the delay, but women were also concerned about the risks to which marriage would expose them (especially the risk of death in childbirth), the loss of some freedoms, and the demands of the new role they were about to take on. Engagement itself also offered delights that a woman might not want to see end, such as the relative freedom with which she could now interact with single men other than her intended husband, and the exchange of frequent love letters. Thus when Jane reminded Harry that they both agreed their absence had strengthened their attachment to each other, she concluded with a plea: "Do not let us be so foolish as to give up hastily the charms of separation."[2]

Whatever the reasons, Jane was consistent in expressing her belief that she and Harry could easily wait a year or more before marrying. She urged Harry to calm himself, and to ignore his family's pressure to marry more quickly. One of the most important reasons for waiting, she reminded him, was the reason he had moved to New York in the first place: he needed to get established, and to prove that he could support a wife and a family. "I can wait patiently for years, if it be necessary," Jane assured him at the start of the new year, "to accumulate the happiness which is in store for us."[3]

Harry's patience was not so great. He complained of Jane's "premeditated procrastination," although he eventually acceded to the need to wait at least until after Louisa Minot had recovered from the birth of her expected child. When it became clear that the baby was due in April, Jane announced her agreement with Louisa's determination that she ought to put off any wedding plans and stay in Boston through the end of the summer.

Faced with this determination, Harry applied all the eloquence he could to his pleading. "I have suffered my hopes to dwell so long and so securely upon the anticipated delights of a home of my own," he admitted, "a home whose more than magic circle should contain all that lovers wish, and better things than poets feign . . . that I cannot at once consent to a protraction of the period when all these imagined joys should be mine." He begged Jane, "do not ask me now to consent to a procrastination of all that I so ardently desire — of all that reason points to and the heart longs for as the source of happiness." But Jane continued to resist, noting that preparations for a June wedding would rule out any other chance Harry might have to visit in spring, and might even force her to reduce the frequency and length of her letters.[4]

Each family seemed to have a position on the timing of the wedding. The Sedgwicks were resolute: the earlier the better.[5] Theodore's encouragement heartened Harry. "He is generally timid," he explained to Jane, "but matrimony is the particular subject on which he is heroic." He recounted for her the events of nine and ten years earlier, leaving out the reason that Theodore "thought his wife had no property" (that is, her stepfather's threat to disinherit her if she married anyone other than his son). The point of the story was, "the result was so happy in his case that he antici- pates the same good fortune for everybody else."[6]

Jane urged Harry to think for himself. Their lives were pleasant, they enjoyed each other's frequent letters, and there was "nothing particularly uncomfortable in either of our situations." His brothers were anxious, she told Harry, because they feared that he would grow tired of her and break off the engagement, "especially as you have hitherto led rather an unsettled life and given your existence to the spirit of occasion." The remark served to remind Harry that he still had something to prove.

One of Harry's most pressing tasks during his first months in New York was to convince William Minot of his prospects for success. In her first letter, Jane assured Harry that her brother missed him, but her ampli- fication of this point was revealing. She believed that William regretted the loss of Harry's "*anticipated* aid in his labors of gallantry" — or, more accurately, that not William but "the ladies" — perhaps Louisa, perhaps some of the friendlies — regretted that Harry would not be present to tutor William in the ways of gallantry. Harry was the expert in that area (it was, Jane reminded him, "a vocation for which nature had designed and education had completed you") and this had always endeared him to the friendlies. The ladies got nothing by the law, which was William Minot's area of expertise, and so were unwilling "to yield a favorite follower to its servile profession." In other words, Harry, the favorite of the ladies, was being *yielded* to the law when they allowed him to go to New York — as if this were to be his first experience of the profession; as if he had never before been fully engaged in its practice.[7]

Harry and his whole family knew of William Minot's reservations when it came to Harry's competence, and even his ethics, as a lawyer. Harry had persuaded Jane and Louisa that these notions were false. "You have certainly been much injured in this town," Jane commiserated with Harry. "No man's character was ever more reversed." But William Minot had to be more cautious in his response. After all, his sister's future and fortune were at stake. So when Jane reminded Harry, "I wish you to suc- ceed in New York chiefly because you will satisfy my nearest relations and be respected as a man willing to make exertions," he knew he had reason to pay attention.[8]

Jane and Harry both wanted to have William Minot's blessing, but it seems clear that they intended to proceed with or without it. In one area, though, William's consent was essential. Any disposition of Jane's property or the income from it would have been nearly impossible without his cooperation.

In the summer of 1816, after confessing to Jane his shameful thoughts regarding Abigail Phillips's great wealth, Harry had assured her "that nothing will ever induce me to accept any portion of a lady's fortune." While both Harry and Jane expected that the income produced by her property would be for *their* use, not for hers alone, he had every intention that the property itself would remain hers, to be protected for her against any claim that might be made by his future creditors, to support her in the event of his death or distress, and to be bequeathed according to her wishes after her death. This had been the customary treatment of property held in trust for women under English law, but the laws of several states (especially the more developed states, where commercial, entrepreneurial, and industrial economies were taking hold) increasingly favored the consolidation of property in the hands of husbands, to be passed on to their sons. In Massachusetts in 1817, to set Jane's property aside in trust required Harry's sworn approval as well as William's.[9]

Harry was ready to sign whatever he needed to sign to grant this approval, but he was uncomfortable bringing it up in a letter to William, Jane's legal guardian since their parents' deaths. Harry referred to these details simply as "the other subject," and put off their discussion until his return to Boston. He knew he still did not have William's entire trust. "The time will come," he vowed, "when he will know me better than he does now."[10]

Harry finally convinced Jane to set a date by a great outpouring of emotion in the letter he composed on Thursday evening, February 20, and Friday, February 21. In this letter he reminded her of many of their previous expressions of love — "Have you not told me that you loved? have you not *looked* your love? have I not *felt* the throbbing of your heart?" — and of the *"perpetual moment"* when he caught her loving glance while walking with her family on Boston Common. He also described the trance (the "mental enchainment") he sometimes experienced while writing to her and imagining her presence. "Our attachment is not the freak of a ballroom, or the infatuation of an hour," he assured her. "We know; we love each other." He urged her to offer him something more than mere hope. "Hope is sweet and delightful," he assured her, "but I would translate it to certainty."

With no new letters of hers to read, Harry was in the midst of rereading all Jane's earlier letters when Jane received this letter from him on Tuesday, February 25. She read it — "devoured" it, she acknowledged — in the privacy of her room. He would receive another letter from her before getting the one she began to write that night, but it is pleasing to contemplate Harry in New York, sighing over months of Jane's letters, at the very moment Jane sat down in Boston to write to him, "My dear Harry I will be all yours in June if at that time you think our union advisable. Why should I wish to delay the event — certainly I can never have anything to fear from you. . . . I believe I am yours beyond the power of recovering myself."[11]

Almost from the moment of their separation, Harry began casting about for opportunities to return to Boston to visit Jane. In one exchange, they laid out the arrangements for their next encounter in Boston. She reminded him to take care what he said to the maid who answered the door. "Tell Joanne when you *next ring at our door* to come up and tell me that *somebody* wants to speak with me in the entry," she instructed. "Charge her not to say who. I would not for the world embrace you before the family and I fear that I could not give you a formal shake of the hand — like when we first met after your return from Stockbridge last winter. There *should be a difference* should not there Harry? Even the most stiff and decorous would allow *that* and we don't pretend to rank among parchment people."

Harry had thought of the details of their next meeting "a thousand times." He agreed with her desire that their first reunion be conducted alone, out of sight of her family. "I could not well bear that any person should be present to give embarrassment and restraint to our meeting," he allowed. He had another plan, though. He knew that he would arrive late at night, so he would plan to call first thing in the morning. "I am sure that it will not be very embarrassing to you," he urged, "to make a little arrangement with Mrs. Minot (who will understand without forcing you to speak out broadly) and contrive to be alone." If they were not able to be alone, they were likely to be observed, "which would dash and disturb the luxury of the most delicious moment of life. I would enjoy the meeting embrace in all its highest and most exquisite delight," he assured her. "I am sure that you will feel as I do upon this subject."

The differences between the two plans were that Jane's called only for the complicity of a servant, while Harry's involved the cooperation of a family member, and that Jane's allowed for a hurried embrace in the entry hall, while Harry's would have made possible a more comfortable reunion in a parlor. The timing was important to Harry. He felt he could count on Louisa Minot's cooperation, but he wanted to arrive after William Minot had left for his office for the day. "I think your plan for our meeting is better than mine," Jane acknowledged. "How many a sweet thought is connected with that. . . . I have enjoyed its prospect almost daily for the last fortnight."

In early March, Harry began to think about making a spontaneous visit to Jane in Boston, and told some of his New York friends that he planned to do so. The thought of an imminent reunion with Jane filled him with "an animation which almost unfits me for connected thought." His friend and client Mr. Wilkins reacted with the amused wisdom of age to the passion in Harry's eyes. "D——n you Harry," the older man said, "you are happy now, you never will be so happy again. You think otherwise but you mistake. Human nature won't bear it. It would kill you to keep up this excitement. D——n it, I know as well as any man." When Harry returned to his office, he resumed writing a letter he had begun earlier. His pulse raced at the thought of seeing Jane. He recounted what Wilkins had said, and assured Jane that the older man's words would not apply to them. "The excitement may subside," he admitted, "but I trust in myself, in you, and in Heaven that confidence, friendship, affection, *love* never will."

"Good night my dearest Jane," Harry concluded with a sigh. "Oh! when we meet. But I will not anticipate. . . . My dear love do be alone." His thoughts were a jumble, filled with references to their earlier plans—what to tell the servants, when William would leave for the office, whether there would be a fire in the parlor fireplace. "I am not sure that I shall come, but—my brain is in a whirl—I can write no more——" At that he broke off—with no closing, no signature, almost an inch of blank space left on the third page of his sheet, and the fourth page completely blank except for the address. Illness, miserable weather, and Jane's trip to Quincy prevented Harry from ever making this visit, but the contemplation of it sustained him for weeks.[12]

Much of Harry and Robert's social activity in the winter and spring of 1817 revolved around the house where Robert boarded, which was owned by a Frenchman. Many of the boarders were French, and much of the conversation around the house was carried on in French. This constant opportunity to practice speaking French explained the lodging's appeal to a young man bent on self-improvement, as Robert Sedgwick was.[13]

In late January, Harry and Robert attended a ball at the boardinghouse. The guests included about eighteen French women, a half-dozen French men and boys, Robert and the other boarders, Harry, the host, and the host's two brothers. The host was another boarder, Benjamin Coles, a native New Yorker who, like Robert, was more a student than a speaker of French.

Benjamin Coles, Harry noted, was "a gentleman of talent and fortune who has seen through and become weary of the insipid fashionable society of the city, and wanted something more spirited, natural, and piquant." He certainly was acquainted with the fashionable society of the city. His father was a wealthy flour merchant, a director of the Bank of New York, and a member of the city's Board of Aldermen. Coles's first French ball was such a success that he decided to reconvene the "Assemblées Françaises" every two weeks for the rest of the season, and Harry and Robert made plans to attend. Within a month the attendance by both sexes, but especially by gentlemen, had increased considerably.

Harry came to consider Benjamin Coles a close friend, and as was so often the case with Harry, he became something of an enthusiast on the subject. He believed Coles was original, spirited, and decidedly *not* orthodox. Coles was in search of something—a search Harry Sedgwick could identify with. He was looking for a refined young woman of high social standing whom he could love; but, Harry lamented, "this city contains no lady whom he thinks suited to him."[14]

Harry and Jane knew a whole roomful of suitable ladies who gathered at the Joneses' house in Boston most Sunday evenings. One in particular stuck in Harry's mind. "I have been thinking," he wrote to Jane in March, "that if chance should bring him and M—— J together, they would just satisfy each other's taste, pride, and affection. I am determined that he shall see her." Harry urged Jane to "accidentally hint" to Margaret Jones that he had mentioned Coles as an interesting man. "Now I don't mean exactly a matchmaking scheme," he assured her, and he did not believe there was much chance for one to succeed. Still, the prospect of making two such good friends happy—the restless, sensitive Benjamin Coles and the high-spirited Margaret Jones—was tempting. Tempting, too, was the chance to secure for Jane "at least one person whom you will certainly like in New York." And in case Margaret was not interested, Harry urged Jane to share his account of Coles with the other friendlies. "Tell the *girls*," he warned, "that they must all guard their hearts against Mr. Coles. He has heard a great deal of the cultivation and attraction of the Boston ladies, and the chance is ten to one that some of them will get *his* heart." Attempting an appearance of candor, Harry wrote that the only negatives he knew about Coles were that he was "too diffident — and too susceptible," and that his health was frail, "though that perhaps will only render him the more interesting."

Since Harry had waived his preference for epistolary privacy, Jane read what he wrote about Coles to "the *girls*." (For a gentleman to use this term to refer to young ladies was a faux pas, but Harry insisted, "I have written it and won't scrape what I have written at the hazard of being deemed impertinent.") The Joneses were delighted to hear about Harry's friend. Jane was especially eager to tell Harry that his report had reached the ears it was most intended for. "M——t is particularly taken with the account of Mr. C. and will do her best to please him," she reported. "That I am sure is enough to satisfy any man."

Harry was surprised by the eagerness Benjamin Coles displayed when he dangled the image of Margaret Jones before his friend's eyes. "The imagination of this gentleman has become very highly excited upon a certain subject — I fear too highly," he told Jane with alarm just a few days later. "He asked me very seriously whether Miss ——— was of a respectable family and was evidently delighted with my answer." But Harry himself could not help but be excited by the prospect of bringing these two friends together.

Coles, who had a great fortune but evidently no profession, or at least not an especially rigorous one, thought about going to Boston alone in late March, armed with letters of introduction from Harry, to be introduced to the friendlies, and especially to the Joneses. Margaret Jones was "elated" at the thought of Coles coming, and considered him "particularly sent to her." Even after Coles dropped his plan of going to Boston alone, the idea of making an April visit with Harry remained under discussion. Margaret told Jane that since Harry would now come with Mr. Coles, there was "no occasion for any effort from her to overcome his diffidence," so she would leave him alone. Jane did not worry about this, for she knew Margaret too well. "If he is pleasing," she predicted, "I rather think her coolness will melt before him."

Harry began to reconsider the idea of an April visit when he realized that it would jeopardize his chance to go again to be married in June. Then two notes of reservation crept into his and Jane's letters about Benjamin Coles. First, Harry mentioned almost casually that Robert believed

Margaret would not like Coles, that he was "not handsome, though his face is one that soon becomes interesting." A few weeks later, Jane suggested that she and Harry might be trying to match Coles up with the wrong member of the friendlies. She wondered if Caroline Danforth would be a more appropriate match for Coles. What she really meant was that Caroline would be a more desirable friend for *her* in New York. "Although M. is the finest companion," Jane insisted, "C. is the most endearing friend. I can get many of the first in New York, but where can I find the last except you?" Their uncertain conclusion seemed to be that Coles was not good enough for Margaret, and Margaret was not good enough for Coles. With an April visit now out of the question, the introductions would have to wait until May, when Coles planned to accompany Harry to Boston for the wedding.[15]

The months of Jane's engagement had been unsettling for Margaret Jones. She was anticipating the loss of a close friend who, it seemed, understood her perfectly and loved her anyway. That friend was marrying a man with whom Margaret felt an easy spiritual and intellectual rapport—and for whom she felt a powerful attraction. Margaret had once been engaged. She acknowledged this in her first note of congratulations to Jane. "Oh Jane how fully I can sympathize with you," she had written. "I have once tasted, like you, the highest state of human felicity." But that engagement had not ended well; at least, that seemed to be the import of Jane's comments during Harry's stay in Boston on Margaret's mournfulness over a recent great loss. "May God avert, any further resemblance in our fates," Margaret had gone on to write.[16]

Harry considered Margaret a friend. Once in December he enclosed an unsealed letter for Margaret inside a letter to Jane. Robert, who had reason to be wary of any social irregularities involving the Jones sisters, told him he had done wrong to presume to write such a letter to one woman while engaged to another, and Jane had an idea that Margaret's family also disapproved. Harry told Jane to read the letter and feel free to destroy rather than deliver it if she thought it at all improper. But, after a few days, Jane sealed the letter and gave it to Margaret.

"Am I to read it now?" Margaret asked.

"Just as you please."

"Well," Margaret decided, "I think I had rather read it when you are gone and sometime I will call and show it to you." Jane did not expect to hear any more of it, but a few days later Margaret read the letter aloud to a group of the friendlies.[17]

The most alarming revelation about Margaret Champlin Jones in Jane's letters was that her older friend was in love—perhaps it should be phrased *still* in love—with Harry Sedgwick, and that she clearly believed he was in love with her. Until April, Jane did not say this in so many words, but in her most troubling nighttime thoughts the implications were clear.[18] Then, after an enjoyable spring evening at a Jones family party, during which Margaret was "everything lovely," Jane stayed up late into the night to finish a letter to Harry. Margaret had asked if she could call on Jane alone the next day. "I believe she has something particular to say," Jane wrote. As she closed her letter, she added a postscript. "I have just been led to think what I have often thought," she wrote, "that you and I would never have come together by ourselves. We are certainly fond of each other *now* and I don't doubt we shall be happy, but whatever may be our condition we shall owe it to others. We had not a natural taste for one another but we have acquired a very good one." Before Jane drifted off to sleep, she added, "Good night dear, I am certain that I love you *now*."

Harry reacted angrily to this passage even before he heard what Margaret had to say the next day. "I cannot divest myself of the imagination that these ideas, which I regret that you should have entertained for a moment, have some connection with Margaret Jones," he replied. "I am sure that she has no unfriendly intentions, but there are some subjects too sacred for any intermeddling." The idea that he and Jane "had not a natural taste for one another" was preposterous. "Had we known each other earlier as we do now we might have loved sooner," he admitted. "I am sure that I should."

Jane waited a week before writing an account of her private conversation with Margaret. In it, Jane learned that Margaret believed Harry truly loved *her*, and had become engaged to Jane almost by accident. "I have no doubt that she believes that the influence of some of your friends in some mysterious cause induced you to offer me your hand while your heart was and is in her possession," Jane wrote in bewilderment. (Margaret was probably referring to Catharine's long-stated preference for Jane as the best choice for her brother among the friendlies.) "Every sign of your regard gives an animation to her feelings," Jane warned Harry, "and she looks forward to your approach with rapture." She did not think Margaret had any "wrong design" or malicious intention—"or rather she has not any design perhaps." But Jane was sure her friend had underestimated her. "She thinks me of an easy happy cast of character," Jane believed, "possessed of those serene affections which are satisfied with general kindness without requiring any peculiarity of feeling."

The conversation was a turning point for Jane. She had been excusing and even exulting in her friend's passionate enthusiasm for years, but now she pulled back. By this point in their correspondence, Jane felt great confidence in Harry's love, and absolute certainty that Harry had no comparable feelings for Margaret. Her problem was not that Margaret threatened her love for Harry, or Harry's for her, but rather that Margaret did not *believe* in her love for Harry or Harry's for her. "However I may admire and esteem a woman of such opinions," the exasperated Jane said, "I could never take one for a bosom friend who should be deficient in such an essential source of sympathy. I cannot feel near to one who does not believe me capable of feeling and inspiring love."

"I did not dream of your being jealous of Margaret J.," was Harry's heated response when he finally received the letter. "I have never entertained an imagination that either of us could be jealous of the *present* sentiments of each other." Of course he had bestowed lavish attention on one of Jane's closest friends during the early days of their courtship and engagement; he had done so to please Jane, he insisted. "I afterwards regretted this," he admitted, "as I perceived it gave pain to some of your friends."[19]

Margaret's beliefs, and the state of her affections, would continue to occupy Jane's and Harry's attention during their final months of preparation for their wedding. But as much as the approaching wedding itself, the April conversation with Margaret began to separate Jane from her old friend, and made it easier for her to think about leaving.

Whenever the friendlies engaged in charitable work, Caroline Danforth took the lead. She would be the organizer of every such undertaking among the friendlies in the months of Harry's and Jane's engagement.

Jane and her friends understood that *charity* had a more particular meaning for the male heads of their families. A historian of this era has written that in Boston "the merchant prince's sense of social responsibility" was the guiding principle, and subscriptions to support various socially responsible causes were the outward signs of such responsibility. Jane was familiar with the details of such giving. She noted that among men of means, the fund-raising for what would become the Massachusetts General Hospital was the current preoccupation, and "How much did *he* give and *he* give?" had replaced "Where have you been?" and "What's the news?" as conversation-opening gambits. The donations for the hospital were so large that their friend John Coffin Jones, Margaret's father, "expressed his mortification that he could afford no more than $500." Of the $80,000 pledged at that point, $20,000 had come from William Phillips, the father of Abigail, whom Harry had courted unsuccessfully three years earlier. No one had subscribed for less than $50. In an age when an urban lawyer would be happy to earn $2,000 in a year and the average farmer or laborer might earn a few hundred, these numbers hint at the magnitude of the wealth concentrated in the hands of a few interrelated families in Boston.[20]

Women had been in control of the fund-raising for the Boston Female Asylum a little more than a decade earlier, and they would pour treasure as well as time and talent into the great humanitarian social reform movements of the antebellum decades. But in 1816 and 1817, as the fund-raising for the hospital was reaching its greatest intensity, women like Jane Minot and Caroline Danforth were isolated from the control of family wealth by law and convention.[21] What they had to share was their time. Caroline was the most assiduous of anyone Jane knew about sharing with the unfortunate. When Jane was out walking in early December, she reported, "who should I meet in a little dark entry but C. D. with her arms full of nice things for the sick. She blushed like Aurora." Caroline was taking these "nice things" to the sick schoolmistress of the church school at Old South Church, and she did not want her father to know. "She is one of those," Jane marveled, "who are good by stealth and blush to find its fame." Yet the example was powerful. Scarcely more than a week later, when Caroline was confined to bed with a cold, Jane kept school in the place of the sick schoolmistress, so the lessons — and the schoolmistress's income — would not be interrupted. And later that week Jane sat up all night with the schoolmistress in the single room that was her home, listening to the bells of Old South chime just outside. The schoolmistress was a widow who suffered from dropsy, and whose three small children all had whooping cough. "In this condition there is no human being upon whose assistance she has any claim," Jane lamented; but she and Caroline honored the unspoken claim.

Despite their efforts, the teacher died early in January, and left her children orphans, to be supported by the more organized charity of Boston's male elite. The plight of this poor woman occupied large portions of three of Jane's letters in December and January, and took up many hours of her and Caroline's time, but nowhere in the letters does Jane mention her name — first or last — or the names of any of her children.[22]

Jane's letters have less to say about Mary Ann Fales than about any of the other friendlies, because of her obvious preoccupation in the months of Harry's absence. Jane and Margaret had visited her on her sickbed on New Year's Eve. Jane apparently believed that Harry would understand what she meant when she said Mary Ann was "sick," because she did not give any hint of it until a week later when she wrote, "Mrs. Fales is well and has another daughter. You might have heard at New York the cheers the friendlies gave on this occasion," Jane told Harry, "not for the little wretch who is come to torment us, but for her dear mother."

The cheering implies (though Jane would never be so indelicate as to say so in a letter, especially one to a gentleman) that the friendlies were together on the occasion of this birth. This was the age of the medicalization of childbirth, with physicians attending deliveries and, at least according to one scholar, with the crowd of female friends and relatives who would have accompanied a midwife in earlier times staying away from the birth chamber. This would seem most likely to be the case among wealthy women in a big city like Boston, with a powerful and fairly sophisticated medical establishment. But Dr. Walter Channing (younger brother of Harry's friend Mary Channing and Unitarian clergyman William Ellery Channing) was Boston's most successful young obstetrician ("male midwife"), and he did not discourage the attendance of his patients' female friends. Whether the friendlies were present for the actual birth of Mary Ann's daughter or not, to some extent they all shared in their friend's experience of childbirth and motherhood. But this experience also separated Mary Ann from them, not least by the sheer physical demands on her body. All the friendlies were aware, as any of their peers would have been, that childbirth was still a perilous event.[23]

Motherhood placed singular demands on Mary Ann Fales's time, and the time of other women of her age, as well as on their bodies. Over the preceding two centuries motherhood had gone from being one of many female responsibilities to becoming the defining responsibility of married women's lives, particularly in the upper classes. Child rearing had gone from a joint parental responsibility, under the direction of the father as patriarchal head of the family, to an almost exclusively maternal responsibility. (Nursing her own child would be one of Mary Ann's additional responsibilities, and another demand on her time, during this period. A few months after this, Louisa Minot would report feeling frustration and pain at sending her infant son to a wet nurse when her milk dried up two months after his birth.) Mary Ann Fales and Louisa Minot had personal knowledge of the responsibilities of motherhood, and the rest of the friendlies did not. To them, the child was just "the little wretch who is come to torment us" — a phrase surely intended in jest, but no less revealing for that.[24]

Mary Ann Fales reentered society six weeks to the day after delivering her child, as Louisa Minot would three months later. There seems to have been some unspoken but well-understood rule about the exact duration of a new mother's confinement from society, for in both cases Jane anticipated the exact end of the hiatus.

Jane's letters are again inconclusive on the subject of her presence during another delivery, that of her nephew, William Minot II, late on the night of April 7. Jane had been in Quincy, staying at the country home of her cousin Mary Speakman, until Saturday, April 5, and she informed Harry that she would have stayed another week but that she had to return to Boston "to attend to some affairs."[25]

Jane had been evasive on the nature of those "affairs" since the beginning of her separation from Harry. Louisa had been no more than four months pregnant when Harry left Boston, but many of Jane's later letters imply that he was aware of her condition. "Until June there cannot be a wedding in this house," she had written in her third letter, after he had begun to press her about setting a date. Harry's unthinking immediate response had been to dismiss this as "some womanish nonsense . . . which manly reason will remove."

If Jane did reveal Louisa's condition to Harry, in person or in one of several letters that do not survive, she must have done so indirectly or euphemistically, to judge by all later references. No forms of the words *pregnant, birth,* or *delivery* (in this meaning) occur in the letters. "Mrs. Minot will be upstairs" in April, Jane informed Harry in late January, when they were discussing their wedding plans. In March they both referred to Mrs. Minot's "health," and Jane later mentioned "my sister's sickness" as the reason for her early return from Quincy. Harry understood that Mrs. Minot's ability to attend was one of the most important factors affecting the scheduling of their wedding, but when he asked Jane for more information on that subject, she informed him, "I cannot tell with exactness until she is sick."

Louisa clearly counted on Jane's presence, if not during the delivery then in the hours and days thereafter. When notified of the birth, Harry from his distance expressed "fervent gratitude" that Louisa's "season of endurance is past, and that life and health have been preserved to a woman of an understanding so elevated, and a heart so true," but he expressed little interest in the child. "I suppose that in two years I shall care something about her—not before," he admitted, and he certainly underscored this point by getting the child's gender wrong.[26]

When young William was three days old, Jane got a fright that must have again reinforced her sense of the experiential chasm that had opened between her and mothers like Mary Ann and Louisa. "I came near killing the poor thing night before last," she admitted to Harry. "I was holding it in my arms while the nurse assisted its mother in rising from the bed when without the least warning I suddenly fell lifeless on the floor." To those around her, and to Jane herself when she came to her senses, "it seemed a matter of course" that the fall must have killed the child. "You may think this occasioned some commotion," she acknowledged to Harry. But the story had a happy ending: "Chance took better care of it than I did, it fell so comfortably upon my arm that it did not even awake until the nurse hastily caught it up."

Two days later, Jane had recovered fully. "It was the silliest freak I ever took into my head," she reflected. "I thought I had outgrown all such ridiculous propensities." But for Jane at twenty-two, a few short months before her scheduled wedding would initiate her into the ranks of prospective mothers, and just after having witnessed two beloved friends give birth, that faint, and her awakening from it unharmed, seemed to signify, and then perhaps begin to resolve, a powerful ambivalence.[27]

Jane's life in Boston in the spring of 1817 was filled with such incidents—events that helped her dramatize her consciousness of the magnitude of the impending change in her life. Another came less than a week after she had fainted and just days after her unpleasant conversation with Margaret Jones.

After the death of the church schoolmistress in January, Jane and Caroline had continued their support of the church school. Jane's appointed day to volunteer her assistance was Wednesday. The new schoolmistress, "Ma'am Green," asked Jane to read a chapter from the Bible aloud to the class. This was something new, she thought. She read chapter 18 from the Gospel according to Matthew, in which Jesus answers the disciples' question, "Who is the greatest in the kingdom of heaven?" As soon as she had finished, she reported to Harry, "about a dozen children ran up to me and all began repeating a line or part of a line of what I had read." Her first thought was that they did this to prove that they had been paying attention. They called out phrases or entire verses. She recalled hearing one child say "kingdom of heaven." Another just said "cast into hell fire." She heard, "There was a little child in heaven." A little one-legged girl on crutches made the most lasting impression on Jane, repeating, "it is better to enter into heaven lame and blind than having legs and eyes to be cast into hell." The whole demonstration, with faces crowding around her and voices clamoring for her attention, startled Jane.

Then Ma'am Green and all the children knelt and prayed. "After noticing the children's wants, she prayed for me," Jane reported. "She particularly noticed the connection I was going to form and begged that it might add to my happiness." Tears rolled down the old woman's cheeks, and she had difficulty getting out the words. Jane was surprised that the schoolmistress was even aware of her personal plans. "I was certainly pleased at this unexpected interest which she manifested," Jane admitted to Harry. "However humble the source of these tears they must have been sincere."[28]

Despite the unpleasant moments with Margaret Jones, Jane's attachment to her friends and her family was a powerful bond holding her to Boston, and to singleness. Harry was intensely aware of this. "For me you have consented to forego all, and more than almost any other had it in her power to relinquish — family, friends, home — all for me." He wondered how he would ever make up the difference when he took her away to the strange and inhospitable world of New York. "I wish you had not such friends — I almost wish you were not so good yourself," he acknowledged. "I should feel less the weight of my duties, and my inadequacy to their discharge." How could he take the place of Mrs. Minot? Of the hospitable Mrs. Fales? Of all the Joneses, mother and daughters? Of the cool and estimable Caroline Danforth? All he could do was promise — and hope. "Trust me I am grateful," he assured Jane. "By the blessing of heaven I will repay you."[29]

Still, once Louisa Minot had given birth to young William and begun to recover from the delivery, it was fairly easy to anticipate the earliest possible date she would be able to welcome guests to her sister-in-law's wedding. Just ten days after the delivery, she would have been well enough to receive visitors from outside the family, but for what Jane called "nurse's rules." (Those rules did not prevent workers from coming into the house

to paint and paper the two parlors.) Louisa came downstairs to have dinner with the family again for the first time on April 27, "but she will not
remain below before a fortnight," Jane reminded Harry. Jane believed she
could take care of all the preliminary details and planning in three weeks.
Making all the preparations for a wedding in just three weeks is not as
outlandish as it might sound to people accustomed to the scheduling
demands of the modern wedding industry. In fact, two weeks of advance
notice and intense planning were more typical during this period. A more
pressing factor, Jane noted, was that "Mrs. M. will not probably be perfectly strong and able to bear a bustle before the first of June."[30]

Harry objected strenuously to waiting much longer than that, and was
distressed to learn that Jane was thinking about the middle of June. "Surely
there is no reason to doubt that Mrs. Minot's health will be reestablished
long, long before that time," he insisted. "What else can there be any occasion to wait for?" But Jane kept casting about for such occasions. "My
soul! How near it is," she marveled. "I declare it's like being on the edge of
Niagara, but I don't much think I shall fall against my inclination." Unable
to restrain herself, she concluded, "Oh Harry I do love you *now* with my
whole soul, whether that can turn or not you will try."

When the discussion of an exact date narrowed to a few weeks, the
Sedgwick family weighed in again. Jane stuck to her insistence that she
and Harry would make up their own minds, for their own reasons. "I shall
pay my brother and sister the compliment of consulting them as to the
time," she insisted, making it clear that the consultation would be nothing
more than a compliment. She hoped Harry would do the same with the
insistent members of his family.

With the appointed month approaching, Harry's arguments for stick-
ing to the date, or advancing it, became relentless. "Believe me my love,"
he concluded his frontal assault on all Jane's actual and potential arguments for delay, "I am not insensible of what you relinquish, of the great-
ness of the change, of the irresolution, the anxious throbbing sensations,
and the thousand conflicting emotions which you must experience." Still,
he went on almost jovially, "the time must come, and there can be no
use in delaying it. It is something like having a tooth out. The pain will
only increase by delay." When Jane received this letter, she expressed a
combination of exasperation and amusement at the way Harry had first
acknowledged her "anxious throbbing sensation" and then reduced it to
a mere toothache. "Why how you hurry me dear," she complained. "Pray
consider that we shall soon be together for life."[31]

The friendlies dreaded Jane's departure, and Harry understood why.

"Such a rare association — a circle so charmed and charming, as that to which we have been so much accustomed," he told her, "it is not probable that we shall again find." By spring he was at least hopeful that she would find *some* friends in New York. Certainly they would also be able to visit Boston every year or so. "Though the chain may be relaxed," he assured her early in their separation, "it will not be broken."

In May, he added with new confidence, "Besides, I feel now that we shall find all that we want in each other." He was ready to be husband, lover, and friend. He would not be locked away in his office through the evening hours, as he was during these months. "Those hours," he promised, "I should consider sacred to love and domestic happiness."[32]

Before they could begin that life of togetherness, though, one major requirement occupied Harry's attention: They needed a place to live.

Harry Sedgwick and Jane Minot discussed the meaning of *home* and the difficulty of moving. Jane had set the tone at Christmas, when she pondered the possibility that she would never again spend that day with her brother and his family, in the city of her birth, "where my parents and relations have so often met in happiness on that day." This thought had occurred to Jane in King's Chapel, as she was taking communion, "and it almost unfitted me for the situation," she admitted to Harry. "If ever the silent petitions of my heart ascended to heaven they did at that moment when the remembrance of my parents who had so often knelt at this altar, my love for you, my surrounding relations, every thought that could excite and solemnize my nature filled my soul and it could only find relief in addressing omnipotence."

Harry recognized that, in the world of 1817, a move like the one Jane would be making was a more formidable undertaking for a woman than for a man. "It is indeed a great thing to leave the place of our ancestors, and which contains all of them that belongs to earth — home — relatives — and dear friends — and to transplant ourselves violently torn from the soil of nature and natural affection to an untried and foreign land," he wrote. "For a *woman* to do it — a woman surrounded as you are with almost everything that can make life desirable — with such a home and such friends — and with no greater inducement than I can offer — seems to me quite wonderful."[33]

Both Jane and Harry were concerned about the cost of living comfortably in New York, so Harry shared with Jane whatever intelligence he could gather on that topic. He learned that the most expensive places to live were in the center of town. Back in Boston Jane noticed, whenever friends or acquaintances asked her if Harry had looked up this or that person in New York, that people of moderate means lived all over the city, often far from the center and from each other. "We shall find our pedestrian powers of more use than ever in that case," Jane noted.[34]

Finding a home proved to be a challenge. Moving day in New York — the day when most annual rental agreements for houses, lodgings, and boarding houses went into effect — was May 1, and most of the arrangements for each year's moves were made in the first week of February. Harry would have rented a house, but in early February Jane was still urging postponement of their wedding until at least the end of the summer. Most of the best and most affordable properties were taken in the first few days of February. "Rents are extravagant," Harry had warned Jane, while their own need for housing was still hypothetical.[35]

By the time Jane had finally agreed to a June wedding, she and Harry were justifiably anxious about their prospects. He couldn't bring her to the boardinghouse on Pearl Street. Boardinghouses were the province of a young, transient, overwhelmingly male population, and there was something vaguely shameful about a young couple from respectable families living in one. Besides, the great advantage the Pearl Street location had offered when Harry was a single professional newly arrived in the city — its close proximity to his office and to the center of mercantile activity on Wall Street — would be a disadvantage when he brought his wife and they attempted to find a place in the city's society. The trend for such families in the early decades of the nineteenth century was to move north to newly developed neighborhoods, often built on landfill near the eastern or western edge of the city. Elite and middle-class workplaces and homes were undergoing a physical and spatial separation that was also mirrored in attitudes as they became gendered "separate sheres," independently and exclusively presided over by men and women, respectively.[36]

April came, and the citywide moving day was less than a month away, but Harry still had found no house. Expecting an imminent visit from Catharine, he decided to wait and rely on his sister to speak for Jane's tastes, requirements, and preferences. But Catharine was late getting to New York, Harry was intensely busy with a rush of clients and cases in April, and there was "uncommon demand" for housing in the bustling New York market of the spring of 1817.

About this time, Theodore Sedgwick heard a rumor concerning his younger brother's intention to sell some of the family's holdings of canal company stock in order to pay for a house and some furniture. Theodore's opposition was quick and decisive. The income from the stock was needed to support Catharine. Much of the property their father had left to her in his will had been lent to their brother-in-law Ebenezer Watson before the Judge died, and was now feared unrecoverable. Theodore disliked selling the stock. "I have unlimited confidence in your honor," he assured Harry, but "Kate is a woman and without anything more than a slender property. You I consider well provided for in your new condition." He had an answer to Harry's seemingly intractable problem: Go, get married, and "go to lodgings as I did for a year." It was commendable of Harry to want to get a house for his new wife, but unnecessary. "She loves you," Theodore reminded his brother. "That's enough. She will be happy with you anywhere. Don't ask the Minots or the Sedgwicks for opinions. Act from yourself."[37] Theodore's advice—and Catharine's, delivered in person when she finally arrived from Albany on Sunday, April 13, carrying Theodore's impassioned letter—convinced Harry of the wisdom of moving into lodgings.

The term *lodgings* referred to a cross between a boardinghouse and what we would call an apartment house. Lodgings were expected to have partly or fully furnished rooms or apartments, with private living quarters but shared parlors, and with shared meals served by the landlord (or more commonly, landlady) in a common dining room. Harry was sure they would be able to find good lodgings—safe, comfortable, and affordable. But before presenting the decision to Jane, he admitted to feeling "half crazy from anxiety and irresolution." Still, circumstances and the housing market had tied their hands. "At the present time," Harry cautioned, "it is literally impossible to obtain a house that would be respectable."

Harry's biggest concern was that Jane's brother would be disappointed. Jane herself claimed not to be bothered in the least. She said she preferred the opportunity to go into lodgings. That way, she could get to know "the mores and customs of the place," and have the leisure to make her own satisfactory arrangements the following year. When she reported that even her brother agreed with the soundness of the decision, Harry was mightily relieved. "I now discard the little that remained of the idea that he is prejudiced and unreasonable upon some occasions," he assured her. Jane had been contemplating the purchase of furniture; now all she planned to bring with her were some linens, some teaspoons, and her "drawing implements." (Of the last, she wrote, "I think they will be a great source of amusement to me at lodgings.") Harry bought some more silverware, a mirror, and some decanters at an auction he attended with Catharine.

Slowly, they began to assemble their household goods. Touching each physical object — each piece of fine silver, or glass, or pewter — or looking at his own reflection in the new mirror, Harry could begin to feel and to see the reality of the change that was about to take place in his life, the change he had so long imagined and desired.[38]

With the help of the visiting Catharine, Harry finally decided on suitable lodgings in May, a week before his scheduled departure for Boston. They settled on a place on Greenwich Street, far from his office but (as he told Jane) close to "those who will be your friends." He considered the house and the location healthy and delightful, noting that it "very much resembles your brother's in its vicinity to and view of the water." (It stood on relatively newly filled land along the Hudson.) There were two other lodgers. The owner, Mrs. Strong, prided herself on taking "only the best of people," and had turned away many applicants. Harry described the appointments to Jane. "There is a charming parlor which we can take in the winter, and in the summer, as Mrs. Strong said, we can 'always have it without taking it' — for her family consists only of her husband and herself and two small children who live chiefly in the back room, and she knows that the *young people* will always like to be by themselves." One chamber was reserved for the lodgers' occasional out-of-town guests, and they were allowed to have visitors in the evening and "one or two to dine." While meals were provided, they were responsible for their own wine, candles, fuel, and other consumables. They would have to be in by eleven o'clock every evening. "I suppose we shall have no difficulty about that," smiled Harry, apparently well reconciled to changing his late-night work habits. Now the life they had so long imagined — coming home from the office, reading to each other, calling to each other, pressing each other in their arms — had a setting outside their imaginations.

With lodgings arranged, his business temporarily caught up, and a few essential household goods in his possession, Harry was ready for the last task that awaited him: the return to Boston. In Boston, Jane contemplated all that return would mean for them both. "June is very near," she wrote at the end of April. "Does it not almost frighten you dear? It does me, for all that I have considered and reconsidered all its possible occurrences for so many months with perfect calmness." Now that the events that had fired her imagination were actually approaching, they had "the effect of perfect novelty," she marveled. She frequently asked herself, "Is it possible that I am going off with Harry Sedgwick to a strange place, leaving every friend and scene with which I have been familiar, going too by my own voluntary act?"

Both Jane and Harry gave evidence of that slight, self-conscious feeling of imbalance that so often agitates us when we anticipate great changes in our lives, for good or ill. The world looks different. We read over the same paragraphs again and again, and go back to redo the tasks we just finished doing. Things we have barely noticed throughout most of our lives suddenly seem almost impossibly real, as we count off events that are "lasts of their kind" or "lasts until" ——

But let them tell it: On the first Saturday of May, Jane received a letter Harry had written the previous Wednesday. Amid some details of his business, travel and wedding plans, and more reaction to Margaret Jones's strange behavior, Harry had written of the thrill his soul felt at the thought that their reunion would be soon, and forever. Sarah Miller, a young cousin (a "lively little girl"), was with Jane as she read this letter, and found it remarkable that her cousin should be so noticeably pleased "just for the sake of a letter." Jane did not bother to describe her feelings to Harry; she let him infer them from her cousin's response. "Now do only read it to me cousin Jane," Sarah had urged, "because I wish to know when you are to be married. After all," Jane's cousin went on, "I think it is because you are soon to have a wedding that you are so pleased."

Two days later in New York, the world looked so new and strange to Harry that he got lost on his way home from the Wilkinses' house, the scene of his most frequent social calls and visits in his entire stay in New York. He recalled that he had gotten similarly lost in Boston the previous July, on the night Jane had accepted his proposal. "I am good for little or nothing here," he proclaimed. It was time to get out of New York and get on with his life.[39]

To both Jane and Harry, the months of letter-writing had made real what they hoped a legal ceremony in Boston would soon make official. "I would sooner embrace a life of misery than renounce the pledges I have given you of love," Jane had written from Quincy, where by the light of the moon the emotions in her heart seem to have risen to flood tide. "I consider myself your wife, I have received from you what no woman ought to receive who did not view herself as irrevocably betrothed. I should consider our separation as a divorce which if my conduct occasioned I should not dare to look to heaven for mercy." Gazing up idly at the sky, the moon, and the stars, she could not think of her physical separation from Harry without weeping.

"Both of us have hearts to which love is necessary," Harry wrote a few short weeks later. "Every evening I think of the calm but exquisite delight I should take in going *home* and seeing you there — hearing you welcome your *dear* Harry — talking — reading — moralizing with you — clasping you to my heart, and calling you my wife. The evening so spent would be worth more — a thousand times more — than all I have enjoyed since I left you." At the end of that month he was even more emphatic. "My whole soul thrills," he proclaimed in the letter Jane would read in the presence of her young cousin, "when I realize the idea that I am so soon to be with you — and for ever — to clasp you to my heart as the dearest and most precious blessing which heaven has given or could give to me. . . . My dearest love I am your husband — you are my wife. Volumes could say no more."

"Now that our separation is so near its close," Jane wrote in one of her last letters, "tell me dear if you do not think it has increased the strength of our ties, and do you regret it?" Harry's reply was unambiguous: "With all my heart I know that we never should have loved each other *quite* so well had it not been for absence."[40]

Both of them, though, had been aware of this transformation long before April turned into May and their promised reunion appeared on the horizon. As early as February, Harry had stated, "I *could* not lose you. I believe that you are more necessary to me — that I think of you more — and love you better than if I had remained in Boston." Everything Jane wrote conveyed her agreement that "absence *does* strengthen attachment." Both of them were on their way to expressing a remarkable truth: their separation, and the correspondence it had inspired, had intensified and purified their love, had brought them to the point where they could already call each other *husband* and *wife*.

They were certain, too, that they would continue to be the people they had become for each other in exchanging those letters. "Whatever other calamities may hereafter befall us," Harry asserted as he prepared to return to Boston, "I feel a delightful confidence that the harmony of our personal union will be as undisturbed as has been that of our epistolary intercourse." For her part, when Jane had learned in the depths of winter that Harry was rereading all her letters, his impulse had struck a chord in her heart. "Your letters have drawn me nearer to you than ever your presence could have done without them," she wrote, her tears flowing as she sensed "my inability to suppress anything from you." Calling him "My love, my best friend, my future husband," she insisted, "I shall always have cause to love you as I do now."[41]

In her last April letter, Jane had told Harry to come to Boston in mid-May. They had not yet chosen a wedding date, but she assured him she would tell him then. Harry knew that his business would keep him in New York no later than Saturday, May 17, and he thought he might be able to get out of town as early as Monday, May 12. In fact, he did finish his business in court that Monday, and made arrangements to depart by steamboat on Wednesday, May 14.

Harry's plan was to take the steamer *Connecticut* as far as New Haven, and then join Benjamin Coles and ride the rest of the way in Coles's gig. (For Coles, a young man and a city-dweller, owning even this small horse-drawn carriage was a sign of his family's great wealth.) Coles left New York on Monday morning, expecting to be in New Haven in plenty of time to visit with friends, refresh his horses, and meet the steamer when it arrived on Thursday morning. If Harry had chosen to stay on the steamboat all the way to New London, he would have been able to reach Boston Friday night. Bringing his friend along, however, would postpone his arrival until Saturday afternoon, May 17, and would make it impossible for him to travel with his sister Catharine. This made him almost sorry he had agreed to go with Coles. "When I did promise," he admitted to Jane, "I did not know how impatient I should be."

In Boston, Jane was immersed in plans for the wedding. They had finally settled on a date: Monday, June 2. Harry hoped that her church would not require that weddings take place in the sanctuary, for he knew she wanted him to dress smartly, and he believed that full dress was "ridiculous" in church. She was pleased to inform him that "you may have all the gratifi-cations which full dress can afford you," as she had no plans for a church wedding. "I own dear," she confessed, "that I like to see you look well to other people." She claimed (quite likely as a joke) to have no intention to indulge in such elegance herself. "I hear it is the height of vulgarity for a bride to be splendidly dressed at her own wedding," she wrote. "You must therefore be content and receive me in a muslin gown." He did not send her a list of people he hoped could be invited until May 12, which meant it probably reached her just a day or two before *he* was scheduled to do so. The list was short, including besides immediate family members and Mr. Coles only eight or ten people.[42]

Jane was determined that as many Sedgwicks as possible should come to Boston for the wedding, insisting that without at least Robert, Catharine,

Charles, and Susan, "I should not consider the ceremony as binding." Harry was at first skeptical of Theodore and Susan's attendance: "let me tell you once for all," he cautioned Jane, "that there never can be any absolute reliance placed on Theodore in any case where energy is required." When Theodore wrote that their attendance was doubtful, Harry advised her, "I never knew anything that was not doubtful with him." Catharine was expected to join some of the friendlies as a bridesmaid, but for a while her attendance also appeared doubtful. She had been seriously sick during the winter, and the long journey would be much more difficult than steaming down the Hudson to New York had been in April. Jane told Harry flatly that she would prefer to delay the wedding for three months rather than go forward without Catharine.

Finally Harry received the good news from Albany that Theodore and Susan would come down the river in time to travel to Boston by the New London steamer. This guaranteed not only their attendance but also Catharine's. (Harry had feared that the overland route might have been so daunting as to discourage her attempting it.) He was impressed by Theodore's display of exertion — "It would have been a less effort for Robert to have gone to Cape Horn," he believed. But he was also troubled. Theodore had somehow gotten the impression that the wedding was to take place on June 6, not June 2, and had made plans to depart from Albany some time after May 26. Harry was not sure his older brother could now be hurried to make the necessary adjustment in his departure date. "Theodore you will know is no starter," he told Jane. Apparently he had forgotten that a wedding was all it took to make Theodore a hero.[43]

"I don't believe that I shall write you much more," Harry informed Jane as early as April 24. "Writing does not answer the purpose at all. I feel a painful sense of inadequacy to express what I feel——" Thus had he abruptly ended his forty-fifth letter to Jane, but in the three more weeks that passed until he boarded the *Connecticut*, he would write six more. The same restlessness and dissatisfaction with the epistolary form surfaced in several of them, but he could not bear *not* to write to Jane, or to receive her letters. His disappointment was keen when William Fales passed through New York and he discovered that Jane had not given him a letter. He urged her to send a letter to him at the New Haven post office, marking it "to remain in the Post Office till called for," so he could collect it when he made his rendezvous with Coles and "solace myself with it on

my journey more than ever a miser did with his well-concealed hoard."
(He even knew the latest possible hour she could send such a letter from
Boston for it to reach New Haven in time.) For his part, he intended to
send her letters along the way from Hartford and Worcester. Yet as he
thought about writing his last letter in this exchange, he began to worry
that "writing is now too feeble and tame a mode of giving expression to
the feelings."[44]

A week before his planned departure, Harry pressed Coles for an accurate prediction of their arrival time in Boston, so Jane "might arrange the
manner of our meeting"; but such a prediction was impossible. If they got
to Boston "at an inconvenient hour" (which apparently meant one that
found William Minot at home), he assured Jane that he would call and
leave a card with one of the trusted servants — Joanne, or Roxy, or Mrs.
Wood — informing her when he would return. "We must not meet before
the family dear," he entreated, yet he knew that Louisa and the children
could be relied on to make themselves scarce for a while. The most likely
arrival time, early in the evening, would be awkward, because William
was sure to be home. But Harry knew he would never be able to sleep in
Boston without seeing Jane, no matter how late he arrived. "Only think,"
he sighed as he went over all these plans, "*next* week I shall be in Boston.
Does not your heart beat a little?"[45]

He kept counting in his next two letters. "Do you know dear," he asked
on Friday, May 9, "how near time has brought us to each other?" As if to
reassure himself of the reality, he announced the tally. "I have only five
more days to stay here," he reported. "In eight days I shall see you." As
he numbered his letter of May 12, he marveled, "Half a hundred letters,
and here they will terminate for the present." Dismissing with barely a
mention his sister Catharine's "superstitious fear" that he and Jane would
never be married, he observed, "This closing the epistolary intercourse,
on my part at least, seems a sort of epoch in our history."

But the epoch was not yet closed. On Wednesday evening, Harry
boarded the *Connecticut*, found a seat at "an inconvenient corner" of a
table, and sat down — to write a letter to Jane. A light rain was falling. "I
have no light or scarcely any to write by," he grumbled. "I thought however that you would like to hear for certain that I am on my way to meet
you." The echo of the crowded barroom at the New London ferry landing
where he had written his first letter at the start of their separation must
have given him a sense of having traveled full circle. Perhaps he thought
of what he had written to Jane on that night, seven months earlier. "If . . .
I shall ever come to anything good," he had promised, "you may consider

yourself as the creator of a new character." Was he returning to her as such a new character? Had their months of correspondence instructed him, or uplifted him, or made him worthy of her?[46]

He gave the letter to an unnamed gentleman on the boat, who promised to deliver it on Friday evening. He closed it with these words:

> Consider me as speaking when you read this— *Tomorrow* we shall meet. I can think of nothing but you, but my heart is too full to write more— God bless you

Epilogue
Volumes Could Say No More

*H*arry's letter to Jane, written on the steamboat on the evening of May 14, 1817, marked the end of their epistolary exchange. What happened next? What was their eventual reunion like? Did they, with the help of Louisa Minot and the servants, find a few minutes or even hours of privacy? How can we ever find out? There are no letters to tell us: unanswerable questions, unknowable moments.

The documentary record does show that Harry Sedgwick and Benjamin Coles arrived in Boston as planned. The exact time of their arrival, the introductions to the friendlies, their reaction to Coles and his to them go unrecorded. We do have strong indication, though, that Margaret Jones was successful in overcoming Coles's famous diffidence.

Reader, she married him.

Margaret Champlin Jones and Benjamin Underhill Coles were married in Boston less than four months after Jane and Harry, and Margaret relocated to New York with her new husband. She was widowed sometime before 1829.[1]

The documentary record also shows that on May 29, 1817, Harry and Jane appeared before a Suffolk County justice of the peace. Jane's brother William and Harry's brother Theodore joined them. They all signed an indenture guaranteeing Jane's right to control her own property, regardless of any debts or obligations Harry might incur, and regardless of "any condition of coverture," and placing that property under William's trusteeship.

Documents record that the wedding ceremony took place on the evening of June 2, 1817, in William and Louisa Minot's Charles Street home.

Dr. James Freeman of King's Chapel, an old family friend, officiated. Margaret Jones, Caroline Danforth, and Catharine Sedgwick were among the bridesmaids. Theodore, his wife Susan, and brother Robert were in attendance as well. Louisa Minot was delighted with Jane's new in-laws, and especially with Susan Ridley Sedgwick, her exact contemporary. But there is virtually nothing in the records to show how Harry and Jane felt on that day, or in the weeks leading up to that day.[2]

One tantalizing hint of Harry and Jane's emotions on their wedding day can be found. In one of the two surviving letters Margaret Jones wrote to Jane Minot Sedgwick during the summer of 1817 — letters in which she pointedly did *not* announce her own engagement to Mr. Coles — the woman who was soon to be married asked the recent bride, "how came you Jane, so soon to be familiarized to the word *Husband*? I half-suspect you must have conned it over, and got it well by heart, ere you legally had a right to use it."

Jane and Harry were married on the evening of June 2, and left Boston early the next day. Almost the only chance Margaret would have had to witness Jane addressing Harry as *Husband* with such easy familiarity would have been at the wedding ceremony itself, or at the ensuing party.[3]

Of course Margaret was right. Jane had used the term *husband* in her thoughts and in her letters for months. "I know that mother, brother, friend, every endearing relation is comprehended in the word husband and that you will be all that to me," she told Harry in February. "I consider myself your wife," she wrote a month later. "I have received from you what no woman ought to receive who did not view herself as irrevocably betrothed." And Harry had echoed it. "My dearest love," he wrote in late April, "I am your husband. You are my wife. Volumes could say no more."[4]

The three youngest Sedgwicks — Robert, Catharine, and Charles — remained unmarried after Harry and Jane were wed in 1817. Charles was married first, in 1819, to Elizabeth Buckminster Dwight, the daughter of his mother's cousin. Robert appeared delighted by the match, writing to Catharine, "Oh what a glorious thing it is to have a heart as young and pure as Charles' and to love fully, freely, undoubtingly, without an apprehension — and such a girl — and to be beloved."[5]

Catharine had numerous suitors. She even accepted, with great ambivalence, a proposal of marriage from the poet William Cullen Bryant, a family friend, during the summer of 1818. But she broke off the engagement the following winter.[6] Virtually the only man outside her family whose physical attractiveness ever drew a comment from her was the poet Fitz-Greene Halleck, whom she met at a ball in New York in 1825. Impressed by his fiery red hair and confident manner, she told her brother Charles that "he dances with grace and talks freely without parade." But Halleck appears to have lived much of his adult life in a committed domestic relationship with another man.[7]

Why did Catharine, attractive, educated, and suitably wealthy, not marry? The experiences of her mother, her older sisters, and even her reviled stepmother provided cautionary tales of married life. "The first tragedy" of her young life was Eliza's 1797 wedding, when "some cruel usurper" snatched away the "mother-sister" who had cared for her. She had sobbed uncontrollably at the wedding ceremony. The groom tried to comfort the seven-year-old. "Your sister may stay with you this summer," he offered. A half century later she still bristled at his comment. "*May!* How my whole being revolted at the word. He had the power to bind or loose my sister!" From that time forward, and for the rest of her life, Catharine carried with her "the impression that a wedding is rather a sundering than a forming of ties." When she considered the outcomes of those "days of sadness," though — the addition of sisters-in-law, nieces, and nephews to her family — she recognized that "by some of them, I have gained treasures that no earthly balance or calculation can weigh or estimate."[8]

Frances's bitter experience with Ebenezer Watson deepened Catharine's doubts about marriage. Shortly before that wedding, Theodore Sedgwick had written to the eleven-year-old Catharine. "Are you willing," the father asked the daughter, "that your sister should leave us and go all the way to New York, and live with a man we hardly know anything about? Are not these girls very strange beings all at once to leave their fathers and mothers, and brothers and sisters, to go and live with a strange man, who possibly will be very cross and abuse them?" He cautioned Catharine, "I hope it will be a good while before you will find a strange man to run off with."[9] Surely the eventual fulfillment of Theodore's unintentional prophecy reinforced Catharine's reservations.

Catharine believed that she could never find a husband whose love would be as complete, or mean as much to her, as the love of her brothers, and especially of Robert, the closest to her in age and the one who had pledged to be her protector after the death of their father. "*Brother* is the most comprehensive word in my vocabulary," she acknowledged to Robert when she was still just twenty-one. "The definition of it with the *various readings* occupy at least a dozen folio pages in the volume of my heart." Robert was equally devoted to Catharine. "As to yourself my dear," he told her, "I am convinced there is nobody in the world half good enough for you. You can never be married without my consent, and that shall never be given to anyone who has not something better to give you than a brother's heart can be."[10]

With Charles married, only Robert and Catharine remained single. Catharine didn't mind. "If worst comes to *worst* dearest Robert," she had stated the winter before Charles's marriage, "you and I will comfort one another's old age — that worst would be to me like that state where there is no marrying nor giving in marriage" — in other words, like heaven — "in more respects than one."[11] Robert was more ambivalent. His dalliances with the friendlies had suggested a reluctance to commit to one woman. But in the closing months of 1821, Robert met and courted a young woman who captivated him as none of the friendlies had. Toward the end of that year the family began buzzing with rumors of Robert's engagement to Elizabeth Ellery, a Newport heiress.

Catharine did not rejoice over the prospect. "Whenever you marry my dear brother," she warned, "I shall have a good deal to suffer." When the announcement finally came in December, it caused Catharine to reflect that she and Robert could not "walk so close together as we have done."

Catharine made an effort to like Elizabeth Ellery ("She is certainly a great provocative to the imagination," she told Frances), but she was devastated. The brother with whom she had dreamed of spending a blissful old age in complementary solitudes had now chosen another as his life's partner. But Robert, approaching age thirty-five, was serious about marrying this young woman of twenty-two. Catharine gave the couple her reluctant blessing. Still, when they were married at the Ellery family's home in Newport on August 21, 1822, Catharine was not among the guests.[12]

That same summer saw the publication of Catharine's first full-length romance, *A New-England Tale*. The work was published anonymously, but many friends and acquaintances knew the tale's true author. They were not surprised by the book's success. Catharine's talent as a writer had long been a subject of admiration. "There is not, in America a little girl of your age, who can write a better letter than you can," her father had told her when she was not yet ten. Harry had arranged for her first paid writing assignments — poems and reviews for Boston newspapers that shared his Federalist sympathies — in the summer of 1812, when she was twenty-two. He also handled the business side of her negotiations with the publisher of

A New-England Tale. She was exceedingly ambivalent about publication of a full-length work. "I have *perfect horror* at appearing in print," she told her brother Theodore, when she and Harry were wrestling with the decision, "and feel as you have seen me when I have been trying to make up my mind to have a tooth out."[13]

The final chapter of *A New-England Tale* describes the death of a minor character, the madwoman Crazy Bet, who resembles all three of the figures Catharine considered parents: Theodore, Pamela, and Mumbet.[14] At least one other time — in her third book, *Hope Leslie*, published in 1827 — Catharine would allow a minor character to run away with the final scene.

In the final pages *Hope Leslie*, after the title character is safely married off to the likeliest and most ardent man around, a female character who had rejected a chance to marry him and had vowed never to marry delivers a meditation on the superior virtues of the single life. "For myself, I have contentment of mind," Esther Downing writes in a letter to the newly married pair. "It hath pleased God to give me glimpses of christian happiness, the foundations of which are not laid on the earth, and therefore cannot be removed or jostled by any of the cross accidents of life. . . . In another strength than mine own, I have overcome, and am of good cheer, and well assured that, as the world hath not given me my joy, the world cannot take it away." When the letter concludes, the author's own calm voice reinforces her point, reminding readers that Esther Downing's letter "illustrated a truth, which, if more generally received by her sex, might save a vast deal of misery: that marriage is not *essential* to the contentment, the dignity, or the happiness of woman."[15]

Yet it was not easy to maintain this stance. Several months after *Hope Leslie* appeared in print, Catharine Sedgwick appears to have suffered a bout of depression. She lamented that she was not first in anybody's heart, and yearned for a home of her own. One scholar who has written with insight about the lives of single women during this era saw "no discernible outward reason" for this 1828 episode, and blamed it on the coming of spring, the time of the earth's fullness, and Catharine Sedgwick's awareness at thirty-eight of the finality of her childlessness. But Catharine's sister Eliza had died the preceding fall; the ancient Mumbet was declining into her final illness; and Catharine was planning a trip to Boston later that year to attend the wedding of Eliza Cabot, one of her closest friends. Cabot, two years older than Catharine, was marrying a man a decade her junior. All of these seem to provide plenty of "outward reason" for her funk.[16]

Nonetheless, Catharine remained steadfast in her chosen commitment to a single life. She published new novels and stories at a prolific pace. All her sisters-in-law survived their husbands, most of them by a decade or more, and none of them remarried. As the years went on they became the inner circle of a group of remarkably creative literary women who gathered around Catharine in Stockbridge. Inspired by Catharine, two of the sisters-in-law (Susan Ridley Sedgwick and Elizabeth Buckminster Dwight Sedgwick) published books of fiction of their own.

Catharine outlived all her sisters-in-law and many of the nieces and nephews to whom she was so devoted. She died in Stockbridge at seventy-seven, in the summer of 1867, having witnessed the consequences of the Civil War that threatened to destroy the Republic her father had helped to create.

Few letters record the day-to-day details of Harry and Jane's marriage. After all, they were usually together during those years. But we have reason to suspect that, despite the best intentions of both Harry and Jane, their marriage did not quite turn out as they had hoped.

Harry's engagement letters to Jane Minot showed him at his best. They revealed intelligence, sensitivity, and a capacity for emotional connection. But if he was brilliant — and all his brothers and sisters considered him the most gifted family member of their generation — he was also bitter, cantankerous, and exasperating.

From the start, Harry raged against his destiny. Disappointed that his father sent him to Williams instead of Yale, he almost got himself expelled in his first term for defying the president. Clerking in his father's law office, he lamented that he was not in his older brother's office in Albany (where he had been earlier), or at Judge Tapping Reeve's law school in Litchfield (where he would be later), or in New York, or in Boston. He fumed when his Federalist allies failed to nominate him for local political office, and still more when they *did* nominate him in 1810 but failed to get him elected. He complained bitterly about his stepmother, so much so that it damaged his reputation in Boston legal circles by creating the inaccurate impression that he had cheated her out of a rightful inheritance. Unable to let go of a slight, Harry cherished the injuries he received from the families of the women he courted.

Marriage did not settle him. In the 1820s, he raged at the stupidity and mean-spiritedness of New York's orthodox Calvinists, as if their view of God's wrath were a personal affront to him. He complained about the lenient treatment of debtors and bankrupts, probably at least in part because one of them was his abusive brother-in-law, Ebenezer Watson. He disparaged the organization of New York's courts. When his eyesight deteriorated, he sued the doctor who failed to cure him, and lost. He deplored the election of Andrew Jackson, and then complained when Jackson did not appoint him to a lucrative political sinecure.

And he failed to keep promises he had made to Jane during their engagement. *She hated risk and speculation*, she told him, but his risky investments in ill-fated attempts to mine coal in Rhode Island and build a coal-fired steamboat engine nearly brought their family to ruin. *She dreaded to live in the country*, she said, but those financial losses and his deteriorating health — not just his near blindness, but a mental derangement similar to what his mother had suffered — forced them to leave New York and relocate to Stockbridge in the late 1820s.

Jane watched and worried as Harry drifted in and out of madness. When the physicians at the new asylum in Boston failed to cure him, he sued them, and lost again. When Robert reluctantly sought the rest of the family's approval to dissolve his legal partnership with his incapacitated brother, Harry sprang into action long enough to threaten Robert with legal retaliation for what he saw as an attempt to steal the business.

In the gloom of December 1831, after months of frenzied derangement and occasional messianic delusions of persecution, Harry Sedgwick slipped into a coma for several weeks and died. Jane became a widow at thirty-seven, with four children, the oldest almost eleven, the youngest just five. She was destined to live out nearly three decades of widowhood in rural Stockbridge, a setting she had once shunned.

The world took only passing notice of Harry's death. "He was a man of talents, of celebrity as a lawyer, but eccentric," former New York mayor Philip Hone remarked in his diary. But Catharine Maria Sedgwick, who waited by her dying brother's bedside with Jane, saw more. "He was changed and impaired in the eyes of the world," she acknowledged, "but like a familiar writing somewhat blotted and effaced, nothing that ever had been there was lost to me."[17]

When Jane Minot Sedgwick thought of all that ever had been there, as she watched Harry's decades of controversy and years of madness wind down into months of incapacity and weeks of grief, the memory of their bittersweet period of separation would have loomed large. "Every one must have some portion of sorrow," Jane had written to Harry in that winter of their engagement. "Probably we are now taking a draught drawn from futurity."[18]

How could she not have seen how far she was from sorrow, as 1816 turned to 1817? How could she not have guessed what she was really borrowing from her future, with each new letter that arrived, bringing heretofore unimagined happiness? This was a Harry unlike any who had ever been seen in Stockbridge or Williamstown during his youth, or in Boston during his earlier courtships; unlike any who would ever be seen in New York legal circles during the 1820s. At the moment of her husband's death, Jane had murmured a final benediction: "Thank God! He is at rest." Then she threw herself on "his poor inanimate body" and cried out, "dear darling Harry!" Nothing that ever had been there was lost to her, either.[19]

Harry Sedgwick and his brothers and sisters were members of a generation for whom *virtue* was being redefined as a characteristic of private domestic life, not the public, civic quality celebrated in their father's generation. The first Theodore Sedgwick had helped to win a revolution, and then guided the entire Federalist legislative program through Congress, from Hamilton's economic reports to the Alien and Sedition Acts, while his wife languished in Stockbridge. A generation later, Harry's engagement to Jane had given rise to his, and their, finest hour. It had ennobled them both. In writing her love letters, Jane had become Harry's inspiration, his muse, the creator of his new character. Writing his love letters had lifted Harry for once above the merely eccentric. Loving Jane, and articulating his love for her, was the purest, happiest, most virtuous thing he had done in his life.

Appendix

ARCHIVAL SOURCES

Boston Area

Massachusetts Historical Society: The vast majority of the Sedgwick
family's papers—at least 176 archive boxes, 21 bound volumes, and
18 reels of microfilm—are held in eight Sedgwick collections at the
Massachusetts Historical Society. Those and other collections I consulted are:

Catharine Maria Sedgwick I–III Papers

 I: Loose correspondence and manuscripts, 1798–1867; journals,
   1826–1863 (9 reels)

 II: Miscellaneous correspondence, n.d.–1867 (4 reels)

 III: Notes and miscellaneous correspondence, 1798–1853 (5 reels)

Sedgwick Family I–V Papers

 I: Mostly papers of Theodore Sedgwick I and his second wife,
   Pamela Dwight Sedgwick (4 boxes, 1 oversize box)

 II: Mostly papers of Theodore Sedgwick II and his family
   (9 boxes, 1 oversize box)

 III: Mostly papers of Theodore Sedgwick III and his family
   (3 boxes, 1 oversize box)

 IV: Mostly papers of Charles Sedgwick and his daughter,
   Katharine Maria Sedgwick Minot (18 boxes, 2 volumes)

 V: Mostly papers of Henry Dwight Sedgwick I, Robert Sedgwick,
   their wives, and their descendants, especially their common
   descendants (139 boxes, 2 oversize boxes, 19 volumes)

 Mark Hopkins Papers

 Sedgwick-Minot Family Papers

 Matthew Ridley Papers II

 John Collins Warren Papers

Massachusetts State Archives, University of Massachusetts, Boston:
Suffolk County Probate Court Records

Houghton Library, Harvard University, Cambridge: Elizabeth Ellery
Sedgwick Journal

New York City

New York City Hall of Records — Division of Old Records, County Clerk's Office: Equity Judgments; Judgments in Chancery; Judgments in Court of Common Pleas; Supreme Court Judgments; Roll of Attorneys
New-York Historical Society: Miscellaneous Manuscripts
New York Public Library: Belles Lettres Club Minutes and Records; Sedgwick Papers (Theodore Sedgwick III and family)

Western New England

Berkshire County Courthouse, Pittsfield, Massachusetts: Proceedings of the Berkshire Court of Common Pleas
Historical Collection, Stockbridge (Massachusetts) Library Association: Bidwell Papers; Miscellaneous Collections
Ingraham Memorial Research Library, Litchfield (Connecticut) Historical Society: Tapping Reeve Law School Records
Manuscripts and Archives, Sterling Memorial Library, Yale University: Bidwell Family Papers
Towns of Great Barrington, Sheffield, and Stockbridge, Massachusetts: Town Records
Williams College Archive: College Records; Record of the Proceedings of the Trustees; Williamsiana Collection

Notes

Abbreviations of Personal Names Used in Notes

AWSD   Abigail Williams Sergeant Dwight (1721–1791), mother of PDS

CMS   Catharine Maria Sedgwick (1789–1867), novelist, ninth child of TS I and PDS

CS   Charles Sedgwick (1791–1856), tenth and youngest child of TS I and PDS

ESP   Elizabeth Sedgwick Pomeroy (1775–1827), first child of TS I and PDS

EW   Ebenezer Watson (1776–1847), husband of FSW

FPS   Frances Pamela Sedgwick (1778–1842), third child of TS I and PDS; later FSW

FSW   Frances Sedgwick Watson, wife of EW

HDS   Henry Dwight Sedgwick (1785–1831; "Harry"), seventh child of TS I and PDS

JM   Jane Minot (1795?–1859)

LDM   Louisa Davis Minot (1788–1858), wife of WM, sister-in-law of JM

PD   Pamela Dwight (1753?–1807), daughter of AWSD; later PDS

PDS   Pamela Dwight Sedgwick, second wife of TS I

RS   Robert Sedgwick (1786–1841), eighth child of TS I and PDS

SRS   Susan Ridley Sedgwick (1788–1867), wife of TS II

TP   Dr. Thaddeus Pomeroy (1764–1847), husband of ESP

TS I   Theodore Sedgwick I (1746–1813; "the Judge"), husband of PDS

TS II   Theodore Sedgwick II (1780–1839), fourth child of TS I and PDS, husband of SRS

TS III   Theodore Sedgwick III (1811–1859), son of TS II and SRS

WM   William Minot (1783–1873), brother of JM

Introduction: The World of the Sedgwicks (pages 1–9)

1. Abigail Williams Sergeant Dwight (AWSD) to Pamela Dwight (PD), 3/14/1774, Sedgwick III Papers. I am grateful to the Massachusetts Historical Society (MHS), Boston, for all they have done to make this book possible, and in particular for permission to quote extensively from the Society's various collections of Sedgwick Family Papers and Catharine Maria Sedgwick Papers

throughout this book. I have silently standardized some spelling, punctuation, and capitalization to assist the modern reader. All quoted passages reprinted in italic, though, were underscored or otherwise marked for emphasis by the manuscript authors themselves.

2. James Axtell, "The Rise and Fall of the Stockbridge Indian Schools," *Massachusetts Review* 27, no. 2 (summer 1986), pp. 367–78; Stephen W. Williams, *The Genealogical History of the Family of Williams in America, More Particularly of the Descendants of Robert Williams of Roxbury* (Greenfield, Mass.: Merriam & Mirick, 1847), pp. 232–33; Electa F. Jones, *Stockbridge, Past and Present; or, Records of an Old Mission Station* (Springfield, Mass.: Samuel Bowles, 1854), p. 57. On the "river gods" in general, and on the home Ephraim Williams built in Stockbridge at about this time, see Kevin M. Sweeney, "Mansion People: Kinship, Class, and Architecture in Western Massachusetts in the Mid-Eighteenth Century," *Winterthur Portfolio: A Journal of American Culture* 19 (winter 1984), pp. 231–55.

3. Timothy Hopkins, *John Hopkins of Cambridge, Massachusetts, 1634, and Some of His Descendants* (Stanford, Calif.: Stanford University Press, 1932), p. 86n, hereinafter cited as *Hopkins Genealogy*; Axtell, "Stockbridge Indian Schools," p. 369; see also Patrick Frazier, *The Mohicans of Stockbridge* (Lincoln: University of Nebraska Press, 1992), pp. 85–88, and Lion G. Miles, "The Red Man Dispossessed: The Williams Family and the Alienation of Indian Land in Stockbridge, Massachusetts, 1736–1818," *New England Quarterly* 67 (March 1994), pp. 46–76.

4. Jones, *Stockbridge, Past and Present*, p. 78; Franklin Bowditch Dexter, *Biographical Sketches of the Graduates of Yale College with Annals of the College History*, vol. 1, *1701–1745* (New York: Henry Holt, 1885), p. 379, hereinafter cited as *Yale Annals*; and Sereno Edwards Dwight, ed., *The Works of President Edwards, with a Memoir of His Life*, vol. 1 (New York: G. & C. & H. Carvill, 1830), p. 449.

5. Edmund S. Morgan, *The Gentle Puritan: A Life of Ezra Stiles, 1727–1795* (New Haven, Conn.: Yale University Press, 1962), pp. 78–89.

6. S. E. Dwight, ed., *The Works of President Edwards*, vol. 1, p. 449; Leverett Wilson Spring, *A History of Williams College* (Boston: Houghton Mifflin, 1917), p. 24.

7. Axtell, "Stockbridge Indian Schools," pp. 372–75; Benjamin W. Dwight, *The History of the Descendants of John Dwight of Dedham, Massachusetts*, 2 vols. (New York: John F. Trow, 1874). General Dwight married AWSD five months after the death of his first wife. Just seventy-five years later, Susan Ridley Sedgwick (SRS) would be "a good deal scandalized" to learn this about her husband's grandparents; see SRS to Theodore Sedgwick III (TS III), 3/20–22/1827, Sedgwick II Papers.

8. On the early days of Theodore Sedgwick (TS I), see Hubert Merrill Sedgwick, *A Sedgwick Genealogy: Descendants of Deacon Benjamin Sedgwick* (New Haven, Conn.: New Haven Colony Historical Society, 1961), hereinafter cited as

Sedgwick Genealogy, and Richard E. Welch, Jr., *Theodore Sedgwick, Federalist: A Political Portrait* (Middletown, Conn.: Wesleyan University Press, 1965), pp. 7–9. On Yale at the time TS I attended, see Franklin Bowditch Dexter, "On Some Social Distinctions at Harvard and Yale, before the Revolution," *Proceedings of the American Antiquarian Society* [new series] 9, no. 1 (October 1893), pp. 34–59; Alexander Cowie, *Educational Problems at Yale College in the Eighteenth Century* (New Haven, Conn.: Yale University Press, 1936), pp. 6, 10–12, 15, 20, 22; and Dexter, *Yale Annals*, vol. 2 (1896), pp. 723–24, 777–80, and vol. 3 (1903), pp. 59, 94–166, 211–12.

9. Dexter, *Yale Annals*, vol. 3, pp. 95–166.

10. Hopkins, *Hopkins Genealogy*; Dexter, *Yale Annals*, vol. 2, pp. 536–37.

11. Antonn-Hermann Chroust, *The Rise of the Legal Profession in America*, vol. 1, *The Colonial Experience* (Norman: University of Oklahoma Press, 1965), pp. 30–39. Chroust presents a fifth way—going to college—but it is clear from his discussion that this would be far more likely to serve as a preliminary step. It would make any of the other four paths that much easier, but it would not eliminate the need to take one of them. The popularity of college education for lawyers varied by colony. Most lawyers in Massachusetts (home of the first colonial college) were college-trained from an early date, but almost none in New York attended college until that colony had its own college, in the 1750s.

12. H. M. Sedgwick, *Sedgwick Genealogy*; Welch, *Theodore Sedgwick, Federalist*, pp. 10–11; Robert J. Taylor, *Western Massachusetts in the Revolution* (Providence, R.I.: Brown University Press, 1954), p. 72; Lee Nathaniel Newcomer, *The Embattled Farmers: A Massachusetts Countryside in the American Revolution* (New York: Atheneum, 1953), p. 12.

13. Dexter, *Yale Annals*, vol. 3, p. 167; Dexter, "Social Distinctions at Harvard and Yale," pp. 54, 57–58; H. M. Sedgwick, *Sedgwick Genealogy*.

14. Steven Mintz and Susan Kellogg, *Domestic Revolutions: A Social History of American Family Life* (New York: Free Press, 1988), pp. 45–48; Ellen K. Rothman, *Hands and Hearts: A History of Courtship in America* (New York: Basic Books, 1984), pp. 26–30; Mary Beth Norton, *Liberty's Daughters: The Revolutionary Experience of American Women, 1750–1800* (Boston: Little, Brown, 1980), pp. 229–32; and Nancy F. Cott, *The Bonds of Womanhood: Women's Sphere in New England, 1780–1835* (New Haven, Conn.: Yale University Press, 1977), pp. 74–80.

15. Linda K. Kerber and Jane Sherron De Hart, "The Law of Domestic Relations: Marriage, Divorce, Dower—Examples from Colonial Connecticut," in *Women's America: Refocusing the Past*, 6th ed., edited by Kerber and De Hart (New York: Oxford University Press, 2004), p. 58 (quoted); Linda K. Kerber, *No Constitutional Right to Be Ladies: Women and the Obligations of Citizenship* (New York: Hill & Wang, 1998), pp. 17–21, 24–32, 94; Joan Hoff, *Law, Gender, and Injustice: A Legal History of U. S. Women* (New York: New York University Press, 1991), pp. 83–84, 93, 107–11; Carole Shammas, "English Inheritance Law

and Its Transfer to the Colonies," *American Journal of Legal History* 31, no. 2 (April 1987), pp. 145–63; Carole Shammas, Marylynn Salmon, and Michel Dahlin, *Inheritance in America from Colonial Times to the Present* (New Brunswick, N.J.: Rutgers University Press, 1987), pp. 42–79; Marylynn Salmon, *Women and the Law of Property in Early America* (Chapel Hill: University of North Carolina Press, 1986), pp. 120–84; Carol Elizabeth Jenson, "The Equity Jurisdiction and Married Women's Property in Ante-Bellum America: A Revisionist View," *International Journal of Women's Studies* 2, no. 2 (March–April 1979), pp. 145–48; Joan Hoff Wilson, "Hidden Riches: Legal Records and Women, 1750–1825," in *Woman's Being, Woman's Place: Female Identity and Vocation in American History*, edited by Mary Kelley (Boston: G. K. Hall, 1979), pp. 11–12, 15–18; and Stanley N. Katz, "Republicanism and the Law of Inheritance in the American Revolutionary Era," *Michigan Law Review* 76, no. 1 (November 1977), p. 28.

16. On the difficulty of obtaining a divorce in Massachusetts and New York, see Hendrik Hartog, *Man and Wife in America: A History* (Cambridge, Mass.: Harvard University Press, 2000), pp. 71–73; Norma Basch, *Framing American Divorce: From the Revolutionary Generation to the Victorians* (Berkeley: University of California Press, 1999), pp. 19–42, 47–48; Glenda Riley, *Divorce: An American Tradition* (New York: Oxford University Press, 1991), pp. 44–46, 52–56; Ann Taves, "Introduction," in *Religion and Family Violence in Early New England: The Memoirs of Abigail Abbot Bailey*, edited by Taves (1815; rpt., Bloomington: Indiana University Press, 1989), pp. 1–13; Salmon, *Women and the Law of Property*, pp. 60–61; Linda K. Kerber, *Women of the Republic: Intellect and Ideology in Revolutionary America* (Chapel Hill: University of North Carolina Press, 1980), pp. 159–60, 181–84: Nancy F. Cott, "Divorce and the Changing Status of Women in Eighteenth-Century Massachusetts," *William and Mary Quarterly*, 3rd ser., 33 (October 1976), pp. 586–614; and Nelson Manfred Blake, *The Road to Reno: A History of Divorce in the United States* (New York: Macmillan, 1962), pp. 49–52, 61–79.

17. On custody, see Hartog, *Man and Wife in America*, pp. 194–95; Mary Ann Mason, *From Father's Property to Children's Rights: A History of Child Custody in the United States* (New York: Columbia University Press, 1994), pp. 60–61; and Michael Grossberg, *Governing the Hearth: Law and the Family in Nineteenth-Century America* (Chapel Hill: University of North Carolina Press, 1985), pp. 237–40. On abuse and confronting abusers, see Mary Beth Sievens, "'The Wicked Agency of Others': Community, Law, and Marital Conflict in Vermont, 1790–1830," *Journal of the Early Republic* 21 (spring 2001), pp. 19–39; Nancy F. Cott, *Public Vows: A History of Marriage and the Nation* (Cambridge, Mass.: Harvard University Press, 2000), pp. 161–62; Randall A. Roth, "Spousal Murder in Northern New England, 1776–1865," in *Over the Threshold: Intimate Violence in Early America*, edited by Christine Daniels and Michael V. Kennedy (New York: Routledge, 1999), pp. 67–69, 76–77; Taves, ed., *Memoirs of Abigail Abbot Bailey*; and Elizabeth Pleck, *Domestic Tyranny: The Making of Social*

Policy against Family Violence from Colonial Times to the Present (New York: Oxford University Press, 1987), pp. 31–33, 53–54.

18. Cott, *Bonds of Womanhood*, pp. 160–68, and Carroll Smith-Rosenberg, "The Female World of Love and Ritual: Relations between Women in Nineteenth-Century America" (1975), rpt. in Smith-Rosenberg, *Disorderly Conduct: Visions of Gender in Victorian America* (New York: Knopf, 1985), pp. 53–76.

19. See, for example, Rothman, *Hands and Hearts*, pp. 51–55.

20. For more on the possibility of such relationships, mostly from two or more decades after Harry and Jane's courtship, see Karen Lystra, *Searching the Heart: Women, Men, and Romantic Love in Nineteenth-Century America* (New York: Oxford University Press, 1989), pp. 14–18, and Rothman, *Hands and Hearts*, pp. 36–42.

21. On women's roles, see Kerber, *Women of the Republic*; Cott, *Bonds of Womanhood*; and Barbara Welter, "The Cult of True Womanhood: 1820–1860," *American Quarterly* 18 (summer 1966), pp. 151–74. On men, see Mark E. Kann, "Manhood, Immortality, and Politics During the American Founding," *Journal of Men's Studies* 5 (fall 1996), pp. 79–103; E. Anthony Rotundo, *American Manhood: Transformations in Masculinity from the Revolution to the Modern Era* (New York: Basic Books, 1993); and Charles E. Rosenberg, "Sexuality, Class, and Role in Nineteenth-Century America," *American Quarterly* 25 (May 1973), pp. 131–53. Other works relating to this topic are cited in chapter 8.

22. On the choice to remain single, see Lee Virginia Chambers-Schiller, *Liberty, A Better Husband: Single Women in America, the Generations of 1780–1840* (New Haven, Conn.: Yale University Press, 1984), pp. 72–77, 169–70; Nancy F. Cott, "Passionlessness: An Interpretation of Victorian Sexual Ideology, 1790–1850," *Signs* 4 (1978), pp. 219–36; and Cott, *Bonds of Womanhood*, pp. 52–53, 76–80.

23. See, for example, Anya Jabour, *Marriage in the Early Republic: Elizabeth and William Wirt and the Companionate Ideal* (Baltimore, Md.: Johns Hopkins University Press, 1998), and William Ellery Channing's 1816 sermon on marriage, reprinted in William Henry Channing, *The Life of William Ellery Channing, D.D.: The Centenary Memorial Edition* (Boston: American Unitarian Association, 1880), pp. 320–23. This sermon of Channing, who was a friend of the Sedgwicks and the Minots, is discussed at length at the end of chapter 8.

24. Welch, *Theodore Sedgwick, Federalist*; Richard E. Welch, Jr., "Mumbet and Judge Sedgwick: A Footnote to the Early History of Massachusetts Justice," *Boston Bar Journal* 8, no. 1 (January 1964), pp. 12–19; Edward Halsey Foster, *Catharine Maria Sedgwick* (New York: Twayne, 1974); Mary Kelley, "A Woman Alone: Catharine Maria Sedgwick's Spinsterhood in Nineteenth-Century America," *New England Quarterly* 51 (June 1978), pp. 209–25; Mary Kelley, "Negotiating a Self: The Autobiography and Journals of Catharine Maria Sedgwick," *New England Quarterly* 66 (September 1993), pp. 366–98; Mary Kelley, introduction to *The Power of Her Sympathy: The Autobiography and Journal of*

Catharine Maria Sedgwick, edited by Mary Kelley (Boston: Massachusetts Historical Society, 1993), pp. 1–41; and several essays in *Catharine Maria Sedgwick: Critical Perspectives*, edited by Victoria Clements and Lucinda Damon-Bach (Boston: Northeastern University Press, 2002).

1. *The Harvest Moon: The Unhappy Life and Mysterious Death of Pamela Dwight Sedgwick (pages 13–36)*

1. On PDS's death, see town records, Office of the Town Clerk, Stockbridge, Mass.; see also Benjamin W. Dwight, *The History of the Descendants of John Dwight of Dedham, Massachusetts*, 2 vols. (New York: John F. Trow, 1874), hereinafter cited as *Dwight Genealogy*; and Hubert Merrill Sedgwick, *A Sedgwick Genealogy: Descendants of Deacon Benjamin Sedgwick* (New Haven, Conn.: New Haven Colony Historical Society, 1961), hereinafter cited as *Sedgwick Genealogy*. On their father's announcement, see Theodore Sedgwick II (TS II) to Henry Dwight Sedgwick (HDS), 6/12/1808, Sedgwick V Papers, Massachusetts Historical Society. HDS did refer to Penelope Russell as "her whom you shall introduce in the place of our mother" in a letter offering his father half-hearted congratulations on his engagement; see HDS to TS I, 11/7/1808, Sedgwick V Papers. For the first clear reference to PDS after her death, see Catharine Maria Sedgwick (CMS) to Robert Sedgwick (RS), 10/4/1811, Sedgwick IV Papers, quoted in chapter 3.

2. Stephen W. Williams, *The Genealogical History of the Family of Williams in America, More Particularly of the Descendants of Robert Williams of Roxbury* (Greenfield, Mass.: Merriam & Mirick, 1847), hereinafter cited as *Williams Genealogy*; Dwight, *Dwight Genealogy*; John Gilbert Holland, *History of Western Massachusetts*, vol. 1 (Springfield, Mass.: Samuel Bowles, 1855), p. 163; Timothy Hopkins, *John Hopkins of Cambridge, Massachusetts, 1634, and Some of His Descendants* (Stanford, Calif: Stanford University Press, 1932), hereinafter cited as *Hopkins Genealogy*; and Franklin Bowditch Dexter, *Biographical Sketches of the Graduates of Yale College with Annals of the College History*, vol. 2, *1745–1763* (New York: Holt, 1896), pp. 536–37, hereinafter cited as *Yale Annals*. *Dwight Genealogy* gives Pamela's date of birth alternately as 6/9/1752 and 6/9/1754; *Sedgwick Genealogy* gives it as 6/26/1753. Several references, in those and other places, to her death in 1807 say that she was fifty-four at that time. On names, see George Rippey Stewart, *American Given Names: Their Origins and History in the Context of the English Language* (New York: Oxford University Press, 1979), p. 207. The other given names in this paragraph appear in this generation in one or another of the families whose genealogies are cited in this note.

3. Dexter, *Yale Annals*, vol. 3, *1763–1778* (1903), pp. 147–48; and Richard E. Welch, Jr., *Theodore Sedgwick, Federalist: A Political Portrait* (Middletown,

Conn.: Wesleyan University Press, 1965), pp. 7–9, 11. Welch, in the only full-length biography of TS I, devotes more space to this marriage than to Sedgwick's thirty-three year marriage to Pamela Dwight. For a summary of the available research on age at marriage in colonial New England, see Michael Gordon, *The American Family: Past, Present, and Future* (New York: Random House, 1978), pp. 171–72.

4. Catharine Maria Sedgwick, "Recollections of Childhood," in *Life and Letters of Catharine M. Sedgwick*, edited by Mary E. Dewey (New York: Harper, 1872), pp. 25–26. This was the first published version of "Notebook of Memories of Her Life Dated 1853," which CMS composed for her grandniece, Alice Minot Sedgwick; the original manuscript is in Catharine Maria Sedgwick I Papers. Mary Kelley has edited a new edition, and written a valuable introduction to it, as *The Power of Her Sympathy: The Autobiography and Journal of Catharine Maria Sedgwick* (Boston: Massachusetts Historical Society, 1993). Some minor differences can be found between the Dewey edition of 1872 and the Kelley edition of 1993, with Kelley showing a more absolute faithfulness to the original "Notebook of Memories." In most passages I have quoted, though, the two are in perfect or almost perfect agreement, differing only in such matters as punctuation or the mention of some names.

5. PD to TS I, 6/1/1773, Sedgwick III Papers; PD to AWSD, n.d. [before 4/17/1774], Sedgwick II Papers; and C. M. Sedgwick, "Recollections of Childhood," p. 26.

6. AWSD to PD, 3/14/1774, Sedgwick III Papers.

7. Mary Kelley, "Negotiating a Self: The Autobiography and Journals of Catharine Maria Sedgwick," *New England Quarterly* 66 (September 1993), p. 375; and PDS to E. Mayhew, 5/25/1782, Sedgwick III Papers.

8. Welch, *Theodore Sedgwick, Federalist*, pp. 27–34.

9. TS I to H. Van Schaack (copy), 3/24/1783, Sedgwick III Papers. Dates in this paragraph come from H. M. Sedgwick, *Sedgwick Genealogy*; most are confirmed by contemporary correspondence.

10. *Brom & Bett v. J. Ashley, Esq.*, Berkshire Court of Common Pleas, Pittsfield, Mass., vol. 4, August 21, 1781, pp. 55–57. (In 1998, sometime after I examined this volume at the Berkshire County Courthouse in Pittsfield, it was moved to the Archives and Records Preservation Division of the Massachusetts Supreme Judicial Court in Boston.) See also Richard E. Welch, Jr., "Mumbet and Judge Sedgwick: A Footnote to the Early History of Massachusetts Justice," *Boston Bar Journal* 8, no. 1 (January 1964), pp. 12–19, and William E. Nelson, *Americanization of the Common Law: The Impact of Legal Change on Massachusetts Society, 1760–1830* (Cambridge, Mass.: Harvard University Press, 1975), pp. 101–2, 228n169. For a typical example of the claim that the argument was based on the state constitution, see Sarah Cabot Sedgwick and Christina Sedgwick Marquand, *Stockbridge, 1739–1939: A Chronicle* (Great Barrington, Mass.: Berkshire Courier, 1939), p. 287; there is also a web site where the original court

records are reproduced, along with portraits of both TS I and Elizabeth Freeman; see Brady Barrows, mumbet.com, <http://www.mumbet.com>. On John Ashley, see Dexter, *Yale Annals*, vol. 1, *1701–1745* (1885), pp. 405–6. On the related case of *Quok Walker v. Jennison*, see F. W. Grinnell, "The Constitutional History of the Supreme Judicial Court of Massachusetts from the Revolution to 1813," *Massachusetts Law Quarterly* 2 (May 1917), pp. 437–41; and Arthur Zilversmit, "Quok Walker, Mumbet, and the Abolition of Slavery in Massachusetts," *William and Mary Quarterly*, 3rd ser., 25 (October 1968), pp. 614–24.

11. For HDS's memories of Mumbet, see [Henry D. Sedgwick,] *The Practicability of the Abolition of Slavery: A Lecture, Delivered at the Lyceum in Stockbridge, Massachusetts, February, 1831* (New York: J. Seymour, 1831), pp. 13–19.

12. C. M. Sedgwick, "Recollections of Childhood," pp. 40–42.

13. PDS to TS I, 7/9/1798, Sedgwick III Papers. For more on HDS's afflictions, see TS I to PDS, 6/9/1786, Sedgwick II Papers; PDS to TS I, 2/24/1788, n.d. [3/1790], 12/11/1792, 1/1/1793, 1/8/1795, and 1/15/[1795; misdated 1794], Sedgwick III Papers; and TS I to PDS, 1/11/1793, Sedgwick V Papers.

14. TS I to PDS, 7/18/1786, Sedgwick II Papers; see also Welch, *Theodore Sedgwick, Federalist*, pp. 40–41, 47.

15. TS I to PDS, 6/24/1786, Sedgwick II Papers.

16. Mary Beth Norton cites TS I's letter in *Liberty's Daughters: The Revolutionary Experience of American Women, 1750–1800* (Boston: Little, Brown, 1980), pp. 232–33. Much of Norton's evidence does demonstrate that the *belief* that lactation acted as a contraceptive was widespread. For an interpretation of this period that stresses both the error of that belief and the fact that at least some people understood that it was erroneous, and that also mentions the souring of the milk, see Catherine M. Scholten, *Childbearing in American Society: 1650–1850* (New York: New York University Press, 1985), p. 73. For examples of Sedgwick family members and friends who recognized that a nursing mother could become pregnant, see H. Van Schaack to TS I, 2/9/1801, Sedgwick I Papers, and TS II to TS I, 6/13/1803, Sedgwick III Papers.

17. A few decades later, TS II would crow about his wife's unexpected success in weaning her firstborn son at thirteen months; see TS II to HDS, 2/14/1812, Sedgwick V Papers. For data from outside the Sedgwick family, see Ross W. Beales, Jr., "Nursing and Weaning in an Eighteenth-Century New England Household," in *Families and Children: Annual Proceedings of the Dublin Seminar for New England Folklife* 10, edited by Peter Benes (1985), pp. 48–63.

18. Welch, *Theodore Sedgwick, Federalist*, pp. 41, 59–65, 66–70.

19. PDS to TS I, 7/7/1789, Sedgwick III Papers.

20. PDS to TS I, 5/23/1790, 6/26/1790, and 2/13/1791; see also PDS to TS I, 5/13/1790, 6/n.d./1790 (fragment), 7/8/1790, and 1/3/1791, Sedgwick III Papers.

21. On the final illness and death of AWSD, see PDS to TS I, 1/24/1791, 1/30/1791, and 2/13/1791, Sedgwick III Papers.

22. C. M. Sedgwick, "Recollections of Childhood," pp. 28, 34, 36. See also J. P. Marquand, Jr., quoted in Jean Stein, *Edie: An American Biography*, edited by George Plimpton (New York: Knopf, 1982), p. 4; Welch, *Theodore Sedgwick, Federalist*, p. 249; and Mary Kelley, *Private Woman, Public Stage: Literary Domesticity in Nineteenth-Century America* (New York: Oxford University Press, 1984), pp. 49–55.

23. On TS I's promises that the current session of Congress would be his last, see TS I to PDS, 1/27/1789, 1/30/1790, and 11/28/1791, Sedgwick II Papers; TS I to PDS, 11/26/1792, 1/5/1794, and 12/12/1797, Sedgwick V Papers; and also PDS to TS I, 7/2/1798, and TS II to TS I, 7/12/1798, Sedgwick III Papers. For references by political allies to TS I's promises, see Rufus King to TS I, 11/6/1796, and H. Van Schaack to TS I, 7/4/1798, Sedgwick I Papers. His reputed desire to quit was a main theme of a campaign oration TS I delivered in what would prove to be his last campaign, in 1798; see TS I manuscript notes, address at Lenox, 9/14/1798, Sedgwick I Papers.

24. Anya Jabour, *Marriage in the Early Republic: Elizabeth and William Wirt and the Companionate Ideal* (Baltimore, Md.: Johns Hopkins University Press, 1998), pp. 137–39, and Philip Greven, *The Protestant Temperament: Patterns of Child-Rearing, Religious Experience, and the Self in Early America* (New York: Knopf, 1977), p. 249.

25. TS I referred to reports on PDS's health (mostly from daughter FPS and from his law partner and PDS's cousin, Ephraim Williams) in TS I to PDS, 11/9/1791, 11/20/1791, and ("thousands of miles") 11/24/1791, Sedgwick II Papers, and TS I to E. Williams, 11/20/1791, 11/24/1791, 11/27/1791, 12/1/1791, 12/4/1791, and ("matronly") 12/6/1791, Sedgwick III Papers. See also H. Van Schaack to TS I, 11/23/n.d. [1791], Sedgwick I Papers.

26. PDS to TS I, 12/4/1791, Sedgwick III Papers.

27. TS I to PDS, 12/16/1791 and 12/18/1791, Sedgwick II Papers.

28. TS I to PDS, 10/10/1793, Sedgwick II Papers; H. Van Schaack to TS I, 11/20/1793, Sedgwick III Papers; TS I to PDS, 1/5/1794, Sedgwick V Papers; and Welch, *Theodore Sedgwick, Federalist*, p. 155n. Pamela was under the care of a Col. Lovejoy in 1793, possibly in Andover, north of Boston and about 150 miles from Stockbridge — almost as far as Philadelphia. In 1796, during the next major bout of insanity, Dr. Erastus Sergeant wrote to TS I: "I found her in as frantic a state — as she was in the summer she went to Andover. . . ." See E. Sergeant to TS I, 1/26/1796, Sedgwick I Papers.

29. TS I to E. Williams, 12/14/1795 (see also 12/7/1795, 12/16/1795, 12/17–18/1795, 12/23/1795, 12/30/1795, and 5/29/1796), Sedgwick III Papers; and TS I to "My finest Loves," 12/16/1795 (see also to "My dearest children," 12/7/1795; to "My dear Children," 12/16/1795; to "My dear good girls," 12/28/1795; and to "My dear children," 3/23/1796), Sedgwick V Papers.

30. E. Sergeant to TS I, 1/26/1796; see also L. Andrews to TS I, 1/28/1796; H. W. Dwight to TS I, 2/18/1796; and Thomas Dwight to TS I, 9/14/1796,

Sedgwick I Papers; and TS II to TS I, 1/20/n.d. [1796], Sedgwick III Papers. On HDS's visit to his mother, see HDS to TS I, 12/31/1795, Sedgwick V Papers. The mentioned tear is near the vertical fold, in a position where it could have been caused by the removal of the seal.

31. TS I to E. Williams, 3/29/1794, 4/4/1794, 4/18/1794, 4/22/1794, 5/6/1794, 5/9/1794, 5/28/1794, 6/5/1794, and 6/7/1794; PDS to TS I, 1/18/[1797; misdated 1796] and 2/[20–28?]/1797; and TS I to H. Van Schaack, 5/4/1797, Sedgwick III Papers.

32. PDS to TS I, 12/18/1797 and 7/2/1798, Sedgwick III Papers; see also TS I to PDS, 12/12/1797, Sedgwick V Papers; and Welch, *Theodore Sedgwick, Federalist*, pp. 193–204.

33. PDS to TS I, 7/2/1798 (see also 7/9/1798), Sedgwick III Papers; Mary Gray Bidwell to Sarah Spring Gray, 8/24/1798, Bidwell Family Papers, Manuscripts and Archives, Yale University Library; H. Van Schaack to TS I, 7/6/1798 and 7/9/1798, and TS I manuscript notes, address at Lenox, 9/14/1798, Sedgwick I Papers; and TS I to H. Van Schaack, 8/8/1798, Sedgwick III Papers.

34. PDS to TS I, 2/11/1799 and 2/17/1799, Sedgwick III Papers, and TS I to PDS, 2/3/1799, Sedgwick V Papers.

35. E. Williams to TS I, 1/14/1800, and H. Van Schaack to TS I, 1/29/1800, Sedgwick I Papers; TS II to TS I, 1/16/1800; PDS to TS I, 2/4/1800; TS II to TS I, 3/1/1800; PDS to TS I, 4/2/1800 ("I can do nothing"); and FPS to TS I, 2/15/1801, Sedgwick III Papers.

36. TS I to PDS, 5/5/1800 ("prisoner"), 5/10/1800 ("no earthly consideration"), and 11/17/1800; see also John Marshall to TS I, 9/8/1800, Sedgwick V Papers. On reactions to the new "federal city," see TS II to TS I, 11/17/1800, and TS I to TS II, 12/23/1800, Sedgwick III Papers; J. Rutledge to TS I, 12/27/1800, Sedgwick I Papers; and TS I to PDS, 1/14/1801 and 1/28/1801, Sedgwick V Papers.

37. FPS to TS I, 2/15/1801, Sedgwick III Papers; CMS to TS I, 2/1/1801, Catharine Maria Sedgwick I Papers.

38. H. G. Otis to TS I, 4/13/1800, and Certificate, 2/1802, Sedgwick I Papers; see also Grinnell, "Constitutional History of the Supreme Judicial Court of Massachusetts," pp. 474–75, 495–507.

39. TS I to TS II, 6/20/1802, and TS I to PDS, 3/6/1803, Sedgwick III Papers; also TS I to PDS, 5/1/1802; RS to TS II, 3/27/1803; RS to TS I, 5/18/1803; and HDS to TS II, 11/22/1803, Sedgwick V Papers.

40. TS I to TS II, 10/7/1805, Sedgwick III Papers; H. Van Schaack to TS I, 5/20/n.d. [1806], Sedgwick I Papers; and HDS to TS II, 12/2/1806, Sedgwick V Papers; also, Mary Gray Bidwell to Barnabas Bidwell, 1/6/1806, 2/10/1806, 2/26–28/1806 (quotations), and 3/31/1806, Bidwell Family Papers, Manuscripts and Archives, Yale University Library. For more on the crisis described in Mary Gray Bidwell's final February letter, see Ebenezer Watson (EW) to HDS, 3/8/1806, Sedgwick V Papers.

41. TS I to TS II, 4/23/1806, and TS I to Henry Van Schaack, 5/23/1806, Sedg-

wick III Papers; see also Theophilus Parsons, Jr., *Memoir of Theophilus Parsons, Chief Justice of the Supreme Judicial Court of Massachusetts* (Boston: Ticknor & Fields, 1859), pp. 193–94.

42. See H. Van Schaack to TS I, 5/20/[1806], 6/4/1806, and 6/7/1806; William Sullivan to TS I, 5/23/1806; H. G. Otis to TS I, 5/25/1806 and 6/20/1806; Jabez Upham to TS I, 5/25/1806 and 9/10/1806; Samuel Dexter to TS I, 5/27/1806; John Hooker to TS I, 5/28/1806; Timothy Bigelow to TS I, 6/2/1806 and 8/6/1806; Daniel Dewey to TS I, 6/3/1806 and 7/28/1806; William Prescott to TS I, 6/4/1806; Samuel Sewall to TS I, 6/15/1806, 7/9/1806, and 7/29/1806; Christopher Gore to TS I, 6/20/1806; Isaac Parker to TS I, 7/10/1806 and 7/25/1806; John Sedgwick to TS I, 7/15/1806; Artemas Ward to TS I, 7/16/1806; Address of 19 Middlesex County lawyers, 8/6/1806; Address of 17 Worcester County lawyers, 9/10/1806; all in Sedgwick I Papers.

43. TS I to ——— [draft], 9/17/1806, Sedgwick I Papers.

44. The first use I have found of this term in this manner occurs in TS II to RS, 8/4/1806, Sedgwick V Papers. See also (by no means a complete list) HDS to TS II, 1/3/1807, TS II to HDS, 6/12/1808, HDS to TS II, 10/30/1808, RS to HDS, 5/8/1810, Charles Sedgwick (CS) to HDS, 3/6/1811, TS II to HDS, 6/[19]/1811, TS II to HDS, 7/10/1811, CS to HDS, 7/15/1811, Thaddeus Pomeroy (TP) to HDS, 12/13/1811, CS to HDS, 4/9/1812, TP to HDS, 5/29/1812, and TS II to HDS, 9/11/1812, all in Sedgwick V Papers; and CMS to RS, 10/4/1811, Sedgwick IV Papers.

45. H. Van Schaack to TS I, 6/4/1806, Sedgwick I Papers.

46. HDS to RS, 11/19/1806, Sedgwick IV Papers; TS I to TS II, 12/9/1806, Sedgwick III Papers; also HDS to TS II, 12/2/1806, and TS I to CS, 1/1/1807, Sedgwick V Papers; and Mary Gray Bidwell to Barnabas Bidwell, 12/29–30/1806, Bidwell Family Papers, Manuscripts and Archives, Yale University Library.

47. RS to CMS, 3/11/1807; CMS to FSW, 3/24/1807 ("cannot expect"); CMS to FSW, 4/15/1807 ("I am bound"); CS to CMS, 4/22/1807; and CMS to FSW, 7/7/1807, Sedgwick IV Papers; TS I to TS II, 5/14/1807, Sedgwick III Papers; HDS to TS II, 5/17/1807 and 6/30/1807, Sedgwick V Papers; and CMS to EW, 7/15/1807, Catharine Maria Sedgwick I Papers.

48. TS I to TS II, 7/23/1807, Sedgwick III Papers; FSW to HDS, 8/12/1807, and HDS to TS II, 8/24/1807 and 9/17/1807, Sedgwick V Papers.

49. TS II to TS I, 9/27/1807, and TS I to TS II, 10/4/1807, Sedgwick III Papers; also EW to HDS, 10/16/1807; HDS to TS II, 10/16/1807; RS to HDS, 10/24/1807; TS I to HDS, 11/7/1807; TS II to HDS, 11/1/1807 and 11/17/1807 (quoted); and FSW to HDS, 11/18/1807; all in Sedgwick V Papers.

50. CMS to FSW, 12/25/1807, Sedgwick IV Papers, and CMS to FSW, 12/28/1807, continued 1/1/1808, Catharine Maria Sedgwick I Papers.

51. The Sedgwick V Papers collection for early 1813 is also filled with letters of condolence from family friends on the death of TS I.

52. TS I to CMS, 1/2/1806, Catharine Maria Sedgwick III Papers, and HDS

to FSW, 2/10/1805, Sedgwick V Papers. For more examples of such retrospective New Year's letters, see TS II to TS I, 1/1/[1801], Sedgwick III Papers; TS I to CMS, 1/3/1809, Catharine Maria Sedgwick III Papers; and Elizabeth Sedgwick Pomeroy (ESP) to HDS, 1/2/1814, Sedgwick V Papers.

53. CMS to Elizabeth Cabot Follen, 8/25/1822, and CMS to Jane M. Sedgwick, 1/10/1836, Catharine Maria Sedgwick I Papers; also C. M. Sedgwick, "Recollections of Childhood," p. 75.

54. [HDS?], "Mrs. Pamela Sedgwick," quoted in C. M. Sedgwick, "Recollections of Childhood," pp. 37–38.

55. Mary Gray Bidwell to Barnabas Bidwell, 9/21–22/1807, Bidwell Family Papers, Manuscripts and Archives, Yale University Library. I first read this letter, and other Bidwell letters cited in this book, in typed copies made by a descendant, Gertrude Catherine Hamilton Bidwell, and kept in the Historical Collection of the Stockbridge (Mass.) Library Association. I am inexpressibly grateful to Polly Pierce, retired curator of the Historical Collection, who, when presented with the story of the Sedgwick family's strange silence and asked if her collections had any record of the circumstances of PDS's death, thought for no more than a few seconds before saying, "Isn't there something in the Bidwell Papers on that?"

56. Mary Gray Bidwell to Barnabas Bidwell, 9/21–22/1807, Bidwell Family Papers, Manuscripts and Archives, Yale University Library. According to a calculation carried out on MoonCalc 4.0, the harvest moon in 1807 would have been at its fullest over Stockbridge when it first appeared above the horizon on the evening of Wednesday, September 16, three nights before PDS's final night of life. When the moon rose above the horizon in Stockbridge just before eight o'clock on Saturday night, September 19 (when PDS would probably have just retired for the night, or have been just about to retire), more than 91 percent of the full moon would still have been visible. Clouds must be considered as a possibility, but Mary Bidwell told her husband that, while the streets were still wet, the rain had come "the preceding night," and the streets were dry enough for her to cross comfortably on Sunday morning. MoonCalc, a program that allows users to calculate the phases of the moon at any place on earth for any date and time between the years 600 and 2100 C.E., was created by Dr. Monzur Ahmed and issued in four versions between May 1993 and June 1997. I downloaded version 4.0, dated June 9, 1997, from Dr. Ahmed's web site at <http://www.starlight.demon.co.uk/mooncalc/> on August 10, 1997. I tested MoonCalc against a mention of a full moon in one of the Sedgwick family's letters (PDS to TS I, 7/7/1789, Sedgwick III Papers). According to the program's calculations, the moon over Stockbridge on July 7, 1789, would have been 99.46 percent full.

57. This paragraph only is based on and quotes from C. M. Sedgwick, "Recollections of Childhood," pp. 38, 43.

58. Compare, for example, the description of a dangerous pool in the Housatonic in *A New-England Tale* to a similar and similarly dangerous spot,

"back of Mr. Sedgwick's," described in Mary Gray Bidwell to Barnabas Bidwell, 6/10/1804, Bidwell Family Papers, Manuscripts and Archives, Yale University Library; see Catharine Maria Sedgwick, *A New-England Tale; or, Sketches of New England Character and Manners* (1822); rpt., edited by Victoria Clements, in "Early American Women Writers" Series (New York: Oxford University Press, 1995), p. 85.

59. C. M. Sedgwick, *A New-England Tale*, p. 7. See also Victoria Clements, "'A Powerful and Thrilling Voice': The Significance of Crazy Bet," in *Catharine Maria Sedgwick: Critical Perspectives*, edited by Victoria Clements and Lucinda Damon-Bach (Boston: Northeastern University Press, 2002); and Edward Halsey Foster, *Catharine Maria Sedgwick* (New York: Twayne, 1974), p. 52. I am grateful to Professor Clements for sharing a draft of her essay in an e-mail message to me dated May 25, 2002. Both Clements and Foster found information about Susan "Crazy Sue" Dunham in the October and November 1900 issues of a short-lived periodical called *The Berkshire Hills*. Clements also notes a significant model for Crazy Bet in the character of Madge Wildfire in Sir Walter Scott's 1818 work, *The Heart of Midlothian*.

60. On Mumbet as "Mother," see CMS to FSW, n.d. [2/1815], RS to CMS, 3/28/1816, and CS to CMS, 1/1/1830, Sedgwick IV Papers; FSW to HDS and RS, 2/9/1817, Sedgwick V Papers; and CMS to CS, 12/17/1829, Catharine Maria Sedgwick I Papers. The attribution of the epitaph to CS is in C. M. Sedgwick, "Recollections of Childhood," p. 43. Based on the evidence of a copy in her handwriting among the family papers, Mary Kelley believes CMS herself wrote the epitaph; see Kelley, ed., *The Power of Her Sympathy*, p. 71n.

61. See C. M. Sedgwick, "Recollections of Childhood," p. 29n.

62. C. M. Sedgwick, *A New-England Tale*, p. 81.

63. See C. M. Sedgwick, "Recollections of Childhood," pp. 25–26.

64. C. M. Sedgwick, *A New-England Tale*, pp. 17, 83–89.

65. C. M. Sedgwick, *A New-England Tale*, pp. 164–65.

2. *The Power to Bind: Eliza, Francis, and Theodore (pages 37–52)*

1. Nancy F. Cott, *The Bonds of Womanhood: Women's Sphere in New England, 1780–1835* (New Haven, Conn.: Yale University Press, 1977), pp. 74–80; Mary Beth Norton, *Liberty's Daughters: The Revolutionary Experience of American Women, 1750–1800* (Boston: Little, Brown, 1980), pp. 229–32; Ellen K. Rothman, *Hands and Hearts: A History of Courtship in America* (New York: Basic Books, 1984), pp. 26–30; and Steven Mintz and Susan Kellogg, *Domestic Revolutions: A Social History of American Family Life* (New York: Free Press, 1988), pp. 45–48.

2. Carole Shammas, *A History of Household Government in America* (Charlottesville: University of Virginia Press, 2002), pp. 100 (quoted), 106. For a

comparative early modern European perspective, see Steven King, "Chance Encounters? Paths to Household Formation in Early Modern England," *International Review of Social History* 44 (April 1999), pp. 26, 32; Beatrice Gottlieb, *The Family in the Western World from the Black Death to the Industrial Age* (New York: Oxford University Press, 1993), p. 62; and John R. Gillis, *For Better, for Worse: British Marriages, 1600 to the Present* (New York: Oxford University Press, 1985), p. 14.

3. Courtship, PDS to TS I, [1/15/1793; misdated and filed as 12/15/1793], and TS I to E. Williams, 6/7/1794, Sedgwick III Papers; Williams's reputation, TS I to E. Williams, 1/9/1795, Sedgwick III Papers, and H. Van Schaack to TS I, 7/9/1798, Sedgwick I Papers. See also Catharine Maria Sedgwick, "Recollections of Childhood," in *Life and Letters of Catharine M. Sedgwick*, edited by Mary E. Dewey (New York: Harper, 1872), pp. 71–72, and Richard E. Welch, Jr., *Theodore Sedgwick, Federalist: A Political Portrait* (Middletown, Conn.: Wesleyan University Press, 1965), p. 160.

4. Engagement, H. Van Schaack to TS I, 11/15/1796, Sedgwick I Papers; biographical details, Calvin Durfee, *Williams Biographical Annals* (Boston: Lee & Shepard, 1871), p. 62 (Pomeroy included because he served for twenty years as a trustee of the college named for and endowed by his wife's great-uncle); ruminations on his own childhood, TP to HDS, 1/29/1812, Sedgwick V Papers; move to Stockbridge, TS I to HDS, 1/2/1806, Sedgwick III Papers, and Mary Gray Bidwell to Barnabas Bidwell, 1/6/1806, Bidwell Family Papers, Manuscripts and Archives, Yale University Library.

5. See Susan E. Klepp, "Revolutionary Bodies: Women and the Fertility Transition in the Mid-Atlantic Region, 1760–1820," *Journal of American History* 85 (December 1998), pp. 910–45.

6. Dates and names of children appear in Hubert Merrill Sedgwick, *A Sedgwick Genealogy: Descendants of Deacon Benjamin Sedgwick* (New Haven: New Haven Colony Historical Society, 1961). On Eliza's illness, see TS II to HDS and RS, 2/15/1805, and TS I to HDS and RS, 2/25/1805; on "N° 9," see TP to HDS, 2/25/1812; and on the "easy" birth of number ten, see CS to HDS, 8/30/1813, Sedgwick V Papers.

7. C. M. Sedgwick, "Recollections of Childhood," pp. 68, 70–71, and TS I to PDS, 1/30/1790, Sedgwick II Papers.

8. The reference to "purity of morals" is applied to "the Bethlehem School" — probably the Moravian Young Ladies Seminary in Bethlehem, Pennsylvania, fifty miles north of Philadelphia and eighty miles west of New York, which opened its doors to non-Moravians in 1785; see PDS to TS I, 2/17/1790, Sedgwick III Papers; TS I to PDS, 2/25/1790 (quoted), Sedgwick V Papers; and Norton, *Liberty's Daughters*, pp. 283–87. Neither Sedgwick parent made any additional mention of Bethlehem or the seminary in letters from these years, so it is impossible to tell whether FPS attended. On FPS in Philadelphia, see TS I to PDS, 11/12/1792, Sedgwick IV Papers. Although there is no specific men-

tion, FPS might have attended the Young Ladies' Academy of Philadelphia, opened under the sponsorship of Dr. Benjamin Rush; see Margaret A. Nash, "Rethinking Republican Motherhood: Benjamin Rush and the Young Ladies' Academy of Philadelphia," *Journal of the Early Republic* 17 (summer 1997), pp. 171–91.

9. On Frances and Andrews "double-dating" with Eliza and Williams, see PDS to TS I [1/15/1793; misdated and filed as 12/15/1793], Sedgwick III Papers. On Andrews's political work, see TS I to E. Williams, 2/20/1794, 3/13/1794, 12/31/1794, and 1/1/1795; and TS I to H. Van Schaack, 2/3/1795, all in Sedgwick III Papers; and nine letters from Andrews to TS I written over a four-month span during the first half of 1796, in Sedgwick I Papers.

10. PDS to TS I, 12/11/1796 and 12/29/1796 (quoted), Sedgwick III Papers. On FPS being in Philadelphia, see also H. Van Schaack to TS I, 1/2/1797, Sedgwick I Papers.

11. L. Andrews to TS I, 1/15/1797, Sedgwick III Papers.

12. PDS to TS I, 1/23/1797 (quoted) and 2/5/1797, Sedgwick III Papers.

13. PDS to TS I, 1/30/1797, Sedgwick III Papers.

14. PDS to TS I, 2/5/1797, Sedgwick III Papers.

15. L. Andrews to TS I, 2/13/1797, 2/20/1797 (quoted), and 4/29/1797, Sedgwick I Papers.

16. PDS to TS I, 2/15/1797, Sedgwick III Papers.

17. D. Penfield to TS I, 4/13/1797, Sedgwick I Papers.

18. PDS to TS I, 12/25/1797 ("fixed"), 1/10/1798 ("distress"), 1/12/1798, and 2/9/1798, Sedgwick III Papers.

19. PDS to TS I, 2/9/1798 ("propriety"), 2/17/1798 ("act for herself"), and 3/5/1798, Sedgwick III Papers.

20. TS I to PDS, 2/3/1799, Sedgwick V Papers; also TS II to TS I, 1/31/[1799; misdated and filed as 1800] and 2/24/1799 (quoted), Sedgwick III Papers.

21. TS II to TS I, 1/31/[1799] ("extravagance") and 2/9/1799 ("scorn," "resentment"), and PDS to TS I, 2/11/1799, Sedgwick III Papers.

22. PDS to TS I, 1/12/1798, Sedgwick III Papers.

23. FPS to TS I, 2/18/1799, Sedgwick III Papers.

24. C. M. Sedgwick, "Recollections of Childhood," p. 70; Martha Tomhave Blauvelt, "The Work of the Heart: Emotion in the 1805–1835 Diary of Sarah Connell Ayer," *Journal of Social History* 35 (spring 2002), pp. 577–92; and Lawrence Stone, "Passionate Attachments in the West in Historical Perspective," in *Passionate Attachments: Thinking about Love*, edited by Willard Gaylin and Ethel Person (New York: Free Press, 1988), pp. 15–26.

25. TS I to PDS, 2/3/1799, Sedgwick V Papers.

26. FPS stayed with the Penfields in 1797, and visited the Tillinghasts as well; see D. Penfield to TS I, 4/13/1797, Sedgwick I Papers, in which Penfield even warns TS I, "I am not without fears that something like a connection with a person in this place is among her intentions." In FPS to TS I, 2/18/1799, Sedgwick

III Papers, this same Mrs. Tillinghast is revealed to be a confidante of Ebenezer Watson (EW), and much later (in RS to HDS, 2/9/1813, Sedgwick V Papers) we learn that EW has long had business dealings with Daniel Penfield.

27. FPS to TS I, 2/18/1799, Sedgwick III Papers.

28. TS II to TS I, 1/13/1801, and FPS to TS I, 2/18/1799, Sedgwick III Papers; see also Cott, *Bonds of Womanhood*, pp. 186–87

29. TS II to TS I, 1/26/1800, and see also PDS to TS I, 2/4/1800, Sedgwick III Papers.

30. TS II to TS I, 3/1/1800; TS I to TS II, 3/10/1800; and TS II to TS I, 3/15/1800, Sedgwick III Papers.

31. FPS to TS II, 10/30/[1800; misdated 1801], Sedgwick III Papers. The letter clearly dates from before FPS's marriage to EW.

32. TS I to TS II, 12/5/1800, and TS II to TS I, 1/25/1801, Sedgwick III Papers; also H. Van Schaack to TS I, 2/9/1801, Sedgwick I Papers.

33. FPS to TS I, 2/15/1801, Sedgwick III Papers.

34. TS II to TS I, 6/13/1803 and 4/1/1804 (quoted), Sedgwick III Papers, and CMS to PDS, 11/15/1805, Catharine Maria Sedgwick I Papers.

35. TS II to TS I, 9/1/1806, Sedgwick III Papers; also EW to HDS, 11/27/1806, and HDS to TS II, 9/17/1807, Sedgwick V Papers.

36. TS II to HDS, 11/17/1807, Sedgwick V Papers.

37. C. M. Sedgwick, "Recollections of Childhood," pp. 55–57.

38. Theodore Sedgwick, Jr. [TS III], *A Memoir of the Life of William Livingston* (New York: Harper, 1833), pp. 411–15; G. T. Ridlon, *History of the Ancient Ryedales* [Ridleys] *and Their Descendants in Normandy, Great Britain, Ireland, and America, from 860 to 1884* (Manchester, N.H.: n.p., 1884), p. 764; Florence Van Rensselaer and William Laimbeer, *The Livingston Family in America and Its Scottish Origins* (New York: n.p., 1949), p. 86; and C. M. Sedgwick, "Recollections of Childhood," pp. 55–57.

39. On Livingston's plans for Susan, see TS II to HDS, 7/22/1807, Sedgwick V Papers. Even though young Robert Leroy Livingston was her stepbrother, their blood relationship was only that of second cousins.

40. TS I to TS II, 10/7/1805, Sedgwick III Papers; also HDS to TS I, 11/24/1805, and TS I to HDS, 12/2/1805, Sedgwick V Papers. The Sedgwick brothers might have known the grim story of another Livingston, John and Kitty's second cousin. He married a young woman who loved another man, but whose influential father preferred the Livingstons' fortune. The marriage of Henry Beekman Livingston and Nancy Shippen was one of the most notoriously unhappy and contentious of the Revolutionary era, ending finally in a squalid divorce. On Henry Beekman Livingston's marriage to Nancy Shippen, see Linda K. Kerber, *Women of the Republic: Intellect and Ideology in Revolutionary America* (Chapel Hill: University of North Carolina Press, 1980), pp. 181–84.

41. HDS to TS II, 12/2/1806, Sedgwick V Papers. The quoted passage alludes to one of Samuel Johnson's *Rambler* essays ("the bloom of roseate virginity")

and to Thomas Gray's "Elegy Written in a Country Churchyard" ("waste your sweetness on the desert air").

42. RS to CMS, 2/23/1807 and 3/11/1807, Sedgwick IV Papers, and HDS to TS II, 3/5/1807 (quoted), Sedgwick V Papers.

43. TS I to TS II, 4/12/1807 and 5/14/1807, Sedgwick III Papers.

44. Susan Ridley does not seem to have informed her mother's sister, Susan "Sukie" Symmes, of her plans; in eight letters over the following year, Sukie never mentions her niece's wedding plans, despite repeated references to the weddings of others; see Susan Symmes to Susan Ridley (eight items), 8/28/1807 through 8/31/1808, Matthew Ridley Papers II, Massachusetts Historical Society.

45. TS II to HDS, 7/22/1807, and HDS to TS II, 7/13/1807, Sedgwick V Papers; see also CMS to FSW, 7/7/1807, Sedgwick IV Papers; CMS to EW, 7/15/1807, Catharine Maria Sedgwick I Papers; and TS I to TS II, 7/23/1807, Sedgwick III Papers.

46. HDS to TS II, with quote from EW, 8/3/1807, Sedgwick V Papers; and TS I to TS II, 4/18/1808, Sedgwick III Papers.

47. TS II to TS I, 10/18/1808 (quoted), Sedgwick III Papers; CMS to TS I, 11/22/1808, Sedgwick IV Papers; and also TS II to HDS, 11/7/1808, and EW to HDS, 12/1/1808, Sedgwick V Papers.

48. Numerous letters from Catherine Livingston to TS II and SRS, 1810–1813, Matthew Ridley Papers II, MHS. On TS II's legal work regarding Catherine Livingston's property, see also TS II to HDS, 7/25/1810; and on Catherine Livingston's death, see H. Bleecker to HDS, 12/14/1813, and TS II to HDS, 12/15/1813 ("inestimable blessing"), Sedgwick V Papers. Disinheritance and exclusion from her stepfather's house were not the last sanctions SRS would suffer: The Livingstons drummed her out of their history as well as their houses and estates, forgetting her so completely that a published Livingston genealogy prepared by family members in the 1940s lists her as not having married at all, and a Ridley genealogy from the 1880s even says that Matthew Ridley and Kitty Livingston Ridley had no children; see Van Rensselaer and Laimbeer, *The Livingston Family in America*, p. 86, and Ridlon, *History of the Ancient Ryedales*, p. 764.

3. Bitterness in the Cup of Joy: A Stepmother, a Death, a Will *(pages 53–69)*

1. On widowers, see Beatrice Gottlieb, *The Family in the Western World from the Black Death to the Industrial Age* (New York: Oxford University Press, 1993), p. 66; on TS I's first marriage, see chapter 1.

2. TS II to HDS, 6/12/1808, Sedgwick V Papers; Samuel Francis Batchelder, *Notes on Colonel Henry Vassall (1721–1769), His Wife Penelope Royall, His House at Cambridge, and His Slaves Tony and Darby* (Cambridge, Mass.: n.p., 1917), in the collection of the New England Historic Genealogical Society; Gerard W.

Gawalt, *The Promise of Power: The Emergence of the Legal Profession in Massachusetts, 1760–1840* (Westport, Conn.: Greenwood, 1979), pp. 48–49; and Catharine Maria Sedgwick, "Recollections of Childhood," in *Life and Letters of Catharine M. Sedgwick,* edited by Mary E. Dewey (New York: Harper, 1872), p. 38.

3. HDS to TS II, 10/30/1808, Sedgwick V Papers, and TS I to TS II, 10/20/1808, Sedgwick III Papers. CMS also expressed concern about the quarrel with Mrs. Tucker in CMS to TS I, 11/22/1808, Sedgwick IV Papers.

4. HDS to TS I (long quote), 11/7/1808, Sedgwick V Papers; and CS, RS, and ESP to TS I (all on same sheet), 11/15/1808, Sedgwick IV Papers.

5. CMS to TS I, 11/22/1808, Sedgwick IV Papers; TS I to HDS, 11/12/1808, Sedgwick V Papers.

6. HDS to TS II, 10/30/1808; HDS to TS I, 11/7/1808; and TS I to HDS, 11/12/1808, Sedgwick V Papers; CMS Journal, 11/29/1829, Catharine Maria Sedgwick I Papers.

7. HDS to CMS, 1/2/1809, Catharine Maria Sedgwick III Papers, and C. M. Sedgwick, "Recollections of Childhood," p. 38.

8. TS II to TS I, 2/10/1809, Sedgwick III Papers; also HDS to TS I, 2/24/1810, TS I to HDS, 10/11/1810, and CS to HDS, 7/2/1812, Sedgwick V Papers. A copy of the TS I Last Will and Testament, dated 3/5/1810, is in Sedgwick V Papers.

9. CMS to RS, 5/27/1811, and CS to RS, 7/29/1811, Sedgwick IV Papers; and also CS to HDS, 6/25/1811, and CS to HDS, 12/6/1811, Sedgwick V Papers. For additional references to Mrs. Sedgwick's health, see CMS to RS, 5/9/1811, and CS to TS I, 11/1/1811, Sedgwick IV Papers; TS II to HDS, 7/10/1811, and TS I to HDS, 11/1811, Sedgwick V Papers; and TS I to TS II, 12/27/1811, Sedgwick III Papers.

10. CMS to RS, 10/4/1811, Sedgwick IV Papers. On the crisis of late 1811, see also HDS to CMS, 9/30/1811; CMS to HDS, 10/20/1811; and CMS to HDS, 11/28/1811, Catharine Maria Sedgwick III Papers; and RS to CMS, 10/16/1811, Sedgwick IV Papers.

11. CMS to HDS, 11/28/1811, Catharine Maria Sedgwick III Papers; CS to CMS, 3/5/1812 and 3/27/1812 ("last view"), and CS to TS I, 4/23/1812, Sedgwick IV Papers; TS II to TS I, 3/29/1812, Sedgwick III Papers; and also CS to HDS, 2/20/1812; stage tickets, 4/27/1812; and TP to HDS, 5/29/1812, Sedgwick V Papers.

12. CMS to RS, 6/3/1812, 6/10/1812, and 6/19/1812, Sedgwick IV Papers; RS to H. Bleecker, 6/9/1812, Sedgwick II Papers; and also TS I to HDS, 6/11/1812; CS to HDS, 6/18/1812; TS I to HDS, with CMS postscript, 8/23/1812; RS to HDS, 8/24/1812 ("Pray come"); and H. Bleecker to HDS, 2/1/1813, Sedgwick V Papers.

13. TS II to HDS, 9/6/1812 ("ridicule") and 9/11/1812; and TS I to HDS, 11/12/1808 ("Had I imagined"), Sedgwick V Papers. Whatever caused the dispute, it happened sometime between HDS's arrival (no earlier than 8/24/1812,

the day RS wrote a letter addressed to him in Boston, cited note 12, above) and TS II's departure (no later than 9/5/1812, the day before he sat down in Albany to write the first of these letters).

14. TS I to HDS, 10/22/1812 ("indescribable"), Sedgwick V Papers, and CMS to RS, 11/12/1812 ("almost necessary"), Catharine Maria Sedgwick I Papers. For more on the status of TS I, see TS II to H. Bleecker, 11/11/1812 and 11/24/1812; RS to H. Bleecker, 11/28/1812; RS to HDS, 12/8/1812; TS II to HDS, 12/8/1812; and HDS to RS, 12/14/1812, Sedgwick V Papers; and CMS to RS, 10/1812 and 12/10/1812, Sedgwick IV Papers.

15. CMS to RS, 12/16/1812, Sedgwick IV Papers; FSW to TS II, 12/21/1812, Sedgwick III Papers; TS II to H. Bleecker, 12/24/1812, and CS to H. Bleecker, 12/25/1812, Sedgwick II Papers; and also EW to HDS, 12/[19 or 26]/1812; TP to HDS, 12/21/1812 ("blissful"); TS II to HDS, 12/28/1812 ("critical"); and FSW to HDS, n.d. [probably 12/21/1812] ("ministering"), Sedgwick V Papers. TS II's and SRS's daughter, Maria Banyer Sedgwick, was born 1/13/1813, joining her brother Theodore (TS III), who had been born 1/27/1811.

16. CMS to FSW, 1/5/1813, and CMS to ESP, 1/15/1813, Catharine Maria Sedgwick I Papers; and CMS to SRS, 1/12/1813, Sedgwick III Papers.

17. CMS to EW, 1/22/1813, Catharine Maria Sedgwick I Papers; HDS to TS II, 1/17/1813 and 1/25/1813 ("without a struggle"), Sedgwick III Papers; and also TS II to H. Bleecker, 1/21/1813; EW to HDS, 1/21/1813; HDS to FSW, 1/23/1813; and HDS to H. Bleecker, 1/25/1813, Sedgwick V Papers. For details on the Judge's funeral, see the [Boston] *Weekly Messenger*, 1/29/1813, p. 3. For a selection of condolence letters on the death of the Judge, see Eliza Susan (Morton) Quincy to HDS, n.d. [2/1813], H. Bleecker to HDS, 2/1/1813, Edward Channing to HDS, 2/4/1813, Mary Channing to HDS, 2/5/1813, and Nathaniel Appleton to HDS, 2/6/1813, Sedgwick V Papers. Appleton and Mary Channing both refer to CMS as "inconsolable."

18. RS to CMS, 3/10/1813, and later CMS annotation on cover, n.d., Sedgwick IV Papers. The substance of CMS's note (that RS fulfilled his promise "by a life of the tenderest fidelity," followed by an exclamation, "Oh my brother — my brother —") leads me to believe that it was written sometime after RS's death in 1841. The fictional account of a parent's funeral is in Catharine Maria Sedgwick, *A New-England Tale; or, Sketches of New England Character and Manners* (1822); rpt., edited by Victoria Clements, in "Early American Women Writers" series (New York: Oxford University Press, 1995), p. 13. After the burial of TS I in Boston, to have his remains removed to and reburied at Stockbridge would have been an awkward and expensive task, but the family did so, as is clear from the discussion of the design of a memorial in RS to HDS, 3/9/1813, Sedgwick V Papers, and the eventual construction of that memorial in Stockbridge.

19. CMS to RS, 2/17/1813 ("beloved Father"), and CMS to FSW, 2/15/1813 ("bitterness"), Catharine Maria Sedgwick I Papers; TP to HDS, 12/21/1812 ("orders"), Sedgwick V Papers; and HDS to TS II, 2/3/1813, Sedgwick III Papers.

20. On the rich and complex subject of changes in inheritance law and women's legal position, I have drawn on Gottlieb, *The Family in the Western World*, pp. 213–20; Joan Hoff, *Law, Gender, and Injustice: A Legal History of U.S. Women* (New York: New York University Press, 1991), pp. 83–84, 93, 107–11; Carole Shammas, "English Inheritance Law and Its Transfer to the Colonies," *American Journal of Legal History* 31, no. 2 (April 1987), pp. 145–63; Carole Shammas, Marylynn Salmon, and Michel Dahlin, *Inheritance in America from Colonial Times to the Present* (New Brunswick, N.J.: Rutgers University Press, 1987), pp. 42–79; Marylynn Salmon, *Women and the Law of Property in Early America* (Chapel Hill: University of North Carolina Press, 1986), pp. 120–184; Carol Elizabeth Jenson, "The Equity Jurisdiction and Married Women's Property in Ante-Bellum America: A Revisionist View," *International Journal of Women's Studies* 2, no. 2 (March–April 1979), pp. 145–48; Joan Hoff Wilson, "Hidden Riches: Legal Records and Women, 1750–1825," in *Woman's Being, Woman's Place: Female Identity and Vocation in American History*, edited by Mary Kelley (Boston: G. K. Hall, 1979), pp. 11–12, 15–18; and Stanley N. Katz, "Republicanism and the Law of Inheritance in the American Revolutionary Era," *Michigan Law Review* 76, no. 1 (November 1977), p. 28.

21. On the frequency of actions to renounce dower rights, see Hoff Wilson, "Legal Records and Women," p. 17; on Europe, see Gottlieb, *Family in the Western World*, p. 206; and on PDS's relative, see PDS to TS I, 12/18/1794, Sedgwick III Papers.

22. HDS to CMS, 4/3/1810, Catharine Maria Sedgwick III Papers; Linda K. Kerber, *No Constitutional Right to Be Ladies: Women and the Obligations of Citizenship* (New York: Hill & Wang, 1998), p. 94 (voting and juries), and pp. 17–21, 24–32 (*Martin* v. *Commonwealth*).

23. On changes in this awkward practice of assigning a widow a room or rooms in, and privileges in other parts of, an inherited house, see Christi A. Mitchell's study of fifty-five cases of court-ordered division in ten southern Maine towns between 1784 and 1845, "Neither His nor Theirs: Dower and Household Relations between Widows, Family, and Friends," *Maine History* 38 (fall winter 1999), pp. 166–85. For the first thirty-six years covered in Mitchell's article, Maine was part of Massachusetts.

24. TS I Last Will and Testament, 3/5/1810, Sedgwick V Papers; HDS to TS II, 2/3/1813, Sedgwick III Papers; TS II to H. Bleecker, 2/4/1813, Sedgwick II Papers; and HDS to RS, 3/12/1813, and [HDS?], manuscript notes, 5/18/1813, Sedgwick V Papers.

25. RS to HDS, 2/9/1813, and HDS to RS, 2/25/1813, Sedgwick V Papers; also CMS to FSW, 3/12/1813, Catharine Maria Sedgwick I Papers.

26. CMS to RS, 3/11/1813, Catharine Maria Sedgwick I Papers; also EW to HDS, 3/9/1813; RS to HDS, 3/9/1813; and CS to HDS, 3/12/1813, Sedgwick V Papers. On EW's debt to the estate of TS I, see chapter 4.

27. HDS to RS, 3/12/1813, Sedgwick V Papers.

28. HDS to RS, 3/12/1813 and 3/18/1813, and HDS to CS, 3/15/1813 (quoted),

Sedgwick V Papers. See also HDS to CMS, 3/11/1813, Catharine Maria Sedgwick III Papers, and TP to HDS, 3/26/1813, Sedgwick V Papers. The Stuart portrait of TS I was donated to the Museum of Fine Arts, Boston, by CS's great-grandson, Charles Sedgwick Rackemann. Black-and-white reproductions of it can be seen in Margaret C. S. Christman, *The First Federal Congress, 1789–1791* (Washington, D.C.: Smithsonian Institution Press, 1989), p. 319, and as the frontispiece to Richard E. Welch, Jr., *Theodore Sedgwick, Federalist: A Political Portrait* (Middletown, Conn.: Wesleyan University Press, 1965).

29. On *Herbert v. Wren*, see Hoff, *Law, Gender, and Injustice*, pp. 109–11; on Hannah Bushrod Washington, see Henry Wiencek, *Imperfect God: George Washington, His Slaves, and the Creation of America* (New York: Farrar, Straus and Giroux, 2003), pp. 299–303.

30. HDS to RS, 3/18/1813, Sedgwick V Papers; see also HDS to CMS, 3/26/1813, Catharine Maria Sedgwick III Papers.

31. CS to HDS, 3/19/1813; HDS to RS, 3/18/1813; and TP to HDS, 3/26/1813, Sedgwick V Papers.

32. HDS to FSW, 4/10/1813, Sedgwick V Papers.

33. RS to HDS, 6/19/1813; HDS to [CMS], n.d. [around 12/11/1813] (fragment); and C. Russell to HDS, 9/29/1815, Sedgwick V Papers. On the quarrel between HDS and EW concerning the income from the English property, see chapter 4.

4. *Brutal Conduct: The Watsons (pages 70–82)*

1. CMS to TS I, 1/27/1809; HDS to CMS, 4/4/1809; and RS to CMS, 11/1/1809, Sedgwick IV Papers; and also HDS to RS, 3/23/1811, Sedgwick V Papers.

2. RS to HDS, 4/2/1811; EW to HDS, 4/[4]/1811; RS to HDS, 4/27/1811 ("safe"); EW to HDS, 5/13/1811; and TS I to HDS, 6/11/1811, Sedgwick V Papers.

3. RS to HDS, 2/9/1813; HDS to RS, 2/25/1813 (*"perfect"*); RS to HDS, 3/9/1813; and HDS to RS, 3/12/1813, Sedgwick V Papers; also RS to CMS, 2/18/1813, Sedgwick IV Papers.

4. HDS to RS, 3/18/1813, and RS to HDS, 3/23/1813, Sedgwick V Papers. On separate estates and women's property in general, see Marylynn Salmon, *Women and the Law of Property in Early America* (Chapel Hill: University of North Carolina Press, 1986), pp. 120–84, and chapter 3.

5. RS to HDS, 5/24/1814, Sedgwick V Papers.

6. HDS to RS, 6/2/1814, and RS to HDS, 7/15/1814, Sedgwick V Papers; also CMS to FSW, 6/5/1814 ("heroic"); CS to RS, 11/10/1814; and RS to CMS, 11/10/1814 and 11/21/1814 ("not so particular"), Sedgwick IV Papers.

7. EW to HDS, 3/9/1813 and 4/7/1815 (quoted), Sedgwick V Papers.

8. EW to HDS, 4/7/1815, and HDS to EW, n.d. [between 4/7/1815 and 4/22/1815], Sedgwick V Papers.

9. RS to HDS, 4/24/1815, Sedgwick V Papers. See also Elizabeth Pleck,

Domestic Tyranny: The Making of Social Policy against Family Violence from Colonial Times to the Present (New York: Oxford University Press, 1987), pp. 31–33, 53–54; Ann Taves, ed., *Religion and Family Violence in Early New England: The Memoirs of Abigail Abbot Bailey* (1815; rpt., Bloomington: Indiana University Press, 1989); and Nancy F. Cott, *Public Vows: A History of Marriage and the Nation* (Cambridge, Mass.: Harvard University Press, 2000), pp. 161–62.

10. FSW to HDS, 6/30/1815 ("I asked"); TS II to HDS, 7/3/1815; RS to HDS, 7/9/1815; TS II to HDS, 9/21/1815 and 10/2/1815; and EW to HDS, 10/15/1815 ("My Dear Brother"), Sedgwick V Papers.

11. HDS to FSW, 10/28/1815; RS to HDS, 11/13/1815; RS to HDS, 1/10/1816 and 1/22/1816; E. Little to HDS, 2/21/1816; RS to HDS, 3/4/1816; EW to HDS, 4/19/1816, with RS to HDS postscript dated 4/26/1816; TP to HDS, 10/30/1816; and TS II to HDS, 3/15/1817, Sedgwick V Papers; also RS to CMS, 3/30/1816, Sedgwick IV Papers, and Copies of Equity Judgments, liber 374, p. 94, Division of Old Records and Condemnation Records, City Clerk's Office, Hall of Records, New York City. On New York's incremental adoption of a series of bankruptcy laws between 1809 and 1831, see Peter J. Coleman, *Debtors and Creditors in America: Insolvency, Imprisonment for Debt, and Bankruptcy, 1607–1900* (Madison: University of Wisconsin Press, 1974), pp. 107–27, especially p. 119.

12. RS to HDS, 3/4/1816; CS to HDS, 4/5/1816 ("last opportunity"); and RS to HDS, 4/26/1816 ("another man"), postscript to EW to HDS, 4/19/1816, Sedgwick V Papers; see also CMS to FSW, 2/26/1816, and RS to CMS, 3/30/1816, Sedgwick IV Papers.

13. FSW to HDS, 2/1/1816, 8/8/1816, and n.d. [9/1816], Sedgwick V Papers.

14. EW to HDS, 10/29/1816, and HDS to JM, 11/12/1816, Sedgwick V Papers. On the contrasting treatment of bankrupts in Massachusetts and New York, see Coleman, *Debtors and Creditors in America*, pp. 41–52.

15. CMS to FSW, 3/7/1816, Sedgwick IV Papers; CMS to RS, 10/8/1817, Catharine Maria Sedgwick I Papers; CMS to RS, 10/20/[1817], Sedgwick IV Papers; and Jane M. Sedgwick to HDS, n.d. 9/[12/1819], Sedgwick V Papers.

16. CMS to FSW, 3/15/1820, Catharine Maria Sedgwick I Papers; also CMS to FSW, 12/20/1820, CMS to ESP, 12/1/1822 (quoted), and CMS to FSW, 1/9/1823, Sedgwick IV Papers.

17. On the difficulty of obtaining a divorce in Massachusetts and New York, see Nelson Manfred Blake, *The Road to Reno: A History of Divorce in the United States* (New York: Macmillan, 1962), pp. 49–52, 61–79; Nancy F. Cott, "Divorce and the Changing Status of Women in Eighteenth-Century Massachusetts," *William and Mary Quarterly*, 3rd ser., 33 (October 1976), pp. 586–614; Linda K. Kerber, *Women of the Republic: Intellect and Ideology in Revolutionary America* (Chapel Hill: University of North Carolina Press, 1980), pp. 159–60, 181–84; Salmon, *Women and the Law of Property*, pp. 60–61; Ann Taves, introduction to *Memoirs of Abigail Abbot Bailey*, pp. 1–13; Glenda Riley, *Divorce: An American Tradition* (New York: Oxford University Press, 1991), pp. 44–46, 52–56; Norma

Basch, *Framing American Divorce: From the Revolutionary Generation to the Victorians* (Berkeley: University of California Press, 1999), pp. 19–42, 47–48; and Hendrik Hartog, *Man and Wife in America: A History* (Cambridge, Mass.: Harvard University Press, 2000), pp. 71–73. On Vermont, see Randall A. Roth, "Spousal Murder in Northern New England, 1776–1865," in *Over the Threshold: Intimate Violence in Early America*, edited by Christine Daniels and Michael V. Kennedy (New York: Routledge, 1999), pp. 67–69, 76–77 (the data on grounds are from Windsor County), and Mary Beth Sievens, "'The Wicked Agency of Others': Community, Law, and Marital Conflict in Vermont, 1790–1830," *Journal of the Early Republic* 21 (spring 2001), pp. 19–39.

18. Michael Grossberg, *Governing the Hearth: Law and the Family in Nineteenth-Century America* (Chapel Hill: University of North Carolina Press, 1985), pp. 237–39; Mary Ann Mason, *From Father's Property to Children's Rights: A History of Child Custody in the United States* (New York: Columbia University Press, 1994), pp. 60–61; Hartog, *Man and Wife in America*, pp. 194–95.

19. Grossberg, *Governing the Hearth*, p. 240, and Carole Shammas, *A History of Household Government in America* (Charlottesville: University of Virginia Press, 2002), pp. 118–22.

20. RS to Elizabeth E. Sedgwick, 8/12/1826 ("that brute"), and FSW to HDS, 8/23/1826 ("I must be driven"), Sedgwick V Papers; CMS to Elizabeth D. Sedgwick, 11/19/[1826] ("serenity"), and CMS to FSW, 8/26/1827 ("hopeless"), Catharine Maria Sedgwick I Papers. The letter on which I have corrected the date was filed as 1820, but the date should be 1826, as attested by the ages of the children mentioned in it.

21. CMS to EW (draft), 1/27/1828, Sedgwick IV Papers. For more on the Unitarian Sedgwicks' critique of orthodox Calvinism, see chapter 8.

22. FSW to HDS, n.d. [before 1828] ("harrowed") and 10/22/[between 1820 and 1824] ("sepulcher"), Sedgwick V Papers; TS II to TS III, 12/27/1828 ("insanity"), and SRS to TS III, 12/28/1828, Sedgwick II Papers; and also CMS to FSW, 12/27/1828 ("severed forever"); FSW to CMS, 1/15/1829; CMS to FSW, 4/12/1829; and CMS to FSW, 6/9/1829, Sedgwick IV Papers.

23. Hubert Merrill Sedgwick, *A Sedgwick Genealogy: Descendants of Deacon Benjamin Sedgwick* (New Haven: New Haven Colony Historical Society, 1961); also Louisa Davis Minot to Mary Minot, 6/3/1842, and Louisa Davis Minot to William Minot, 6/17/1842, Sedgwick IV Papers.

5. The Heart That's Worth Possessing: Two Disastrous Courtships
(pages 85–97)

1. For HDS's surprise at the size of his inheritance ("I had no anticipation that our affairs would turn out so well"), see HDS to RS, 3/12/1813, Sedgwick V Papers. On readiness for love, psychologist Ethel Spector Person noted

that some "special moments in one's individual development and particular kinds of life circumstances do appear likely to foster love. Falling in love often falls closely on the heels of anticipated or actual separation and loss. . . ." She included the death of a parent and a move away from home as examples of such loss. See Person, *Dreams of Love and Fateful Encounters: The Power of Romantic Passion* (New York: Norton, 1988), pp. 31–32.

2. On the age of Mary Channing (later Mary Channing Rogers, 1782–1843), see Frank Carpenter, "The Channing Family," 1998, <http://www3.edgenet.net/fcarpenter/chanfam.html>.

3. RS to HDS, 11/30/1811 (quoted); see also RS to HDS, 2/18/1812, 3/25/1812, 4/15/1812, and 10/1812, Sedgwick V Papers.

4. Love letters and letters to family members about love affairs in the 1810s were extremely revealing of passions and emotions, but not at all revealing of names and personal information. The two women HDS courted in 1813 and 1814 were never named in his letters to CMS or RS in those years, or in copies of letters he sent to or received from the women he was courting, but they can be identified, using street directories, genealogies, initials, and hints about their fathers' identities that crop up in the letters. HDS later wrote a full account of both courtships, to explain his behavior to the woman to whom he would eventually become engaged. That letter (HDS to JM, n.d. [summer 1816], Sedgwick V Papers) helped to put the scattered, often undated and unaddressed letters of 1813 and 1814 into context. I have relied on it heavily in what follows, and quotations from HDS in the remainder of this chapter that are not otherwise credited come from it. (See chapter 6 for more on the letter of summer 1816 and the occasion of its composition and delivery.) Even in that letter, though, the women were only identified as "Miss S" and "Miss P"—that is, by the first letters of their family names. Those family names were finally mentioned in later letters; see JM to HDS, 11/[19]/1816 (mentions Miss Phillips), and 1/3/1817 (mentions Miss Sumner), and another reference to Miss Phillips in an undated fragment discussed in greater detail in note 9, below, HDS to [E. Sumner?] (copy or draft), n.d. [11 or 12/1813]; all are in Sedgwick V Papers.

5. On the Phillips family, see Benjamin B. Wisner, *A Sermon Occasioned by the Death of the Hon. William Phillips, Preached on the Third of June, 1827, Being the Sabbath after the Funeral* (Boston: Hilliard, Gray, Little, and Wilkins, 1827), esp. Note A, pp. 34–48; see also extensive references in Claude M. Fuess, *An Old New England School: A History of Phillips Academy, Andover* (Boston: Houghton Mifflin, 1917), and in [Anonymous], *The First National Bank of Boston, 1784–1934: A Brief History of Its 150 Years of Continual Existence with Emphasis on the Early Days of Its Forebear, the Massachusetts Bank* (Boston: n.p., 1934). On Old South Church, see Conrad Wright, *The Beginnings of Unitarianism in America* (Boston: Beacon, 1966), p. 261.

6. HDS to JM, n.d. [summer 1816], and M. Channing to HDS, 8/1813, Sedgwick V Papers; for CMS's distant and puzzled observation of the events of this month, see CMS to HDS, 8/26/1813, Catharine Maria Sedgwick III Papers.

7. For evidence of HDS's earlier acquaintance with the Sumner family, see W. Sumner to HDS, 6/16/1810, Sedgwick V Papers.

8. Quotations from CMS, postscript to CS to HDS, 11/9/1813; RS to HDS, 12/14/1813; and HDS to JM, n.d. [summer 1816], Sedgwick V Papers. See also CMS to HDS, 12/[13]/1813 [dated "Monday"], Catharine Maria Sedgwick III Papers, and TP to HDS, 11/2/1813, CS to HDS, 11/13/1813, and RS to HDS, 11/23/1813, Sedgwick V Papers. HDS's dream letter to Elizabeth Sumner does not survive, only his 1816 account and references to it in the CMS and RS letters cited here. For more on the intricate rules of courtship, see chapter 6.

9. HDS to [E. Sumner?] (copy or draft), n.d. [11 or 12/1813], dated from internal evidence and a reference in RS to HDS, 12/14/1813; both in Sedgwick V Papers.

10. RS to HDS, 12/14/1813, and HDS to [CMS], with passage from "Miss Sumner" to HDS, n.d. [around 12/11/1813] (fragment), Sedgwick V Papers. Only the last page of HDS's letter survives; apparently the full letter contained accounts and transcriptions of the whole affair, including the dream. RS had read and reacted to HDS's copies of the correspondence by 12/14, which means Mehetable Sumner's letter must have been written no later than early December. In HDS to JM, n.d. [summer 1816], HDS remembered it as possibly dating to January, though he admitted he was unsure. On ways of interpreting Elizabeth Sumner's intent, see also CMS to HDS, 12/13/1813, Catharine Maria Sedgwick III Papers.

11. HDS to H. Bleecker, 12/7/1813, and HDS to [CMS], n.d. [around 12/11/1813] (fragment), Sedgwick V Papers.

12. The letters are undated, but they are numbered. The contents make it clear that they do not refer to HDS's relationship with Abigail Phillips, about which Mary Channing had written earlier, in a letter (quoted above) that she dated August. See M. Channing to HDS (numbers 2, 6, and 8 of 12), n.d. [1813], Sedgwick V Papers.

13. CMS to HDS, 1/8/1814 (quoted), Catharine Maria Sedgwick III Papers; see also RS to HDS, 1/1/[1814]; TP to HDS, 1/1/1814; and ESP to HDS, 1/2/1814, continued 1/18/1814, Sedgwick V Papers.

14. "Tremont Street" [A. Phillips] to HDS (copy), 1/20/1814, Sedgwick V Papers. All four January 1814 letters from Abigail Phillips to HDS survive only as copies in HDS's hand. This at least raises the question, unanswerable and probably unduly skeptical, whether the entire second phase of the courtship of Abigail Phillips was a fiction whipped up by HDS to deceive his family, to redirect their attention and conceal his disappointment over the ending of the courtship of Elizabeth Sumner, or for some other unfathomable reason; but perhaps one has read too many modern novels.

15. HDS to [CMS], n.d. [after 1/20/1814], Sedgwick V Papers. Interestingly, psychologist Ethel Spector Person spoke of the transitional moments of readiness for love (such as the death of a parent or a move away from home; see note 1, above) as times when "one can be infatuated with two different people almost

simultaneously. Here the would-be lover admires two prospective candidates for his affection and fantasizes that one or the other relationship might evolve into love given the right circumstances. This capacity for simultaneous or sequential infatuation speaks to the question of when we fall in love, suggesting that there are psychological moments at which one is ripe, regardless of whether there is an appropriate love object at hand. Though such a lover appears to be fickle, it may only be his longing for a beloved who will reciprocate that makes him seem so. . . ." See Person, *Dreams of Love and Fateful Encounters*, pp. 31–32.

16. HDS to [A. Phillips] (draft), n.d. [1/1814], Sedgwick V Papers.

17. "Tremont Street" [A. Phillips] to HDS (copy), 1/24/1814; n.d. [1/28?]/1814; and another n.d. [1/29]/1814, Sedgwick V Papers. On HDS's report that Abigail Phillips told him she would accept his proposal, see CMS to RS, 6/7/1814, Catharine Maria Sedgwick I Papers.

18. TS II to HDS, 2/4/1814, and ESP to HDS, 2/[n.d.]/1814, Sedgwick V Papers; see also CMS to HDS, 2/4/1814, Catharine Maria Sedgwick III Papers.

19. TS II to HDS, 2/23/1814, and TP to HDS, 3/1/1814; see also CS to HDS, 2/18/1814, and RS to HDS, 2/28/1814, Sedgwick V Papers. RS believed that William Phillips suspected his brother was a fortune-hunter; see RS to HDS, 3/7/1814, Sedgwick V Papers, for his proposal of a plan that would enable HDS to refute the suspicion.

20. FSW to HDS, 2/17/1814, Sedgwick V Papers.

21. HDS to [William H. Sumner], n.d. [1814] (draft or unsent) ("puppet"), and HDS to JM, n.d. [summer 1816] ("civility"), Sedgwick V Papers. For confirmation that HDS sent some version of this letter and that he believed William Sumner had accepted his explanation, see HDS to CMS, 3/8/1814, Catharine Maria Sedgwick III Papers, and CMS to RS, 6/7/1814, Catharine Maria Sedgwick I Papers.

22. On HDS's travels, see CS to HDS, 6/1/1813, T. Woodbridge to HDS, 4/19/1814, and RS to HDS, 5/24/1814 and 6/27/1814, Sedgwick V Papers.

23. FSW, postscript to EW to HDS, 3/29/1814, Sedgwick V Papers; HDS to CMS, 3/8/1814, Catharine Maria Sedgwick III Papers; CMS to ESP, 3/12/1814, and CMS to RS, 6/7/1814, Catharine Maria Sedgwick I Papers; and RS to HDS, 6/27/1814, Sedgwick V Papers.

24. HDS to JM, n.d. [summer 1816], and CMS to HDS (quoting Deut. 33:15 and Rev. 6:14), postscript to CS to HDS, 11/9/1813, Sedgwick V Papers.

6. *The Perils of Badinage: Harry and Robert among the Friendlies* (pages 98–126)

1. J. M. Ely to HDS, 6/23/1814; RS to HDS, 6/27/1814; HDS to SRS, 7/4/1814; HDS to H. Bleecker, 7/22/1814; and RS to HDS, 8/23/1814, Sedgwick V Papers; also CS to RS, 11/10/1814, Sedgwick IV Papers.

2. RS to HDS, 11/18/1814, Sedgwick V Papers.

3. TS II to HDS, 12/6/1814; N. Hale to HDS, 4/21/1815; N. Hale to HDS, 7/10/1815 (quoted); HDS to E. P. Ashmun, 8/23/1815; TS II to HDS, 9/21/1815; and TS II to HDS, 10/2/1815, Sedgwick V Papers.

4. RS to HDS, 10/4/1815, Sedgwick V Papers. For the timing of RS's visits to Stockbridge, see RS to CMS, 5/9/1815, 6/28/1815, and 9/[2–4? or 9–11?]/1815, Sedgwick IV Papers; on the trip to Boston, see also EW to HDS, 10/15/1815, and H. W. Dwight to HDS, 11/3/1815, Sedgwick V Papers; and CS to CMS, 10/19/1815, Sedgwick IV Papers.

5. On HDS's first encounter with William Minot [WM], see HDS to TS II, 11/28/1804, Sedgwick V Papers. On George Richards Minot and Mary Speakman Minot, see James Jackson Minot, *Ancestors and Descendants of George Richards Minot, 1758–1802* (n.p., 1936), pp. 14–15, and Last Will and Testament of Mary Speakman Minot, dated 1/10/1811, Sedgwick V Papers. On the Sedgwicks' connection to Daniel Davis, see TS II to HDS, 5/27/1810, Daniel Davis to HDS, 6/10/1810, and RS to HDS, 6/17/1810, Sedgwick V Papers; and also HDS to CMS, 3/11/1812, Catharine Maria Sedgwick III Papers. On LDM's first impression of WM, see Minot, *Ancestors and Descendants of George Richards Minot*, p. 18. On the house and its location, see *The Minot Family: Record of Births, Marriages and Deaths, 1754–1934, Copied from Family Bibles* (n.p., 1934), in the collection of the Massachusetts Historical Society; Walter Muir Whitehill, *Boston: A Topographical History*, 2nd ed. (Cambridge, Mass.: Harvard University Press, 1968), pp. 55–64; and Allen Chamberlain, *Beacon Hill: Its Ancient Pastures and Early Mansions* (Boston: Houghton Mifflin, 1925), pp. 7, 31–32, 80–81. On legal business with the Davis family, see RS to HDS, 5/3/1811, TS I to HDS, 6/11/1811, and William Davis to William Dawson, 1/11/1812, Sedgwick V Papers, and also CMS to RS, 5/9/1811, Sedgwick IV Papers. On legal business with WM, see Charles Denison to HDS, 10/12/1813, Sedgwick V Papers.

6. HDS would later refer to Mr. Murray, at whose home JM and RS first conversed, as RS's best client; see HDS to JM, 11/29/1816, continued 12/1/1816, Sedgwick V Papers.

7. For JM's later recollection of the impression RS made on her, see JM to HDS, n.d. [1/8/1817, continued 1/9/1817], Sedgwick V Papers. Other quotations in this paragraph are from JM to "My dear Friends," Travel Journal, July–September 1815, Sedgwick V Papers. For the first part of the journey, see also twelve letters from WM to LDM, 7/3/1815 through 8/18/1815, and D. Davis to WM, 8/24/1815, Sedgwick IV Papers. On RS at Ballston, see RS to CMS, 8/25/1815, Sedgwick IV Papers.

8. RS to HDS, 10/4/1815, HDS to FSW, 10/28/1815, and RS to HDS, 11/13/1815, Sedgwick V Papers; see also CMS to Robert Watson, 11/30/1815, Catharine Maria Sedgwick I Papers; RS to CMS, 12/4/1815, Sedgwick IV Papers; and Thomas B. Wait & Sons to HDS, 12/5/1815, Sedgwick V Papers.

9. On the meeting with Elizabeth Sumner, see HDS to JM, n.d. [summer

1816], Sedgwick V Papers. RS knew HDS's most grievous anxiety concerned a woman of great wealth, and Abigail Phillips's father was probably the wealthiest man in Boston; this leads me to believe that when RS told HDS, "You did right *a l'autre*," the reference was to Abigail Phillips; see RS to HDS, 10/4/1815 and 11/13/1815, Sedgwick V Papers.

10. RS to HDS, 4/4/1816, Sedgwick V Papers.

11. The taboo against the use of ladies' first names was described as something that ought to have been universally understood in JM to HDS, 2/2/1817, Sedgwick V Papers, and was observed by HDS and RS in almost all their correspondence of this period. The first uses of the term "friendlies" that I have found occur in CMS to HDS, 3/15/1816, and JM to CMS, 4/8/1816, Catharine Maria Sedgwick III Papers.

12. Daniel Kilbride, "Cultivation, Conservatism, and the Early National Gentry: The Manigault Family and Their Circle," *Journal of the Early Republic* 19 (summer 1999), pp. 221–56; Susan Branson, *Those Fiery Frenchified Dames: Women and Political Culture in Early National Philadelphia* (Philadelphia: University of Pennsylvania Press, 2001), pp. 125–42; Carroll Smith-Rosenberg, "The Female World of Love and Ritual: Relations between Women in Nineteenth-Century America" (1975), rpt. in her *Disorderly Conduct: Visions of Gender in Victorian America* (New York: Knopf, 1985), pp. 53–76; and Nancy F. Cott, *The Bonds of Womanhood: Women's Sphere in New England, 1780–1835* (New Haven, Conn.: Yale University Press, 1977), pp. 160–68. For much more about the friendlies, see chapters 7 and 9.

13. References to JM's age are contradictory; they allow us to narrow her date of birth down to sometime between February 1794 and August 1795. See JM to WM, 8/5/1805, and JM Commonplace Book, 1811–1815, Sedgwick V Papers; and Death Records, Office of the Town Clerk, Stockbridge, Mass. All of this illustrates the relative carelessness about reporting exact calendar dates by women and for events in women's lives that was seen in PDS's letters to TS I (see chapter 1) and would be seen again in the correspondence between HDS and JM that is the subject of chapters 7–9.

14. JM Commonplace Book, 1811–1815, Sedgwick V Papers, is the best source for information about the friendlies' activities and emotions, but not about their ages or family histories. The available genealogies do not indicate the relationship between Caroline Danforth and Mary Ann Gray Fales, but in a letter JM refers to Mary Ann's father as Caroline's uncle — he must have been her dead mother's brother; see JM to HDS, 11/[19, continued 11/20 and 11/21]/1816, Sedgwick V Papers. In addition to what is contained in JM's Commonplace Book, Fales family information comes from De Coursey Fales, *The Fales Family of Bristol, Rhode Island* (Boston: n.p., 1919), pp. 116–17. Jones family information comes from Probate no. 29075, John C. Jones, November 9, 1829, Suffolk County Probate Court, Boston, in the Massachusetts State Archives; Clifford K. Shipton, *Sibley's Harvard Graduates*, vol. 17: *1768–1771* (Boston: Massachusetts

Historical Society, 1975), pp. 49–54; and Ross H. Gast, *Contentious Consul: A Biography of John Coffin Jones, First United States Consular Agent in Hawaii* (Los Angeles: Dawson's Book Shop, 1976), pp. 17–19. (The subject of Gast's book is Margaret's brother, not her father.) Danforth family information comes from Shipton, *Sibley's Harvard Graduates*, vol. 14: *1756–1760* (1968), pp. 250–54.

15. Throughout this chapter, residential information is taken from the letters, from *The Boston Directory; Containing Names of the Inhabitants, Their Occupations, Places of Business and Dwelling Houses, With Lists of the Streets, Lanes and Wharves; the Town Officers, Public Offices and Banks, and Other Useful Information* (Boston: Cotton, 1816), and from Annie Haven Thwing, *Suffolk Deeds, 1630–1800, Compiled by Streets*, 22 vols. (Boston: n.p., 1916). On Boston churches, see Conrad Wright, "Ministers, Churches, and the Boston Elite, 1791–1815," in *Massachusetts and the New Nation*, edited by Conrad Edick Wright (Boston: Massachusetts Historical Society, 1992), p. 135; on "liberal Christianity," see chapter 8.

16. Nancy F. Cott, "Passionlessness: An Interpretation of Victorian Sexual Ideology, 1790–1850," *Signs* 4 (1978), pp. 219–36. Lee Virginia Chambers-Stiller found evidence of a related ideal, which she called a "Cult of Single Blessedness"; see Chambers-Stiller, *Liberty, A Better Husband: Single Women in America, the Generations of 1780–1840* (New Haven, Conn.: Yale University Press, 1984), p. 18.

17. "Sketch of Miss Danforth," JM Commonplace Book, 1811–1815, Sedgwick V Papers.

18. "Sketch of Miss Jones," JM Commonplace Book, 1811–1815, Sedgwick V Papers, and JM to CMS, 4/8/1816, Catharine Maria Sedgwick III Papers.

19. On JM's piano lessons, see JM to WM, 8/5/1805, Sedgwick V Papers. On the association of wealth and city-dwelling with education for young women, see the discussion of a young woman eight or nine years JM's junior in Richmond, Virginia, in Anya Jabour, "'It Will Never Do for Me to Be Married': The Life of Laura Wirt Randall, 1803–1833," *Journal of the Early Republic* 17 (summer 1997), p. 197.

20. JM Commonplace Book, 1811–1815, Sedgwick V Papers. There are obvious differences between JM's self-portrait and her characterization of Caroline Danforth, but the similarities reinforce the availability and importance of the ideal of passionless femininity that Nancy Cott has attributed to this period and the years just before it; see Cott, "Passionlessness."

21. JM to HDS, 4/[12]/1817, and RS to HDS, 4/4/1816, Sedgwick V Papers. For evidence of a previous instance in which HDS and JM had interacted without noticing each other, see J. W. Hulbert to HDS, 6/22/1812, and JM to WM, 6/25/1812, Sedgwick V Papers, and HDS to CMS, 6/22/1812, Sedgwick IV Papers.

22. On HDS's return to Boston and determination not to go back to Stockbridge, see Thomas B. Wait & Sons to HDS, 12/5/1815, and CS to HDS, 1/10/1816,

Sedgwick V Papers, and also RS to CMS, 1/17/1816, Sedgwick IV Papers; on his office-sharing with Fales, see CS to HDS, 3/7/1816, Sedgwick V Papers; on RS's visits, see RS to HDS, 1/10/1816, 1/22/1816, 2/27/1816, 5/22/1816, and 6/11/1816, Sedgwick V Papers, and RS to CMS, 1/17/1816, Sedgwick IV Papers.

23. CS to HDS, 2/20/1816 and 8/5/1816, Sedgwick V Papers; CMS to FSW, 3/25/1816, Catharine Maria Sedgwick I Papers; and TP to HDS, 2/5/1816 and 2/22/1816 (quoted), Sedgwick V Papers.

24. SRS to HDS, 3/1/1816, continued 3/15/1816, Sedgwick V Papers, and CMS to HDS, 3/15/1816, Catharine Maria Sedgwick III Papers. HDS would certainly have recognized the allusions, biblical and contemporary, in SRS's letter. "How long will you halt between two opinions?" is the exhortation of the prophet Elijah to Ahab, unfaithful king of Israel, in I Kings 18:21, and "Be wise, redeem the time, for the days are evil" is from the letter to the Ephesians 5:16. In addition, "Time has not thinned my flowing hair" is the first line of a popular madrigal or "canzonet" by English composer William Jackson (1730–1803) — Thomas Jefferson owned a copy of the sheet music as early as 1783; see Helen Cripe, "Appendix I, Jefferson's Catalogue of 1783: Transcription of the Music Section," *Thomas Jefferson and Music* (Charlottesville: University of Virginia Press, 1974), online since January 1996 at <http://www.lib.virginia.edu/dmmc/Music/Cripe/cripe.html>. The phrase "tide of *successful* experiment" is from Jefferson's 1801 inaugural address; the experiment to which Jefferson referred was the republican form of government. CMS's letter also contains a biblical allusion, to "birds of the air," from the parable of the lilies of the field, Matt. 6:26. Clearly, if playfully, SRS and CMS want HDS to know that the family awaits a momentous decision.

25. RS to CMS, 12/4/1815, Sedgwick IV Papers; RS to CMS, 12/13/1815, Catharine Maria Sedgwick I Papers; CMS to HDS, 2/29/1816, Catharine Maria Sedgwick III Papers; and RS to HDS, 3/1/1816, Sedgwick V Papers,

26. JM to CMS, 4/8/1816; HDS to CMS, 4/9/1816; and CMS to HDS, 5/12/1816, Catharine Maria Sedgwick III Papers; on the brothers' indecision, see also RS to HDS, 6/11/1816; RS to HDS, 7/28/1816; JM to HDS, [1/8/1817, continued 1/9/1817]; HDS to JM, 1/20/[1817]; and JM to RS, 1/[21]/1817, Sedgwick V Papers.

27. RS to CMS, 3/30/1816, Sedgwick IV Papers.

28. On conduct manuals, see C. Dallett Hemphill, *Bowing to Necessities: A History of Manners in America, 1620–1860* (New York: Oxford University Press, 1999), pp. 111–19.

29. This account has been reconstructed from RS to HDS, 6/11/1816, 6/17/1816, and 6/22/1816, Sedgwick V Papers, and also CMS to HDS, 6/13/1816 and 6/25/1816, Catharine Maria Sedgwick III Papers. Most quoted passages come from the first of RS's three letters. The references to criminal trifling, to laughing heartily, and to saying extravagant things; Margaret's version of RS's parting line; the final request for HDS's judgment of Mary; and RS's complaint about HDS's reading of the letter to Margaret all come from his third, as do

my inferences about the responses in HDS's letter of 6/20/1816, which does not survive. On CMS's agreement with HDS regarding the consequences of another visit to Boston, see her two cited letters and RS to HDS, 7/9/1816, Sedgwick V Papers.

30. RS to HDS, 7/9/1816, 7/18/1816, 7/28/1816 ("second sight"), 8/4/1816 ("whimsical"), 8/5/1816, and 8/10/1816, and HDS to CMS (copy), 7/27/1816 ("unappropriated"), Sedgwick V Papers; also RS to CMS, 7/27/1816, Sedgwick IV Papers, and CMS to HDS, 8/8/1816, Catharine Maria Sedgwick III Papers.

31. JM to HDS, 10/30/1816 ("Miss E") and 12/[21]/1816 ("Mrs. Snow" and "matrimonial opportunity"); also RS to HDS, 7/28/1816 and 8/4/1816, Sedgwick V Papers.

32. HDS to JM, 12/28/1816, continued 12/30 and 12/31/1816 ("shame-facedness"); 1/9/1817 ("Boston stage"); 1/20/[1817]; 2/7/1817, continued 2/8/1817 ("Robert will come"); 2/20/1817, continued 2/21/1817 ("deeply regret"); and 3/3/1817, continued 3/4/1817 ("distant"); also, JM to HDS, 2/[25]/1817 ("*That man*"), Sedgwick V Papers. See also CMS to HDS, 2/22/1817, Catharine Maria Sedgwick III Papers.

33. On RS's marriage to Elizabeth Ellery, see the epilogue; on Caroline Danforth, see "C D——" to Dr. Warren, n.d. ["Probably 1827? Dec. 30?"], John Collins Warren Papers, Massachusetts Historical Society, and Fales, *The Fales Family of Bristol, Rhode Island*, pp. 116–17.

34. On the January handshake, see JM to HDS, 3/1/1817, and on the June parting, see JM to HDS, 12/22/1816, Sedgwick V Papers; on JM's belief that HDS was captivated by Margaret, see JM to CMS, 4/8/1816, and on CMS's high opinion of JM, see CMS to HDS, 4/21/1816, Catharine Maria Sedgwick III Papers; see also RS to HDS, 6/22/1816, Sedgwick V Papers.

35. HDS to JM, 12/9/1816, continued 12/10/1816, Sedgwick V Papers.

36. RS to HDS, 7/18/1816 ("went through me"), Sedgwick V Papers; concern about WM's approval, CMS to HDS, 7/18/1816, and JM to CMS, n.d. [1816], Catharine Maria Sedgwick III Papers; and also RS to CMS, 7/27/1816, Sedgwick IV Papers; announcement of WM's consent, HDS to CMS, 7/27/1816, Catharine Maria Sedgwick III Papers; HDS to JM, 12/9/1816, continued 12/10/1816, Sedgwick V Papers.

37. RS to HDS, 4/4/1816 ("cannot be") and HDS to JM, 2/20/1817 ("*perpetual moment*"), Sedgwick V Papers. On the 1818 ruling of Chief Justice Isaac Parker in the case of *Wightman v. Coates*, see Michael Grossberg, *Governing the Hearth: Law and the Family in Nineteenth-Century America* (Chapel Hill: University of North Carolina Press, 1985), pp. 35–37.

38. HDS to CMS (copy), 8/2/1816; JM to HDS, 3/23/1817, continued 3/24/1817; see also LDM to JM, 7/28/1816, Sedgwick V Papers.

39. HDS to JM, 12/19/1816, and JM to HDS, 12/22/1816, Sedgwick V Papers.

40. On CMS's journey to Boston, see RS to HDS, 8/10/1816, and Edward Channing to Elizabeth Ellery, n.d. [8/16 or after/1816]; on the arrival of JM,

CMS, and HDS at Stockbridge and activities there, see HDS to JM, 12/19/1816; JM to HDS, 12/[21?]/1816 ["Saturday"]; CS to HDS, 1/12/1817; and HDS to JM, 3/29/1817 (quoted), Sedgwick V Papers.

41. The letter written at Stockbridge is HDS to JM, n.d. [9/1816]. My dating of this letter depends on the implication in a letter of FSW's that she had witnessed this episode: "you kept her letter to Catharine — and you did as you should — one man in a thousand would not have given so beautiful an instance of proof of love to his beloved." For FSW to be aware of the controversy over the letter to CMS, it must have taken place at Stockbridge in September, because FSW never left Stockbridge that summer or fall, and HDS arrived there after September 2; see FSW to HDS, n.d. [9/1816], and CS to HDS, 1/12/1817. The earlier letter on the Phillips and Sumner affairs is HDS to JM, n.d. [summer 1816]; see chapter 5 for a discussion of its contents. All letters cited in this note are in Sedgwick V Papers. On the absolute centrality of *sincerity* in love letters and other communications between lovers at this time, see Karen Lystra, *Searching the Heart: Women, Men, and Romantic Love in Nineteenth-Century America* (New York: Oxford University Press, 1989), pp. 14–18, and Ellen K. Rothman, *Hands and Hearts: A History of Courtship in America* (New York: Basic Books, 1984), p. 42. This term is discussed at greater length in chapter 7.

42. RS to HDS, 4/16/1814, Sedgwick V Papers. For other references to RS's plans, see RS to HDS, 9/7/1808 and 10/11/1810, Sedgwick V Papers; and RS to CMS, 12/13/1815, Catharine Maria Sedgwick I Papers.

43. RS to HDS, 7/9/1816, Sedgwick V Papers. RS's letter concerning HDS's offenses is similar to the advice offered in some of the late-eighteenth-century "courtesy books" cited by Richard L. Bushman in *The Refinement of America: Persons, Houses, Cities* (New York: Knopf, 1992), pp. 38–46, and especially p. 42.

44. SRS to HDS, 3/1, continued 3/15/1816, Sedgwick V Papers.

45. WM to HDS, 9/20/1816, Sedgwick V Papers.

46. RS to HDS, 9/30/1816 and 10/10/1816; CS to JM, 10/15/1816; and TS II to HDS, 10/23/1816 and 10/28/1816, Sedgwick V Papers; also CMS to HDS, 11/21/1816, Catharine Maria Sedgwick III Papers.

47. The events of their last days together are discussed in JM to HDS, 1/[26]/1817, continued 1/[27]/1817, and 2/[25]/1817 ("tenderness"), and HDS to JM, 2/20/1817; the first letters written by each after their parting are JM to HDS, 10/30/1816 ("agonizing" and "melancholy"), and HDS to JM, 10/30/1816 ("new stimulus"); all in Sedgwick V Papers.

7. The Only Consolation of Absence: Love Letters (pages 129–154)

1. HDS to JM, 10/30/1816, Sedgwick V Papers. (Unless otherwise specified, all manuscript letters cited in the notes to this chapter can be found in Sedg-

wick V Papers at MHS. Undated or partially dated letters, because they are so numerous, are simply indicated by brackets around all or part of the estimated dates.)

2. HDS to JM, 11/9/1816, continued 11/11/1816 ("whirling"); 11/6/1816 (Pearl Street); 11/11/1816 (second of that date); and 11/12/1816. On New York "surrounded with masts," see [Anne Newport Royall], *Sketches of History, Life, and Manners in the United States* (New Haven, Conn.: n.p., 1826), pp. 242–44. Royall's complete description of her stay in New York in 1824 (pp. 241–69) is invaluable; for more on New York as it looked to Royall, see Bessie Rowland James, *Anne Royall's U.S.A.* (New Brunswick, N.J.: Rutgers University Press, 1972), p. 130. On "swamps of shipping" and "huge masses of buildings," see Mark Hopkins to parents, 5/12/1820, in Susan Sedgwick Hopkins, ed., *Early Letters of Mark Hopkins* (New York: John Day, 1929), p. 44. Hopkins was a young second cousin of HDS, and like him a Stockbridge native and a Williams College graduate. For more on New York at this period, see Edwin G. Burrows and Mike Wallace, *Gotham: A History of New York City to 1898* (New York: Oxford University Press, 1999), pp. 429–518; Robert Greenhalgh Albion (with Jennie Barnes Pope), *The Rise of New York Port, 1815–1860* (New York: Scribner, 1939); and Dixon Ryan Fox, *The Decline of the Aristocracy in the Politics of New York, 1801–1840* (New York: Columbia University Press, 1919; rpt., New York: Harper & Row, 1965).

3. JM to HDS, 11/[27]/1816 and 4/3/1817 ("good habits"); and HDS to JM, 11/11/1816, 11/14/1816 ("native Bostonian"), 11/29/1816, and 1/27/1817, continued 1/29/1817 ("swarms"). On New York as a city swarming with New Englanders, see Albion, *Rise of New York Port*, pp. 241–56, and Burrows and Wallace, *Gotham*, pp. 337–38 and 452–55.

4. The letters are in Sedgwick V Papers (also known as the Henry Dwight Sedgwick Papers) at MHS. Most are in Box 8 (1816) and Box 9 (1817); some previously undated or unattributed ones of JM's are in Box 82, and one of HDS's written on legal paper (HDS to JM, 11/14/1816) is in a box of oversized papers. My selective transcription of portions of the 90 surviving letters runs to 144 typed, single-spaced pages. On reactions to the size and scope of the letters from both CMS and a college classmate of HDS and RS, see S. Howe to HDS, 12/1/1816.

5. HDS to JM, 11/29, continued 12/1/1816.

6. For this apology, see HDS to JM, 3/8/1817.

7. JM to HDS, 2/[25]/1817 ("sanctuary"); 3/[8]/1817 ("a week's silence"); five-day letter, 12/6/1816, continued 12/8 and 12/11/1816. The one-week gaps in JM's letters are bounded by letters dated 1/[14]/1817, and (JM to RS), 1/[21]/1817; and 3/1/1817, 3/[8]/1817, and 3/[15]/1817. JM's last surviving letter in the exchange is dated 5/4/1817, and HDS refers to his receipt of a letter "yesterday" in HDS to JM, 5/14/1817. Nine days was an unusually long time for a letter to travel from Boston to New York by U.S. mail, as this one did. It is not clear whether on

5/13/1817 HDS received her letter of 5/4/1817, or (more likely) a subsequent letter that has been lost.

8. JM dated her Thanksgiving letter to HDS "November about the 25th," but from internal evidence it was written on the day before Thanksgiving and Thanksgiving Day, which are the dates I have assigned to it; see JM to HDS, 11/[27, continued 11/28]/1816. JM correctly dated JM to HDS, 11/30/1816; for HDS's congratulations, see HDS to JM, 12/4/1816. It is possible that the 11/30 letter was only JM's eighth, although someone (probably HDS or JM) has numbered it "No. 9" in a corner. If it was the ninth, then both the fifth and sixth letters, dated between 11/14 (or possibly 11/7) and 11/19, are missing. HDS to JM, 1/20/[1817] is dated incorrectly; see JM to HDS, 1/24/1817, for JM's comment.

9. HDS to [LDM], 1/10/1817, Sedgwick IV Papers.

10. Note that the extract set aside here is one long sentence. HDS effectively communicated some of the breathless confusion experienced by the witnesses to the fire by writing an astonishing 113 words before finally coming to the main verb, *presented*.

11. HDS to JM, 12/4/1816, continued 12/5, 12/6, and 12/7/1816, and JM to HDS, 12/13/1816, continued 12/15 and 12/16/1816. For more on this fire, see the *New-York Evening Post*, 12/4/1816, pp. 2–3. The fire was not fully under control until 4:00 A.M., but the *Evening Post* managed to include it as the lead story in that day's paper, and Mr. Blunt managed to insert an advertisement announcing his thanks to his friends for their efforts to save his property. In Boston, JM and her family might have learned of the fire in the *Weekly Messenger*, 12/12/1816, p. 138 (the tenth page of a sixteen-page issue).

12. On seals, see HDS to JM, 12/28/1816, continued 12/30 and 12/31/1816 ("*inspectable*"), and JM to HDS, 3/[19]/1817, continued 3/20/1817 ("so many letters"); on office expenses and on FSW and postage, see JM to HDS, 1/[26]/1817, continued 1/[27]/1817, and HDS to JM, 2/3/1817, continued 2/4/1817; on WM's involvement, see JM to HDS, [1/8/1817], 1/24/1817, and 2/[6]/1817, continued 2/[7]/1817; and on the late letter, see HDS to JM, 2/25/1817, continued 2/26/1817.

13. JM to HDS, [1/8/1817] ("presuming"); 11/[19, continued 11/20, 11/21, and 11/22]/1816 ("opportunities every hour"); and 12/[29/1816] ("cannot animate"). See also JM to HDS, 1/1/1817, and HDS to JM, 12/28/1816, continued 12/30 and 12/31/1816, and 1/1/1817, continued 1/3, 1/4, and 1/6/1817.

14. The Munson letter is JM to HDS, 1/[14]/1817; she referred to it and wondered about its whereabouts in JM to RS, 1/[21]/1817, JM to HDS, 1/24/1817 ("Have you received a letter from me by Mr. Munson?"), and JM to HDS, 1/[26]/1817. HDS was almost exactly correct: Popham delivered the letters to JM at her home on January 19, a Sunday so stormy that no one at the Minots' had even gone to church, and RS's letter arrived in time for JM to write a response to it on Tuesday, January 21. See JM to HDS, 1/24/1817, and JM to RS, 1/[21]/1817; and, for HDS's later resolutions, HDS to JM, 1/23/1817 ("penny-post" and "most expeditious"); 1/27/1817, continued 1/29/1817 ("his trunk" and "only conveyance"); and 2/3/1817, continued 2/4/1817.

15. Mr. Cunningham delivered JM to HDS, 1/[29]/1817, continued 1/[30]/1817 (an undated postscript apparently composed 2/1/1817 is filed separately); receipt was acknowledged in HDS to JM, 2/3/1817, continued 2/4/1817. Mr. Bulfinch and Mr. Tudor also managed to deliver letters in two days, as had Mr. Coolidge in December, once he finally got on his way; see JM to HDS, 2/[21]/1817, continued 2/[23]/1817, and 5/4/1817; and HDS to JM, 12/28/1816, continued 12/30 and 12/31/1816. On the reaction of witnesses, see JM to HDS, 1/24/1817 and 3/[15]/1817. Both these examples involve the same messenger, Helen Davis's suitor, John Popham. The second Munson letter, HDS to JM, 2/6/1817, is mentioned in JM to HDS, 2/17/1817; the letters she received earlier were HDS to JM, 2/7/1817, continued 2/8/1817, and 2/13/1817. The word *he* is used throughout this discussion because the carriers of letters in these private opportunities were, like Popham and Munson, almost always men. JM's ten letters in late January and February include an apparently missing letter dated between 1/28/1817 and 2/2/1817.

16. HDS to JM, 11/11/1816.

17. HDS to JM, 12/28/1816, continued 12/30 and 12/31/1816 (party plans), and 1/1/1817, continued 1/3 and 1/4/1817 (New Year's visits).

18. JM to HDS, 1/24/1817; CS to JM, 12/17/1816; and HDS to JM, 1/1/1817, continued 1/3 and 1/4/1817.

19. HDS to JM, 2/25/1817, continued 2/26/1817; 3/3/1817, continued 3/4/1817; and 3/8/1817.

20. Karen Lystra alludes to the importance of the ritual aspects of the act of reading a love letter in the nineteenth century in *Searching the Heart: Women, Men, and Romantic Love in Nineteenth-Century America* (New York: Oxford University Press, 1989), p. 24.

21. JM to HDS, 2/[9]/1817, continued 2/[13]/1817; HDS to JM, 2/18/1817, continued 2/19/1817 ("jostling"), and 2/20/1817, continued 2/21/1817 ("never enjoyed").

22. HDS to JM, 11/26, continued 11/27/1816 ("conjecturing"), and 1/23/1817 ("a stranger"); JM to HDS, 1/[26]/1817 ("diffidence"); HDS to JM, 2/3/1817, continued 2/4/1817 ("such fits"); and JM to HDS, 4/[27]/1817 ("obtain a letter").

23. HDS to JM, 2/18/1817, continued 2/19/1817, and 2/25/1817, continued 2/26/1817; JM to HDS, 3/1/1817; 3/23/1817, continued 3/24/1817; and 3/25/1817; HDS to JM, 3/21/1817, 3/25/1817, and 3/29/1817; and JM to HDS, 4/1/1817, continued 4/2/1817 (quoted).

24. HDS to JM, 2/6/1817 ("imagination"); JM to HDS, 11/6/1816, continued 11/7/1816 ("widowhood"), [11/7 or 14/1816] ("consolation"), and 12/[29/1816] ("opposite states"); and HDS to JM, 11/11/1816 ("stay where I am").

25. JM to HDS, 2/[6]/1817 ("hourglass"), and HDS to JM, 3/14/1817 ("monotony") and 5/9/1817 ("Robert wonders").

26. HDS to JM, 1/27/1817, continued 1/29/1817 ("without any circumlocution"), and 11/26, continued 11/27/1816 ("secure *home* feeling"); and JM to HDS, 1/[14]/1817 ("I care not") and 1/3/1817 ("delicate and tender"). Karen Lystra has written about the meaning and importance of *sincerity* in love letters, in

Searching the Heart, pp. 14–18; see also Ellen K. Rothman, *Hands and Hearts: A History of Courtship in America* (New York: Basic Books, 1984), p. 42, on the importance of sincerity for lovers of the preceding two generations.

27. JM to HDS, 11/[27]/1816; 12/[21]/1816 ("heart-felt pleasures"); 2/2/1817; 2/[6]/1817; 2/[9]/1817, continued 2/[13]/1817; 3/1/1817; and 4/[12]/1817.

28. On the friendlies' compliments and "affectionate interest," see (for example) JM to HDS, 2/[9]/1817, continued 2/[13]/1817; 4/[17]/1817, continued 4/18/1817; and 4/[21]/1817, continued 4/[23]/1817; see also "Gretina" [Margaret C. Jones] to JM, [July or August 1816; second of two] ("delightful tie"), and JM to HDS, [11/4/1816] (*"evening* sigh"), 3/23/1817 ("nearest to a woman"), and 1/[29]/1817, continued 1/[30]/1817 ("no danger"); and Nancy F. Cott, *The Bonds of Womanhood: Women's Sphere in New England, 1780–1835* (New Haven, Conn.: Yale University Press, 1977), pp. 168–72.

29. JM to HDS, 11/30/1816.

30. The entire account of the meeting with Clerc is in HDS to JM, 11/1/1816. For more encounters with Clerc in New York, see HDS to JM, 11/21/1816; 12/28/1816, continued 12/30/1816; 1/9/1817; [1/10]/1817, continued [1/13]/1817; 1/20/[1817]; and 5/12/1817. Biographical information on Clerc, and an account of his fund-raising tour, can be found in Harlan Lane, *When the Mind Hears: A History of the Deaf* (New York: Random House, 1984), pp. 213–22, 442–43. The school for the deaf opened in Hartford, Conn., on April 15, 1817; see RS to CMS, 6/11/1817, Sedgwick IV Papers, for an account of a visit that RS, TS II, SRS, and SRS's brother-in-law, Robert Watts, made to the school shortly thereafter. Nearly two centuries later, it is still in operation, in West Hartford. A statue of Clerc, who remained at the school until his death in 1869, stands at its main entrance.

31. JM to HDS, 11/6/1816, continued 11/7/1816, and 11/30/1816 ("primness").

32. HDS to JM, 12/4/1816, continued 12/5, 12/6, and 12/7/1816. JM might have obliged to some extent, although in March both LDM and Mary Ann Fales exhibited extensive familiarity with the contents of his recent letters; see JM to HDS, 3/[19]/1817, continued 3/20/1817.

33. HDS to JM, 12/4/1816, continued 12/5, 12/6, and 12/7/1816, and JM to HDS, 12/13/1816, continued 12/15/1816; and Lystra, *Searching the Heart*, pp. 14–18.

34. JM to HDS, [11/7 or 14/1816], and HDS to JM, 11/14/1816 and 11/21/1816. Lystra saw this apprehension of love letters as symbolic physical visits from the absent lover as a sign of the growing intimacy that love letters created, which makes the speed with which HDS and JM arrived at this understanding (within two weeks of HDS's departure from Boston) all the more remarkable; see Lystra, *Searching the Heart*, pp. 22–27.

35. HDS to JM, 11/19/1816, and JM to HDS, 12/[29/1816] and 12/[21]/1816. The letter with the obliterated postscript, addressed to RS, does not survive. For more on HDS's quarrels with New Yorkers over religion, see chapter 8.

36. JM to HDS, 1/24/1817 ("vainly endeavoring"); separately filed postscript

[2/1/1817] to 1/[29]/1817, continued 1/[30]/1817 ("invigorated"); and 2/2/1817 ("no delight more exquisite").

37. HDS to JM, 2/3/1817, continued 2/4/1817, and JM to HDS, 2/[6]/1817, continued 2/[7]/1817.

38. HDS to JM, 2/20/1817, continued 2/21/1817 ("late and silent hours"); JM to HDS, 2/[25]/1817 ("devour") and 3/1/1817 ("harrowed"); HDS to JM, 4/1/1817 ("beating heart"); and JM to HDS, 4/3/1817, continued 4/5, 4/6, and 4/7/1817 ("deadly pale").

39. HDS to [LDM], 1/10/1817.

40. Rothman, *Hands and Hearts*, pp. 51–55; the quotation is from p. 54. John R. Gillis has noticed similar boundaries, sometimes ignored by engaged couples, in early modern Britain; see Gillis, *For Better, for Worse: British Marriages, 1600 to the Present* (New York: Oxford University Press, 1985), pp. 52–54, 109–14.

41. JM to HDS, [1/8/1817], and HDS to JM, 12/9/1816, continued 12/10/1816.

42. JM to HDS, 1/3/1817, and HDS to JM, 2/20/1817.

43. HDS to JM, 3/29/1817 ("moonlight"); JM to HDS, 2/[25]/1817 ("behind the buildings") and 1/[26]/1817, continued 1/[27]/1817 ("when I bade"); HDS to JM, 2/20/1817 ("throbbing"); and JM to HDS, 10/30/1816 ("parting look").

44. JM to HDS, 1/[26]/1817, continued 1/[27]/1817 ("testimony"); [11/7 or 14/1816] ("on the sofa"); and 11/[19, continued 11/20 and 11/21]/1816 ("make my fire").

45. JM to HDS, 4/1/1817, and HDS to JM, 4/1/1817.

46. HDS to JM, 12/19/1816, and JM to HDS, 12/22/1816, continued 12/26/1816, and 1/[14]/1817.

47. HDS to TS II, 1/3/1807.

48. HDS had acknowledged receipt of JM to HDS, 2/17/1817, continued 2/18/1817, on the previous Thursday, and lamented at that time that he would be "destitute of my usual Sunday refection"; see HDS to JM, 2/20/1817, continued 2/21 and 2/22/1817.

49. HDS to JM, 2/25/1817. I certainly join him in this lament: HDS's mention of letters from JM predating his move was the first I had heard of such letters, which apparently do not survive.

50. JM to HDS, 2/[21]/1817, and HDS to JM, 3/3/1817, continued 3/4/1817.

8. *That I Might Be Worthy of You: Roles and Responsibilities* (pages 155–171)

1. "Gretina" [Margaret C. Jones] to JM, [July or August 1816; first of two], Sedgwick V Papers. (Unless otherwise specified, all manuscript letters cited in the notes to this chapter can be found in Sedgwick V Papers at MHS. Undated or partially dated letters, because they are so numerous, are simply indicated by

brackets around all or part of the estimated dates.) Coming from an educated woman like Margaret Jones, the allusion in the salutation to Gabriel's annunciation to the Virgin Mary and her sister Elizabeth's recognition of her joy (Luke 1:28, 42) was surely not accidental.

2. Karen Lystra, *Searching the Heart: Women, Men, and Romantic Love in Nineteenth-Century America* (New York: Oxford University Press, 1989), p. 129. For more on the doctrines, ideas, and ideologies referred to by Lystra, see the introduction, and especially note 21 there.

3. On the nineteenth century, see Charles E. Rosenberg, "Sexuality, Class, and Role in Nineteenth-Century America," *American Quarterly* 25 (May 1973), pp. 131–53; on the founding era, see Mark E. Kann, "Manhood, Immortality, and Politics During the American Founding," *Journal of Men's Studies* 5 (fall 1996), pp. 79–103.

4. Jan Lewis, *The Pursuit of Happiness: Family and Values in Jefferson's Virginia* (New York: Cambridge University Press, 1983), pp. 198–201. (The quotation is from page 199.) The most detailed portrayals we have of specific Southern marriages during this period differ on the possibility of the kind of mutuality Harry and Jane strove for. Its possibility is hinted at in Melinda S. Buza, "'Pledges of Our Love': Friendship, Love, and Marriage among the Virginia Gentry, 1800–1825," in *The Edge of the South: Life in Nineteenth-Century Virginia*, edited by Edward L. Ayers and John C. Willis (Charlottesville: University of Virginia Press, 1991), pp. 9–36; it is desirable but probably unattainable for Elizabeth Gamble and William Wirt in Anya Jabour, *Marriage in the Early Republic: Elizabeth and William Wirt and the Companionate Ideal* (Baltimore, Md.: Johns Hopkins University Press, 1998), pp. 21–22, 54–58; but it is definitely absent (though conceivable, and intensely desirable) for the Wirts' daughter, Laura Wirt Randall, in Jabour, "'It Will Never Do for Me to Be Married': The Life of Laura Wirt Randall, 1803–1833," *Journal of the Early Republic* 17 (summer 1997), pp. 192–236, and *Marriage in the Early Republic*, pp. 136–38.

5. Like many others, Richard L. Bushman implies that the removal of virtue to the private, domestic sphere — or, as he calls it, "the domestication of gentility" — dates to the Victorian era. In the chapter on "Literature and Life" in which he develops this theme, all but two of his primary references (including quite a few quoted from CMS's novels) date to 1835 or later, and the two exceptions are eighteenth-century courtesy books cited for still being widely read during the antebellum decades; see Bushman, *The Refinement of America: Persons, Houses, Cities* (New York: Knopf, 1992), pp. 280–312, 473–76. E. Anthony Rotundo, on the other hand, sees the domestication of virtue as taking place in the post-revolutionary era and specifically as a result of the Revolution; see Rotundo, *American Manhood: Transformations in Masculinity from the Revolution to the Modern Era* (New York: Basic Books, 1993), pp. 16–17, 23.

6. HDS to JM, 3/[16]/1817 ("festering") and 3/25/1817 ("magnitude"); and JM

to HDS, 3/[19]/1817, continued 3/20/1817 ("startled"); 3/23/1817; 3/25/1817; and 4/3/1817.

7. On HDS's two courtships, see HDS to JM, n.d. [summer 1816], and chapter 5.

8. JM to HDS, 11/30/1816 ("a notion") and 1/3/1817 ("delicate"); HDS to JM, 2/3/1817, continued 2/4/1817 ("fluctuations"); and JM to HDS, 2/[6]/1817 ("very thinking people").

9. JM to HDS, [12/17–20/1816] ("confidence") and 12/22/1816 ("consideration").

10. HDS to WM, postscript to HDS to JM, 11/14/1816, continued 11/15/1816 ("theological"); HDS to JM, 11/9/1816, continued 11/11/1816; and JM to HDS, 1/1/1817. Boston has long been recognized as the birthplace of this belief system in America; see, for instance, Conrad Wright, *The Beginnings of Unitarianism in America* (Boston: Beacon, 1966), pp. 261–63, 266. For uses of the term *unitarian* (sometimes capitalized, sometimes not) see HDS to JM, 3/14/1817, and JM to HDS, 3/[19]/1817, continued 3/20/1817. See also William Ellery Channing, "Unitarian Christianity: Discourse at the Ordination of the Rev. Jared Sparks, Baltimore, 1819," in *William Ellery Channing: Selected Writings*, edited by David Robinson (New York: Paulist Press, 1985), pp. 70–102.

11. HDS's beliefs are laid out most fully in HDS to JM, [1/10]/1817 and 3/25/1817. On Unitarianism in Boston, see Conrad Wright, "Ministers, Churches, and the Boston Elite, 1791–1815," in *Massachusetts and the New Nation*, edited by Conrad Edick Wright (Boston: Massachusetts Historical Society, 1992), pp. 118–51; and Mary Kupiec Cayton, "Who Were the Evangelicals? Conservative and Liberal Identity in the Unitarian Controversy in Boston, 1804–1833," *Journal of Social History* 31 (fall 1997), pp. 85–107. In a lengthy entry in the commonplace book that she used between 1811 and 1815, JM once compared the beliefs and attitudes of liberal and orthodox Christians in terms strikingly similar to the ones identified by Cayton; see JM Commonplace Book, 1811–1815.

12. HDS to JM, 12/22/1816. Mary Kupiec Cayton has pointed out that the avowed desire to avoid controversy was a defining characteristic of Channing and other liberal Christians in Boston, at least until Channing's 1819 sermon on Unitarianism; see Cayton, "Who Were the Evangelicals?" p. 88.

13. Wright, *Beginnings of Unitarianism in America*, p. 202.

14. HDS to JM, 12/22/1816, continued 12/23, 12/24, and 12/25/1816; see also HDS to CMS, 12/22/1816, Catharine Maria Sedgwick III Papers.

15. JM to HDS, 12/22/1816, continued 12/26/1816, and 12/[29/1816] ("from curiosity"); HDS to JM, 12/28/1816, continued 12/30/1816 ("cooled down"); JM to HDS, 1/3/1817 ("for the future"); and HDS to JM, 1/1/1817, continued 1/3, 1/4, and 1/6/1817.

16. JM to HDS, 12/[21]/1816 (Romagno) and 12/[29/1816] ("misgivings"), and HDS to JM, 1/1/1817, continued 1/3, 1/4, and 1/6/1817.

17. For more on their theological agreement, see JM to HDS, 2/[21]/1817,

continued 2/[23]/1817; for the earlier comparison of liberal and orthodox Christians, see JM Commonplace Book, 1811–1815; for JM's warning, see JM to HDS, 12/[29/1816].

18. For RS's critique of HDS's manners, see RS to HDS, 7/9/1816, and chapter 6.

19. On the Romayne controversy, see HDS to JM, 3/8/1817, 3/12/1817, 3/[16]/1817, 3/21/1817, and 3/25/1817; and JM to HDS, 3/[15]/1817; 3/[19]/1817, continued 3/20/1817; and 3/25/1817.

20. JM to HDS, 3/23/1817 ("plumage") and 4/[27]/1817, continued 4/28 and 4/29/1817 ("kitten").

21. HDS to JM, 4/19/1817, continued 4/20/1817.

22. On New York during the embargo, see TS II to TS I, 11/1/1808, Sedgwick III Papers; CMS to TS I, 1/27/1809, Sedgwick IV Papers; and RS to HDS, 9/28/1811. See also Dixon Ryan Fox, *The Decline of the Aristocracy in the Politics of New York, 1801–1840* (New York: Columbia University Press, 1919; rpt., New York: Harper & Row, 1965), pp. 102–3.

23. JM to HDS, 2/[6]/1817, 2/17/1817, 3/23/1817 (Fales), and 5/4/1817; HDS to JM, 3/21/1817, 3/29/1817, and 5/9/1817 ("mercantile failures").

24. JM's journal entries are quoted in HDS to JM, 12/9/1816.

25. For JM as "preacher," on his industrious exertions, see JM to HDS, 11/6/1816, continued 11/7/1816; on his temper, see JM to HDS, 3/[19]/1817, continued 3/20/1817; and on living up to her own advice, see JM to HDS, 4/1/1817.

26. JM to HDS, 11/[27]/1816 ("virtue"); 12/13/1816, continued 12/15/1816 ("deficiency"); and 3/[19]/1817, continued 3/20/1817 ("hacknied").

27. "Gretina" [Margaret C. Jones] to JM, [July or August 1816; two items]; JM to HDS, 4/1/1817 ("religion and love") and 2/17/1817 ("even in your unhappiness"). Ellen K. Rothman has written of the importance in this era, especially to women, of subjecting love to the restraint of reason; see Rothman, *Hands and Hearts: A History of Courtship in America* (New York: Basic Books, 1984), pp. 36–41. JM did not deny that importance in these letters, any more than she and HDS would ever have denied the importance of reason in religion, but rather recognized its limits.

28. JM to HDS, 3/1/1817.

29. JM to HDS, 2/[21]/1817, continued 2/[23]/1817 ("not religious"), and 3/[19]/1817, continued 3/20/1817 ("acting contrary"); HDS to JM, 2/3/1817, continued 2/4/1817 ("more than I deserve"); and JM to HDS, 2/[6]/1817, continued 2/[7]/1817 ("total depravity").

30. HDS to JM, 1/1/1817, and JM to HDS, 1/[14]/1817. A clue about why this subject came up here: JM mentioned reading in November a sermon on marriage in which Jeremy Taylor, a seventeenth-century Anglican bishop, had denied its eternal duration. "At the resurrection there shall be no relation of husband and wife, and no marriage shall be celebrated but the marriage of the Lamb," Taylor had preached, "yet then shall be remembered how men and

women passed through this state, which is a type of that; and from this sacramental union all holy pairs shall pass to the spiritual and eternal, where love shall be their portion, and joys shall crown their heads, and they shall lie in the bosom of Jesus, and in the heart of God, to eternal ages." The sermon appears in an 1816 Boston edition to which JM had access; she might have also mentioned it previously in one of the November or December letters that do not survive. See "The Marriage Ring; Or, the Mysteriousness and Duties of Marriage," in Jeremy Taylor, *Discourses on Various Subjects*, vol. 2 (Boston: Wells & Lilly, 1816), p. 365.

31. JM to HDS, 1/3/1817, continued 1/5/1817 ("responsible"), and 3/23/1817 ("I am told").

32. William Henry Channing, *The Life of William Ellery Channing, D.D.: The Centenary Memorial Edition* (Boston: American Unitarian Association, 1880), p. 323.

33. Channing's 1816 sermon on marriage is reprinted in W. H. Channing, *Life of William Ellery Channing*, pp. 320–23.

9. To Translate Hope to Certainty: Setting the Date (pages 172–198)

1. On JM's earlier courtships, see JM to HDS, 2/[25]/1817, Sedgwick V Papers. (Unless otherwise specified, all manuscript letters cited in the notes to this chapter can be found in Sedgwick V Papers at MHS. Undated or partially dated letters, because they are so numerous, are simply indicated by brackets around all or part of the estimated dates.) On HDS's courtships of Elizabeth Sumner and Abigail Phillips, see chapter 5. The literature on age at marriage in the colonial and early national periods is fragmentary and anecdotal. Some useful findings include those of Michael Gordon, who summarized a number of local studies of colonial New England by noting that the average age of men at first marriage seemed to be 26 to 28, for women 22 to 25; see Gordon, *The American Family: Past, Present, and Future* (New York: Random House, 1978), pp. 171–72. Daniel Scott Smith found a slight decline in women's average age at first marriage (from 23.7 years to 23.3 years) when he compared the sixty years after the Revolution to the preceding sixty years in Hingham, Massachusetts; see Smith, "Parental Power and Marriage Patterns: An Analysis of Historical Trends in Hingham, Massachusetts," *Journal of Marriage and the Family* 35 (1973), p. 426. The most detailed study of age at marriage using reliable official records focused on a later period (1845–1948). In it, Thomas P. Monahan saw a gradual but noticeable upward trend in the average ages at first marriage of both men and women; see Monahan, "One Hundred Years of Marriage in Massachusetts," *American Journal of Sociology* 56 (May 1951), pp. 534–45. Based on what he acknowledged was more limited evidence, Peter Ward found a similar slight upward trend in English Canada from 1817 to 1900; see Ward, *Courtship,*

Love, and Marriage in Nineteenth-Century English Canada (Montreal: McGill-Queen's University Press, 1990), pp. 51–54.

2. Ellen K. Rothman, *Hands and Hearts: A History of Courtship in America* (New York: Basic Books, 1984), p. 54, and JM to HDS, 2/17/1817, continued 2/18/1817; see also chapter 7. In colonial times, according to Rothman, the transition from engagement to marriage had been smoother, and the feelings of men and women more uniform, because young women enjoyed fewer freedoms in their parental homes, and because in the agriculturally organized society of colonial America, marriage brought with it an actual increase in real authority for women; see *Hands and Hearts*, pp. 70–75.

3. JM to HDS, 11/6/1816 and 1/3/1817 (quoted).

4. HDS to JM, 11/12/1816 ("premeditated"); JM to HDS, 1/[29]/1817; HDS to JM, 2/3/1817, continued 2/4/1817 ("anticipated delights"); and JM to HDS, 2/[21]/1817, continued 2/[23]/1817.

5. TS II to HDS, 3/15/1817; CS to HDS, 1/1/1817; JM to HDS, 4/1/1817, continued 4/2/1817; and CS to JM, 4/3/1817. See also CMS to JM, 12/12/1816, Catharine Maria Sedgwick III Papers.

6. JM to HDS, 11/6/1816, continued 11/7/1816, and HDS to JM, 3/21/1817 and 4/1/1817 (quoted). On John Livingston's attempt to keep SRS from marrying TS II, see chapter 2.

7. JM to HDS, 3/25/1817, continued 3/28/1817 ("nothing particularly uncomfortable"), and 10/30/1816 ("gallantry"); see also HDS to JM, 11/1/1816.

8. JM to HDS, 5/4/1817 ("much injured") and 11/[19, continued 11/20 and 11/21]/1816 ("satisfy my nearest relations"). See also HDS to [LDM], 1/10/1817, Sedgwick IV Papers, and LDM to CMS, n.d. [1816], Catharine Maria Sedgwick III Papers.

9. HDS to JM, [summer 1816] (quoted), and JM to HDS, 2/[25]/1817. In her will, JM's mother instructed her to secure her property in such a trust; see Last Will and Testament of Mary Speakman Minot, dated 1/10/1811, Sedgwick V Papers. WM was the executor of his mother's will, and it is also likely that he drafted it or had a hand in drafting it. On changes in inheritance law and the treatment of women's property in this period, see Joan Hoff, *Law, Gender, and Injustice: A Legal History of U.S. Women* (New York: New York University Press, 1991), pp. 107–11; Jane H. Pease and William H. Pease, *Ladies, Women and Wenches: Choice and Constraint in Antebellum Charleston and Boston* (Chapel Hill: University of North Carolina Press, 1990), p. 91; Carol Elizabeth Jenson, "The Equity Jurisdiction and Married Women's Property in Ante-Bellum America: A Revisionist View," *International Journal of Women's Studies* 2, no. 2 (March–April 1979), p. 147–48; and Joan Hoff Wilson, "Hidden Riches: Legal Records and Women, 1750–1825," in *Woman's Being, Woman's Place: Female Identity and Vocation in American History*, edited by Mary Kelley (Boston: G. K. Hall, 1979), pp. 17–18. On overall changes in the law that favored rising American entrepreneurs but diminished some traditional protections, includ-

ing those of married women and widows, see Hoff Wilson, "Legal Records and Women," pp. 11–12, and Morton J. Horwitz, *The Transformation of American Law, 1780–1860* (Cambridge, Mass.: Harvard University Press, 1977). For much more on family, property, and inheritance law as it affected the Sedgwicks, see the discussion of HDS's execution of TS I's will in chapter 3.

10. HDS to WM, 5/2/1817, and HDS to JM, 5/2/1817 (quoted) and 5/9/1817.

11. HDS to JM, 2/20/1817, continued 2/21/1817, and JM to HDS, 2/[25]/1817.

12. JM to HDS, 3/1/1817; HDS to JM, 3/3/1817, continued 3/4/1817, and 3/8/1817; and JM to HDS, 3/[8]/1817.

13. On RS's boarding arrangements, see RS to CMS, 7/17/1816, Catharine Maria Sedgwick III Papers. This was not a new experience for the Sedgwick brothers. RS had boarded with a French family in Albany in 1807 for similar reasons, and HDS had sought his father's permission to do so in 1805 shortly before he instead returned from Albany to Stockbridge; see RS to HDS, 9/3/1807, and HDS to TS I, 12/24/1805.

14. HDS to JM, 1/27/1817, continued 1/29/1817 ("gentleman of talent"); 2/7/1817, continued 2/8/1817; 2/18/1817; and 3/12/1817 ("suited to him"); and JM to HDS, 2/2/1817. On the Coles family, see "Walter Barrett, Clerk" [pseud.— Joseph Alfred Scoville,] *The Old Merchants of New York City*, 2nd ser. (New York: Carleton, 1863), pp. 41–45, 69–71.

15. HDS to JM, 3/12/1817 ("I have been thinking"); 3/[16]/1817 ("tell the *girls*"); 3/21/1817 ("excited"); 3/25/1817 ("imagination"); 4/1/1817 ("not handsome"); 4/12/1817; 4/19/1817, continued 4/20/1817; and 4/[23]/1817, continued 4/[24]/1817; and JM to HDS, 3/[19]/1817, continued 3/20/1817 ("do her best"); 3/25/1817, continued 3/28/1817 ("particularly sent"); 4/3/1817, continued 4/5, 4/6, and 4/7/1817; and 4/[12]/1817, continued 4/[13]/1817 ("no occasion" and "finest companion").

16. JM to HDS, 4/[12]/1817; 12/22/1816, continued 12/26/1816; and 3/25/1817, continued 3/28/1817; and "Gretina" [Margaret C. Jones] to JM, [July or August 1816; first of two] (quoted).

17. On the letter to Margaret Jones (which does not itself survive), see HDS to JM, 12/4/1816, continued 12/5, 12/6, and 12/7/1816; and 12/9/1816, continued 12/10, 12/11, and 12/12/1816; and also JM to HDS, 12/13/1816, continued 12/15 and 12/16/1816. The lines given as dialogue are quoted verbatim from JM's letter.

18. JM to HDS, [11/4/1816]; 11/[19, continued 11/20]/1816; and 2/[21]/1817, continued 2/[23]/1817.

19. JM to HDS, 4/[12]/1817, continued 4/[13]/1817, and 4/[21]/1817, continued 4/[23]/1817; and HDS to JM, 4/19/1817, 4/[23]/1817, and 4/30/1817.

20. JM to HDS, 11/6/1816 and 1/1/1817 (quoted), and, on incomes, HDS to JM, 4/1/1817. On charitable activity in Boston, see Paul Goodman, "Ethics and Enterprise: The Values of a Boston Elite, 1800–1860," *American Quarterly* 18 (fall 1966), p. 444 ("merchant prince"), and Ronald Story, *The Forging of an*

Aristocracy: Harvard and the Boston Upper Class, 1800–1870 (Middletown, Conn.: Wesleyan University Press, 1985), pp. 160–63.

21. On the Boston Female Asylum, see Kathleen D. McCarthy, *American Creed: Philanthropy and the Rise of Civil Society, 1700–1865* (Chicago: University of Chicago Press, 2003), pp. 38–45; on the antebellum decades, see Lori D. Ginzberg, *Women and the Work of Benevolence: Morality, Politics, and Class in the Nineteenth-Century United States* (New Haven, Conn.: Yale University Press, 1990), pp. 36–66; and on women's isolation from fund-raising for the hospital, see McCarthy, *American Creed*, pp. 93–95, and Story, *Forging of an Aristocracy*, pp. 10–12.

22. JM to HDS, 12/6/1816, continued 12/8/1816 ("who should I meet"); 12/13/1816, continued 12/15 and 12/16/1816; [12/17–20/1816] ("no human being"); and 1/[14]/1817.

23. JM to HDS, 1/1/1817, and 1/3/1817, continued 1/5 and 1/6/1817 (quoted). See also Catherine M. Scholten, *Childbearing in American Society: 1650–1850* (New York: New York University Press, 1985), pp. 46–49, and Amalie M. Kass, *Midwifery and Medicine in Boston: Walter Channing, M.D., 1786–1876* (Boston: Northeastern University Press, 2002), pp. 71–87. On the death in childbirth during this year of Emily Gibbs Bradish, a cousin of the Channings and the wife of HDS's and RS's college classmate and RS's onetime law partner Luther Bradish, see HDS to CMS, 4/9/1816, Catharine Maria Sedgwick III Papers.

24. Scholten, *Childbearing in American Society*, p. 98; John Demos, "Digging Up Family History: Myths, Realities, and Works-in-Progress" (1982), and "The Changing Face of Fatherhood" (1982), rpt. in *Past, Present, and Personal: The Family and the Life Course in American History* (New York: Oxford University Press, 1986), pp. 10, 49; and Joseph F. Kett, "Growing Up in Rural New England, 1800–1840," in *Anonymous Americans: Explorations in Nineteenth-Century Social History*, edited by Tamara K. Hareven (Englewood Cliffs, N.J.: Prentice-Hall, 1971), pp. 2–3. See also Nancy F. Cott, *The Bonds of Womanhood: Women's Sphere in New England, 1780–1835* (New Haven, Conn.: Yale University Press, 1977), pp. 84–92. On nursing, see Mary Beth Norton, *Liberty's Daughters: The Revolutionary Experience of American Women, 1750–1800* (Boston: Little, Brown, 1980), pp. 90–91; Carl N. Degler, *At Odds: Women and the Family in America from the Revolution to the Present* (New York: Oxford University Press, 1980), pp. 79–80; and Scholten, *Childbearing in American Society*, pp. 72–73. On LDM's difficulties in nursing young William, see LDM to JMS, 6/11/1817.

25. JM to HDS, 2/[6]/1817; 2/[9]/1817, continued 2/[13]/1817; 2/17/1817; 3/25/1817, continued 3/28/1817; 4/3/1817, continued 4/5, 4/6, and 4/7/1817 (quoted); 4/[17]/1817; 4/[21]/1817, continued 4/[23] and 4/[24]/1817; and 4/[27]/1817.

26. JM to HDS, 11/6/1816 ("until June"); HDS to JM, 11/12/1816 ("womanish"); JM to HDS, 1/[29]/1817 ("upstairs"); HDS to JM, 3/[16]/1817; JM to HDS, 3/[19]/1817 ("sickness"); HDS to JM, 3/21/1817; JM to HDS, 4/3/1817, continued 4/5, 4/6, and 4/7/1817 ("I cannot tell"); HDS to JM, 4/12/1817 ("fervent grati-

tude"); *The Minot Family: Record of Births, Marriages and Deaths, 1754–1934, Copied from Family Bibles* (n.p., 1934); and James Jackson Minot, *Ancestors and Descendants of George Richards Minot, 1758–1802* (n.p., 1936), in the collection of the Massachusetts Historical Society.

27. JM to HDS, 4/[12]/1817.

28. JM to HDS, 4/[17]/1817. The Gospel passage referred to is Matt. 18:1–20. JM makes particular reference to Matt. 18:1 (the opening question); Matt. 18:9 ("And if thine eye offend thee, pluck it out, and cast it from thee; it is better for thee to enter into life with one eye, rather than having two eyes to be cast into hell fire."); Matt. 18:2–4 ("And Jesus called a little child unto him, and set him in the midst of them, and said, Verily I say unto you, Except ye be converted, and become as little children, ye shall not enter into the kingdom of heaven. Whosoever therefore shall humble himself as this little child, the same is greatest in the kingdom of heaven."); and Matt. 18:8 ("Wherefore if thy hand or thy foot offend thee, cut them off, and cast them from thee; it is better for thee to enter into life halt or maimed, rather than having two hands or two feet to be cast into everlasting fire.") All bible quotations are from the King James version.

29. HDS to JM, 11/19/1816.

30. JM to HDS, 4/[17]/1817 ("nurse's rules"), 4/[27]/1817 ("fortnight"), and 4/[21]/1817, continued 4/[23] and 4/[24]/1817 ("bear a bustle"); and Rothman, *Hands and Hearts*, pp. 77–81.

31. HDS to JM, 4/12/1817; 4/19/1817, continued 4/20/1817; and 4/[23]/1817, continued 4/[24]/1817 ("long, long" and "relinquish"); and JM to HDS, 3/25/1817, continued 3/28/1817 ("compliment"); 4/[12]/1817; 4/[17]/1817 ("edge of Niagara"); 4/[23]/1817, continued 4/[24]/1817; and 4/[27]/1817, continued 4/28/1817 ("you hurry me"). See also CMS to HDS, 4/3/1817, Catharine Maria Sedgwick III Papers.

32. HDS to JM, 11/29/1816, continued 12/1/1816 ("a circle so charmed"), 2/13/1817 ("sacred"), and 5/6/1817 ("all that we want"); see also JM to HDS, 4/[17]/1817, continued 4/[18]/1817.

33. JM to HDS, 12/22/1816, continued 12/26/1816, and HDS to JM, 3/3/1817, continued 3/4/1817. Ellen K. Rothman points out how frequently marriage entailed a move for one partner, and stresses its greater impact on women, in *Hands and Hearts*, pp. 68–69.

34. HDS to JM, 11/11/1816; JM to HDS, 11/[19, continued 11/20 and 11/21]/1816; and HDS to JM, 2/13/1817.

35. HDS to JM, 2/3/1817, continued 2/4/1817 (quoted), and JM to HDS, 4/[27]/1817, continued 4/28/1817. May would continue to be the season for moving in New York for many years; see CMS to FSW, 5/2/1830, Sedgwick IV Papers, and SRS to TS II, 4/21/1837 and 4/30/1837, Sedgwick II Papers. See also Mark Hopkins (a Sedgwick cousin, later president of Williams College) to parents, 5/12/1820, on a visit to the Sedgwicks in New York—"It was May day or the first of May and they were all moving as the law obliges them to, on that

day if at all" — in Susan Sedgwick Hopkins, ed., *Early Letters of Mark Hopkins* (New York: John Day, 1929), pp. 44–45; a diary entry of Philip Hone, a merchant and one-time mayor, 5/9/1831 — "The city is now undergoing its usual annual metamorphosis" — in Allan Nevins, ed., *The Diary of Philip Hone, 1828–1851*, vol. 1 (New York: Dodd, Mead, 1927), p. 41; and Edwin G. Burrows and Mike Wallace, *Gotham: A History of New York City to 1898* (New York: Oxford University Press, 1999), pp. 392–93, 476, 767.

36. On boardinghouses, see Elizabeth Blackmar, *Manhattan for Rent, 1785–1850* (Ithaca, N.Y.: Cornell University Press, 1989), pp. 134–36, and Wendy Gamber, "Tarnished Labor: The Home, the Market, and the Boardinghouse in Antebellum America," *Journal of the Early Republic* 22 (summer 2002), pp. 177–204. On changes in the Manhattan housing market during these decades, see Blackmar, *Manhattan for Rent*, especially pp. 72–148. On "separate spheres," see Barbara Welter, "The Cult of True Womanhood: 1820–1860," *American Quarterly* 18 (summer 1966), pp. 151–74, and Cott, *Bonds of Womanhood*.

37. JM to HDS, 3/25/1817, continued 3/28/1817; HDS to JM, 4/1/1817; 4/4/1817, continued 4/7/1817; and 4/12/1817 ("uncommon demand"); and TS II to HDS, 4/11/1817 ("you do wrong").

38. HDS to JM, 4/19/1817, continued 4/20/1817 ("half crazy" and "literally impossible"); JM to HDS, 4/[21]/1817, continued 4/[23]/1817 ("mores and customs"); HDS to JM, 4/[23]/1817, continued 4/[24]/1817; JM to HDS, 4/[27]/1817, continued 4/28 and 4/29/1817 ("drawing implements"); and HDS to JM, 4/30/1817 ("discard").

39. JM to HDS, 4/[27]/1817, continued 4/28 and 4/29/1817 ("almost frighten you" and "is it possible"), and 5/4/1817 (Sarah Miller); also HDS to JM, 5/6/1817 (description of lodgings and "good for little or nothing").

40. JM to HDS, 3/25/1817, continued 3/28/1817 ("I consider myself your wife"), and 4/[27]/1817 ("near its close"); also HDS to JM, 4/12/1817 ("love is necessary"), 4/30/1817 ("whole soul thrills"), and 5/6/1817 ("with all my heart").

41. HDS to JM, 2/6/1817 ("necessary"); JM to HDS, 2/17/1817, continued 2/18/1817 ("absence"); HDS to JM, 5/12/1817 ("other calamities"); and JM to HDS, 3/1/1817 ("drawn me nearer").

42. HDS to JM, 4/[23]/1817, continued 4/[24]/1817; JM to HDS, 4/[27]/1817, continued 4/28 and 4/29/1817; HDS to JM, 4/30/1817 ("ridiculous") and 5/2/1817; HDS to WM, 5/2/1817; JM to HDS, 5/4/1817 ("gratifications" and "muslin"); and HDS to JM, 5/6/1817 ("how impatient"), 5/9/1817, and 5/12/1817. JM shared the wedding date with HDS in a lost letter dated around 4/30/1817; it is referred to in HDS's letter of 5/2/1817.

43. JM to HDS, 3/25/1817 ("binding"); HDS to JM, 4/30/1817 ("absolute reliance"); JM to HDS, 5/4/1817; and HDS to JM, 5/6/1817 ("doubtful") and 5/9/1817 ("Cape Horn" and "no starter").

44. HDS to JM, 4/[23]/1817, continued 4/[24]/1817 ("sense of inadequacy"); 5/6/1817 ("till called for"); and 5/9/1817 ("too feeble"); see also JM to HDS,

5/4/1817. If JM did send a letter to the New Haven post office, or HDS did send one from Hartford or Worcester, they do not survive.

45. HDS to JM, 5/6/1817.

46. HDS to JM, 5/9/1817, 5/12/1817, and 5/14/1817; see also HDS to JM, 10/30/1816.

Epilogue: Volumes Could Say No More (pages 199–206)

1. See *Index of Marriages in Massachusetts Centinel and Columbian Centinel, 1784–1840*, 8 vols. (n.p., n.d.), in the collection of the Massachusetts Historical Society; apparently prepared around 1942 at the American Antiquarian Society, Worcester, Mass., and Probate no. 29075, John C. Jones, November 9, 1829, Suffolk County Probate Court, Massachusetts State Archives, Boston. Seven years after Margaret Jones married Benjamin Coles, her sister Martha, the youngest of the friendlies, married his brother, Isaac Underhill Coles. They had many children. He took over his father's flour business, and lived a long life, retiring in 1835 at a fairly young age and "then becoming aristocratic." See "Walter Barrett" [pseud. — Joseph Alfred Scoville], *The Old Merchants of New York City*, 2nd ser. (New York: Carleton, 1863), p. 44.

2. Indenture, 5/29/1817; JM to HDS, 4/[21]/1817, continued 4/[23]/1817, and 5/4/1817; Mary Robbins to JMS, 6/5/1817; LDM to JMS, 6/6/1817; JMS to LDM, 6/[8]/1817, all in Sedgwick V Papers; also JMS to FSW and CMS, 6/19/1817, Catharine Maria Sedgwick III Papers, and the [Boston] *Weekly Messenger*, 6/5/1817, p. 544 (the last page of a sixteen-page number).

3. "Gretina" (Margaret Champlin Jones) to JMS, 6/[16]/1817, and JMS to LDM, 6/[8]/1817, Sedgwick V Papers.

4. JM to HDS, 2/[25]/1817 and 3/25/1817, and HDS to JM, 4/30/1817, Sedgwick V Papers.

5. RS to CMS, 3/1/1819 (quoted), CMS to RS, 3/8/1819, and CS to CMS, 3/14/1819, Sedgwick IV Papers.

6. For discussion of an early suitor, see RS to HDS, 3/19/1811, Sedgwick V Papers; on Bryant, see CMS to RS, 3/24/1819, and CMS to FSW, 3/28/1819, Catharine Maria Sedgwick I Papers. Richard D. Birdsall says that Bryant proposed to CMS in 1819, and that she turned him down; see his *Berkshire County: A Cultural History* (New Haven, Conn.: Yale University Press, 1959), p. 291; but CMS's 1819 letter to RS on the subject speaks clearly of her "last Summer's arrangement" with "Mr. B," and states, "He has been so generous as to relinquish the promise I then gave him, and all is now ended forever."

7. CMS to CS, 1/20/1825, Catharine Maria Sedgwick I Papers, and Nelson Frederick Adkins, *Fitz-Greene Halleck: An Early Knickerbocker Wit and Poet* (New Haven, Conn.: Yale University Press, 1930), p. 47. For more on Halleck's frequent interactions with Bryant, HDS, and RS in the months after Bryant's

relocation to New York, see Bryant to Frances F. Bryant, 4/29/1824, in *The Letters of William Cullen Bryant*, edited by William Cullen Bryant II and Thomas G. Voss, vol. 1 (New York: Fordham University Press, 1975), p. 154; CMS to CS, 2/22/[1825] and 3/27/1825, Catharine Maria Sedgwick I Papers; and separate memorial addresses delivered by Bryant more than forty years later for CMS (quoted in Parke Godwin, *A Biography of William Cullen Bryant, with Extracts from His Private Correspondence*, vol. 1 [New York: Appleton, 1883], p. 209) and for Halleck ("Fitz-Greene Halleck," read before the New-York Historical Society, 2/3/1869, in *Prose Writings of William Cullen Bryant*, edited by Parke Godwin, vol. 1 [New York: Appleton, 1884], pp. 369–93).

8. See Catharine Maria Sedgwick, "Notebook of Memories of Her Life Dated 1853," Catharine Maria Sedgwick I Papers; Catharine Maria Sedgwick, "Recollections of Childhood," in *Life and Letters of Catharine M. Sedgwick*, edited by Mary E. Dewey (New York: Harper, 1872), p. 69; and *The Power of Her Sympathy: The Autobiography and Journal of Catharine Maria Sedgwick*, edited by Mary Kelley (Boston: Massachusetts Historical Society, 1993), p. 84.

9. TS I to CMS, 1/30/1801, Sedgwick III Papers.

10. CMS to RS, 6/10/1811, and RS to CMS, 7/27/1816, Sedgwick IV Papers.

11. CMS to RS, 11/15/1818, Sedgwick IV Papers.

12. CMS to RS, n.d. [11/1821] ("good deal"), and 12/1821 ("walk so close"), and CMS to FSW, 2/[1822] ("provocative"), Sedgwick IV Papers. For more on the family's reaction to Elizabeth Ellery, see RS to CMS, 2/19/1822 and 8/9/1822, Sedgwick IV Papers, and HDS to JMS, 9/1/1822, Sedgwick V Papers. See also Mary Kelley, "A Woman Alone: Catharine Maria Sedgwick's Spinsterhood in Nineteenth-Century America," *New England Quarterly* 51 (June 1978), pp. 213–18. I believe Kelley underestimates the importance of the whole family's genuine initial dislike for Elizabeth Ellery as a factor contributing to CMS's grief and depression over the marriage of her last remaining single brother.

13. TS I to CMS, 12/24/1799, Sedgwick III Papers; HDS to CMS, 6/22/1812, Sedgwick IV Papers; CMS, postscript to TS I to HDS, 7/9/1812, Sedgwick V Papers; and HDS and CMS to TS II, 3/29/1822, Sedgwick II Papers.

14. On the last chapter of *A New-England Tale* and its possible evocation of the circumstances of the death of PDS, see chapter 1.

15. Catharine Maria Sedgwick, *Hope Leslie; or, Early Times in the Massachusetts* (1827); rpt., edited by Mary Kelley, in "American Women Writers" Series (New Brunswick, N.J.: Rutgers University Press, 1987), pp. 345–50.

16. Lee Chambers-Schiller, *Liberty, A Better Husband: Single Women in America, the Generations of 1780–1840* (New Haven, Conn.: Yale University Press, 1984), pp. 72–77, 169–70, 235n12. On Eliza Cabot's marriage to Charles (or Karl) Follen, see CMS to FSW, 9/20/1828, Catharine Maria Sedgwick I Papers.

17. Diary entry, 12/26/1831, in Philip Hone, *The Diary of Philip Hone, 1828–*

1851, edited by Bayard Tuckerman, vol. 1 (New York: Dodd, Mead, 1889), p. 42; CMS to LDM, 1/29/1832, Sedgwick IV Papers.

18. JM to HDS, 1/3/1817, Sedgwick V Papers.

19. SRS to TS III, 12/23/1831, Sedgwick II Papers.

Index

abuse, spousal, 6–7, 72–74, 76–77, 79–80, 82, 161, 164; as ground for divorce, 78

Adams, John, 20, 140, 170

Addicks case, 79

age at marriage, 14, 15, 172, 249n1

Ahmed, Monzur, 220n56

Albany, New York, 37, 39, 42, 45, 70, 81, 124, 196; Catharine Maria Sedgwick visits, 109–10, 191; Pamela Dwight Sedgwick visits, 24, 41; Theodore Sedgwick II in, 27, 30–31, 47–48, 57, 109–10, 204

Alien and Sedition Acts, 206

Andrews, Loring, 39–45, 76, 95

arranged marriages, 6, 36–37, 43–46, 51, 170

Ashley, John, 16

Assemblées Françaises, 178

asylum (Boston), 205

Back Bay (Boston), 100, 125

badinage, 112–14, 116, 119, 120

Ballston, New York, 100–101

Bank of New York, 178

bankruptcy laws, Massachusetts, 76; New York, 75, 205

Battery (New York), 129

Beacon Hill (Boston), 100

Bedell case, 79

Bell, Mrs. (schoolmistress in Albany), 48

Berkshire County (Massachusetts), 1, 5, 16, 22, 27, 32, 122; Court of Common Pleas, 16

biblical allusions, 97, 109–10, 155, 186–87, 202, 234n24, 238n24, 245–46n1, 253n28

Bidwell, Barnabas, 25, 30

Bidwell, Mary Gray, 23, 25–26, 30–31, 220n55

Bleecker, Harmanus, 59, 64, 90

Blunt, Mr., 132–34, 242n11

boardinghouses, 130, 132, 190; French, 177–78

Boston, 7, 99–100; Catharine Sedgwick visits, 54, 99, 101, 195–96; charitable activities, 144, 182–83; compared to New York, 130, 138, 158, 160; death of Theodore Sedgwick, 59–61; Harry Sedgwick in, 7, 56, 58, 65, 69, 85–96, 97, 99, 164–65, 199–200; Harry Sedgwick plans to visit Jane Minot in, 176–77, 179; Penelope Russell Sedgwick in, 54, 57–60, 64–66, 68–69; Robert Sedgwick visits, 54, 99, 101, 105, 108–10, 111–15, 119, 195–96, 200; rumors and reports in, 88, 90, 94, 114, 117–18, 120, 122, 174, 204; Supreme Judicial Court sessions, 25, 30, 58

Boston Common, 100, 121, 125, 150, 175

Bradish, Luther and Emily Gibbs, 252n23

Brattle Street Church (Boston), 104

breast-feeding. *See* nursing

bridesmaids, 88, 196, 200

bridges, in Harry and Jane's letters, 122–23, 125, 146, 150–52, 172

Brom & Bett v. Ashley, 16, 215–16n10

Brower, Mr., 165

Brush, Mrs. 139

Bryant, William Cullen, 200–201, 255–56nn6–7

Burma, 81

Cabot, Eliza, 203
Cabot, George, 66
Calvinism, 2, 80, 86, 158–62, 168, 205, 247n11
Cambridge, Massachusetts, 53–54
Canada, 100
canal stock, 64, 190–91
Canal Street (New York), 129
Channing, Mary, 85–87, 91, 147, 184
Channing, Walter, 184
Channing, William Ellery, 60–61, 104, 147, 158, 169, 184, 247n10, 247n12; sermon on marriage, 169–71
Charles River, 100, 125
Charles Street (Boston), 100, 121, 125, 148–49, 199
child custody, laws concerning, 7, 77–79; tender years doctrine, 79
child rearing, 170, 184
childbirth, 21, 173, 184–186, 252n23; medicalization of, 184; mothers' confinement after, 185, 187–88
Christmas, 28, 160, 189
Civil War, 204
Clap, Thomas, 4, 5
Clerc, Laurent, 144–45, 244n30
Codd case, 79
Coles, Benjamin Underhill, 177–80, 195–97, 199; as possible match for Margaret Jones, 178–80; befriends Harry Sedgwick, 177–78; marries Margaret Jones, 199–200
Coles, Isaac Underhill, 255n1
Coles, John B. (father of Benjamin and Isaac), 178
College of New Jersey (Princeton), 3
common law, 6, 61–62, 175
commonplace book, Jane Minot's, 103–8, 120, 162, 236n14, 237n20, 247n11
condoms, 152
Connecticut (steamboat), 195–98
Connecticut Courant (newspaper), 43
Constitution, Massachusetts, 16, 215–16n10

Constitution, U. S., 18–19, 62
Continental Congress, 15, 17–18, 48
Coolidge, Mr., 136
Cornwall, Connecticut, 3
Cott, Nancy F., 103–4, 144, 237n20
courtship rules, 7, 87–91, 95–97, 112, 114–15, 119
coverture, 63, 199
Crazy Bet (character in *A New-England Tale*), 32–35, 203, 221n59
Cunningham, Mr., 137

dancing, 138
Danforth, Caroline, 103–4, 108, 116–19, 145, 172, 180, 187; bridesmaid at wedding of Harry Sedgwick and Jane Minot, 200; charitable activities in Boston, 144–45, 182–83, 186; Jane Minot sketches her character, 104–5
Danforth, Martha Hall Gray, 103
Danforth, Samuel, 58, 69, 103, 108, 119
dates, on letters, 132, 236n13, 242n8
Davis, Daniel, 100, 120, 164
Davis, Helen, 136
Davis, Louisa. *See* Minot, Louisa Davis
Dedham, Massachusetts, 121
divorce and separation, laws concerning, 7, 77–80
domestic violence, 6–7, 72–74, 76–77, 79, 82, 161, 164
Don Quixote, 110
dower ("widow's third"), 6, 62–65, 67–68, 69
Downing, Esther (character in *Hope Leslie*), 203
dreams, 151–52
Dwight, Abigail Williams Sergeant, 2–3, 5, 14, 21; death of, 20; disapproves of daughter's marriage to Theodore Sedgwick, 15, 51; marries John Sergeant, 2; marries Joseph Dwight, 3, 210n7
Dwight, Elizabeth Buckminster, 200, 204

Dwight, Henry, 3
Dwight, Joseph, 3, 210n7
Dwight, Pamela. *See* Sedgwick, Pamela
  Dwight

education of women, 48, 106, 169
Edwards, Jonathan, 2–3
Ellery, Elizabeth, 202, 256n12
Embargo Act of 1807, 70, 165
engagement, 7, 46, 50–51, 102, 121–22,
  172–74, 204–6
English common law, 6, 61–62, 175
English property of Penelope Russell
  Sedgwick, 56, 63–68, 72–73

Fairman, Sally, 30–31
Fales, Caroline Danforth (daughter of
  William and Mary Ann), 119
Fales, Jane Minot (daughter of William
  and Mary Ann), 165, 184–85
Fales, Mary Ann Gray, 103–4, 108, 116,
  143, 165, 186–87; gives birth to Jane
  Minot Fales, 184–85
Fales, William, 108, 111, 165, 196
Federal Street Church (Boston), 61,
  104, 169
Federalist Party, 37, 39, 41, 47, 86, 202,
  204; and Theodore Sedgwick I, 1, 23,
  25–26, 206
female friendships, 7, 103–4. *See also*
  friendlies
feme covert, 63, 199
fertility transition in early nineteenth
  century, 37–38
fire, 132–34, 145, 242nn10–11
Follen, Karl and Eliza Cabot, 203,
  256n16
Franklin, Benjamin, 20
Freeman, Elizabeth. *See* Mumbet
Freeman, James, 200
French boardinghouse, 177–78
friendlies, 7, 102–6, 121, 138,
  143–45, 178–80, 187–89, 202, 236n11;
  bridesmaids at wedding of Harry
  Sedgwick and Jane Minot, 196,

200; charitable activities in Boston,
  182–83, 186–87; courted by Sedgwick
  brothers, 108–19, 202; presence at
  birth of friends' children, 184–85

gender roles and expectations, 7,
  155–56, 172–73, 190. *See also*
  husband's ideal characteristics; wife's
  ideal characteristics
Gray, Sarah Spring ("Aunt Gray"), 21,
  23
Great Barrington, Massachusetts, 4, 5
Green, "Ma'am" (church school-
  mistress), 186–87
Greenwich Club, 138–39
Greenwich Street (New York), 192
Greenwich Village (New York), 129
Greven, Philip, 20
Grossberg, Michael, 79

Halleck, Fitz-Greene, 201, 256n7
Hamilton, Alexander, 206
Hampshire County (Massachusetts), 5
Hartford, Connecticut, 197; School for
  the Deaf, 144–45, 244n30
Hartog, Hendrik, 79
Harvard College, 37, 100
Heard, Mr. and Mrs., 136
Henry, Patrick, 4
Herbert v. Wren, 67–68
Higginson, Stephen, Jr., 66–69
Hone, Philip, 205, 253–54n35
Hope Leslie, 203
Hopkins, Electa Sergeant, 4, 15
Hopkins, Mark (cousin of Theodore
  Sedgwick I), 4–5, 15
Hopkins, Mark (grandson of earlier
  Mark Hopkins), visits New York,
  129, 241n2, 253–54n35
Hopkins, Samuel, 4
Housatonic River, 122, 220–21n58
house hunting in New York, 146,
  189–92
Hudson River, 47, 48, 101, 192, 196
Huguenots, 130, 131

husband's ideal characteristics: even temper, 158, 161, 163–64; honesty, 157; industry, 164–65, 174; love, 157–58; sincerity, 157; worthiness, 156–57

incomes, typical, 183
infant mortality, 15–16, 170
inheritance law, 6
Intolerable Acts, 15
invention of petting (Rothman), 149, 172

Jabour, Anya, 20
Jackson, Andrew, 205
Jackson, William, 238n24
Jay's Treaty, 22
Jefferson, Thomas, 20, 25, 70, 165, 238n24
Joanne (maid in Minot household), 176, 197
Jones, Elizabeth (daughter of John Coffin and Elizabeth Champlin), 103
Jones, Elizabeth Champlin (mother of Margaret, Elizabeth, Mary, and Martha), 103, 187
Jones, John Coffin, 103, 136, 139, 183
Jones, Margaret Champlin, 103–4, 108, 111–16, 118–19, 143–44, 187; as a possible match for Benjamin Coles, 178–80; bridesmaid at wedding of Harry Sedgwick and Jane Minot, 200; congratulates Jane Minot on engagement, 155–56, 167; corresponds with Harry Sedgwick, 137, 180–81; earlier engagement, 105–6, 110–11, 180; in love with Harry Sedgwick, 180–82; Jane Minot sketches her character, 105–6; marries Benjamin Coles, 199–200; private meeting with Jane Minot, 181–82, 193
Jones, Martha Ellery, 103, 255n1
Jones, Mary, 103–4, 108, 111–17

Kelley, Mary, 215n4, 256n12
Kerber, Linda K., 6
King's Chapel (Boston), 104, 160, 189, 200
Knickerbockers, 130

legal education, 4–5, 211n11
Lenox, Massachusetts, 78
letters, 7, 8, 232n4; after death of Pamela Dwight Sedgwick, 27–29; New Year's, 28–29; privacy, 116. *See also* love letters
Lewis, Jan, 156
liberal Christianity. *See* Unitarianism
Litchfield (Connecticut) law school, 27, 50, 204
literacy, rise of, 43
Livingston, Brockholst, 51
Livingston, Catherine ("Kitty"), 48–51, 53, 225n48
Livingston, Henry Beekman, 224n40
Livingston, John, 48–51, 53, 174
Livingston, Nancy Shippen, 224n40
Livingston, Robert Leroy (stepbrother of Susan Ridley Sedgwick), 48–49
lodgings, 191–92
Lovejoy, Col., 217n28
love letters, 7, 8, 130–32, 134–37, 139–54, 204–6, 232n4; address panel, 134; as symbolic visits, 145–48, 175–76; dates on, 132; dreams in, 151–52; early, 153–54; effects on lovers, 193–94; erotic aspirations in, 148–52; format, 134; postage, 135, 137; "private conveyances," 135–37, 242–43nn14–15; reading, 139, 146–47, 153, 176; reading aloud and privacy, 144–45; sincerity in, 123, 142–43, 145; U.S. mail, 135, 140, 196–97; writing, 130–32, 137, 141, 143
Lystra, Karen, 145, 155–56

mail, U. S., 135, 140, 196–97
Maine, district of, 25, 228n23
male midwives (obstetricians), 184
Marshall, John, 67

Massachusetts Bank, 86–87

Massachusetts Constitution, 16, 215–16n10

Massachusetts General Hospital, 182–83

Massachusetts Historical Society, 8, 13, 207, 209n1

Massachusetts State House, 100

Matthews, Mr., 160–61

May Day, moving day in New York, 190, 253–54n35

Mayhew, Elizabeth, 15

measles, 131, 136–37, 148

medicalization of childbirth, 184

Metcalf, Mrs., 166

Miller, Sarah, 193

Minot, George Richards (father of Jane and William), 99–100, 189

Minot, George Richards (son of William and Louisa), 121

Minot, Jane, 7, 99–101, 108, 111, 117–18; accepts Harry Sedgwick's proposal, 120; advises Harry Sedgwick to avoid religious squabbles, 160–63; advocates delay in wedding date, 172–74, 188, 196; age, 103, 172, 236n13; agrees to June wedding date, 175–76; at Harry's deathbed, 205–6; befriends Catharine Sedgwick, 103, 105, 110, 122; charitable activities with Caroline Danforth, 183, 186–87; children, 205; commonplace book, 103–8, 120, 162, 236n14, 237n20, 247n11; courted by Harry Sedgwick, 119–20; description of her own character, 106–8; education, 106; effects of being orphaned, 99, 107, 175; engaged to Harry Sedgwick, 121–26, 129–98, 204–6; faints while holding newborn nephew, 186; introduces Sedgwicks to the friend-lies, 102, 108–9; "Ma'am Green" prays for, 186–87; marries Harry Sedgwick, 199–200, 204–6; prepares for move to New York, 188–89, 191–92; presence at births of friends'

children, 184–86; private meeting with Margaret Jones, 180–82, 193; religious beliefs, 162, 166–69, 247n11; thoughts on child rearing, 106–7; travel journal, 100–101; visits New York, 101; visits Stockbridge, 122–23; warns Harry Sedgwick about Margaret Jones, 181–82

Minot, Louisa Davis, 99–101, 107–8, 121, 146, 160, 174, 176, 197, 199–200; advises Jane Minot on setting wedding date, 187–88; corresponds with Harry Sedgwick, 132, 148; gives birth to William, Jr., 141, 173, 185–186; visits New York, 101

Minot, Mary (daughter of William and Louisa), 108

Minot, Mary Speakman (mother of Jane and William), 99, 189

Minot, William, 99–100, 107–8, 135, 146, 148, 158, 177, 188, 197, 199; consent required for sister Jane to marry Harry Sedgwick, 120–21, 124–25, 174–75, 191, 199; practices law in Boston, 100, 124–35, 136

Minot, William, Jr. (son of William and Louisa), 100, 141, 173, 185–87

"Miss E," 117–18

Mohawk Indians, 3

moon, 19; at death of Pamela Sedgwick, 30, 33–34, 47; in Harry and Jane's letters, 122–23, 150–51, 193

MoonCalc, 220n56

Moravian Young Ladies Seminary (Bethlehem, Pennsylvania), 222n8

Mount Vernon (Boston), 100

Mumbet (Elizabeth Freeman), 16–17, 32–33, 34, 66, 203; as midwife, 21, 28, 56; leaves Sedgwick family's service, 55–56; on death of Pamela Sedgwick, 30–31; sues for freedom, 16, 215–16n10

Munson, Mr., 136–37, 139, 142, 153

Murray family, 101, 235n6

Museum of Fine Arts (Boston), 229n28

names, impropriety of speaking or writing ladies', 102, 232n4, 236n11

Naples, Italy, 69

New-England Tale, A, 32–35, 61, 202–3

New Haven, Connecticut, 136, 195–97

New London, Connecticut, 125–26, 129, 195, 197

New Year's Day, letters, 28–29; visits, 138

New York city, 43–44, 50, 55, 94; becoming nation's commercial capital, 165, 190; compared to Boston, 130, 138, 158, 160; effect of Embargo Act, 70, 165; Harry Sedgwick in, 118, 129–31, 136–39, 142, 149, 158–65, 173, 190, 192; house hunting in, 146, 189–92; Minots in, 101; Robert Sedgwick in, 27–28, 64, 73, 101, 123–25, 177–78; Watsons in, 28, 46–47, 56, 59, 72, 75; 78, 201; Yankee immigrants from New England, 130

Newport, Rhode Island, 104, 110, 202

Niagara Falls, 188

Northampton, Massachusetts, 3

Norton, Mary Beth, 17–18, 216n16

nursing, 17–18, 184–185; folk belief in contraceptive effects of, 18, 216n16

obstetricians ("male midwives"), 184

Old South Church (Boston), 86, 183, 186–87

Pamela (novel by Samuel Richardson), 14

parental involvement in choice of marriage partners, 6, 36–37, 51–52; John Livingston, 48–49, 174; Theodore Sedgwick I, 41, 43–46,

Parker, Isaac, 66

Parsons, Theophilus, 26

passionlessness (Cott), 104, 237n20

Pearl Street (Boston), 108, 111–12, 143, 181

Pearl Street (New York), 130, 190

Penfield family, 43, 223–24n26

"perpetual moment," the, 121, 150, 175

Person, Ethel Spector, 231–32n1, 233–34n15

Philadelphia, 21–24, 39–41

Phillips, Abigail, 86–87, 89, 91–99, 102, 122–23, 157, 175, 232n4, 233n14

Phillips, William, 86–87, 92–96, 183, 204

Pierce, Polly, 220n55

Pomeroy, Elizabeth Mason ("Eliza") Sedgwick, 5, 15, 22, 36; and her children, 24, 28, 37–38, 41; and the Watsons, 77, 80; courted by Ephraim Williams, 37, 39, 51; death of, 203; marries Dr. Thaddeus Pomeroy of Albany, 37, 40–41, 43, 201; moves back to Stockbridge, 25, 37; on Harry and Robert's courtships, 94; reaction to father's marriage to Penelope Russell Sedgwick, 55, 66, 68; religious beliefs, 60, 80

Pomeroy, Thaddeus, 37–38, 55, 60, 61; marries Eliza Sedgwick, 37, 40–41, 43, 201; on Harry and Robert's courtships, 95, 109

Popham, John, 136, 146

postage, 135, 137, 140

Prather v. Prather, 79

pregnancy, 185; premarital, 149

Presbyterian Church on Murray Street (New York), 159, 162–64

primogeniture, 6, 62

Quincy, Massachusetts, 121, 140, 147, 150–52, 185, 193

Quok Walker v. Jennison, 16, 216n10

reading together, husbands and wives, 170–71, 194

Reeve, Tapping, 27, 50, 204

republicanism, 62, 156

Revolution, American, 6, 15, 47–48, 53–54, 62, 206

Rhode Island coal, 205

Richardson, Samuel, 14

Ridley, Catherine ("Kitty") Livingston, 48–51, 53, 225n48

Ridley, Matthew, 48–49, 225n48

Ridley, Susan. *See* Sedgwick, Susan Ridley

river gods, 1–2

Romagno, Major, 161

romances, reading, 38, 43

Romayne, Dr., 162–64; insulted by Harry Sedgwick, 162–63

Rothman, Ellen K., 148–49, 172–73

Roxy (maid in Minot household), 197

Royall, Ann Newport (traveler to New York), 129, 241n2

Rush, Benjamin, 223n8

Russell, Catharine, 67, 68

Russell, Penelope. *See* Sedgwick, Penelope Russell

Scott, Sir Walter, 221n59

Sedgwick family burial plot (Stockbridge), 13, 56, 82, 227n18

Sedgwick, Alice Minot, 215n4

Sedgwick, Anna Thompson, 3

Sedgwick, Benjamin, 3

Sedgwick, Catharine Maria, 5, 15, 19, 47, 63, 172, 200; *A New-England Tale* (novel), 32–35, 61, 202–3; advises Harry and Robert on courtships, 85–86, 88–91, 92, 96, 98, 109–11, 115–17, 119–20, 124, 181; attends Mrs. Bell's school in Albany, 48; befriends Jane Minot, 103, 105, 110, 122, 181; begins career as writer, 31–32, 202–3; bequest from father's estate, 64, 71, 191; bridesmaid at Harry and Jane's wedding, 196, 200; briefly engaged to William Cullen Bryant, 200–201; death of, 204; debt owed by Ebenezer Watson, 71–73; decision to remain single, 8, 201–4; depression in late 1820s, 203–4; helps Harry with house hunting in New York, 190–92; *Hope Leslie* (novel),

203; initial dislike of Elizabeth Ellery, 202, 256n12; "Notebook of Memories of Her Life Dated 1853," 15, 16, 20, 29, 31, 38–39, 43, 215n4; on death of her father, 59–61; on death of her mother, 13, 29, 31, 32–35, 57–58; on deaths of siblings, 81, 203, 205, 227n18; on father's retirement from Congress, 24; on Mumbet, 16–17, 31–32, 55; on Watson's abuse of Frances, 77, 80, 81; reaction to father's marriage to Penelope Russell Sedgwick, 54–58, 64–65, 67; special relationship with brother Robert, 61, 201–2; superstitious fear that Harry and Jane will never marry, 197; visits Albany, 109–10, 191; visits Boston, 54, 99, 101, 195–96; visits New York, 75, 191–92, 196, 201

Sedgwick, Charles, 5, 19, 21, 25, 38, 60, 98, 196; and the Watsons, 72, 75–78; inherits family home in Stockbridge, 64, 68, 76, 78; marries Elizabeth Buckminster Dwight, 200, 202; on Harry and Robert's courtships, 109; reaction to father's marriage to Penelope Russell Sedgwick, 55, 57–59, 65, 68; visits New York, 27, 75, 138

Sedgwick, Elizabeth Buckminster Dwight (wife of Charles), 200, 204

Sedgwick, Elizabeth Ellery (wife of Robert), 202, 256n12

Sedgwick, Elizabeth Mason (first wife of Theodore Sedgwick I), 14, 33–35, 53, 214–15n3

Sedgwick, Elizabeth Mason (oldest daughter of Theodore and Pamela Sedgwick). *See* Pomeroy, Elizabeth Mason ("Eliza") Sedgwick

Sedgwick, Frances Pamela. *See* Watson, Frances Pamela Sedgwick

Sedgwick, Henry Dwight ("Harry"), 5, 19, 22, 25; advises Robert on courtships, 111–19; advocates early

Sedgwick, Henry Dwight *(continued)*
wedding date, 172–74, 188; arrives
in Boston to marry Jane Minot,
199–200; assists Catharine with
writing career, 202–3; attempts to
establish legal career in Boston, 56,
58–59, 65, 69, 94, 97, 98–99, 101–2,
124, 164, 204; attends Judge Reeve's
Litchfield law school, 27, 50, 204;
attends Young Men's Missionary
Society debate, 159–162; befriends
Benjamin Coles, 177–80; courts
Abigail Phillips, 86–87, 91–93, 98,
157; courts Elizabeth Sumner, 87–92,
94, 98, 157; courts friendlies, 7, 102,
108–11; courts Jane Minot, 119–20;
dealings with Ebenezer Watson,
71–74, 76–77, 80, 82, 98, 122; death
of, 205–6; engaged to Jane Minot,
121–26, 129–98; executor of father's
will, 63–68, 70–71, 74, 85, 94, 98, 120,
164, 204; friendship with Margaret
Jones, 180; friendship with Mary
Channing, 85–87, 91; gets measles,
131–32, 136–37, 148; house hunting in
New York, 189–92; in Stockbridge,
28, 72, 96, 98–99, 101, 108, 119,
122–24, 148–50, 204–6; insults Dr.
Romayne, 162–63; loses eyesight,
205; manners, 123–24, 163; mental
illness of, 205–6; moves to New
York, 118, 125–26, 129–30, 173; office
in New York, 131, 136, 142, 149, 160,
190, 192; on birth of William Minot,
Jr., 185–86; plans to visit Jane Minot
in Boston, 176–77, 179; prepares to
go to Boston for wedding, 192–93,
195–97; proposes to Jane Minot,
120; reaction to father's marriage
to Penelope Russell Sedgwick,
53–56, 67; religious beliefs, 158–63;
sickly as a child, 17–18; social life
in New York, 137–39, 189; temper
of, 67, 72–73, 158–164; understands

language of feelings and emotions,
143–44, 174; urges Theodore to
propose to Susan Ridley, 48–49;
writes letter to Margaret Jones,
180–81; writes obituary for mother,
29–30
Sedgwick, John, 3
Sedgwick, Maria Banyer (daughter
of Theodore II and Susan Ridley),
60
Sedgwick, Pamela Dwight, 3, 201,
203; death of, 13, 27, 29–35, 53,
57–58, 60; family's silence about
her death, 27–29, 57–58; fond of
Loring Andrews, 39–40, 41–42;
marries Theodore Sedgwick, 1, 5,
14–15, 51; mental illness of, 6, 20,
21–24, 25–26, 32; nursing, 17–18;
reacts to death of infants, 15–16;
reacts to husband's absence from
home, 19–20, 206; visits husband in
Philadelphia, 22
Sedgwick, Penelope Russell, 53–54, 69,
94, 120, 201, 204; dislikes country
life, 53, 56–57; English property
of, 56, 63–69, 72–74; in Boston,
54, 57–60, 64–66, 68–69; in
Stockbridge, 56–57, 61, 63–64,
65, 66–67, 69; intemperance of,
57–58, 66–67, 69; marries Theodore
Sedgwick, 6, 13, 55; Sedgwick
children's reaction to, 53–59, 61,
64–65, 67–68
Sedgwick, Robert, 5, 18, 19, 25, 38, 54,
59–60, 200; advises Harry on courtships, 85–86, 88–90, 96–97, 98–99,
102; advises Theodore on courtship,
48–49; boards at French boardinghouse in New York, 177–78; clerk
in Theodore's Albany law office,
27, 30–31, 49; courts friendlies, 7,
101–2, 108–11, 202; courts Jones
sisters, 111–16, 180; dealings with
Ebenezer Watson, 71–75, 77, 79–80;

defends Harry to Dr. Romayne, 163;
dissolves partnership with Harry,
205; imagines courting Caroline
Danforth, 116–19; invites Harry to
join him in New York, 123–25; marries Elizabeth Ellery, 202; opinion of
Benjamin Coles, 179–80; practices
law in New York, 27–28, 64, 73, 109,
114; reaction to father's marriage
to Penelope Russell Sedgwick, 55,
65; religious beliefs, 159; special
relationship with sister Catharine,
61, 201–2; visits Boston, 54, 99, 101,
105, 108–15, 119, 195–96, 200
Sedgwick, Susan Ridley, 48, 60, 109–10,
124, 210n7, 225n44, 225n48; advises
Harry on courtships, 109; attends
Mrs. Bell's school in Albany, 48;
courted by Theodore Sedgwick II,
48–50; marries Theodore Sedgwick
II, 51–52, 174; travels to Boston for
Harry and Jane's wedding, 195–96,
200; writes novels, 204
Sedgwick, Theodore I ("the Judge"),
3–6, 8, 201–4; absences from home,
6, 17–18, 19, 21–22, 24, 25, 30–31, 35,
56, 58, 170; arranges daughters' marriages, 37, 41, 43–46, 51; called "the
Judge" by his children, 26, 219n44;
death of, 6, 28, 60–61, 70, 85, 93,
191, 201; disapproves of Frances's
courtship by Andrews, 39–43, 45;
dreams of dead first wife, 14, 33–35;
early political career, 15, 17, 18–19;
encourages young Theodore to
marry Susan Ridley, 50, 52; expelled
from Yale, 4; final illness, 58–60, 86,
103, 108; in U.S. Congress, 18–19,
20, 21–24, 37, 206; last will and
testament, 56–57, 61, 63–68, 70–71,
191; legal career, 5, 16, 54, 63; loan to
Ebenezer Watson, 70, 191; marries
Pamela Dwight, 1, 5, 14–15, 51; marries Penelope Russell, 6, 13, 53, 55;

on Massachusetts Supreme Judicial
Court, 24–25, 26–27, 58–59, 100;
promises to retire, 20, 22–23, 26, 57;
religious beliefs, 15, 60; Speaker of
the House, 23–24
Sedgwick, Theodore II, 5, 28, 36–37,
59, 64; courts Susan Ridley, 48–50;
dealings with Ebenezer Watson,
81; marries Susan Ridley, 51–52,
55, 174; mediates between Frances
and their father, 42, 44–45, 47; on
Harry and Robert's courtships, 94,
109–10; practices law in Albany,
27, 30–31, 47–48, 57, 204; reaction
to father's marriage to Penelope
Russell Sedgwick, 53, 56, 59; retires
to Stockbridge, 78; travels to Boston
for Harry and Jane's wedding,
195–96, 199–200; urges Harry to
set early wedding date, 173–74, 188,
190–91
Sedgwick, Theodore III, 38
separate spheres, 8, 155–56, 190
Sergeant, Abigail Williams. *See* Dwight,
Abigail Williams Sergeant
Sergeant, Electa, 4, 15
Sergeant, Erastus, 22, 217n28
Sergeant, John, 1–2
servants: in Minot household, 135,
176–77, 186, 197, 199; in Sedgwick
household, 27, 55–56, 64, 66
Shammas, Carole, 36
Shaw, Lemuel, 79
Sheffield, Massachusetts, 3, 4, 5, 14, 22
Shippen, Nancy, 224n40
slavery in Massachusetts, 16, 215–16n10
Smith–Rosenberg, Carroll, 103
Snow, Mrs., 117
Society for the Propagation of the
Gospel in New England, 1
Socinians, 159
South, differences from North, 156
Speakman, Mary, 121, 140, 152, 185
Spring, Gardiner, 159

Stamp Act, 3–4

steamboats, 125–26, 129, 144, 195–98, 199, 205

Stockbridge, Massachusetts, 1, 25–26, 39, 40–41, 94, 204; Charles Sedgwick inherits family home, 64, 68; death of Pamela Sedgwick, 27, 30–31, 32, 206; Harry Sedgwick in, 28, 72, 96, 98–99, 101, 108, 119, 122–24, 148–50, 204–6; Indian school and mission, 1–3; Penelope Russell Sedgwick in, 56–57, 61, 63–64, 65, 66–67, 69; Watsons in, 47, 58, 70, 75–78, 81

Strong, Caleb, 26

Strong, Mrs., 192

Stuart, Gilbert, portrait of Theodore Sedgwick by, 66, 68, 69, 229n28

Suffolk County (Massachusetts), 199

Sullivan, Mrs. William, 145

Sumner, Elizabeth, 87–91, 94–97, 102, 122–23, 157, 232n4

Sumner, Increase, 87

Sumner, Mehetable, 87–88, 90, 94–97, 204

Sumner, William, 87, 95–96

Supreme Court of the United States, 6, 67–68

Supreme Judicial Court (Massachusetts), 16, 24–27, 58–59, 66, 100, 120–21

Symmes, Susan ("Sukie"), 225n44

Tacitus, 25

Taylor, Jeremy, 248–49n30

tender years doctrine, 79

Thanksgiving holiday, 101, 132, 242n8

Tillinghast family, 43, 223–24n26

Tories, 53–54

travel journal, Jane Minot's, 100–101

Tremont Street (Boston), 86

Tucker family, 54, 61

Unitarianism, 60, 80, 94, 104, 156, 158–59, 162–63, 167–71, 247nn10–12

United States Constitution, 18–19, 62

Van Schaack, Henry, 21, 26, 46

Vassall, William, 54

Virginia, 156

virtue, domestication of, 156–57, 166, 169, 206

Wall Street (New York), 129, 190

War of 1812, 87, 130, 164

Washington city, 24

Washington, Bushrod, 67

Washington, George, 47, 67

Washington, Hannah Bushrod, 67

Watson, Catharine Sears, 47, 77–78; missionary in Burma, 81

Watson, Ebenezer, 27, 43–44, 50–51, 61; abuses Frances, 72–74, 76–77, 79–82, 164, 201; business failures, 47, 70–72, 75, 81; courts Frances Sedgwick, 44–46; death of, 82; debt owed to father-in-law's estate, 65, 70–72, 74, 122, 191; marries Frances Sedgwick, 6–7, 46–47, 51, 201; religious beliefs, 60, 73, 80, 159

Watson, Ebenezer, Jr., 47, 77

Watson, Frances Pamela (daughter of Ebenezer and Frances Pamela Sedgwick Watson), 77–78, 79, 81

Watson, Frances Pamela Sedgwick, 5, 27, 28, 36–37, 38, 50, 58, 61, 135; abused by Ebenezer Watson, 72–74, 76–77, 79–82, 164, 201; and death of son Theodore, 77, 81; bequest from father's estate, 64, 70–72; courted by Ebenezer Watson, 44–46; courted by Loring Andrews, 39–43, 51, 76, 95; death of, 81; in New York, 47, 56, 59, 72, 75, 78, 201; marries Ebenezer Watson, 6–7, 46–47, 51, 201; moves back to Stockbridge, 70, 75–78, 81, 159; on Harry and Robert's courtships, 95, 96, 109; religious beliefs, 38, 60, 80, 159

Watson, Robert Sedgwick, 77–78, 81

Watson, Theodore Sedgwick, 47; death of, 77, 81

wedding date, setting, 172–176, 185, 187–88, 193, 195

wedding parties, 138, 199–200, 202; planning, 187–88, 193, 195

West Hartford, Connecticut, 3

West, Stephen, 3, 60

Western Star (newspaper), 39–40

Whiting & Watson, 70–71, 75, 81

Whiting, Samuel, 70

widows, legal status of, 6, 61–63, 67, 228n23

wife's ideal characteristics: happiness, 166; love, 166–67; mutuality and reciprocity, 165–67; piety, 167–69

Wilkins family, 139, 153, 177, 193

Williams College, 19, 25, 54, 85, 99, 204, 241n2

Williams, Abigail. *See* Dwight, Abigail Williams Sergeant

Williams, Elizabeth, 3

Williams, Ephraim (cousin of Pamela Dwight Sedgwick), 22, 39, 41, 58; courts Eliza Sedgwick, 37

Williams, Ephraim (grandfather of Pamela Dwight Sedgwick), 1–3

Wirt, William and Elizabeth, 20

women's charitable activity, 182–83

women's property rights, 63, 71, 75, 175, 199

Wood, Mrs. (cook in Minot household), 135, 197

Worcester, Massachusetts, 197

Yale College, 1, 3–4, 14, 42, 206

Young Ladies' Academy (Philadelphia), 222–23n8

Young Men's Missionary Society, breakup, 159–62